MICHAEL J. MACLEOD

THE
BRAVE
ONES

A Memoir of Hope, Pride, and Military Service

**GRAND
HARBOR**
PRESS

Published by Grand Harbor Press, Grand Haven, MI
www.brilliancepublishing.com

Amazon, the Amazon logo, and Grand Harbor Press are trademarks of Amazon.com, Inc., or its affiliates.

ISBN-13: 9781503945425
ISBN-10: 1503945421

Cover design by: Charles Brock, Faceout Studio

Printed in the United States of America

THE
BRAVE
ONES

For Corporal Antonio Burnside, Private First Class Michael Metcalf, First Lieutenant Jonathan Walsh, Private First Class Christian Sannicolas, Sergeant Jacob Schwallie, Specialist Chase Marta, Private First Class Dustin Gross, Staff Sergeant Nick Fredsti, and Private First Class Blake Hagert

Never Forgotten

TABLE OF CONTENTS

PART IV: Warfare

AUTHOR'S NOTE:

The stories in this book were composed from memory without additional research and some of the names and identities of the characters have been altered to protect privacy.

MILITARY ACRONYMS

AAB Advise-and-Assist mission, or Advise-and-Assist Brigade

ACU Army Combat Uniform

AIT Advanced Individual Training

AO Area of Operations

APFT Army Physical Fitness Test

AWT Air Weapons Team

BCT Basic Combat Training

BDU Battle Dress Uniform

CHU Containerized Housing Unit

COP Combat Outpost

FET Female Engagement Team

FNG Fucking New Guy

FOB Forward Operating Base

HLZ Helicopter Landing Zone

HQ Headquarters

IED Improvised Explosive Device

ISR aerial Intelligence, Surveillance, and Reconnaissance

JOAX Joint Operational Access Exercise

JRTC Joint Readiness Training Center

LGOPs Little Group of Paratroopers

MiTT Military Transitions Team

MOS Military Occupation Specialty

NCO Noncommissioned Officer

NOD Night Observation Device

OPFOR Opposing Forces

PAO Public Affairs Office/Officer

PIR Parachute Infantry Regiment

PID Positive Identification

POG Person Other than Grunt

POO Point of Origin site

PRT Anbar Provincial Reconstruction Team

PSD Personal Security Detail

PT Physical Training

PTDS Persistent Threat Detection System

PTSD Post-Traumatic Stress Disorder

QRF Quick Reaction Force

R&R Rest and Relaxation

RCPs Route-Clearance Patrols

SF Special Forces

SIGACTS Significant Actions

SOP Standard Operating Procedure

SP Start of Patrol

Swick – used in place of the mother of all acronyms, **USJFKSWCS**, which stands for US Army John F. Kennedy Special Warfare Center and School

TBI Traumatic Brain Injury

TC Truck Commander

TCS Temporary Change of Station

TICs Troops In Contact

TOC Tactical Operations Center

TTP Tactics, Techniques, and Procedures

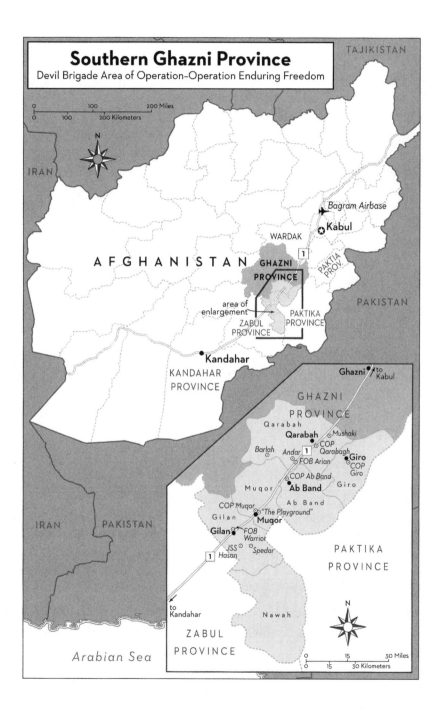

Southern Ghazni Province
Devil Brigade Area of Operation–Operation Enduring Freedom

TAJIKISTAN

IRAN

AFGHANISTAN

WARDAK

Bagram Airbase

Kabul

GHAZNI PROVINCE

area of enlargement

PAKTIA PROV.

PAKISTAN

ZABUL PROVINCE

PAKTIKA PROVINCE

Kandahar

KANDAHAR PROVINCE

IRAN

PAKISTAN

Arabian Sea

Ghazni
to Kabul

GHAZNI PROVINCE

Qarabah

Qarabah

Mushaki

Barlah

Andar

COP Qarabagh

FOB Arian

Giro

COP Giro

COP Ab Band

Giro

Muqor

Ab Band

Ab Band

COP Muqor

"The Playground"

Gilan

Muqor

Gilan

FOB Warrior

JSS Hasan

Spedar

PAKTIKA PROVINCE

to Kandahar

Nawah

ZABUL PROVINCE

30 Miles
30 Kilometers

INTRODUCTION

The day I graduated college, a boy was born to Ceejay and Kimberly Metcalf in Coral Springs, Florida. It was May 15, 1989. I was twenty-two, ready to begin my adult life. I went on to earn a master's degree in wildlife biology, taught college for a few years, started a photography business, then a publishing business, then did more graduate school, and finally built houses to subsidize a writing habit until the housing bust of 2008. All the while, young Michael Metcalf was being nurtured into an able young man, eventually splitting time between his father in Ashtabula, Ohio, and his mother in Boynton Beach, Florida. He played baseball, football, and hockey, but he also developed a fondness for bull riding and tattoos. In the spring of 2011, Michael enlisted in the army.

Ceejay was not pleased. His own father had been a young child when Ceejay's grandfather, a soldier, was killed during World War II. Clarence Joseph Metcalf had not been there to teach his son, Ceejay's father, how to be a man or to raise his four children. As a result, life for the family had been very difficult and Ceejay grew up determined to change the future. In his son Michael, Ceejay saw an opportunity to rectify the past. Then Michael enlisted.

"I knew the price my family had paid, but I wanted my boy to have freedom of choice," said Ceejay. He'd driven his only son to the recruiting station in Miami. Ceejay was only six years older than me.

In the army, Michael earned his silver jump wings and became a paratrooper. He was immediately assigned to the 82nd Airborne Division based in the sandhills of North Carolina at Fort Bragg, home of the Army's Airborne and Special Operations. A year after enlisting, "Cowboy Mike Metcalf" deployed to Afghanistan, where our paths would finally cross. He was twenty-two.

As for myself, in 2008, with the housing market on the verge of collapse and my age dancing with the upper limit of the army's post-9/11 expanded recruitment window, I decided to fulfill a lifelong ambition that, if not acted upon, would soon become a lifelong regret. At just shy of forty-one, with my wife's blessing, I enlisted in the Army. I became a combat correspondent, using my already seasoned skills of writing and photography to "tell the soldier's story." After basic training, I went on to airborne school and was soon assigned to the army's 1st Brigade Combat Team, 82nd Airborne Division, or 1/82. The 504th Parachute Infantry Regiment, to which Metcalf would be posted two years later, was the infantry component of 1/82.

Our brigade combat team of thirty-five hundred paratroopers deployed to Iraq from 2009 to 2010, the year after Metcalf's senior year at St. John's Northwestern Military Academy in Delafield, Wisconsin. In Iraq, we built upon a relative peace made possible by the successful 2007 troop surge, "advising and assisting" Iraqi soldiers and police in a mostly successful defense of their own country from Al Qaeda-linked insurgents.

Upon returning to Fort Bragg in August 2010, we began training for the role of America's always-ready "Global Response Force," or GRF, a role we were assigned to hold for a year. However, as it often did, our mission changed. In the summer of 2011, 1/82's paratroopers began preparations for a year-long deployment to the birthplace of the Taliban in Kandahar, Afghanistan. A few weeks after that, we were re-missioned again, to a locale few had heard of, called Ghazni.

Ghazni province sprawls across a high plain midway between Afghanistan's two largest cities, Kabul and Kandahar. Arid mountain ranges cover much of the land. The rest is, as our brigade commander put it, "densely sparsely populated" agricultural fields and vineyards whose beds of dust and mud are irrigated by ancient networks of subterranean tunnels called *karezes*, which draw from the water table to reclaim what is essentially dustbowl wasteland. It's a land of calloused hands and strong, stooping backs, where shovels are more common than tractors and male literacy hovers around 35 percent. Villagers have dirt floors and cell phones, yet no service after dark because of a Taliban threat to blow up the towers, and in spite of a token Polish military force, the Taliban has had near-complete freedom of movement since NATO forces arrived in 2001. Villagers in outlying areas mistook us for Russians, though the Russian occupation ended the same year Michael Metcalf was born.

Running north-south across the dull countryside is Highway 1, the most important road in Afghanistan because of the promise of commerce and connectedness that it holds for the country's future. Yet it has the feel of a two-lane North Dakota rural route, frozen, baked, beat up by heavy tires, and repaired with wheelbarrows. It is the only pavement connecting Kabul and Kandahar. Traffic is often heavy with civilian vehicles—long-haul rigs, local traders and craftsmen in small vans and three-wheeled pickups, whole families on a single motorcycle, buses, farm tractors, and cars of cross-country travelers—that belie the dangerous nature of the road. On this highway, people have died and continue to die, literally by the busload, in fiery head-on crashes, by massive fertilizer-based bombs that terrorists bury beneath the asphalt, by Taliban highwaymen looking for non-Pashtuns to make examples of.

Big Army, the equivalent of "corporate" in the business world, told us we were going to conduct the last major "clearing operation" of the war. Our mission was to beat down the insurgency and make the road safe in southern Ghazni Province. For six months beginning in March 2012, we did just that in places whose names became seared into the lexicon of our thoughts and dreams: Qarabagh, Hassan, Muqor, and Giro. Our paratroopers killed or captured over four hundred insurgents in over one hundred seventy engagements, conducted thirty-five hundred partnered patrols with Afghan soldiers and policemen, and neutralized two hundred improvised explosive devices and weapons caches. Over a hundred paratroopers were awarded for valor on the battlefield, and over 160 earned Purple Hearts. Eight were killed during combat operations, including PFC Michael Metcalf, who died when the vehicle he was driving hit a massive roadside bomb on April 22, 2012. The explosion was so powerful that both soldiers within were blown from the armored vehicle.

Twenty-three years and two days from the date of his birth, Metcalf was buried at Arlington National Cemetery in Section 60, where our country's recent war-dead are laid to rest. I visited his grave while on leave in November 2012, a few months after leaving Ghazni. Cowboy Mike was settled in a littoral zone in which a slow tide of tidy green turf and white headstones was taking over bare soil, the soil demarcated by taught string-lines waiting for future rows of soldiers yet to die, perhaps yet to deploy.

I cried like a baby. Though I had only briefly known Metcalf, and two more of our paratroopers buried nearby (Sergeant Jacob Schwallie and Specialist Chase Marta), as part of my job, I had researched their lives and written the notices of their passings. I had taken the final photos of each with his mates, at his memorial in Afghanistan, and then sent them on to the family. And while I called these soldiers brothers in a professional sense, they were all my surrogate sons as well.

They were my peers, but by age I am their parents' peer. As a father of two teenagers, I am keenly aware of the human cost of rearing a child to adulthood. Imagining the loss of a child, if I dare go there, I can feel the loss of those many years, the tears and heartache, the triumphs, the love and joys. Arlington was quiet. Always quiet.

In Afghanistan, I had been threatened by IEDs and lived through more than a dozen firefights and mortar attacks, yet there I was standing on this young man's grave, closing out my second set of twenty-two years and moving into the next set, what would have been another whole life for Michael Metcalf. What was I doing with this gift? Were my many years well spent? Would I wake up tomorrow appreciating Mike's sacrifice, and his father's as well?

For any parent standing at the grave of another parent's child, in that most hallowed cemetery, in what I still believe is the greatest country in the history of the world, the question is unavoidable. More sobering, and cutting to the core of who I was: would I want my own son to serve in today's US Army?

A rancher friend says it takes five years of doing something to really understand it. That's a number that seems to square with the experimental probability of Life in General. It's not too difficult to imagine the bell curves of knowledge acquisition, competition, and complexity intersecting at the number five like some fixed value of the Universe, like the atomic weight of hydrogen. It's just that way.

The post-9/11 military occupies a unique time, with smart phones, drones, and even Facebook and YouTube in a decade-long, two-front war fought by less than 1 percent of the country's citizenry. For the civilian outsider, military culture, with its byzantine castes of ranks and badges, convoluted and arcane traditions of ceremony and operations, circular jargon and metastasizing acronyms, and seeming stare-downs against efficiency and common sense, all guarded by snarling sergeants and exploding things, can cement itself into a formidable redoubt of fastness. That wiki of Hollywood is not much help. No, it's not like the movie *The Hurt Locker*.

The nearly five years I spent in the US Army's 82nd Airborne Division has had a profound impact on my life, and because I was a civilian for over forty years prior, I'm in a unique position to explain what that might look like to a nonmilitary reader.

Four decades of civilian life never cured me of the idea that I was special, and though the army quickly liquidated that canard, they replaced it with a much better idea—that I might be useful. Here's something else I learned. Soldiers don't say, "Never forget the fallen." They say, "Never forgotten." It's true—not a day goes by that we don't think of those we've lost in combat. They come like a breeze and leave the same way. They're always welcomed in our thoughts, and in that way, they are never forgotten. So long as they're remembered, their lives are not wasted, regardless of what happened next or *why* in whatever shithole they were lost in. That is something soldiers understand, and by the end of these pages, I hope you will too.

This book is the story of the enlisted soldiers and junior officers of the 82nd Airborne Division—American paratroopers—how they train, how they fight, and what they endure so that the other 99 percent of their countrymen don't have to.

Why paratroopers? Because they volunteer three times—to serve in the army, to become airborne-qualified, and to serve as paratroopers. They are the best of America's conventional fighting forces.

Would I want my son to become a paratrooper? If he wanted to, yes. From a father's perspective, I am about to tell you why. The route is not direct because there is no direct route, but hang on for the next few hundred pages. From time to time, I'll ask you to keep your head down, exercise some noise discipline, and maybe even pull some rear security. There will be swearing, awful swearing. There may be some off-color humor. We'll get there. It might get vulgar before it gets better, so don't shit yourself. In the words of an old first sergeant, "You can't shit yourself clean."

Stand by.

PART I:

Boot Up—Training the Xbox Generation to
fight the War on Terror

CHAPTER 1:
SCRATCH 'N' SNIFF

"I love me some soldiers. The Army can kiss my ass, but I love my soldiers."

—Old veteran at Pope Army Airfield greeting paratroopers
returning from Afghanistan, September 2012

TC and I were college buddies back in the late 1980s when our roommate, Feigenbaum, was killing rabbits for ROTC field training "survival exercises." Feigenbaum, a former Daytona Beach surfer dude, had already graduated Airborne School and Ranger School as a college cadet, but a rappelling accident in his senior year ended his Army career before it began.

A decade after college, TC joined the army as an officer and became a nurse anesthetist. In 2008, he deployed to Camp Bucca in the southern Iraqi desert, just over the Kuwaiti border. With twenty thousand detainees of the Iraq War, Bucca was the coalition's largest detention facility.

More than any other person, TC was responsible for me enlisting in the army at nearly forty-one. In a phone call from Bucca, he shared stories of Iraqi bomb makers on his operating table, several brothers de-limbed literally by their own device, threatening to rip TC's throat out if they only had hands. It was 120 degrees in the desert, and the giant Caterpillar generator that cooled TC's hooch was broken. A chaplain—a captain in rank—was whining that nobody would salute him because he was "just a chaplain." Nobody's end-of-tour medals were matching what they contributed to the war effort. And why was the army paying local contractors to ship in sand from Kuwait?

"We're in the fucking desert surrounded by sand, and the army's buying sand," TC said. His voice had that low-key command presence imbued by the army that said, doubt me and you'll see. Then came the most prophetic words I would hear before enlisting. "The trouble with the army," he said, "is that the army hates soldiers."

How right he was. Consider that, with a workforce of 3.2 million, the US Department of Defense in 2012 was the world's largest employer (next were the Chinese People's Liberation Army at 2.3 million, and Walmart at 2.1 million). Imagine working at a two-century-old institution that, while proud of its efforts today, holds nothing so dear as what its "greatest generation" did during World War II. Realize that promotions are based on what the army deems one's potential rather than one's accomplishments. Understand that few soldiers in the army hold a certain job for more than a year or two, so there is often scant momentum or incentive for substantive solutions to long-standing problems. The result is a system that more resembles an unmovable mountain of Band-Aids than a living institution. Soldiers are often buried beneath it. It has been this way since Christ was a corporal.

Pit against this staggering bureaucracy a single soul who has vol-untarily surrendered great portions of his or her First, Third, Fourth, Fifth, Sixth, Seventh, Eighth, Ninth, and Tenth Amendment rights and all of his or her time for many years in an arrangement that can only be terminated early in a very bad way. A deployed private first class, even with hazardous duty pay, earns less than workers at McDonalds. Where are the labor unions?

TC also told me that, in the army, I would experience the highest highs and lowest lows of my life. Spot-on, TC. Only in the army had I ever literally pinched myself hoping the great wash of misery I was experiencing was only a nightmare. It never was.

I could expect to go to war within a year of entering service. I could expect to be away from my family for extended periods, not only during deployments but also stateside. For my trouble, I might play a role in the leading world events of the current generation, be a part of the most powerful force and brotherhood the world has ever known, and know that I would forever be among the ranks of citizen soldiers who said yes when our nation asked for volunteers to defend the interests of its people.

Finally, TC warned, "Do not under any circumstance enlist. Become an officer, or don't do it." The army is actually several armies, he explained. TC belonged to AMEDD, the medical army, where many of the rules of Big Army do not apply because the emphasis is on patients. Within Big Army, there are at least three other armies: one for officers, one for noncommissioned officers, and one for junior enlisted (mostly privates). Each is its own distinct experience. For the most part, the officers—male and female—belong to a gentlemen's club. Being on the enlisted side is to exist in a gritty Jack London tale ruled by the "law of club and fang," in which the most senior NCOs—the command sergeants major—have an almost despotic lock on the rest of the enlisted.

Hell's bells. I wanted to be an army journalist, and an unfortunate fact about the army is that its journalists are junior enlisted. I enlisted. Five months before my forty-first birthday, I left my wife and children and our home in Montana for boot camp at Fort Knox, Kentucky, to become instant peers with kids just a few years older than my own. What followed was a period of serious awkwardness.

My recruiter was a slight, zit-faced chain-smoker, less than half my age, who'd already been to Iraq twice. On the way to the Butte airport, he reassured me that, even though things were about to get really bad, they would also get better. True, but for the next year, not a day would pass that I wouldn't have opted out were it at all possible. It wasn't. Name another job you can't quit from. There aren't any. Prison maybe—and prison supposedly has better food. So why would anyone do it? I'll tell you why.

CHAPTER 2:
HEROES AND
EFFING RE-RES

Surrounded by pleated wheat fields between the Tobacco Root and Elk Horn Mountains, I signed the papers on the trunk of the young recruiter's little gray Mazda at a windblown gas station outside of Three Forks, Montana. We were driving west on I-90 toward the Military Entrance Processing Station in Butte where I would be officially inducted into the army.

The kid was still working through post-pubescent acne, my beard was half gray. I struggled to pin down the flapping forms long enough to sign them. He dragged expectantly on a cigarette.

Three construction workers on lunch break walked past. One, a burly young rough hand who must have been the boss, catcalled, "Damn, the army's hard up for people, making deals in the parking lot, ain't it?"

I felt like I was going to a slumber party with the friends of my kids and was just busted. What was I doing here?

"Nice, huh?" said the recruiter, unaffected by the locale of our paperwork. It was July 2009. The kid had just returned from a second combat tour in Iraq and was trying to make sense of a country that didn't seem to know it was still fighting two wars. In fact, less than 1 percent of America was serving in the conflicts, and some of those were returning for four, five, six combat tours or more. In Vietnam, few served more than one tour unless they volunteered for more.

But the construction worker was correct in his general assessment. In the year before I joined up, the army and marines paid out some $640 million in bonuses to entice young people to enlist, even accepting over a thousand felons in 2008, then accepting recruits up to the age of thirty-five, and eventually up to forty-one. (1)

Enlistment bonuses for our all-volunteer military have ebbed and flowed during the wars in Iraq and Afghanistan, but nearly a decade after 9/11, the army was still offering up to forty thousand dollars for a six-year commitment. My bonus was fifteen thousand dollars, a combination of regular cash incentive, the calculated value of my job type (in short supply in the army at the time), and reward for higher education. I was also eligible for over forty thousand dollars in GI Bill tuition assistance if I wanted another degree.

I didn't enlist on the trunk of a car, but rather signed off on some relatively inconsequential last-minute paperwork. All the important ink would be spilled down the road in Butte, along with the fingerprinting, screening for unauthorized tattoos (e.g., no swastikas), explanation of the eight-year shadow commitment within which my five-year active-duty contract was nested (i.e., stop-loss), the last-chance-before-you-sign speech, the really-last-chance-before-you-sign speech by a civilian auditor, and my pledge to defend the Constitution of the United States of America.

I'll admit that last part was a pretty heady ending to a rather unseemly accession process that included standing in my briefs in a lineup with a dozen catfish-ribbed boys for tattoo and bad ankle screening. It was, as the soldiers say, all "asses and elbows," like being part of a mass induction into the juvenile court system, and I was the undercover narc.

One of these things is not like the others.

One of these things just doesn't belong.

At any minute, I half expected one of the adults in the room to approach me and whisper, "You know this is just for kids, right?"

Accession—I had to look it up. It was on my enlistment contract. It means attainment of a dignity or rank, as in the queen's accession to the throne. Based on my education and other accomplishments, my rank would be specialist, four up from the bottom but still in the sweaty bowels of the ship. Being an Eagle Scout, bringing buddies in with you, or completing some fitness and soldiering tasks also influence one's initial rank: buck private, private, private first class, specialist. Specialist is an odd term, because those bearing the rank are really special at nothing but ordering privates around and shirking responsibility since they're not yet noncommissioned officers. (A corporal is essentially a specialist who's an NCO, but corporals are rare in today's army.) The next rank is sergeant, what I wanted to be, but that requires at least two years of service, regardless of age, accomplishment, or my own nagging need to be the adult in the room. Until then, I would be some twenty-something sergeant's soldier—Specialist MacLeod.

I slept little on the eve of my formal accession. Two days later, I rode a Greyhound bus into Fort Knox, Kentucky. On the phone, my ten-year-old son wanted to know if the army would give everyone a bar of gold for graduating the ten-week basic combat training course. It wasn't exactly like that.

Two words and one blasphemy: Oh. My. God. The first week was a vaudeville adaptation of *Lord of the Flies*, with only loose supervision provided by drill sergeants unlucky enough to be cast into reception with us. They hovered like tower guards, their primary function to prevent escape, suicide, or internecine chaos. Reception was really just a holding pond until we were sluiced into the first thirty minutes of another show, the opening of *Full Metal Jacket*. Life became art became life.

The teardown began immediately. In reception, we were as a herd weighed, measured, inoculated, shorn, and unceremoniously assigned army combat uniforms and other equipment. We filled out paperwork: Who will get my last paycheck if I die? Who will collect my remains? Where do I want to be buried? What song do I want played? Even at forty-one, the questions were unnerving.

My wife would get my last paycheck. My father-in-law would collect my remains. Easier for him than my own parents, I surmised. I would be buried in Arlington. I left the song blank. I received the dog tags that would stay on my person through Iraq and Afghanistan, and every time I jumped out of an aircraft.

MACLEOD

MICHAEL J

XXX-XXX-XXXX

A POS

ROMAN-CATH

It was like carrying my own tombstone.

"Today, you will meet with a civilian liaison," a drill sergeant told us. "He or she will ask you to select your top three choices for your first active-duty station. Just so you know, you have almost no chance of getting what you want." He continued without a hint of irony in his voice, "Your liaison cannot help you with either of the things you want at this point. He cannot get you out of the army, and he cannot change your MOS." MOS is a soldier's military occupation specialty, his job.

Call him cynical—the sergeant surely enjoyed watching adolescent hope die en masse—but he also knew what they as yet did not, that managing one's expectations would be key to their success in the army.

The drills loved to quote Marine Corps Gunnery Sergeant Hartmann:

"How tall are you, private?"

"Drill sergeant, five foot nine, drill sergeant."

"Five foot nine. I didn't know they stacked shit that high!"

Or: "Were you born a fat, slimy, scumbag puke piece o' shit, private, or did you have to work on it?"

Though I had spent years in the rough-and-tumble construction industry, never had I heard the English language debased to such a sustained oily flock as I did during my time of service. It was off-putting, to say the least, this infinite arsenal of f-bombs the army seemed to supply its soldiers with. As a writer, I'd always considered casual swearing a form of sloth, bending the f-word instead of finding the right word. Eventually I would come to understand vulgar language simply as shop talk designed to help survive the always-abundant unpleasantness and find a way forward as reality fornicated with orders, regulations, and the Good Idea Fairy. (Foul-mouthed soldiers still knew how to talk to their mothers.) Now I know that a string of f-bombs can come as a sweet breeze in the right situation. Vulgarity is steam to the military pressure cooker, ballast to the suck, and the suck began at basic training.

For those nine weeks, there would be no caffeine or tobacco products, no snacks, no calling home, no time alone; no *chairs* anywhere but the chow hall, no sitting or leaning or hands in pockets; no music, no books or magazines or computers; no effective rank, no First Amendment, no first name. Except *private*.

Afforded only minutes to eat each meal, we would scramble for calories like rats in a dumpster—in packets of ketchup, and salad dressings ripped and slurped, licked from the foil tops of yogurts and butters, even picked out of the dirt, even those foods we hated. Boiled okra. Beets. Brussels sprouts. Cabbage in bacon grease. Several times, no sooner had I sat down than I was ordered to get up and dump my untouched meal in the trash to make room in the overcrowded chow hall for others. (The last time this happened, just days from graduating, the adult in me was so angry at wasting food that I yelled and cursed all the way to the door.) During basic, I lost fifteen pounds from an already trim physique.

The Game, of course, was to reformat our little hard drives. It came from the same indoctrination playbook used worldwide to bring civilians into military culture: strip recruits of their identities, break them down to nothing, and then build them back up into the desired ideal. The primary lesson for recruits is that freedom is not free and neither are soldiers. It's not a very American attitude, and youngsters, even the timid, immediately push back.

I can't say how basic training occurs at the army's other initial entry training sites—Forts Benning, Leonard Wood, Sill, and Jackson—but at Fort Knox, the "building up" phase never really happened, nor did it occur at my Advanced Individual Training that followed. I've come to believe that the buildup process really starts when a new soldier arrives at his first duty station and begins doing his job with his unit, where he finally gets his first name back, but then it's "Joe." As in, "I need five Joes to clean the latrine."

Parents, do your sons and daughters a favor. Impress upon them that the lockdown and deprivation of boot camp prepares them for the army, but it is not the army. It is, however, as dramatic as the reformatting of a computer hard drive.

The first official day of boot camp was a cleaving point, an absolute weaning more primal than exists anywhere in civilian culture outside of prison, though at my age, it was mostly entertaining. In formation, boys were boiled pallid by their own imaginations and vomited even before the drill sergeants showed up. Several passed out. For sixty-three days, a coarse martial order was imposed upon the four training platoons of Delta Company, 1/46 Infantry, two hundred of the 169,000 recruits that the army would train in 2008. (Army Exceed Recruiting Goal for Fiscal Year 2008, 2008) (2)

Qualities of little use to the combat soldier, such as physical or mental sloth, personal expression and the need to be heard, minding one's own business, pandering to comfort and enjoyment, and objection to objectionable orders—be they digging weeds from sidewalk cracks with a pen cap or ostensibly killing another human being—all had to go.

The drill sergeants came in pairs and threes, cool-heeled ruffians beneath the slant-set campaign hats of the Great War, the "brown rounds" adorned with the Great Golden Seal of the United States, slung by a single black strap to grip shaved scalps. They approached with predatory swagger and wore scrimshaw expressions. All but one had seen combat in ongoing wars.

My platoon of fifty recruits was assigned three drill sergeants, each with two combat tours. Our senior drill sergeant was a short, bulldog-faced career soldier who clearly didn't want to be anybody's friend. Sergeant First Class Steven Boer was an army mechanic, tapped for drill sergeant duty. His most endearing quality was the use of double and triple negatives as threat.

"If you think you're not going to war because of something your recruiter did or didn't tell you," yelled Boer, "think again. I'm here to tell you, ain't none of you not going downrange. And when you get downrange and they run out of work for your MOS, don't be surprised if you don't end up behind a .50 cal [machine gun] or kicking in doors with the infantry. So pay attention to what you learn here. It may save your life, and if it don't save yours, don't think it won't save your battle buddy's life." We were all non-infantry, just engineers, truck drivers, cooks, and the sort. Boer's soliloquy got our attention.

The Young Turk of our drills was Staff Sergeant Kristopher Berube, a quick stepping, gung-ho, hardbodied infantryman from the Northeast who had seen extensive combat in Iraq and Afghanistan. He was "new school" compared to the other drills and hadn't quite bought into the idea of hating on privates to make them respect authority. He was an instant hit.

The last and largest drill sergeant was a soon-to-be retiree, which, in the enlisted ranks, usually occurs after twenty years of service around the age of forty. He was a giant black man with a shiny bald dome, ample beltline, and horse-like eyes. Drill Sergeant William Boddie was a common-sense machine. He was paternal in a familiar manner and too old for this shit. Everyone loved him, even when he was chewing butt.

"Listen up," Boddie said. "Basic training is a cakewalk today. When I went through in '87, my drill sergeant had us do push-ups on the tarmac in the hottest part of the day. It was 110 motherfucking degrees. We could smell our skin cooking. Ninety-five percent of us burned the motherfucking skin off our motherfucking hands. When the drill sergeant finally let us go to sick call to get our fucked-up hands taped, he said, 'Now you can do push-ups again.' That's what we did. That motherfucker made us do more push-ups on the hot motherfucking tarmac. You can't do that today. You can't even touch one of these motherfuckers."

Cherish the day when a drill sergeant could slap a motherfucking recruit. Not in today's army. The primary tool of discipline and the number one demoralizer of fanciful exceptionalism was the "smoke session," push-ups and other calisthenics applied until muscle failure.

It's important to understand that few people join the army to become a drill sergeant. The job is generally a two-year assignment, a promotion tool for noncommissioned officers. Some NCOs volunteer for the duty; some are "voluntold." Either way, the long hours and often intense dramas of turning raw civilians into soldiers are formidable enough to earn the assignment its own epithet: on the trail.

During the two years that a drill sergeant is on the trail, he or she will train eleven cycles of recruits. That's 550 soldiers. If a drill doesn't learn to be mean at drill sergeant school, building new soldiers on four to five hours of sleep a night for two years is likely to make him so.

KILLING THE INDIVIDUAL

"I want you to try that individual shit in Iraq, because when everybody else is ducking, you gonna end up in the motherfucking newspaper, deceased, because you had to be a motherfucking individual and didn't duck."

–Drill Sergeant Boddie

It's difficult to overemphasize the army's success at killing "the individual" in spite of our cultural obsession with identity politics and granting concession to every special case of personhood. The army doesn't want you to do it your way, because if you do, when you get "blown-the-fuck-up," the person next in line to do your job won't know where you kept the ammo, and then he's going to get blown-the-fuck-up. Respect in the army is afforded based on how well a soldier soldiers, not how brightly colored his parachute is. Everybody's parachute is green. War is always a team sport.

Though I had played baseball, soccer, and football, it was basic training that taught me to be a real team player, and here's why: in the army, the concept of the classic give-me-the-ball "superstar" is nonexistent. The best soldiers, sergeants, and officers are also the best team players, and those who sacrifice for others are afforded the highest honors. In fact, drill sergeants often use *superstar* and *hero* sarcastically when correcting junior enlisted: "Hey, Hero. Why did you leave your battle buddy alone and without water back there?" So it's out with, "I can't because I have this individual need." Soldiering on is transcending self for the team, especially when the end of your rope is at hand.

One of the more conspicuous edifices of basic training is the so-called confidence course, i.e., the obstacle course. In combat, I've never had to climb anything more challenging than a head-high wall, but that's not the point. The ropes and ziplines look fun, and they are fun.

Navigating mildly treacherous physical obstacles does build confidence. Because I was an avid participant in just about every outdoor activity and a veteran of many years of framing houses in Montana in all types of weather, little in basic pushed me physically, but as a father, I could appreciate how it challenged these young men for the good.

Soaked with sweat and back on terra firma after surviving an hour-long ordeal on the Jacob's ladder, our corpulent country boy, Private Jones, gushed, "I don't care if I get smoked for hugging Drill Sergeant Berube. I'm gonna do it anyway. He better be ready for 270 pounds of sweaty love." So there was confidence.

What really was accomplished through competitive vehicles like the confidence course, combatives (hand-to-hand combat), and pugil sticks (padded poles) was the construction of a new paradigm of self. In the army, the most irreducible body is the team. A single soldier is just a piece of that body. The smallest team in the army is the battle buddy team of two. Nobody in the army is not on your team.

This social redesign takes a year or two to fully flower, but the seeds are planted at basic training. For example, following a win in an obstacle course race, my platoon whooped it up, thinking we were showing "warrior spirit." Drill Sergeant Boddie rained down on us with an f-filled ass-chewing storm: "Look at them," he spat, pointing at the other platoons with one of his reticulated tree-limb arms. "Y'all motherfuckers fucked up! It ain't about the winning, it's about the training. They on your motherfucking team too."

Of course, they weren't. Competitions were platoon on platoon, and drills not only stacked teams to win but were most belligerent to privates not in their platoons. That's just human nature. But the drills were still fundamentally focused on the unit in a way we were not. With time, indoctrination, and forced feedback from the combat-hardened cadre, every soldier became "brother," even the ones we didn't like. Five years down the road, I'm no longer shocked when a full-bird colonel—someone who outranks me by ten notches—calls me "brother." We are all brothers because we all sacrificed the same thing, *all of our time*, and risked the same thing, *everything*. In that regard, service is an equal endeavor across ranks. (Don't get me wrong, in garrison, generals still live in mansions.)

For many youngsters, basic training is the first time in their lives they're held to what Staff Sergeant Sal Giunta, the first living Medal of Honor awardee since Vietnam, refers to as an "unyielding moral compass."(16) The army calls itself a values-oriented organization, with its writ of core values contained in the word *leadership*: loyalty, duty, respect, selfless service, honor, and personal courage. In a sense, it's like the Boy Scouts, but with guns.

Removing personal effects such as clothing, cell phones, and designer sunglasses is one way the cadre kills the individual. (I was amazed at how leveling the simple act of separating the cool kids from their cool phones was.) The other way is through smoke sessions.

In front of our barracks was a giant sandpit where our company was repeatedly smoked for hours, generally for high crimes only the cadre could enumerate. No matter. The point was never the crime, only the admonition to police our own ranks before they did. Become our brother's keeper.

It's not as easy as it sounds. To get into your brother's business— even if he is half your age—flies in the face of our cherished American liberty, but I was learning quickly that the army was one of the most un-American institutions I'd ever run afoul of. Once committed, I had no vote, no liberty, no privacy or private property, and no voice. The American freedom I had enjoyed for four decades apparently came with a regressive tax, one that was paid entirely by its service members.

The great feat of basic training was how it gathered a mixed geology of personalities and backgrounds, and pressed a simple, consistent, and reliable stone. Kill the individual. Make a Joe. Make a brick wall of Joes. Consistent building materials are the key to any construction, be it a sandcastle, an orchestra, or a brigade combat team.

Who joins today's army? Who *doesn't?* Heroes and heels, and every-one in between. Among the soldiers in the army journalism office where I last worked, Sergeant "K" chose the army because there was less paper-work to fill out than for the Air Force, Navy, or Marines. "Shawsome" joined after failing freshman college physics for the third time. A Texan that I met in AIT enlisted in a "go to war or go to jail" scenario. On the other hand, Staff Sergeant Mary Katzenberger wanted to be a soldier since she was old enough to comprehend what it meant that her father had served in Vietnam. She believed it was her duty as an American.

My friend Dan Loeffler enlisted Sept. 12, 2001. He was a senior in college with a lucrative technology job lined up when the Twin Towers came down. Among the forty enlisted soldiers in his first platoon, a dozen were college graduates. "We had a couple guys who had master's degrees, but at the end of the day, they were still just Specialist So-and-so," he says with typical understatement. He and his fellow paratroopers were about to enter the meat grinder of pre-surge Iraq.

The initial inflow of over-qualified, patriotic Americans had mostly run its course by 2008 when I enlisted, but there were still a few. Here is what I found at boot camp:

Makarov, twenty-five years old, a Russian from Siberia. Makarov was assigned the bunk below mine. I asked him why he hadn't joined his country's army. Lean, pale, and hoarse from cigarettes, he looked me square in the eye and replied in a rolling Slavic accent, "Russian army is shit." The name was Makarov, with emphasis on the *CAR*, but most everybody pronounced it with the same emphasis as in *mackerel*. As a teenager, he had immigrated to Houston with his mother, tried to enter college, but American universities would not accept his Siberian high-school diploma. An oblique brush with the law further clouded his future. "I joined the army to get my shit together," he said. Halfway through our training cycle, Russia briefly went to war with Georgia, nearly drawing the United States into a conflict that might have pitted Makarov against his former neighbors, on the side of the Georgians, who, according to my Russian friend, had faked several incidents—artillery barrages, planes shot down—to gain the world's sympathy. Makarov's MOS was transportation specialist.

I tried to imagine the resolve required of him to join our military after being shunned by our education system. He was a Dostoevsky character, it seemed to me, my Brother Makarov. "I always enjoyed Russian literature," I told him.

"Who do you like?" he asked. "And please don't say 'Dostoevsky.' I hate that guy."

Gordon, the Oklahoma hayseed. "Two things," he told me. "One: my best friend is Buster. He's a golden retriever. My dad took him out to the woods one Saturday for killing chickens. He showed up on the porch Sunday morning with a bullet wound to the head. He was like, 'I'm home.' Two: my girlfriend only loves me for my truck. That's all you need to know about me."

Ok. Let's move on then.

Whitefeather, a classic apple-shaped native off a Southwest reservation, quiet as a kangaroo mouse. At fourteen, he was an honor student and captain of the soccer team. He got drunk one night and was taken advantage of by a seventeen-year-old girl, he said. She had the child. Following high school, he worked for the railroad but girl trouble followed him with his other bad habit, drinking. More alcohol, more girls, more babies. He taught his fiancée some martial arts because sometimes he "drinks like crazy," and she might need to defend herself, but instead, she karate-kicked one of his old girlfriends. Whitefeather joined the army to get away from girls and alcohol, he said.

Joseph, a coal miner's son, who quit Walmart to be an army truck driver when truck drivers were hard to keep because of the number and effectiveness of roadside bombs in Iraq. To the eye, Joseph was a cartoon hillbilly, but in truth, he was a hard-working, self-sacrificing, determined son. He lost over thirty pounds in six weeks and passed the final physical fitness test despite a double hernia. With his twenty-thousand-dollar enlistment bonus, Joseph was going to buy a new car. "But I decided that would be selfish," he said. "I told my daddy that I was able to stand on my own now, and he should retire. Because coal mining kills people."

Big Johnson was a journeyman electrician from Orange County, California. He wasn't particularly big, but he wasn't Little Johnson. Little Johnson, who was little, enlisted to be a cook to support his young family.

Roberts projected inner-city thug. A young black man who might have been a good infantryman, he enlisted to be a truck driver. To the end, he refused to be part of the team. "I came into this army alone. I'm a be alone now too," he'd say.

Massey was Roberts's antithesis: a tall, well-spoken, self-aware black man who was leveraging the army's educational benefits for business school. Always dependable and one of the smartest recruits in our platoon, Massey would do whatever it took to get through this part of his life and onto the next.

Hinds, a sandy-haired, soft-spoken, lanky cowboy off a working Texas cattle ranch. His wife mailed him a card every day of basic training. The drills made him do ten push-ups for each letter of each word she wrote on the backs of the envelopes. Hinds would become a helicopter mechanic.

Masson, our beautiful Haitian, whose pidgin-English poetry I corrected nightly in his letters to his "baby-mama" in New York City.

Heckerman, a natural if unorthodox leader and his own chubby comic foil, slotted for administration, still hoping for combat medic.

Materne, a street-tough Hispanic rumbler from Hinesville, Georgia. He was going to fight the good guys or the bad guys; might as well make him a good guy.

Hacker, a Pan-like goat kid, who couldn't seem to find the energy to make his own bed; hippie parents from the Seattle area. He was headed for a rude awakening in the 82nd Airborne Division.

Sekulow, a wafer-thin, hypercaffeinated carrottop from Nebraska who loved sci-fi, coffee, and his grandparents. He spoke in an elf's voice, began every sentence with "Dude, I . . ." and carpet-bombed liberally with high-pitched ineffectual f-bombs, but I really liked his energy and resilience. He planned to one day use his enlistment bonus to open a nightclub in Sweden. His grandmother had taught him to love fantasy books and use them to escape the sobering reality of an alcoholic father and manic-depressive mother. In the army, he hoped to find a surrogate parent, and I was happy to be that for him, if only for a short while.

Pulaski, an old guy like me. He was balding and out of shape, looked and talked corporate. Something had happened in Florida. He had been making six figures for a big real estate developer before the bust. Now he was in basic training, missing his wife and children.

And so on.

Second Platoon included citizens, semi-citizens, and cold-war enemies; African American Hispanics, Japanese Hawaiians, Scandinavian Nebraskans, and Turkish Muslims; GEDs, master's degrees, and one Ph.D. We represented the low and high enlistment age limits, with recruits of seventeen to forty-one. One thing was certain: these were men of action. Some enlisted for college money or adventure. For others, enlisting was an answer to a crappy home life, botched college scholarship, or petty crime. I can understand how some who have followed a career progression without dalliance might view service in the army as Stephen King so famously described just months before our basic training commenced. If you can't read, he said, ". . . then you've got the army, Iraq, I don't know, something like that. It's, it's not as bright."

Most Americans, I think, would recognize fellow travelers. Rather than giving in to victimhood, many saw service as a means to a brighter future, in a life they recognized as 100 percent mortal, on a path they knew traveled directly through war. In each was a measure of bravery and sufficient will to act. Did some enlist because they sincerely wanted to serve their country at a time of war? Yes. That is what they had in common.

Watching our platoon form up before the barracks was like watching paint mix at the hardware store. In no time, lack of sleep and food, along with the loss of personal space, time, and status mixed us into indistinguishable goo, so that our Muslim, Kosay, was attending synagogue on Sunday for the free donuts, another kid was eating southern Kentucky's oversized horseflies for money, and the boys downstairs snuck out one night in their issued brown polypropylene long johns to buy candy bars at a post convenience store. When they were caught reselling Snickers for twenty dollars, the drills tore the barracks apart for the contraband (wall lockers emptied and toppled, bunks upended), and the entire company was severely smoked through the night and road-marched in the morning.

TC says the army's greatest success is its integration of races and ethnicities. In basic training, the only minority was recruits who were failing to become soldiers. Those who felt they were owed never fit in. Others couldn't cope with the lack of notoriety.

"Out in the civilian world, I was hot shit," one young man told me. "I come into the army, and I can't do the obstacle course, I can't fire my weapon, I can't do anything right." I felt bad for him and suggested that he be patient and keep trying, but the truth is, some recruits belonged in the army, and some did not. The trouble is, once they were in, they had to stay in unless the army didn't want them.

The privation of basic training has the boys-to-men effect one would expect on young recruits. For those with more miles on the odometer, it can be equally instructive. One day as our platoon was sweating in the shade of a sprawling hickory, waiting for our turn to clear a building of opposing forces, Pulaski was in a contemplative mood. "In my life, I was so angry at everyone, at my wife, at my father, my business partners. It was their fault that my life wasn't working out as I expected it would."

He removed the helmet from his balding, sunburned head and wiped the salt from his eyes. "Ski" had replaced twenty-five pounds of flab with a vitality that he previously lacked. In fact, during the "shark attack" of drill sergeants on day one that had us running up and down staircases in the mid-August Kentucky heat, we thought he'd had a heart attack.

"Something's changed in me, though, and it changed here," he said. "I see these kids like Roberts. They just don't give a crap about anything. I used to be so hard on my own kids. I didn't want their lives to turn out like mine, and I just thought that if I controlled all the little details and made them into little perfect people, that they'd be happy."

"Little did you know you'd come to basic training and have to raise other people's kids," I said. "This army is the country's largest finishing school."

"Exactly. My kids are already so perfect," he said. "My life is already so blessed, and I just had no idea."

One is never too old to kill the individual.

OBEDIENCE

"They'll learn that, if the drill sergeant says the sky is green, it's green. If they don't, they'll die. They are children. They have no idea they are about to get slapped in the mouth by Iraq."

–Drill Sergeant Berube

Obedience. During my first three years in the army, I believed it was the only message any sergeant major had to deliver. "You will obey me." It didn't matter what the subject was. In Afghanistan, a command sergeant major named John Wayne Troxell was visiting our forward operating base in southern Ghazni Province. I was returning to the FOB on one helicopter, and he was arriving on another. As I humped my body weight in gear off the landing zone a quarter mile or so to headquarters, he and his entourage rode comfortably in an SUV next to me. Just before the HQ, the vehicle stopped and he jumped out, screaming in my face, "Those are not authorized eye pro! I'll bet you think they are, well they are not! Get that garbage off your face!"

Now, the army is serious about its "eye pro," or eye protection. It publishes an Authorized Protective Eyewear List of approved glasses. I guess during the long ride, he had time to consider mine. The ones I was wearing were on the list, but they were not on the simplified poster that the sergeant major was referring to. (Photographing through issued eye pro made me shoot off-center. I think it had to do with the increased distance between my eye and the viewfinder.)

With a nom de guerre of The Duke, one would hope John Wayne Troxell might have something better, or at least more inspirationally Duke-like, to say in a combat zone, perhaps slap me on the shoulder and coach me: "If you've got Stan Taliban by the balls, his heart and mind will follow." Nope. He wanted to talk eyewear. I was right, but he was the sergeant major. I hated mandatory obedience to institutionalized stupidity as much as any soldier, but I still appreciated how enforcement of standards produced a predictable and reliable soldier.

Since exiting the army, I've had so many people tell me the reason they never served was an inability to blindly obey stupid orders. It's a self-serving prophecy, of course, by those who have never had to depend on the reliability of another's actions or equipment in battle.

It doesn't help that lack of personal communication skills among the NCO corps, whether never learned or purposely not employed, makes the enlisted ranks clank along like a steel machine in perpetual need of oil, with hot metal gears sparking and grinding away at each other, causing premature wear-out and a constant need for new parts. Obedience is the electric current that runs the machine. Because authority can, authority does.

If told to wipe up a loogie he spat on the drill grounds using his T-shirt, a recruit does it. When drill sergeants empty the contents of fifty lockers in a pile while smoking their owners in a sandpit until one in the morning and then decree that the barracks floor, lockers and bodies will be spotless by 4:30 a.m. wakeup, and all the cleanup must be done by red-lens flashlight since it's already past lights-out, army recruits do it. Or, if a platoon sergeant tells a soldier to gather the grisly chunks of his best friends who have just been blown apart by daisy-chained 155mm artillery rounds buried beneath a street in Samarra, Iraq, he does that. And when he returns to base, he will help medics match the pieces to put his friends back together in separate bags before they're shipped home. Just ask my friend, Dan Loeffler, who lost three best friends who were like his brothers (and three other former squad mates) in that blast.

GETTING PHYSICAL: A SCHOOL FOR THOSE WHO HATE SCHOOL

"I hate boring classes. So when we learn how to handle enemy prisoners-of-war, we are gonna learn it hands on."
                                                    –Drill Sgt. Boddie

The enlisted ranks often appeal to those who never cared for school. That applies to drill sergeants as well, since they are the bloom of the corps. This of course makes them neither stupid nor unmotivated. In fact, over 92 percent of military enlistees have a high-school diploma, and 70 percent score in the upper half of the Armed Services Vocational Aptitude Battery, a test that all recruits take before they can enlist. (Stevens, 2008) (3)

Soldiers are a kinetic lot, so it's no surprise that classroom learning at basic training was awful. For all of their hard-won knowledge on the battlefield, as a group, the drill sergeants were terrible lecturers. They read PowerPoint slides as best they could, often stumbling over expensive words such as *discernible* or *proficiency*, but pounding each syllable with authority nonetheless. Post-lunch lectures in closed class-rooms lacking air conditioning begat a zombie class that only proved it was possible to sleep and snore while standing. The drills kept us awake by yelling "grenade" into the sleep-depleted, insulin-drugged audience, to which we responded "bang!" while backhanding our neighbors in the chest.

Grizzled old Drill Sergeant Engler loved to prowl for nodders. He would close nose-to-nose before spit-yelling in some sandbagged face, or pull the chair from beneath the dozer, or throw a rubber ball at him while screaming, "Wake up, you effing re-re!" Effing re-re was a practical and apparently allowable substitute for "fucking retard." Drills were allowed to call a recruit an effing this or effing that, but not a retard. Occasionally the old bull would hurl a chunk of two-by-four with calculated poor aim. It was a type of "man-up" correction common in a boy's world, a sort of "chastise-tainment."

To be sure, PowerPoint after lunch can challenge even the lustiest student, and it was no small bonding moment when, in Iraq a year later, a platoon of Iraqi soldiers told me that our American trainers could best improve teaching squad movement tactics by incorporating less PowerPoint in their lessons.

Unfortunately, physically-oriented recruits are not necessarily physically fit. A lieutenant colonel told our class that the army was finding stress injuries in male soldiers that were only found in women ten years earlier, particularly hip-neck fractures in which the ball joint of the hip breaks off. "The American male is no longer raised to be athletic," he said.

Coupled with lax recruiting standards to fill the ranks in a time of multiple wars, when up to 20 percent of incoming recruits were admitted with physical waivers, the challenges for basic training staffs to build a fit soldier were greater than ever. (Michaels, 2008) (4)

Of fifty recruits in our platoon, five failed the Army Physical Fitness Test, or APFT, even after ten weeks of training. (At Fort Jackson that year, three recruits died during PT.) For an eighteen-year-old male, the minimum requirement is fifteen push-ups, fifty-five sit-ups, and a two-mile run in 20:06, a feat my twelve-year-old daughter handily accomplished in middle school while I was in basic training.

Blame for a less fit generation is surely due in part to the electronic gizmos that none of us can put down. Critics have suggested that the twenty-billion-dollars-a-year video game industry produces products that fulfill many of the roles that team sports once did for American youth—opportunities for "physical" achievement, freedom, and connection to other players—and keeps kids on their butts and off their growing bones. (Pawlik-Kienlen, 2007) (5) Studies have shown that adults who were more active as children have denser bones that are more durable and resistant to fractures, such as those hip-neck fractures we were warned about. And their muscles are stronger. And their brains are more developed. (Those Who Exercise When Young Have Stronger Bones When They Grow Old, 2010) (6)

Yet video games, particularly first-person shooter games such as *Halo* and *Call of Duty*, are also credited by some with preparing soldiers for what might be their greatest challenge in the military—killing people. In 2006, Lieutenant Colonel Scott Sutton, director of the technology division at Quantico Marine Base, told a *Washington Post* reporter that soldiers in the current generation "probably feel less inhibited, down in their primal level, pointing their weapons at somebody . . . [which] provides a better foundation for us to work with." (Vargas, 2006) (7)

As it turns out, the army has been wrestling with this problem for some time. Teaching a recruit how to operate a rifle or machine gun is easy; teaching him to fire at a human is more complex.

WHAT WE KILL WITH

One, two, three, four.
Shoot 'em in the head, shoot 'em in the head, kill!
One, two, three, four.
Reload and shoot 'em again.

—First cadence after being issued our rifles

We were issued our M16s on a Sunday after church. The army refers to the M16 as a "lightweight, air-cooled, magazine-fed, shoulder-fired" weapon. The familiar Vietnam-era assault rifle was first issued in 1964, the same year Shea Stadium opened in New York, the Rolling Stones released their debut album, and the Gulf of Tonkin Incident gave President Lyndon Johnson broad powers to use conventional military forces in Southeast Asia. Our training rifles weren't that old, but most had seen better days. Every time I fired mine, the rear sight adjuster spun a few clicks, raising the peep sight. I had to compensate by aiming ever lower on a target or stop firing and reset it. It was a real piece of crap. Yet it accomplished the "good-enough" standard that the army adheres to for basic training. In 2008, most troops in Iraq and Afghanistan were using the more compact M4 carbine, a shorter version of the M16 suitable for close-quarters combat. However, the M16 would work just fine to teach us muzzle awareness and basic marksmanship.

Because I was a hunter accustomed to hardwood stocks and polished steel barrels, the M16 felt like refuse angle iron that had fallen off a passing train. It was short, matte-black with knobby steel and a profane plastic stock, what was left of a rifle once relieved of aesthetic considerations. The iron peep sight was nearly identical to what was used on the M1 Garand, the .30-caliber, semi-automatic rifle that our infantrymen carried in World War II. Worldwide, there are some seven million M16s in circulation. Compared with modern hunting rifles, the M16 has almost no kickback. Like the M4 we would eventually carry into battle, its 5.56mm bullet was much smaller and lighter than the old .30-caliber slugs of the World War II rifle, allowing infantry to carry many more rounds for the same weight. The tradeoff was that each round was less lethal, especially compared with the enemy's AK47 that fired a 7.62mm round, a rough equivalent to the .30 caliber. In theory, wounding an enemy still removed him from the battlefield, but in practice, enemies hit by a 5.56mm round can often continue to fight in the short term. Tellingly, most of the long-barrelled sniper rifles used by US forces are chambered for bullets closer in size to .30 caliber.

The army teaches rifle marksmanship in a safe, simple progression that, in addition to providing the skill of consistently hitting a target, infuses in the soldier two balancing propensities—to treat live ammunition as an agent of death and to fire it quickly. Instructors manage risk through strict allocation and accountability of live ammo at rifle ranges, unforgiving rules of range etiquette such as which direction to point the barrel, shakedown for errant rounds filched or accidentally caught up in gear, and the omnipotent decree, "Take all commands from the [range boss] tower."

Think about it. In basic training, large groups of young men are purposely pissed off, underfed, and deprived of sleep, then given assault rifles with live ammunition. But because of the strict rules that the drills adhered to at the ranges, I never felt in danger.

Drill Sergeant Boer had his own way of teaching muzzle awareness. When Private Helland carelessly pointed the empty weapon at Boer's stomach, the drill sergeant forced him to pull the trigger . . . "click," and then write a two-thousand-word essay to Boer's wife explaining why her husband was dead. The task actually brought Helland to tears.

HOW WE LEARN TO KILL

Young Drill Sergeant Berube walked solemnly down the "Pride Zone," the sacred, mural-painted center aisle of the barracks upon which no recruit was allowed to walk. At the far end, Berube turned and faced us.

"Listen. We talk glibly in the army about killing people. How many people have I killed with my weapon? Enough. It's not something that I am proud of. I pray to God—and he and I don't talk much—that you never have to take a human life. It's not an easy decision. Unless you are deranged, you carry it with you. There's not a day that goes by that I don't think about it."

For once, our platoon of Chatty Cathies was silent.

"The United States creates more ideals and freedoms than any country on earth," Berube said. "Yet there's a price to all that. Soldiers lose freedoms so they can protect the freedoms of others. Some of those freedoms—like freedom from taking a human life—you can never win back.

"When I returned home from Afghanistan, the governor of New Hampshire gave me a certificate of merit, and on that piece of paper was the number of enemy combatants that I had killed—14. I ripped it to pieces and threw it away."

Retired Lieutenant Colonel Dave Grossman, a former Army Ranger, 82nd Airborne paratrooper and West Point psychology instructor, contends in his so-called killology treatise, *On Killing*, that since World

War II, the Army has radically altered its weapons training to make it significantly easier for a soldier to pull the trigger on another human being. (Grossman, 1996) (8) His work is based on data suggesting that during World War II, less than a quarter of infantrymen were willing to fire their rifles at the enemy, half fired in Korea, and over 90 percent fired in Vietnam. What had changed?

It's the pop-up targets, he says. Modern military rifle ranges employ what recruits call "little green men," or human-shaped, green plastic targets that pop up at varying distances and time intervals for a rifleman to knock down with his fire. The sequencing trains soldiers to fire first and feel later, thus overcoming what Grossman says is a species-saving resistance to killing. (Some critics suggest the resistance to killing is less a phenomenon of our biology and more of our Judeo-Christian culture.) Grossman implicates the feel-later aspect as a primary culprit in post-traumatic stress disorder, or PTSD, which, according to a Rand Corp. study, has affected at least a quarter of the two million troops deployed to Iraq or Afghanistan since 2001. (K2, 2008) (9)

It may be difficult to imagine green plastic cutouts providing the realism necessary to shove a soldier over that curb against killing, but they must be real enough. A fellow recruit, a Mexican immigrant and the son of a borderland drug lord, confided to me one day at the range, "When I point my weapon at them, I cannot shoot. They are like people."

According to Grossman, the Army was also desensitizing us to killing through the "boot-camp deification of killing," a culture "almost unheard of in World War I, rare in World War II, increasingly present in Korea, and thoroughly institutionalized in Vietnam." We sang cadences about shooting people in the face and "watching them die, so early in the morning." We sang songs about clubbing baby seals (if a guy can kill a baby seal, he can surely kill an armed enemy). At the bayonet range, we attacked an army of old tires and tubular steel made into men while Drowning Pool's *Bodies* thumped over loudspeakers. Amidst the clang of bayonets and the occasional helmeted noggin thudding against the enemy's steel arms, we shouted, "Kill, kill, kill!" and like half-giddy supplicants playing along to a god we knew was also playing along, we gave the drill sergeants the answers they wanted to hear.

What is the bayonet for?

To kill, kill, kill, with cold blue steel!

Why is the grass green?

Blood, blood, bright red blood makes the green grass grow!

What are the two kinds of soldiers?

The quick and the dead!

Who are you?

The quick!

Who are they?

The dead.

Why is the sky blue?

Because God loves the infantry!

Our bloodlust rose with the energy in the lyrics, but for all the drama, it was a lot like learning to dance the salsa. It didn't necessarily make us want to eat tacos. It was make-believe and designed to condition us, and I think we all knew it.

Grossman says that violent video games are programming civil society much as the army is programming its soldiers, wearing away our resistance to killing. Can video games train warriors to fight and kill? Do violent gamers make violent combatants? I can tell you that gaming consoles are ubiquitous in garrison and deployed environments. A forward artillery observer friend said that after every contact with the enemy in Afghanistan,[1] his platoon would return to their base and play *Halo* and other first-person shooter games all night long. Clearly, there is a link.

---

1   The sergeant served as a forward observer with the 173rd Airborne Brigade Combat Team during its 2007-08 deployment to the Hindu-Kush area of Afghanistan.

The army certainly thinks so. We started rifle training on a weapons simulator that combined projected video and M16s modified with laser "projectiles" and a pneumatic operating system that provided realistic kickback each time the trigger was pulled. Though the graphics were clunky by contemporary gaming standards, the simulator provided a safe opportunity for new soldiers to become familiar with the weapon.

In a straw poll, I found that only seven of fifty-two recruits in my platoon had never played a combat-related video game. One young man from Boston told me that, after playing *Call of Duty* for many years, he was ready to get to Afghanistan to "kill so many people." Another said the day he touched his first real M16 that he was already an expert with it. He was preening before peers but one thing was certain: These young men wanted to be that Bad Muldoon blazing away in the video game, and, whereas prior generations of youngsters have only dreamt of going to war and returning as men, worthy and full, this generation has come closer than any to fooling itself into believing it has already done this.

In a rebuttal to Grossman's gamer-turned-killer hypothesis, Henry Jenkins, director of the comparative media studies program at the Massachusetts Institute of Technology, points out that, in classic studies, even apes make basic distinctions between play-fighting and actual combat. (Jenkins) (10) We understand play as entering a "magic circle" that allows us to express feelings and impulses without real-world consequences.

"We assume that [gamers] unwittingly apply what they learn in a fantasy environment to real world spaces," writes Jenkins, who also teaches courses on comics, animation, and graphic storytelling. He may have a point. We all know that it's all fun and games until someone pokes an eye out.

One of our final marksmanship lessons was a visit to the close-quarters shooting range where we used the shorter M4 carbine fitted with close-combat optics, the same type of weapon that most of us would be issued within a year and shortly before deploying to Iraq.

(Even in Big Army, weapons are tightly controlled in garrison and only issued by one's current company during training events.) Instead of little green men, the targets were full-color, lifelike representations of Iraqis and Afghans on pop-up armatures. There were six types of targets on the range: an Afghan with an AK47, an Arab with an RPG, an Arab with a machine gun, two Arab women with AK47s, and an Arab grandmother.

Before flipping up the targets, the range boss in the tower would call out what we were to fire at: "Shoot anyone with an AK47," or, "Shoot all armed males," but whatever the tower called, we were never to shoot the grandmother. We were learning to make positive identification before firing ("PID" is generally required before our soldiers engage enemy forces in today's war zones).

What basic training doesn't teach that real combat does is that to shoot at the enemy, a soldier must expose himself to getting shot. Especially when a firefight first kicks off, the most difficult task is locating where the fire is coming from, and to do that requires even more exposure. I've seen soldiers so terrified in a firefight that they were unable to shoot back. They simply wouldn't expose themselves. I've also seen reluctant warriors, clearly shaken, risk being shot at repeatedly to fire at the enemy. Some excel at war. Personality and genes, life experiences, varying degrees of training, and yes, moral values, all come into play. Is the man who hides a coward? One hates to say yes without knowing his story, and yet, the man who engages is clearly brave. The only way to know how a man will react in combat is to put him in combat.

HOW WE TRAIN TO FIGHT

The bond of brotherly love that holds small units of soldiers together has been written about and portrayed in film extensively. As Sebastian Junger writes in *War*, the chronicle of small-unit fighting by American paratroopers in Afghanistan, the essence of military tactics is soldiers moving as a single-minded organism. It should be no surprise then that a soldier is loyal to his bones. If he is loyal to the unit, the unit survives. If the unit survives, its members are more likely to survive. The strength of the wolf is the pack. Soldiers have a term to describe those who are not loyal. It is "blue falcon," code for buddy fucker.

In the decentralized wars in Iraq and Afghanistan, soldiers fight in small, close-knit units. What is a unit? It depends. The word *unit* is a relative term that changes depending upon who wants to know. If a civilian were to ask me, I would say that my unit is the 82nd Airborne Division. To another soldier, my unit is the 1st Brigade Combat Team of the 82nd Airborne Division. To a soldier within our brigade, I would say brigade public affairs. An infantry soldier in the same position might respond with his platoon and company, e.g., Third Platoon, Delta Company.

Beyond the battle-buddy pair, the smallest unit in the infantry is the four-man "fire team." Two fire teams and a squad leader make a squad, the smallest unit that can move on a fixed enemy position or execute an ambush. Four squads make up a platoon, which is led by a platoon leader (a lieutenant) and a platoon sergeant. Many operations in Iraq and Afghanistan are executed at the platoon level since platoons have an officer, a medic, machine gun teams and a forward observer (to call in artillery or close air support). An infantry platoon consists of about forty soldiers.

A company is made up of three to four platoons. It is commanded by a captain and is run by an executive officer and a top NCO called a first sergeant. In general, it's the captain's job to let the Good Idea Fairy fly and the first sergeant's job to kill it before it reaches the men. A more generous analysis might suggest that the officer inspires and gives direction, and the first sergeant ensures discipline and functionality. Companies contain the additional assets of mortar teams, attached sniper teams, and a headquarters element that can manage several ongoing operations. While military units are further grouped into battalions, brigades, divisions, etc., it's at the company level and lower that a soldier finds familiar faces, a home, and brotherly love. Parents supporting their soldier's unit during the holidays should send gifts and supplies to his company.

While multi-player video games attempt to replicate small-unit warfare, they lack the cohesive bonds formed between soldiers who continually place their lives in each other's hands. Who needs love when you have the reset button?

Basic training wasn't much more effective at engendering those bonds, probably because we knew that each soldier would be heading off his own way at its conclusion. We learned the techniques of small-unit warfare by attacking mortar teams in a forest, clearing villages by firing blanks at cardboard insurgents, and defending an FOB in a weeklong culminating exercise. Even though together we suffered the heat, lack of food and sleep, and drill sergeants, we loved each other only as much as we had to.

Case in point, it was finally our squad's turn to assault Sideyah, a mock Iraqi village made of old Western-style storefront facades and a pre-recorded soundtrack of Muslim call to prayers, automatic rifle fire, and barking dogs. We were taking fire from multiple positions, and Lambert had already accidentally shot the friendly mayor. We bounded up Main Street from building to building, one team covering as the other moved, when a simulated IED killed Makarov, who was playing a team leader.

I was the squad leader. "Somebody has to carry Makarov," I ordered.

"You carry his ass," Boggs told Lambert.

"Fuck no, I didn't get him killed. He's too heavy."

Maxwell, the biggest man in the entire company by a head, tried to look inconspicuous. On a balcony, a barrel fell over, uncovering an Arab. Maxwell and a slight Hawaiian kid opened up with their M16s, more or less so they would not have to carry Makarov. They shot an unarmed boy. Strike two for winning the hearts and minds.

"Good *gravy*," cried Drill Sergeant Boer.

Materne, the scrappy Hispanic, hoisted Makarov onto his shoulder and wobbled off toward the forest, cursing in Spanish.

"You only have to carry him to the edge of the woodline," called Boer. With that, Materne unceremoniously dumped Makarov on the ground, the "woodline" apparently being a relative term that included tall grass.

Our teamwork during FOB Week was a little better because the opportunity to get it over on the drills once before graduating was like a shiny thing in the grass. The idea of FOB Week was simple: go out on "missions" to nearby villages and rifle ranges during the day, and defend the FOB at night from attacking insurgents (drill sergeants). We could sleep after graduation.

Our FOB was an acre of large tents secured by a perimeter of railroad ties, concertina wire, and guard towers fixed with machine guns loaded with belts of blank ammunition. We had blanks for our M16s as well. Each platoon was responsible for manning a section of the perimeter. One platoon was assigned the main gate and towers. The drills relished this phase of training and took turns attacking us.

Midnight, our first night on the FOB, Makarov and I have front-gate guard duty. There was no moon, no stars. "You know how they say you hear crickets when nobody knows an answer that everyone should know?" Makarov asks. "Well I hear these crickets now."

"Those are cicadas," I say, correcting him.

"Whatever the fuck they are. Little fucking insects. I hear them."

We wait for four hours. Nothing happens. Not until we're back in the tents sleeping do the drill sergeants attack. Mortars come screaming in (simulated by controlled explosives in a steel barrel) as insurgents attack with machine guns. Gonzales runs out of the dark and yells, "We need more men. They're all dead at the front gate! Gurule got his throat slit, and Heckerman was killed by point-blank machine gun fire." After the guard is annihilated, the attackers walk through the front gate, and while the rest of the company stands dumbstruck, they capture our headquarters. Game over.

The point of the mortars, machine gun fire, and sleepless nights was to give us a taste of chaos under fire, but also to get us thinking as a group. Before, during and after each attack, we had to account for each soldier's whereabouts and condition. This was where soldiers began to learn about never leaving a fallen comrade. The easiest way to leave another soldier is to lose track of him.

In one particularly ferocious engagement, nearly our entire company was slaughtered. At the casualty-collection point, rows of dead and wounded looked like the grim pavers of some misbegotten highway. Makarov, as usual, provided comic relief. "I saw General Jones Patton by the front gate," he said, calling out our platoon's king of one-ups-manship. "He was killed twenty-seven times. He thinks we should attack."

"Wow, he must be lucky," I replied.

"Lucky?" Makarov asked. "Is not lucky. In my country, we have this saying. If you were born lucky, even your rooster will lay eggs. I don't see Jones's rooster laying eggs. I think Drill Sergeant will cook him tonight."

"Really?"

"We have this other saying in Russia. Rooster today, feather duster tomorrow."

There was no blood, no torn and shattered limbs, gray matter, sucking chests, or any of the other combat wounds we had been trained to treat, just self-loathing by forty of the army's newest Bad Muldoons.

When Second Platoon was again bedded down, I resumed guard duty with Hinds, the Texas ranch hand. From a cobalt, pre-dawn sky came a low rumble as two hulking angular forms materialized in the west just above treetop level. They were Apache attack helicopters. "Good Lord," I muttered. The drill sergeants just had to keep beating us down. Helicopters? Really? I sat paralyzed, as did Hinds. Above the front gate, the helicopters suddenly flared and turned south. We watched them fly beneath Orion and disappear. They were awesome. "Were you thinking what I was thinking?" I asked, relieved that we didn't have to rouse the boys to fight helicopters.

"Yep."

"That would have been ridiculous."

It would have been. Incorporating a $36 million helicopter would have been too expensive for basic training. If nothing else, FOB Week taught us how basic our basic training had been and how little we still knew. Though we might be dressed like heroes behind our bullet-proof ceramic plates and Kevlar helmets, we were not even experienced enough to be called Cherry, let alone Soldier. The real training, the life-preserving training, would happen once we reached our unit.

FAMILY

"And remember, once you qualify with your weapon, unless you are just a worthless motherfucker, you are gonna gradu-ate this motherfucking place. Remember this: At graduation, your mothers are going to want to meet the man who made the men. Send them my way."

–Drill Sgt. Boddie

Much was made of graduation and Family Day, of the mothers who would stare unrecognizing at the chisel-faced warriors in place of their sons. My children were still in school, so I would not see my family until later that fall.

In many respects, leaving my wife and kids for basic training was the most jarring of any of the family separations I've experienced as a uni-formed service member, including deployments to Iraq and Afghanistan. At least then I called my wife every week and emailed almost daily.

During the nine weeks of basic, I was allowed two three-minute phone calls and the post office. The only wives and mothers in America still receiving handwritten letters have a loved one in basic training.

Privation does make for an appreciative heart. The family separation that I've endured as a soldier has made me a more thankful, patient husband and father. It's the one thing I'd like my own children to experience in some meaningful capacity before they set out into the world.

The drills told us that basic training would prepare families for deployment separation. I suppose it does. Young wives and girlfriends are forced to confront an often unwelcomed autonomy, not why they wanted a relationship. Some young wives spend their soldiers' paychecks frivolously, sometimes with other men. This happened extensively during the Iraq troop surge of 2007, during which some troops were away for 15 months. On the phone, daughters fret and sons refuse to talk. Those left behind get a week of flag-waving support from well-meaning friends and relatives, and then all is quiet on the home front. It's that way every time.

During basic training, we lost many family days but a limited number of life events. Sekulow's grandfather died and then his grandmother fell ill, with only his younger brother to care for her. Boggs' wife left him. Sunsets languished unused on the porch, and the dogs moped on the kitchen floors.

Downrange would be much different. Downrange is a military term used to describe the dangerous end of a rifle range, or being deployed to a war zone. Downrange, life moments fall away like loose sand carried in your hands for twelve months. You know it's too long not to lose most of it.

Twelve months is a long time to hold one's breath. Ask any Army wife. With a soldier downrange, a spouse can retreat into the ensuing silence, fearful of "news" in any form. On the phone, she asks you to be careful, and because she's driving to see her folks over the weekend, you ask her to be careful, and you hold your breath, too. Children put on growth rings, the car depreciates, and the dog can no longer straighten its hip while lying on the vent. After a year in Iraq, many of my fellow soldiers came home to babies they'd never held. One came home to a funeral for his two-year-old who had drowned.

TC had forewarned me. Every separation is more difficult than that last. His girls' sweet sixteens and graduations were lost long ago—they're in college now. His last trip to Afghanistan was cut short when his wife developed breast cancer. He left a remote FOB where young men of my division were coming in shot up and bleeding out so that he could be with his wife of twenty years in case that year was her last. He was told he was going back to Afghanistan in a few months, for a year. I'm not sure what to make of that.

APPEARANCE IS REALITY

"You watch. There's always one motherfucker gonna pass out in his pimp suit right there on the graduation field. Somebody gonna say, 'You see that motherfucker fall down?' And somebody else gonna say, 'Huh?' then 'Hey, he's out of step!'"
—Drill Sgt. Boddie

In the army, a thing is not always its name. The M16 is never to be carried by its carrying handle; trash is never to sit in the trashcan; the water fountain in our basic training barracks was never for drinking. Velcro is hook-pile-loop tape. Rubber bands are retainer bands. Hands don't go in pockets; walls don't hold up soldiers; the push-up is the front leaning rest; a smoke session is neither hazing nor punishment but rather, corrective training.

In the army, what you wear is who you are. Soldiers wear their résumés. We look at people's chests first because that is where the important stuff is, beginning with rank. The nametape sits above the right breast pocket. "US Army" is on the opposite side, "above the heart" as the drills liked to tell us. Of course, the heart is actually center-mass, and more appropriately, directly beneath the rank.

Like money, rank is not a big deal until you get some. As a grown man new to the army, rank reverence irritated me, but after a while, I grew to appreciate how quickly rank indicated what another soldier's presence meant for you.

On the left shoulder goes a soldier's unit insignia, such as the 82nd Airborne Division's famous All American "AA" patch. That's also where any tabs go, and tabs are all good—Ranger, Special Forces, Sapper, etc. Tabs are certifications. For instance, a soldier who graduates from Ranger School gets a Ranger tab, but that only makes him Ranger-qualified. To be a Ranger, one has to be assigned to the 75th Ranger Regiment.

The right shoulder is the "heavy shoulder," because that's where the combat patch goes. Most of our drills had seen combat in Iraq with the 101st Airborne Division, so they wore the iconic "Screaming Eagle." A soldier who had 101st patches on both shoulders, meaning that he'd gone to war with and was still part of the 101st, had a "chicken sand-wich." Rival units might refer to the patch as the "gagging chicken."

Black skill identifiers go on the left breast above "US Army." These include jump wings, combat badges, and the like.

What does it all mean? Practically speaking, rank has the most weight, followed by tabs, then badges and patches. However, as in life, it's important not to confuse rank with authority. Rank dictates, author-ity leads. Rank is what grade you are, authority is what you've done, what you can do, and how you act. A Ranger-tabbed specialist may have more real authority than a non-tabbed sergeant. In close combat, authority almost always trumps rank. However, rank never goes away. It's like military kryptonite.

Soldiers are taught to project authority, to walk erect with shoul-ders back and eyes forward, and to speak with "big boy voices." I was amused at my hometown recruiters for dropping their voices several octaves when answering the phone, but four years later, I was doing the same thing, speaking in my "sergeant's voice" as my wife likes to call it. Project authority, and others will concede it to you. Back it up with confident posturing and those of higher rank will largely let a soldier go about his business.

MARCHING ORDERS

"If you need help with the army, under no circumstance will you call me. If I see you in Iraq and you wave, I'm going to raise my motherfucking M4 and shoot you in the face. If you need help, ask your platoon sergeant. If he turns out to be a turd, tell him your drill sergeant said he should be helping you, then you call me. Be motherfucking soldiers. Be motherfucking men. Otherwise you just gonna be a motherfucking turd."

–Drill Sgt. Boddie

In the Big Army, twelve thousand soldiers will rehearse for eight hours to prepare for a division change-of-command. That may sound like egos-on-fire for the two-star generals swapping places, but here's the thing: in the army, officers generally get swapped out of command positions every two years. With that kind of tenure, the division was never really General So-and-So's in the first place. He was just the custodian of its soldiers and colors for a while.

However, the military loves its ceremony. Following our final twelve-mile ruck march back to the basic training barracks, we stood in formation preparing to don our black berets for the first time. Tiki torches lit up a space in the dark, and Lee Greenwood crooned "God Bless the USA" from a boom box. In just a week, we would again be free in America, if just for a single afternoon, to visit with our families, to fill our bellies, to wear *civvies*, to go and see and be and say. We could smell the liberty. We were proud.

To my right was Makarov, the Russian national, to my left, Jose Ceno of the Dominican Republic. There was Guevara from Mexico, Masson from Haiti, Kosay from Turkey. To be an American soldier required no American at all, only eligibility and a signature.

Within days, we would each receive orders to relocate to another post for training specific to our MOS. Forward observers would go to Fort Sill, Oklahoma, home of the artillery. Makarov and other transportation specialists were headed to Fort Lee, Virginia. I was bound for Fort Mead, Maryland, and the Defense Information School.

I removed the black beret from the front pocket of my body armor, where it had been stowed throughout FOB Week. I prepared to put it on. Drill Sergeant Chapman, a giant linebacker type from the 101st, was telling Boggs a story about coming home from Iraq and turning down a hundred dollars in an airport bar from a businessman trying to show his appreciation. (Chapman had once asked a recruit from West Virginia whether all the houses in his county were trailers, and had he ever eaten possum stew. He was not a sensitive man.)

"Drill sergeant, my daddy raised us to always accept gifts," Boggs said.

"See, we're raising you a new way," replied Chapman.

And with that, we donned our berets. We were soldiers, raised a new way. I was proud, even though Drill Sergeant Berube said I looked like a pizza delivery boy. Now we each wanted a combat patch.

Hours before sunup on the final day of basic training, Makarov and I were jogging back from the mailbox. "Hey, do you think we'll get good chow this morning?" he asked.

"No," I replied, "but do you know what's funny? When we passed the new recruits who just got here, did you feel any nostalgia?"

"Hell no. I hate this place."

"Me too," I said. "You know what they say?"

"What do they say?"

"Basic training is supposed to suck."

He laughed. It did suck. "Is that what they say?" he asked.

"In my country," I replied.

A year later, Makarov became a US citizen. I was in Iraq.

CHAPTER 3:
STRIKE HOLD, ALL THE WAY, AIRBORNE!

"There's a lot of things you're going to see here that are a little messed up or a little different. Don't try to change it. We're the 82nd Airborne and that's the way we do it. We like it that way."

—An officer at a newcomers' brief, Hall of Heroes, 2011

AIT: PROM NIGHT EVERY NIGHT

TC always said that race integration is the army's greatest accomplishment but that its integration of the sexes is its greatest failure. That's hardly fair but perhaps true. Undiscovered and un-invented is the institution that has successfully corked the animal spirits of human nature, and the army is no different.

What I will say is this: every night I spent at Fort Meade was like high-school prom night. Boys and girls sequestered for months in the lockdown of boot camp were able to mingle once again. AIT was still initial entry training, so we still exercised, marched, pulled duty and ate when and where the army told us to, all in a restrictive manner. Ever the forbidden fruit, female soldiers were locked up at night on the barracks' third floor, which was surveilled 24/7 by closed-circuit television. That slowed the party down but hardly stopped it. In the barracks day room, in the back seats of cars, in the poison ivy patch across the road, in combat boots and ACUs.

For male soldiers who had attended one of the male-only basic training facilities, it was not just their first experience with uniformed female soldiers but their first encounter with any woman in over ten weeks. In the male-heavy, limited lockdown of AIT, many girls were for the first time in their lives de facto beauty queens, and lacking the developed social skills necessary to navigate their newly elevated positions. They transformed overnight into tramps or prima donnas. Female platoon sergeants became governesses, openly scolding overly flirtatious female soldiers; male platoon sergeants treated male soldiers like soldiers and female soldiers like their daughters or girlfriends. The army officially discourages the potentially pejorative terms *lady*, *girl* and *woman* to reference the female soldier. That's probably a wise choice given the challenges that women must confront that men don't, especially in superior-subordinate relationships. None of this is to say that the army and especially AIT is a great venue to pick up dates, only that the Army's ability to fundamentally change behaviors happens over time, and so far as the human condition goes, not at all.

Of course, socializing wasn't the official point of AIT. I was there to learn army-style journalism. Having worked in the publishing industry for many years prior to enlistment, I found the journalism training to be quite good, albeit abbreviated. As with boot camp's marksmanship training, it was more about knocking the target down than hitting the bull's-eye. All of my instructors were dedicated professionals. Many were prior-service civilians who brought Big Media experience to the schoolhouse.

For budding journalists, the military is an outstanding option for learning the craft without starving. New hires in civilian journalism write obituaries and wait tables. My first assignment was covering the war in western Iraq, mixing with top reporters from the *New York Times*, *L.A. Times*, and the *Washington Post*.

The downside is that military journalists are more like members of a corporate in-house news staff than independent voices of news. We write for the boss, megaphoning what the military calls "command information." Is it propaganda? Not really. The military has another branch for that called Information Operations. I would peg the job somewhere between journalism and cheerleading, certainly no more biased and often more accurate than the major news outlets of today, particularly in war zones that are simply too dangerous for civilian reporters to penetrate effectively.

Another downside: news-staff dynamics will always default to rank in the military. A senior sergeant may shut you down through force of rank, even though his "opinion" introduces four grammatical errors and two errors in fact—but there are few opportunities like military journalism for young people to gain critical experience, particularly in a time of war.

Finally and importantly, I have never been told or encouraged to lie or mislead the reader.

JUMP SCHOOL

All I really have to say about airborne school is that it worked. My parachute opened every time. In the January cold, a cough that I picked up in AIT developed into pneumonia at Fort Benning, Georgia. Paratroopers are a tough breed, I learned, and don't need "snivel gear," or clothing designed to keep a person warm. Snivel gear includes Army-issued long johns, fleece jackets, wind-proof parkas, etc. Not allowed.

A high fever from the pneumonia made jump week pretty rough (it was fourteen degrees during the combat-equipment night jump), but I didn't report it for fear of being recycled. I'd heard too many stories of soldiers being caught in that unpredictable spin cycle, sequestered for weeks at Benning doing "details" like pulling weeds or mowing grass, waiting to fall back into the jump-school queue. One thing about the all-voluntary military: it's easier to render the obligations one makes than attempt to shed them. Just because a person quits something he volunteers for, be it basic training or airborne school, doesn't mean he's going to be on the next bus home. Or the next bus, or the one after that. Everyone at jump school was a volunteer, and many had to beg to get there. Quitters were not well received.

There was a plus to being sick. Misery inside the aircraft, I found, provided a very compelling reason for jumping out of it. That was particularly true during the "combat jump" when we were laden with heavy rucksacks and weapons, preparing to huck en masse into the pitch-black night over an unseen earth. Sickness, heat, cold, full bladders—they all contribute toward one's willingness to jump out of that perfectly good aircraft.

THE DEVIL BRIGADE

Earning the silver wings of a US Army paratrooper was a proud experience for me. My seventy-year-old father pinned them on my chest. Ironically, he had served in the Air Force between the Korean and Vietnam Wars to avoid being drafted into the army.

I remember from childhood his stories of how the tedium and pointlessness of standing guard over barrels of oil in the jungles of Guam spurred him to make something of himself in business, and how the military's starched uniforms, sharp creases, and tactically-folded T-shirts permanently wrecked his opinion of his mother's ability to properly do laundry. Yet he was proud of his service and glad to be a part of the ceremony.

Like all new soldiers graduating jump school, I did not learn to what duty station I would be reporting until the final day of jump school. I called my wife. "Honey, we're moving to Fort Bragg, North Carolina. I've been assigned to the 82nd Airborne Division."

"Is that good?" she asked.

The 82nd Airborne Division. Had the late Stephen Ambrose never written the book *Band of Brothers*, the 82nd might still be the most well-known airborne division in the world. In fact, it's the only one left in America's army.

In the fall of 1942, the World War I era 82nd Infantry Division was reactivated as the 82nd Airborne Division at Camp Claiborne, Louisiana. The following day, the troops mustered in a large field. Everyone on one side would remain in the 82nd. Everyone on the other side would become part of the newly formed 101st Airborne Division. Together, the two divisions would make history with the largest combat airborne operations the world would ever know.

The mass parachute assault was a relatively new approach to warfare and one that Supreme Allied Commander General Dwight D. Eisenhower enthusiastically embraced, in spite of the German Army's poor results. (During the assault of Crete in 1941, *Fallschirmjäger* losses were so heavy that Hitler forbade their further use except in special operations.)

Dropping troops from the sky seemed ideal for seizing enemy airfields, bridges, and key road intersections, or for pincer movements against enemy forces attacking beachheads. In either case, paratroopers were expected to capture an objective and defend it just long enough to link up with traditional ground forces.

The 82nd was the first American division to conduct a large-scale drop, during the invasion of Sicily in the summer of 1943. Two of its parachute infantry regiments, the 505th and the 504th, joined

British airborne forces for the initial assault. It was the 504th Parachute Infantry Regiment—Michael Metcalf's future unit—that I would join at Fort Bragg.

Allied naval forces mistook the C-47 transports for German bombers and opened fire, downing twenty-three planeloads of 504th paratroopers and scattering the rest across the countryside. Yet once on the ground, the highly-trained, tenacious paratroopers became a decisive force, stalling the advance of German armor against a nascent Allied beachhead until a force large enough to defend itself had landed.

Two months later, the 504th jumped into Salerno, Italy, to reinforce the 5th Army beachhead there. While the rest of the 82nd shipped back to England to prepare for the invasion of northern France, the 504th stayed with the fight in Italy, assaulting Anzio in January 1944. During fierce fighting there, the regiment earned its nickname, taken from the diary of a German officer killed in combat:

"American parachutists . . . devils in baggy pants . . . are less than a hundred meters from my outpost line. I can't sleep at night; they pop up from nowhere and we never know when or how they will strike next. Seems like the black-hearted devils are everywhere . . ."

Following months of difficult fighting in the rugged hills of Italy, the "Devils in Baggy Pants" returned to England to refit while the rest of the 82nd joined the 101st in the parachute assault on Normandy to open the Allied invasion of France. Sainte-Mère-Église was the first French town to be liberated. Paratroopers of the 82nd drove the Germans out at four in the morning, June 6, 1944. General Matthew B. Ridgway, the division's commander, described his paratroopers' battle in Normandy as ". . . 33 days of action without relief, without replacement. Every mission accomplished. No ground gained ever relinquished." By the time the division returned to England, 5,245 troopers were killed, wounded, or missing. An excellent account of the fighting around Sainte-Mère-Église is *The First Men In: US Paratroopers and the Fight to Save D-Day* by Ed Ruggero. (18)

During Operation Market Garden in the Netherlands, the 504th earned fame at Nijmegen near the German border for a daring and costly daylight crossing of the Waal River under heavy machine gun and artillery fire, recounted in brutal detail in James Megellas' autobiographical book, *All the Way to Berlin: A Paratrooper at War in Europe.* (17)

During the winter of 1944–45, as the "Band of Brothers" of Easy Company, 506th PIR, were preparing to defend Bastogne, Belgium, 82nd Airborne Division paratroopers were also marching forward past American troops fleeing the German surprise offensive through the Ardennes. Famously, a young paratrooper, a private, told a sergeant in a retreating tank destroyer to ". . . pull your vehicle behind me—I'm the 82nd Airborne, and this is as far as the bastards are going!"

Since World War II, the 82nd Airborne Division has seen action in a number of small conflicts, including a civil war in the Dominican Republic, the defeating of a military coup in Haiti, and the 1989 invasion of Panama to oust Manuel Noriega. Because of its quick-strike capability, the division was held in strategic reserve for the Korean War and much of Vietnam. It played active roles in both Desert Shield and Desert Storm in the early 1990s.

By the time I caught up with the Devils in Baggy Pants in March of 2009, most of its mid-level sergeants had three, four, even five deployments under their belts. Many were part of the initial invasions in Afghanistan or Iraq, or both. Most had lost friends. They had held through the shifting sands of modularization as the army reorganized its forces from large echelons designed to fight the Soviets into smaller self-sustaining brigade combat teams to meet the demands of the asymmetrical warfare it was now confronting. The smaller teams negated the need to deploy an entire division of twenty thousand soldiers when most of a division's warfighting functions could be contained within a single BCT of 3,500.

The old "regimental" system was, for the most part, a thing of the past, as infantry, artillery, scout, and support regiments were diced and collated into standalone BCTs. The 82nd Airborne Division's 1st Brigade Combat Team retained the 1st and 2nd Battalions of the 504th Parachute Infantry Regiment as its infantry component. To that nucleus were added a squadron of cavalry scouts (a squadron is similar to an infantry battalion), an airborne field artillery battalion (yes, they jump with their howitzers), and two support battalions that included military police, logisticians, engineers, intel cells, medics, and mechanics. Except where the demand of certain MOSs exceeds supply, every soldier is airborne-qualified.

All this was new to me as I stepped off the bus onto sun-bleached and cracked Ardennes Street in Fort Bragg, North Carolina. Ardennes, as in Ardennes Forest, pronounced with the *S* because we're in America, not France, and pronouncing it the French way would only make a soldier stick out.

"You sound like a varnished turd, specialist," a staff sergeant scolded me when I said it wrong.

"Ardennes," I repeated, this time with an *S*.

"Airfuckingborne!" he replied.

At the north end of Ardennes beyond rows of lofty longleaf pines lay Pope Army Airfield. From Pope come the rumbling Hercules C-130 propeller-driven paratroop planes that streak the blue skies daily over Ardennes, the red thumping artery of the 82nd Airborne Division. The growl of those four turbine engines already evoked in me visceral machinations of stand up, hook up, shuffle to the door, the sudden rush, the prop blast, and silk snapping overhead.

Jump school seemed the natural entrance to this place. From north to south, Ardennes was rife with 82nd history: Graves, Waal, Mederet, and Messina Streets; La Fiere Loop; Bastogne, Salerno, and Sicily Drives—all World War II references. There was York Theatre and Pike Field, named for a courageous sergeant and lieutenant colonel who fought in World War I; Deglopper Street, Towle Stadium, and Funk Gym, for two heroic privates and a first sergeant who fought in

World War II. All five were Medal of Honor awardees. One of the more endearing qualities of military culture is how courage and self-sacrifice are held above all else, even rank. Because those qualities are in greatest demand on the battlefield, and because the battlefield is mostly filled with privates and young sergeants, they are most likely to be awarded for valor. Generals salute Medal of Honor awardees, even privates.

As I watched a crowd of young paratroopers in gilded dress uniforms, canted maroon berets, and glinting black jump boots pour from York Theater, it occurred to me that the only combat veterans I had ever seen were wrinkled vestiges of the 1940s or ponytailed 'Nam vets. These men were something altogether different. They walked like weaponized energy. They were vital, jovial, and strong, leaving from some ceremonial gathering in twos and threes. I think it was their conspicuous youth that made me think of my son, Douglas, who was still in middle school. Most of them were likely in middle school when we first invaded Afghanistan. My son will be of age in a year.

I watched with some awe, but also thinking of TC's one story that stuck, from when he and his wife lived here on post. When a paratrooper living a few houses down was killed in Iraq, the house was swarmed with visitors for a few days, and when they left, for five days the wife did not come out of the house. Then the house was vacant.

The nerd variant of the infantrymen I had seen at York Theater was Staff Sergeant Patrick Malone. He was my new immediate supervisor and would be my boss for the next eighteen months. Malone had arrived a month earlier, from Vicenza, Italy, where he was a broadcaster for the Armed Forces Network.

Malone was a quick riser, a knock-kneed, bespectacled, nose-to-the-grindstone geek in the subculture of army public affairs. In a month, he would be promoted to sergeant first class, achieving the eponymous "E-7 in seven years" only common to wartime fast trackers. I would come to appreciate his work ethic, loyalty, and big-hearted nature over time, but it was a bit of a Mexican standoff at the beginning. Tall, with small hands and a bit of a paunch, my new sergeant had never been to college and was half my age. I was about to "drink through the proverbial fire hose" as he conducted my first "counseling" in the dilapidated husk of a red-brick building that was apparently my new office.

In the army, counseling has a specific meaning. It's a formal sit-down with one's supervisor with a worksheet to guide and document expectations, plans, and outcomes. NCOs are required to counsel subordinates once a month, though they may do so at any time for any reason, good or bad.

Young Malone gave me a stern talking to. That initial counseling session was a harbinger of mostly unfavorable things to come:

THE ARMY OWNED
ALL OF MY TIME

No measure is so keenly kept in the army as is time. That includes a soldier's time in service, time in rank, time in grade, time for formation, time for chow, time for reveille and retreat; there is leave, absence without leave, temporary duty leave; hard time and army time, and of course, "time now." Army time is ten minutes prior to the hard time, and it accumulates at each level of authority: the captain says 0630, so the first sergeant says 0620, the platoon sergeant says 0610, the squad leader 0600, the team leader 0550. Joe shows up at 0545 for the 0630 formation, to be "on time."

From years of self-employment, I was keenly aware that time is money and courted cardiac arrest at the hours I would squander in lines waiting to accomplish a simple task or no task at all. Because the army owns all of a soldier's time (it's right there in the contract), there is no pressure to use it efficiently. Nobody cares if your time is wasted in cetacean-sized chunks, because those who might care are subject to the same affliction. A four-hour layover at an airport is loose change to a soldier. On jump days, it's common for paratroopers scheduled for a mid-morning jump to muster for manifest at 2 a.m. It takes less than five minutes to don a parachute and another fifteen to board a plane.

The sheer inventory of soldier time is often a burden for the army, which is why bucket brigades are so popular. Why have two do a job for two when you can have ten?

The truth is, an army's purpose is to wage war, and when there is no war (as in garrison), keeping Joe busy is often the goal of work. Soldiers can only train so much. What to do with them then? For starters, count them first and count them often. First formation is at 6:30 a.m. to count bodies, to salute the flag to the sounds of reveille, receive the day's orders, and conduct physical training, or PT. Soldiers exercise for about an hour with their platoon or staff section. Paratroopers run a minimum of four miles at least three times per week and road-march with a thirty-five-pound (or more) rucksack once a week, minimum.

Managers such as company first sergeants may arrive as early as 4 a.m., and there is no bonus, overtime, or commission for extra time or effort, not even brownie points, only the avoidance of getting "crushed" by one's superior.

The official workday is something like nine to five, but those are tidal marks. One's duty as a soldier often changes with no advance notice. My wife and I quickly learned to avoid plans more than two weeks out. At least once a week, I would tell her that I would be home in fifteen minutes, only to arrive hours later or even the following day.

Finally, there is little time for sleep. Troop movements, some training, and much of combat occur in the dead of night. Also, junior enlisted serve various forms of twenty-four-hour guard duty several times a month, which massively interrupts the sleep cycle.

Malone began my counseling session by listing my chores: I would empty the office trash daily, vacuum the floor, and clean the latrines for the building's forty occupants every Friday. I would be at least ten minutes early for formation.

ACCOUNTABILITY IS EVERYTHING

"You better never end up drunk in a strip joint on Bragg Boulevard," the broadcaster said, sounding like a scolding Tom Brokaw. The penalty if I did not comply, particularly on the whoring and boozing? "I will crush you."

In the army, superiors *crush* subordinates when they commit inappropriate acts that embarrass the command. It means to punish in a way that leaves no pockets of resistance or opportunity for rebuttal. You take the punishment and soldier on. Malone's point was that, if I were "man down" and he couldn't find me, *he* would get crushed.

The army goes to war whenever and wherever war happens. It can't go to war if it doesn't know where its soldiers are. In battle, commanders cannot maneuver without knowing the status of their troops. Thus, it is *never* none of your NCO's business where you are.

If a soldier wants to drive from Fort Bragg to Myrtle Beach over the weekend (135 miles), before doing so, he must complete some ten pages of paperwork that includes getting his car inspected by his NCO, declaring a travel route and safe-driving plan, and taking a driving safety quiz (the same one he took last weekend and the weekend before that). If he wants to drive farther than 150 miles, he also needs a mileage pass, signed by his company commander. Sometimes the Friday-afternoon paperwork takes longer than the drive.

Every junior enlisted soldier in the Devil Brigade must also submit a plan of what he intends to do each weekend and every holiday, and his sergeant must perform a risk assessment against that plan. I am not making this up.

NCOS GET IN YOUR BUSINESS

The army's entire goal in garrison is to achieve combat readiness. On an organic level, what the army does is develop people. At a tactical level, it's a boardinghouse finishing school for American youth where small group leaders keep tabs on almost every aspect of their soldiers' lives.

Malone asked me the questions that he was required to ask: How many times had I had unprotected sexual intercourse during the last twelve months? With how many partners? How many drinks (beer, liquor, wine) per week did I consume? In the past thirty days, how many times had I operated a motor vehicle within one hour of drinking alcohol? How often, in the last thirty days, was I in an environment where illegal drugs were used? In the last five years, how often had I used cocaine or crack? How often, during the last thirty days, had I had thoughts of cutting or killing myself? How much credit card debt did I have? Would I tell someone in my chain of command if I knew of a peer who exhibited high risk behavior? Imagine a civilian employer asking any one of these questions. For soldiers, all business is the army's business.

OFFICERS GET FIRED, ENLISTED GET RETRAINED

Every army regulation is in response to some pressure, and most have to do with "what Joe will do if you let him." I am reminded of a fellow paratrooper, Phil, whose unit received a care package of tennis equipment (of all things) from a church while deployed to a remote outpost in Afghanistan. When night fell, they began pelting flaming, fuel-soaked tennis balls over the outpost walls, and when they ran out of balls, they kitted up and played three-on-three warfare with the rackets and rocks. "You wouldn't believe the sound a stone makes when you hit it with a tennis racket," he said.

Imagine if you could never get fired from your job, as a private cannot get fired; imagine what you might try to get fired anyway. Imagine what an officer might do to keep you, who can't get fired, from getting him fired.

Enlisted soldiers who do wrong get "retrained" through punishment, loss of pay, and/or loss of rank. Older specialists, I learned quickly, are often regarded as dirtbags because soldiers assume they lost rank for repeated offenses.

THE ARMY IS NOT A MERITOCRACY

Malone must have been reading my mind, for he reminded me that older soldiers often had difficulty "staying in their lanes" and that I had better keep my nose out of "sergeants' business," which meant anything with real responsibility.

Oh dear God.

It's not that competence is ignored in the army, it's just rewarded in a roundabout fashion and on the army's airborne-like timeline. The army is very good at codifying who can get promoted and when. However, promotion rates vary by needs of the army in specific job fields so that some very good candidates never make senior ranks before the twenty-year retirement mark, and others make it with milk on their lips. Soldiers who work very hard at getting promoted don't necessarily get promoted more quickly than those who do not. Soldiers who enlist during times of war are much more likely to get promoted quickly because the need for leadership increases as the number of troops increases.

In the civilian world, becoming proficient at one's job and getting promoted go hand-in-glove. In the army, they are two separate endeavors. Job skills specific to one's MOS have little to do with getting promoted.

Promotion skills focus on general soldiering and often have little to do with one's day-to-day work. They include memorizing policy code, creeds, field manual specs, and form numbers. That's not a bad thing. It's just different than the civilian world. When a soldier becomes an NCO, much of the memorized information will become useful as he guides younger soldiers through the army's byzantine and often unconnected mazes.

Awards and medals are conferred in a manner often surprising to civilians. When troops complete a deployment in a war zone, they are awarded "end of tour" medals whether they see combat or not. Everybody gets something. One would assume that awards match a soldier's contribution to the fight, but alas, they generally match rank. Clearly with rank comes responsibility and the army argues, more contribution. Yet every soldier has seen the incompetent major awarded the Bronze Star because all majors got one.

The hackneyed part is that award recommendations are due halfway through the tour to allow adequate processing time. Everyone knows this, yet, every time the award tray is trotted out, soldiers get butt-hurt for being under-rewarded. After the ceremony concludes, soldiers unpin their awards and place them back on the tray. They must buy their own when they get home.

(When my enlistment ended, I actually had to prove to the army what medals the army had awarded me so they could properly fill out my DD214 Military Service Record.)

Superiors acknowledge a soldier's superior performance by awarding them "coins of excellence." These silver-dollar-sized coins, stamped with unit logos and hooah slogans, are handed out by commanders and senior NCOs, and many soldiers collect and even trade them. They seem silly at first, like the prize in a cereal box, but they grow on you for the memories they hold.

Coining is hardly a perfect award system either. The cute blonde who performed the same work I did in Iraq garnered forty-five coins to my five, three from the same sergeant major. I got my first coin for being old.

THE ARMY IS A RIVER OF PEOPLE AND A MOUNTAIN OF BAND-AIDS

Malone was the first of four managers that I would have while doing the same job for four years. In my first year, our company had three different commanders, executive officers, and first sergeants. These three positions provide most of the administrative services for the senior soldiers who staff the headquarters of a 3,500-strong brigade combat team, as well as the brigade's legal, public affairs, and civil affairs departments. Imagine "the program" changing every four months. In the army, few soldiers are in a position long enough to fix problems; only mitigate them and move on. When the army does attempt a fix, it's with a broad brush. For instance:

YOU WILL SIGN FOR THIS EQUIPMENT, NEED IT OR NOT

In five years, I was issued enough never-used, everybody-gets-this equipment to fill four duffel bags: galoshes; a winter dress overcoat; two unused hydration-pack cleaning kits; three plastic canteens; a Vietnam-era pistol belt; four sets of brand-new, fire-resistant uniforms that I received too late in a deployment to use (can't use them in garrison); two full sets of extreme cold-weather "Michelin Man" tops and bottoms; four fleece jackets; three different kinds of rain suits; a heavy winter jacket that I was only allowed to wear during AIT; three sleeping bags and a sleeping pad; several awkward ammunition bandoleers; shoulder armor that only people who stay on FOBs ever wear outside the wire; and a green plastic whistle.

Even though the fleece jackets and Michelin Man suits were army-issued, paratroopers in the 82nd Airborne Division were not allowed to wear them because they did not look tough and paratrooper-like.

Ironically, we were required to pack them for deployments to both Iraq and Afghanistan. Other "snivel gear" such as long underwear was allowed to be worn as long as the garment was not visible.

I found the equipment that did get used generally more than adequate for the job, though there exists a strong aftermarket economy for everything from rifle buttstocks and magazines to backpacks and boots.

A PT BELT MAKES EVERYTHING RIGHT

The army's PT uniform includes a mandatory two-inch-wide, fluorescent yellow reflective belt, worn around the waist or diagonally across shoulders. To the chagrin of soldiers, the PT belt has become the cornerstone of the army's safety program. Soldiers at Fort Bragg were required to wear the PT belt while motorcycling, bicycling, ruck marching, and mowing grass, day and night.

The army takes the same heavy-handed approach to keeping its soldiers safe over the weekend by requiring all to attend a Friday afternoon "safety brief," typically presented by the company commander or first sergeant. It usually goes something like this: don't do drugs, don't drink and drive, don't beat your wife/girlfriend/husband/children/pets, practice safe sex, don't do anything dangerous alone, and don't embarrass the uniform. Or as one company commander was fond of saying, don't drink and drive, always bring a wingman, and always wrap it up. Also, wear a PT belt.

YOU GET WHAT YOU GET

When Malone asked me if I had any questions, I asked if the office we were in would be our permanent home. I was shocked at the slum-like conditions, with its mold-colonized and drooping ceiling, torn carpets, dead and living cockroaches, cracked windows, and peeling paint. Malone said the old brick three-story would be razed while we were in Iraq. Unfortunately it wasn't, and long after Malone was gone, I was still working in that condemned rathole. When the Public Affairs Office, or PAO, was finally moved into a newer building, we were stashed in a dank storage cage underneath a grated metal staircase, then into an unvented, windowless concrete supply closet in the same building. Because we were assigned no keys to the building, we had to enter each morning by picking the lock on exterior double-doors with a pocketknife, then open a combination lock on our old storage cage to retrieve the one office key that three enlisted soldiers shared to open the supply closet "office" door.

At that point in my army career, especially after the austere conditions of Iraq and Afghanistan, having a crappy office stateside no longer fazed me. I had come to understand that, while perhaps not the best conditions, it was army good-enough. Structures were not the army; soldiers were, and we trained and worked outdoors.

THE ARMY HAS ITS OWN LANGUAGE

"Any other questions before we pop smoke?" Malone asked. Popping smoke, I would discover, is what infantrymen do to signal the helicopters to swoop in and whisk them away. Metaphorically, it's almost always deliverance from an unpleasant fix, which fit the current counseling. I tucked the phrase into my kitbag and continued drinking from the fire hose. The army makes short phrases long and long phrases short. For instance, "Swick" is used in place of the mother of all acronyms, USJFKSWCS, which stands for US Army John F. Kennedy Special Warfare Center and School. But then, Velcro becomes "hook-pile tape."

My favorite army vernacular is the archaic-sounding expression "on digits," as in, "Hey, Sergeant Mac, did you put that photo on digits?" In other words, did I upload a digital copy of a photo onto the computer network? Was the first soldier to use that phrase really asking if a document were available in binary 0s and 1s?

Many army terms have been around so long that nobody knows their original meaning. For instance, a soldier's basic combat equipment is his "TA50." Everyone knows what it is; nobody knows what it means.

Field language is coined as much for titillation and operatic value as usefulness. For instance, every motor pool has a "donkey dick" or two for funneling fuel. On the artillery gun line, the smell of cordite from an outgoing round is "wolf pussy" or "dragon quif." "Dick-beaters" and "ass-clowns" in the operations planning shop create nightmarish "goat-fucks" and "fuck-fests" in the field, causing soldiers to jump through their own assholes to complete missions. That company commander who wants to storm Normandy during every field exercise is "Captain America." Soldiers don't shoot an enemy twice, they "double-tap" them. They don't head for home, they "pop smoke" or "cut slingload." When they're ready to continue the mission, they "Charlie Mike."

It's almost time to pop smoke on this chapter. First, one word of advice:

NEVER TELL ANYONE WHAT YOUR RECRUITER TOLD YOU

My recruiter said that as an army journalist, I would deploy for a month or two at a time and keep regular 9-5 hours. Clearly, he didn't know what he was talking about. In the army, I woke most mornings at 4:45 a.m. and returned home around 6 p.m. or so, and then edited projects until about 10 p.m. My drill sergeant promised me that I would be in Iraq within a year, for at least a year. He was right.

For the most part, I took Malone's boardinghouse rules in stride, reminding myself every ten minutes that I had inflicted this new reality on myself, that part of the lure of enlisting had been that *I couldn't quit* in spite of whatever unseemly challenges were to come my way. But know this: during my first eighteen months in the army, not a day went by that I wouldn't have quit were quitting an option. My real life peers were majors, lieutenant colonels, and colonels, and I was paying my dues as a forty-one-year-old specialist alongside kids only a few years older than my own. It was often humiliating, even denigrating, to be lectured by young sergeants, captains, and—the worst—newly-minted second lieutenants, but over time, two things changed.

First, in the middle of my tour to Iraq, I would climb from the military boardinghouse and become a noncommissioned officer, a sergeant. Second and more importantly, I witnessed so many soldiers and families sacrifice so much for little more than the honor to serve that the significance of my own toils diminished sharply. In time, my "sacrifices" would petrify into a pride for serving those who served and sacrificed so much more. In time, I learned to "love me some soldiers." But that was down the road a bit.

MISERY LOVES A COMPANY OF INFANTRY AT THE JOINT READINESS TRAINING CENTER

The most important event in a combat unit's training cycle is a month-long rotation at either the National Training Center at Fort Irwin, California, or the Joint Readiness Training Center at Fort Polk, Louisiana. At both, army units war-game against opposing forces, or OPFOR, using blank ammunition and a weapon-mounted laser-tag system to simulate combat. For most soldiers, it is the most realistic training they will get prior to deploying to a war zone.

Across the ranks, JRTC is loathed as a necessary but miserable experience. It's a full-fledged deployment to a place with little or no communication back home; painfully infantilizing rules; swamp vermin such as mosquitoes, ticks, and chiggers; poor food, laundry, and showers; and scant chance of anything but that for a month. For most junior soldiers, it entails a whole lot of pulling guard against imaginary enemies that never materialize (OPFOR are expensive) and waiting for their commanders to finish lengthy meetings with role-playing village elders in plodding scenarios.

The cost to train our 3,500 paratroopers was seven million dollars, or two thousand dollars per helmet. The personal cost was another month away from the family just before a deployment, at a time when most soldiers were afforded at most twelve months at home between deployments. Subtract time away for various schools such as Ranger, air assault, or NCO development, plus multi-week field exercises, and then JRTC, and a soldier's time at home shrinks to perhaps nine months at the most. In 2009, I routinely met young soldiers who had spent more of their military life in Iraq than America.

Rumor was that 1st Brigade would be deploying to Afghanistan, but no, we would deploy to western Iraq's Al Anbar Province. Our mission there would dictate how our JRTC rotation was structured.

Prior to 2008, Anbar was home to some of the most violent fighting of the Iraq War, including the sieges of Fallujah and Ramadi, and later, the clearing of Al Qaim, Hit, and Haditha. In 2007, the provincial seat of Ramadi was the headquarters of Al Qaeda in Iraq and declared the most dangerous city on earth, but following the so-called "Anbar Awakening" or uprising of the Sunni tribes against Al Qaeda that coincided with the American troop surge, a relative peace had been established there. The Devil Brigade's mission was to become the first in a series of "advise-and-assist" brigades to help train and grow Iraq's security forces, i.e., its army, police, and border patrol.

According to the advise-and-assist blueprint, a couple dozen midlevel officers would be added to our BCT specifically tasked to help plan the growth of Iraq's military and civil institutions. The brigade's overall mission was to enable the binding institutions of Al Anbar Province—the governor, governing counsels, and mayors; the police departments, army brigades, and border police; the business community, school systems, and the electorate—to provide citizens with stability and security via Iraqi hands, and ultimately, an Iraqi-style "pursuit of happiness." It was no coincidence that the plan was originating from the office of the Undersecretary of the United States, the same office occupied by George C. Marshall, whose Marshall Plan allowed post World War II Japanese and Germans to rebuild their countries as they saw fit. This foreign internal-defense mission, so long the terrain of Special Forces, was being rolled out to conventional troops as President Bush's timeline to leave Iraq drew near.

Anbar was still a very dangerous place, with ratlines of arms and foreign fighters running in from Syria and elsewhere, massive roadside bombs, deadly snipers, and always the potential for open conflict, but for the most part, it was not the Iraq of 2007. A new status-of-forces agreement between the United States and Iraq would, for the most part, confine coalition troops to the FOBs and combat outposts and severely limit our ability to wage war. For the American soldier, the Iraq War was practically over.

Like most new paratroopers, I was disappointed. Like many, perhaps most, I had enlisted to go to war and regarded a five-year enlistment without seeing combat as a huge waste of time. It wouldn't have been, but that's how I regarded it then. I can hear Drill Sgt. Boddie saying, "Listen up, Second Platoon. If you can't kill motherfucking people with your motherfucking weapon, you ain't no use to the motherfucking army. That's what we do, we kill motherfucking people."

We weren't going to Iraq to "kill Hajji," but to advise and assist him, teach him how to use our weapons and tactics, previously used against him. That's a tall order for a bunch of Joes who joined the army for the adventure of combat. It's a tall order for the sergeants and young commanders who knew that many Iraqis they would train had only recently been killing American soldiers. By the end of our month in the piney swamps of Fort Polk, most agreed that the upcoming advise-and-assist mission was going to suck. Paratroopers train hard to fight hard. They don't train to train others to fight. Among the infantry, this was "going to be some bullshit."

With JRTC over, it was time for "war," whatever that was going to be.

PART II:

Iraq—No More Hajjis to Kill

CHAPTER 1: DUST TO DUST: THE STORY OF ANBAR

Mike wasn't terribly fond of Arabs. He was born in Baghdad, yet he was of Chaldean descent. Chaldeans were a people of Babylon who predated Arabs in Iraq, he explained. He spoke English and Arabic, but his people had once spoken Aramaic, the language of Jesus. Saddam's wars had destroyed his family and left them heavily in debt. Mike was an interpreter, or "terp," for US forces. From Mike, I heard firsthand what Anbar had been like during the worst of the fighting, two years before we arrived.

"These guys were camel jockeys, and now they all want to be kings," he told me one day at Al Asad Air Base. "They forgot where they came from. They say Islam is peace, but it does not mean that. It means submission. That's why the United States should say, 'Work with us here or we'll fuck you up.' They are Arabs. They understand that."

I met Mike midway through my Iraq deployment. In his mid-twenties, he was clean, muscular, and articulate, yet he blazed through filthy Iraqi cigarettes and moved as if he were trying to avoid his own shifting shadow. He was clearly struggling through post-traumatic stress disorder. Mike had seen much of the worst fighting that preceded our brigade's arrival in Anbar.

As a terp, Mike had accompanied the marines on their second assault on Fallujah (November 2004) that had resulted in the deaths of over 1,350 insurgent fighters at the cost of 95 US military personnel. Most of the city's three hundred thousand residents had fled before the fighting erupted.

Fallujah had been an epicenter for the convergence of international jihadists wanting to fight the American invaders. "How stupid to go up against the US Army and Marines," Mike said. "There were three guys in every house. I didn't see a single Iraqi the whole time I was there. I spoke to people from Afghanistan, Pakistan, Qatar, Tunis, and Egypt. They would say, 'My wife is sick,' or 'For my kids, I needed money.' They were being paid. They had four thousand dinar on them. I know because I had to inspect the dead bodies as part of the human interrogation team."

Mike described the house-to-house combat in detail. "I saw a marine, this kid, get lifted by an IED. You know how it is when you kick a soccer ball? The boy was like that. We were all fucked up in the head from many days of insane combat, and then I turn and there the same kid is asking me, 'How is it going?' I just saw him get blown up, but all he had was a small stone embedded in his face. I thought I was losing my mind, but the insurgents had buried the bomb too deep.

"We would be in these buildings and hear RPGs slam into [them] one after another, ten in a row. We assaulted Fallujah with eleven thousand marines over three weeks of nonstop fighting. There would be a tank and then twenty marines, a couple [armored troop carriers] and then more marines. The tanks would fire a couple rounds twenty feet away from us, and it was like my head was going to explode even though I had earplugs in. My ears kept ringing all the time. Then the tanks would go to the other side of the house and fire more rounds. There were also UAVs,[2] fighter planes, and A-10s.[3]

"I saw a plane dive down and heard its mini gun go off, and I saw the bullets go from rooftop to ground level through two stories, just ripped the building apart. Whole houses were demolished. I saw kittens eating the flesh off a man's leg and a skull with no skin on it."

Mike's PTSD burned red like the ash of his cigarettes as he spoke. "There were four guys in one house. The marines asked me to go up and talk to them. I said, 'No way, they're probably all suicide bombers. Why go in there and get killed?' A staff sergeant agreed. He could hear them talking. The marines used the .50 caliber [machine gun] on the building, and when they went in, all four of the guys were dead on the floor with grenades in their hands.

"I would lie to my sister and family and tell them that I never went out, was never in danger," he said. Inexplicably, he emailed photos of the gore to his sister in Michigan, but the emails never went through. "I knew then that I was fucked up in the head," he said.

"When we captured the insurgents, they would say, 'We can't believe how you are treating us. Our papers told us you were just butchering Iraqis.'"

Listening to Mike's stories reminded me of a time in my childhood when my vacationing parents had left us kids with a live-in sitter named Beverly, a tiny elderly British lady who had been a nurse in the bunkers of London during the sustained Nazi bombardment of 1940–41. It's one thing to read about epic human violence; it's quite another to meet a survivor and to wrap one's head around his mere survival of such cataclysm. Yet Mike was more than a survivor. Like a soldier, he had bravely left security to fight the evil gripping his country. He was a son wearing the mantle of manhood and following in his father's footsteps.

---

2   Unmanned aerial vehicles used primarily for surveillance

3   A-10 Warthog, an airplane designed to destroy tanks and provide close air support to infantry

After Fallujah was captured from Al Qaeda, insurgents fled westward to Ramadi and on to the border towns of Husaybah and Al Qaim, he said. Near the Syrian border in Husaybah, Mike's marines conducted foot patrols day after day, with a Cobra attack helicopter in the air and a field ambulance behind them. "We were going around a corner once and the marine right behind me got sniped, but he was saved by his body armor." The terp who replaced Mike was killed the week after he left the battlefield.

Mike's account of the fighting in Anbar was one of many that I recorded as a journalist to give context to the Devil Brigade's mostly benign mission to leverage the gains made during the Surge. A number of books provide excellent overviews of how Al Qaeda overplayed its hand with the Sunni tribes, forcing marriages into influential families, terrorizing the citizens, murdering academics, intellectuals, and politicians, hanging teenagers in the streets, and kidnapping the children of anyone brave enough to stand up to the terrorists.

My brigade arrived in Ramadi in late summer 2009. Our main base, Camp Ramadi, was a former Iraqi army barracks northwest of the city on the banks of the Euphrates River that was once a prison for draft dodgers and deserters. In earlier years, it housed some ten thousand marines, soldiers, and Navy SEALs as Coalition Forces battled the insurgency for control of the city. After losing Fallujah, Al Qaeda established Ramadi as the capital of their so-called caliphate, the Islamic State of Iraq. Anbar, and Ramadi in particular, became the bellwether for the War in Iraq.

At the aid station there, I interviewed Senior Chief Hospital Corpsman Christopher Rebana, a warm, Filipino, 15-year veteran from San Diego. Rebana had deployed to Ramadi before. "This place was like Chechnya then," Rebana told me. "One day we had a Special Forces operator come in with a live RPG[4] round embedded in his spine. We

---

4 Rocket-propelled grenade

had to call in EOD[5] before we could do anything with him. In 2007, we were still clearing parts of the city, and we'd watch Apaches and A-10 Warthogs[6] go to work. We used to drop so many five-hundred-pound bombs and JDAMs,[7] it was incredible." As he talked, his medics were treating a marine computer technician who had dropped a ladder on his toe. Different times.

"In '05 we used to say the problem with Iraq is that it is full of Iraqis. Now that's the solution," he said. "Let's let the Iraqis take the lead on this. As an infantry regiment, we want to go out there and engage the enemy. Now we're engaging the people." It was a nod to the advise-and-assist concept, early assurance that the army knew what it was doing by bringing us here. During the rough days in Anbar, Rebana kicked in doors and rooted out insurgents with the same marines and Iraqi soldiers he patched up. Iraqi soldiers called him *Muharib*, or warrior, which he wore in Arabic on his helmet.

Though only one-fifth of US troops were deployed in Anbar when Rebana was there, they accounted for two-fifths of Coalition casualties. The desert province had been on fire. I had considered enlisting just after 9/11, and had I, Mike's and Rebana's war would have been my war too. But why would I have wanted to risk dying in a place so foreign to any reference in my life that I had created thus far? What great feat would that have accomplished, at the price of two fatherless kids and a widowed wife? The intellectual hopscotch from establishing peace in Iraq, to bringing "freedom," to making a stable ally, to defending our Constitution seemed like a trick shot on a pool table that I wasn't willing to risk my family's future on. In my head, I was comparing the future of Iraqi children to the future of American children, but the

---

5 Explosive-ordnance disposal, i.e., the bomb squad

6 US Army AH-64 Apache attack helicopter and Air Force A-10 Thunderbolt (Warthog) ground attack aircraft

7 Joint Direct Attack Munition, a smart-bomb dropped from an aircraft

American children were mine. As I listened to Rebana, suddenly, a combat-free tour didn't seem so terrible.

The first female marine officer killed in Iraq, Major Megan McClung, 34, was also a public affairs officer. One of the responsibilities of public affairs officers is to escort journalists embedding with troops in war zones, and that is what McClung was doing when her Humvee was shattered by a roadside bomb in downtown Ramadi in 2006. She had just dropped off Oliver North and his *Fox News* crew at the Government Center (which would be hit by car bombs several times during our deployment) and was escorting a *Newsweek* correspondent on the ten-minute return to Camp Ramadi when the blast occurred. Two soldiers were also killed, but the correspondent, Sarah Childress, was uninjured. McClung was the granddaughter of a Greatest Generation soldier and a navy pilot, and the daughter of a marine officer who fought in the Tet Offensive. She was a triathlete and marathoner, the first female graduate of the United States Naval Academy to be killed in action, one of eight female marines who would die during the War in Iraq, and one of twenty-four marines who died there that month.

Service runs deep in some families, and it's not always father-to-son. I could say "even daughters carry on the tradition," but I have met so many young women who joined the army for that very reason that it would seem insincere. Better to ask why the other 99 percent aren't serving, I think.

McClung had died during a transformational and heroic moment in Anbar, when US and Sunni Iraqi forces came together to root out Al Qaeda from western Iraq. As a journalist, would she have considered her sacrifice worthwhile?

The marines who we replaced in Anbar fired only seven rounds during their six-month deployment. The only injuries came from Ramadi's infamous snipers and the occasional roadside bomb. Attacks by violent extremists on both US personnel and Iraqis were down from 1,350 in March 2007 to 50 in September 2009, a 96 percent reduction that approaches what might be an irreducible minimum, i.e., a "crime rate." One of the most tangible signs of progress in fact was the drawdown of coalition forces in Anbar from 18,000 marines to our 3,500 paratroopers. We were all there was, one unit from one block of Ardennes Street at Fort Bragg, responsible for a province the geographical size of North Carolina.

A kind of peace was spreading across Iraq, and Anbar seemed to be its birthplace. But at what cost to Iraqis? I asked "Leo," an interpreter from Fallujah, why all Iraqis don't hate Americans. It was an oblique form of two questions that everyone back home seemed to want to know. 1) Do the Iraqi people understand that we are trying to help them help themselves? 2) Are they grateful? The second question speaks to the ego of American exceptionalism, but only superficially. Really people just want to know whether the loss of our sons and daughters killed in Iraq was worth it.

"You have to remember our history," Leo told me. "Before 2003, it was a massacre in Iraq. Saddam was killing people. He was a criminal, killer, murderer. He was corrupt. He was everything. Americans will never be able to appreciate how bad life was under Saddam. How you say is, 'You can't get there from here?' I think the five thousand you guys lost is more than the millions we lost. Do you know why? We in Iraq are a tribal community. We are a family community. So if one in our family survives, we're good. We still have the same family. In the US, let's say there is a husband and a wife, and the husband got killed. The wife is done. The family is gone. From my point of view, the five thousand are more than the millions."

Albeit typical of Leo's Iraqi lurch toward overstatement in several directions (estimates of Iraqi deaths range from a hundred thousand to a half million), I understood him to mean that Iraqi society was structurally very different from ours, and removal of Saddam made Iraqi life better by at least an order of magnitude.

An Iraqi mechanic from Hit said it this way: "George Washington and Abraham Lincoln are also great American presidents like George W. Bush. They also freed people like Bush did." It was shocking to me that anyone in 2009 considered George W. Bush one of America's great presidents; that the man considered Washington and Lincoln worthy of Bush's company and not vice versa; that the mechanic doing the talking was Iraqi. Life in Saddam-era Iraq must have been worse than I had previously imagined, and Leo's "million dead" was from an Iraqi's perspective of a slaughter that began with Saddam's rise, continued through the Iran-Iraq War, and ended with the quelling of the insurgency and the apparent defeat of Al Qaeda.

This much is true: Many Iraqis did not hate Americans even though exponentially more Iraqi lives were lost than American. (We forget that nearly twenty thousand French civilians were killed during the Invasion of Normandy, mostly by Allied bombing.) The tribes of Anbar uprooted Al Qaeda during the Awakening. The tribes supplied the hundreds of new local police when the streets were still war zones. The tribes worked with the US Marines and Army to improve the schools, utilities, and governance.

The tribes were key to Anbar. Well, Anbar was meeting another tribe, the Devils in Baggy Pants.

CHAPTER 2: GETTING DIRTY IN ANBAR

Q: What's the difference between a second lieutenant and a private first class?
A: The private has been promoted twice.

In spite of all the razzing that newly commissioned second lieutenants or "butter bars" endure for being in charge but lacking experience, compared with newly enlisted privates, they lead pretty charmed lives. Even the sergeant major of the army calls a new lieutenant "sir."

Officers in general have a much different deployment experience than enlisted soldiers. For instance, majors in a brigade staff deploying to Iraq would, but for short periods of time, keep company only with other majors, captains, and colonels of the army's upper middle class. They would get a separate tent during the layover in Kuwait. Arriving at a forward-operating base such as Camp Ramadi, they would be assigned to and helped into their own "wet CHU" or containerized housing unit with running water. This treatment is not necessarily because they are lazy or feel privileged, though certainly some are both. Being essential to the command-and-control of the brigade, they *are* more privileged. For senior noncoms, the deployment experience is similar, though some might have to share a dry CHU.

In contrast, Private Snuffy begins his deployment by getting put on a "baggage detail," and before he even leaves the departure airfield, he's "sweating his balls off," dragging the duffle bags and rucksacks of officers, sergeants, and fellow soldiers into the belly of the airliner. When the aircraft stops for fuel and a new crew somewhere in Europe and everybody else deplanes for a break in travel, Snuffy stays aboard and guards all the weapons. After landing in Kuwait, he's part of the bag-drag again, but this time, it's 120 degrees outside. Eventually he rides a CH47 Chinook helicopter into Camp Ramadi, where he and the rest of the Joes are shuffled into the dark and narrow, rat-infested quarters that once housed the lice-infested draft dodgers of Saddam's army. The poor bastards don't get the scurvy or bubonic plague or anything like that. My fellow Joes and I killed the rats, mopped and bleached the barracks, and made the place livable. We were grateful that we weren't living in the sand, eating MREs every meal, and never showering, like Joes did during the invasion. (There is no bottom to the suck, especially for the enlisted.)

To the uninitiated like me, Camp Ramadi was a monoscape of ankle-deep dust, concrete blast walls, and drab windowless buildings ringed by berms, trenches, c-wire, and a barren no-man's land that created a cold draft in one's being. But for sparse colonies of hardy weeds, the only plants were a handful of date palms that provided shade near the tactical operations center, or TOC. The only birds were sparrows, doves, and birds that ate doves. We never saw the raptors, only the feathers they left behind. The occasional feral cat or coyote-like jackal might pass through the beam of one's flashlight at night (the base was, of course, blacked out), and occasionally there were more rats needing killing in the barracks, but for the most part, Camp Ramadi was a biosphere that supported only weapons, armor, tires, and tracks. I never saw a child on the base.

There was a life to be had, though. The departing marines had jettisoned everything they couldn't stuff into steel shipping containers or carry in their bags, including microwaves, televisions, refrigerators, bedside lamps, and chairs. Specialist Dahlman, a gaunt forward observer who lived off of Mountain Dew and tobacco products, found me a lamp and some other niceties. I draped my *wooby* (poncho liner) between my bunk bed and the one paired up against it, hung a sheet over the end and angled my locker off the wall for a little nook of privacy. That worked until the kid on the adjoining bunk—he was literally inches away through my wooby—began masturbating repeatedly in the night, shaking my bunk along with his own. I guess I became the grumpy old man for insisting that he quit. Eventually, the FOB fire marshal ordered all "spank blankets" and other dividers be removed, and that ended much of the solo sex in the barracks.

On the other side of my bunk was Gupta, an airman of Indian descent whose job was to coordinate air force assets with ground forces in Anbar. Gupta had it all: the fridge, microwave, and TV monitor, a trifecta for comfortable video gaming and Internet surfing. Within the drabness of the FOB, he had constructed a pleasant micro habitat, augmented with daily workouts at the gym, gourmet brew from the Green Beans coffee shop, and takeout meals from the Subway trailer (both run by TCNs, or third-country nationals, usually Filipinos or Bangladeshis). Whatever Gupta lacked could be had within ten days via Amazon.com. Gupta was a fobbit. During his entire four-month deployment, he would never leave the security of the FOB.

Unfortunately for our infantry, who mercilessly derided fobbits as something less than true soldiers, their fates were not that different due to the recently signed status of forces agreement that sequestered most of our troops on FOBs unless requested and accompanied by Iraqi forces, making them more or less a combat fire department.

Unlike years past, the infantry would not be living among the Iraqis in small outposts, engaging insurgents in firefights or patrolling the *mulhullas* (neighborhoods) and alleyways of Ramadi. Rather, our paratroopers would have their own multicultural experience within the FOB walls. We learned more Swahili than Arabic (from Ugandans contracted to man the guard towers, gates, and internal checkpoints), had our laundry done by Filipinos, and got haircuts from Bangladeshis and Koreans. The third-country nationals who manned the gym counter could belt out Jason Aldeen's "Big Green Tractor" without understanding a lick of English.

Many staff officers began priding themselves on passing through internal security gates while speaking only Swahili.

Habadi?

Missuri, habadi?

I'm fine, thank you.

The Ugandan guards were only too happy to converse with American troops, particularly those of recent African descent. While their $600 monthly wage was enormous for impoverished Uganda, they knew that even a lowly Joe earned $1,500 and most Americans made more than that. How might they enlist?

Because the army offers a fast track to US citizenship, there seems to be one or two African nationals in every unit. The Ugandans idolized our Americanized Africans. "They would join the army tomorrow if they could," Specialist Chica Nkata told me. A handsome Nigerian who became a US citizen in 2008 shortly after enlisting, the combat medic and self-described history junkie often probed the Ugandan guards about life under the rule of Idi Amin, the immensely popular but controversial dictator. In turn, they asked him how he joined the US Army. "I tell them I am from Nigeria, but because of my name, they think I am from a royal family in Uganda," he said, laughing. "I am not, but I *am* someone with better prospects. I am an American."

FOB life was driven by the "optempo" or operations tempo, and within the 82nd Airborne Division, the optempo was famously high. Daytime staffers began as early as 6 a.m. and stayed on until around midnight. Joes, NCOs, and junior officers who manned TOC communications posts put in twelve-hour shifts, seven days a week. The only break came on Sunday morning for attending worship services (or sleeping in).

The irascible heat of Anbar begged the question, who in their right minds would choose to live in Iraq? The answer is, not Americans. Almost all of the American military bases in Anbar lay on or near the Fertile Crescent, that cradle of civilization bound in the west by the Euphrates River along the eastern edge of a vast desert. The soil there is not like beach sand, but rather a fine red-tinted powder that is sometimes packed into rock-hard desert pan, sometimes pooled into shin-deep, talcum-like deposits, and when sucked into the atmosphere by convective currents boiling off a super-heated earth, storms of choking dust can last for hours or days. These are real apocalyptic skies that roll over the land like they are feeding on the earth, and when combined with thunderstorms, they shower mud-drops back on the land in the world's worst, non-life-threatening weather.

For the most part, life on the FOB was safe, but the violence of war was never far away. Well before sunrise one long night, I was watching a bootleg copy of *The Hurt Locker* on a DVD player given to me by a marine who got it from a marine who was killed by a roadside bomb. Suddenly the hardened barracks quaked as a thunderous explosion concussed across the FOB. Haloes of dust danced from our steel bedframes, walls, and lockers. Sleeping soldiers around me were jolted awake. Dahlman rushed in from the TOC: a dump truck packed with five thousand pounds of explosives had just detonated on the main highway bridge across the Euphrates, ripping out the northbound lanes. There was no follow-on attack, only word that Al Qaeda was spreading the "news" that Americans had blown up the bridge with a missile so that we couldn't leave Iraq like we promised. Even as a soldier new to the fight, it was maddening to be part of this colossal effort to raise Iraq, only to feel powerless against simple *words*.

Camp Ramadi was occasionally rocketed by insurgents, but for most of the fobbits who inhabited the base in 2009-10, the only connection to the war outside the wire was the quake and boom of VBIEDs and SVESTS (vehicle-born improvised explosive devices and suicide vests) from outside the perimeter walls. In fact, the closest call I had that first month was on an early morning run along the backside of the FOB's ring road. While keeping an eye out for snipers among outside structures that rose above the wall, I was nearly struck by a golf ball. No doubt the offending club had been passed along from some marine grunt to some Joe, who was trying to chip out of the biggest sand trap ever.

The disconnect between a soldier and the war he was there to "fight" could be dramatic. During an Iraqi Army change of command, a young American helicopter mechanic once asked me, "Are all these Iraqi officers against Osama bin Laden?" The army term for that soldier is "lost in the sauce." He was a fobbit. More importantly, he was a POG, a person other than grunt (infantry), and as such, he was never outside the wire.

Fobbits and POGs are similar but not the same. Both are derogatory terms used mostly by the infantry. The word fobbit reflects a habitat, while POG reflects a job. I was a POG but not a fobbit because I was off the FOB as much as on it. Traditionally, most of the suck occurs outside the wire. While we like to say that the absence of front lines in today's asymmetrical battlefield makes everyone a combatant, it's still true that, by far, the infantry sustains the most casualties because warfighting is their primary role.

By 2009, it was rare for conventional marines or soldiers to leave the wire in anything less armored than a Mine Resistant Ambush Protected vehicle, or MRAP. The giant, V-hulled, rubber-wheeled troop carriers had reduced troop casualties by 90 percent. Humvees were only used on FOBs, by Special Forces, or for navigating tight roads in villages that were deemed relatively safe. Most of our infantrymen had never been inside an MRAP until they arrived in Anbar.

Yet MRAPs were far from impenetrable. Well-aimed EFPs sliced through their armor like butter. Hand-thrown RKG-3 grenades that employed small parachutes to orient a shaped charge posed a danger to the less-protected roofs, and even a well-aimed RPG could cause significant damage. Even if the gun turret was armored, the machine gunner was always at significant risk from small-arms fire, roadside bombs, and rollovers. As with Humvees, the gunner's turret—a big round hole in the roof—let the weather in.

In spite of their size, MRAPs were cramped inside, as were all military vehicles. Add a half dozen soldiers in body armor, backpacks, MREs, bottled water, and extra machine gun ammunition, and there was little room to move around. The ride was stiff (some are built on a dump truck chassis). The sound of an MRAP is a diesel growl, whining transmission, and hissing airbrakes, the clickety-clack of the gun turret rotating in its mount, and squelching beeps of the intercom on the headset radio. Outlawed banter on the internal radio was what made travel in an MRAP bearable, as in this exchange during a hunt for roadside bombs:

"Turner, is it only around bridges that we watch for RKG-3 grenades?"

"Negative, sar'nt," Turner replied. "Urban areas or any area with cover for people to hide."

Turner was behind the .50 cal in the gunner's turret of an RG-33, one of the more common, larger MRAPs used in Iraq. It was well after dark, and his platoon of combat engineers was locating and clearing roadside bombs on a highway between Ramadi and Fallujah.

Turner was a nineteen-year-old private first class from Nashville, and he was crooning a country song at the mic between inquiries from Sergeant Jorgensen, the truck commander.

"*That's the story of my life right there in black and white,*" Turner sang. "*You should have seen it in color.*"

It was a popular country song.

"Turner, do you see the low-hanging wires?"

Turner was eyeball level with the wires as the high-profile MRAP threaded through the narrow streets of downtown Ramadi. "Doing big things up here, sar'nt. I got the wires," he replied.

Over the radio, there was chatter between the vehicles. "Husky," someone called, "be advised there is a vehicle between me and you." Then a wisecrack, "Do not be afraid. I am here to protect you."

A favorite pastime of soldiers on long mounted patrols was testing each other with impossible hypotheticals. They were an endearing yet vulgar form of moral drama, but only because the alternative was to contemplate being blown up by an illiterate goat herder's morning project.

"What would you rather do, have sex with your sister or shoot your mother?"

"Would you rather pick up a baby with a pitchfork, or throw a paraplegic in a fire?"

In one form or another, these young men were weighing the relative value of human life in real terms, perhaps as a surrogate for murkier thoughts that might otherwise be in the forefront, such as, "Why am I risking my life in this wasteland?" or "Whose life is worth more, that of my best friend in the gun turret or of some Iraqi kid I've never met?" It passed the time.

Dismounted patrols, i.e., "foot patrols," were altogether different. There was very little banter. The infantry was out of its cage, unfolding into a tactical column or wedge. Every paratrooper knew his job. Every doorway, window, alleyway, even roadside trash, represented a potential threat and had to be vetted.

Foot patrols were work. A platoon on patrol consisted of three squads of nine soldiers armed with rifles, grenade launchers, and light machine guns, and a weapons squad bearing two medium machine guns and ammo. Ammunition for the M240B medium machine gun weighs seventeen pounds per hundred rounds of its 7.62mm ammunition (recall that 7.62mm is similar in size and weight to the relatively heavy .30-caliber ammunition that our troops in World War II carried). The gunner might carry two hundred rounds in addition to his twenty-eight-pound weapon, and eight hundred additional rounds—136 pounds worth—are carried by the assistant gunner and ammo bearer. The platoon will also carry anti-tank weapons, mine detectors, radios and radio jammers, perhaps a mortar and extra rounds, food, and extra water and ammunition. Added to each soldier's thirty-five pounds of body armor, eight to thirty pounds of primary weapon, and at least 210 rounds of ammunition, the average weight that a soldier carried while on patrol was 90-120 pounds. For multi-day patrols, it was much more.

How did they patrol in 120-degree heat? They just did what they had to do. Our paratroopers conditioned hard, and then, like the marines and soldiers who had come before them, they drank plenty of water, learned to appreciate a sweat-saturated uniform, and embraced the suck. It wasn't unheard of for an entire squad to rehydrate themselves with IV bags. If they were lucky enough to be based on one of the larger FOBs, reward for a day's work might include video-chatting with the family back home or playing combat on the gaming console while sipping a hyper-caffeinated energy drink from the PX.

In World War II, the Devils in Baggy Pants jumped into combat and were immediately surrounded by the well-trained, well-equipped Wehrmacht. They had crappy food, lived in the dirt and snow, and had little assurance of what shelter, if any, they would have on any given night. When I talk with veterans of the Big War, they often marvel at what today's soldiers have dealt with in Iraq and Afghanistan. Perhaps it's just humility talking when they remark on the difficulty of not knowing who the enemy is, or where he lives, or where the front lines are, or what constitutes success. They seem sincere.

CHAPTER 3:
ADVISE AND ASSIST

A brigade combat team, even "light infantry" like the 82nd Airborne Division, is hung with an awesome amount of firepower. A single infantry company is equipped with over two thousand pounds of assault rifles, heavy and light machine guns, grenade launchers, pistols, mortars, and anti-tank weapons. Our brigade comprised a dozen such companies. In fact, a single platoon had more firepower than an entire company in World War II. That's a lot of potential energy just itching to be released.

That itch was never scratched during our "advise-and-assist" role because of the dedication and discipline of our young riflemen, who worked directly with Iraqi soldiers and policemen. In part, that was because, as Americans, they truly wanted to gift the Iraqi people with the peace and prosperity of America. Mostly, they were kept very busy with the details of the advise-and-assist mission as pumped out by a relentless plans shop.

It is worthwhile to consider what we did accomplish in Iraq, because it speaks to the flexibility of today's soldier and the battlescapes he is likely to face in future wars. It also set the stage for the violent tour in Afghanistan that would follow. The brigade's energy was channeled into three main efforts: to train Iraqi army, police, and border security forces; to conduct partnered missions with them; and to support ongoing organic Iraqi successes against insurgents. The strife in Iraq always felt more like tension between political classes than between religious sects or even between insurgents and invaders. To be sure, the war was a complex struggle that went through many phases, but after the fall of Saddam, it was a rush between Sunni and Shia political forces to capture the flag, with Al Qaeda playing the role of agitator. I don't think most rank-and-file Iraqis ever gave up on the eventual outcome being a peaceful, stable country.

Within weeks, our paratroopers were meeting and working with dozens of Iraqis who had already stepped forward to cure the ills of their country. Finding and supporting those individuals will be an enduring feature of frontless, future wars. The Ramadi area had several homegrown heroes, such as "The Hatchetman," a police colonel who fought fire with fire, planting fear in the hearts of terrorists by butchering them in the streets with a hatchet. Colonel Ahmed Hamid Sharqi was also one of the first officials to publicly proclaim that Al Qaeda was evil, and that US forces were trying to do something good for Iraq.

Colonel Shabban Barzan Ubaidi, head of the provincial SWAT team, shared the Hatchetman's outspoken contempt for the insurgents. Defiantly dressed in mirrored aviators and snappy, freshly-laundered camouflage fatigues, Shabban had lived under Al Qaeda bounty for years. His house was blown up, one brother was killed by Al Qaeda, and another lost a leg to a roadside bomb. Shabban conducted operations with our Special Forces, but also helped our MPs train Iraqi police.

North of Ramadi and just south of Haditha Dam, one of our artillery companies partnered with the mayor of Barwanah, a town of several thousand. The mayor's name was Myeser Abdol Mohsin Freh. When insurgents began encroaching on Barwanah in 2005, the former mayor quit, and other city leaders fled to Baghdad. The town fell under control of the so-called Islamic State of Iraq. "They used to do just one thing in the city," said Myeser, "killing." Insurgents strangled the city, killing anyone they wanted to and leaving the bodies in the streets for people to see. If they knew of anyone working with the government, police, or military, they would slaughter him, cut off his head, and send it to his family. In 2007, American and Iraqi troops entered Barwanah and cut off all access at its two bridges and the few roads leading across the desert. Within six months, policemen were again walking the streets without helmets or body armor.

One of the artillerymen, Specialist Travis Benefiel, remembered a very different Barwanah just a few years earlier. A marine then, Benefiel had been stationed just upriver in Haditha. "We endured constant IEDs, small-arms fire, mortar fire, and rocket fire," he said. "It was very dangerous—lots of suicide bombers and vehicle-born IEDs. I lost quite a few friends."

His current platoon sergeant, Sergeant First Class Jason Reininger, said the friends he lost during earlier deployments would be proud of how the people of Barwanah were honoring the sacrifices they and their families had made and continue to make for Iraqi freedom. "If people want to know what we're doing over here, they should look at this community. I would hope that other communities around Iraq would look at what they're doing to make themselves better."

They were looking and doing. Between Barwanah and Ramadi, the city of Hit was home to Lieutenant Colonel Waleed Mohammed Salman al-Hiti, the commander of an anti-terrorism police unit. Waleed bravely stood up to Hit's one-time savior-turned-gangster police chief, General Ibrahim Hamid Jaza, prior to the general's arrest by US forces in May of 2007. In January 2009, Al Qaeda operatives planted bombs outside the bedroom window of Waleed's home, killing his mother, two sisters, and his four-year-old son, and wounding his father. Yet Waleed was still aggressively pursuing the town's enemies.

A common theme for the media and Hollywood during the Iraq War was that US troops nurtured low-brow hatred for Hajji, the stereotypical Iraqi. To be sure, after losing close friends in combat for a people who often seemed complicit with the enemy that was destroying their country, many American soldiers had no love for Iraqis. That theme certainly fit the trickle-down theory of "bad" war begetting only badness, peddled by those who should have been objectively reporting the war. Yet most Iraq War veterans have Iraqi friends and know true Iraqi heroes such as Waleed, Myeser, and Sharqi.

There were many more. In the northwest corner of Anbar, two Iraqi policemen guarding the district police headquarters shot and killed a suicide bomber before he could detonate seven thousand pounds of explosives in his truck. Three schools with twelve hundred students in attendance were adjacent to the station. Soldiers with the 747th Military Police Company of the Massachusetts National Guard, supported by our brigade, had been working with the Iraqi police and alerted them of a likely attack.

In April 2010, bomb-sniffing dogs and their Iraqi handlers supported and trained by our Army K9 Corps scored their first major find, when a woman who had planted an explosive belt on a fifteen-year-old boy near Fallujah was sniffed out of a ten-woman lineup. "Arko nibbled on her clothes and sat next to her," said Husian Saadoun Kareem, the German shepherd's handler. "I felt like the wealthiest man on earth because of what we had achieved and the innocent lives we saved." The Iraqi government had plans to deploy a thousand dogs countrywide, with an additional twenty-one in Anbar. That's a big deal in a Muslim culture in which dogs are regarded as unclean.

Everywhere, bolstered by American support, there were Iraqis taking back their country. Staff Sergeant Allen House, an acquaintance from a rifle company, who had lost close friends in Iraq, described the advise-and-assist mission as "boring as fuck." Yet, in spite of the tedium of training "a people who won't even help themselves," he was seeing a country get back on its feet. His company was one of dozens partnered with Iraqi army forces to teach air assault, combat lifesaving, running an aid station, logistics, mechanics, communication, and even public affairs.

Our brigade even attempted to find enough Iraqi paratroopers for a partnered airborne training operation. We brought in instructors and parachute riggers from Fort Bragg's Advanced Airborne School, welded training apparatuses, and even conducted two training jumps at Al Asad Air Base, where the hardpack drop zone busted up a number of our paratroopers (one even suffered an eye popped from its socket). The trouble was, we couldn't find any Iraqi paratroopers. The brigade staff decided to ask for Iraqi soldier volunteers, conduct a mini airborne school, and make the partnered jump.

Airborne!

Fortunately, that ended quickly when the head of all US forces in Iraq, four-star General Raymond Odierno, saw one of my photos of the training jump while checking his email. Though Odierno had given the original go-ahead, I think he was concerned the jump might take away from efforts to secure the upcoming national elections.

A sure sign of camaraderie developing between forces was the not-so-gentle ribbing of each other. An Iraqi soldier who noticed my gray hair asked me, "Do you drink whiskey? Whiskey bad. Do you have H1N1 [swine flu]?"

During air assault training with Iraqi helicopter-borne commandos in northern Anbar, First Lieutenant Theron Tingstad told his Iraqi counterpart, First Lieutenant Tahseen, that the Americans were going to make posters of Tahseen and cover Anbar with his likeness, which would have been a particularly Iraqi thing to do. Everyone laughed, but not Tahseen. Another Iraqi lieutenant, Ali, asked Tingstad why he was making fun of Tahseen. "You know, he is from Diyala Province, a very dangerous place," Ali advised. "Between 2006 and 2007, lots of innocent people were killed there. It is still dangerous for him to be an officer. If his neighbors in Diyala found out, they might kill him or his family."

Tingstad said, "My mistake. We will put the posters in Diyala." That split guts on both sides and even made Tahseen smile. Willingness to go for the soft underbelly is like blowing a kiss in a grunt's world.

At times, training the re-emergent Iraqi army took enormous patience for everyone. For instance, the Iraqi Helicopter Quick Reaction Force had no helicopters (the entire Iraqi army owned only two). Tingstad's infantrymen trained the Iraqi commandos at sun-stroked Camp Kassam, a crater-like Iraqi army base covered in moon dust on the edge of the Al Jazirah Desert. The camp lay a mile or two north of Rawah, a hillside town on the banks of the Euphrates that still harbored an active insurgent presence. Living out of a barn that reached 140 degrees during the day, the paratroopers built the 7th Iraqi Army Division's first MI-17 twin-turbine, medium transport helicopter out of dry-rotted two-by-fours and sun-warped plywood torn from a nearby abandoned shed using a ball-peen hammer, two claw hammers, and a fire ax. Army cots were used to replicate the helicopter's bench seats. The photos that I took of the training are hysterical.

Staff Sergeant Robert Burnett, a veteran of previous Iraq deployments, said that many of the Iraqi soldiers had fought for years with American special operations forces. "They picked up a few techniques from us such as shooter stance and the way we handle noncombatants versus combatants, but we're definitely going with the way they've been trained on room clearing because they are proficient at it right now."

During the loading and unloading of the "helicopter" and the tactical movement across a field that followed, neither Americans nor Iraqis would comment on the absurdity of training in something that looked like a poorly made stage for a high school play, when there were known bombmakers down the road in Rawah building sophisticated weapons against them. Tingstad's platoon sergeant, Sergeant First Class Gary Wilson of Baltimore, Maryland, said later that the day's enterprise had been "worth the ass-pain" to him because the Iraqi officers had led the training for the first time. Iraqi soldiers might fistfight their NCOs, but they respected their officers.

On the other hand, on a shuttle bus back to Al Asad a few days later, I overheard one of Wilson's soldiers say to another, "Get this shit: we just trained the dumbest Hajjis known to mankind. They completely forgot the wedge [formation] from last week. We built a helicopter. Out of wood. It gets dumber and dumber." I was about to ask him to tell me more when he leaned into his buddy and said, "Dude, I still say I'd like to do the girl in *Roger Rabbit* with the 3-inch waist and huge rack." In the army, everyone has his lane.

Much of the Iraqi police training was done by National Guardsmen attached to our brigade. According to one of our terps, Moe, "If you have ten marines, they are no different to each other. You look to Army Guard unit and there is fat guy, short guy, tall guy, old guy, another fat guy, and what the fuck? This is not an army."

The so-called weekend warriors of the Army National Guard and Reserves were not the guys to assault a fortified enemy position, but for professionalizing a growing Iraqi police force, the wide array of technical expertise and practical knowledge they offered was ideal. For instance, when the Ramadi police department was issued two thirty-thousand-pound, fire-truck-like riot control vehicles with no manual and no trainer, the 585th Military Police Company of the Ohio National Guard drew from its ranks three firefighters, a commercial driving instructor, and an instructor from the Ohio Military Police Regional Training Institute. The company had just finished serving a term as Ohio's quick response force for riot control. In three days, the firefighters had the truck's pumps, targeting systems, and maintenance not only figured out, but documented in an Arabic-language manual they had created with the assistance of interpreters. A training team coached a few Iraqi police officers, who then trained forty-five Iraqi policemen. In fewer than ten days, the Guardsmen had accomplished a task that the average regular army unit would have struggled with.

Iraqi police were key to rooting out insurgents, because, unlike the army, they were all locals and knew who was doing what. The downside was that, because they were locals, they were far more susceptible to corruption. My friend Leo, the terp from Fallujah, used to tell me that the local police were "100 percent" corrupt. When the governor of Al Anbar province was attacked by two suicide bombers just after Christmas (he lost a hand in the second blast), it was believed that police were complicit with the assassins.

On my second trip outside the wire, I was almost shot in the face by a sniper at Ramadi's Jazirah police station while Iraqi cops stood by laughing. A company commander was meeting with the police chief there, and while they were talking, I was interviewing a soldier whose wife was also in our brigade, but stationed at a different FOB. While we trotted back to the MRAPs, Sergeant Kevin Novak was hit in the shoulder by a sniper. Novak had been standing by a vehicle in front of me. Iraqi police just yards away shrugged and laughed. Were they complicit? I don't know, but a day later our intel cell found a video posted on a jihadist website. Watching it, I realized that the sniper had missed his target altogether, but only by inches. I was the star of the video, with a big red circle around my head. The title was, "A sniper kills an American soldier instantly in Al Jazeera area."

On the other hand, police were often the choice targets of Al Qaeda and other insurgent groups. They always seemed to be the ones getting blown up by car bombs. Shortly after our arrival at Camp Ramadi, a VBIED tried to run a checkpoint just outside the north gate. When stopped, it detonated. The explosion killed seven policemen and wounded twenty others. In January 2006 at the glass factory just outside the FOB gate, a car bomb killed over fifty police recruits.

Most of that type of violence had abated by the time our paratroopers began partnered operations with Iraqi soldiers and police. That allowed them to make highly visible contributions to the rebuilding of Iraq, such as the reconstruction of the Saqlawiya Bridge to open commerce to rural areas north of the Euphrates. An Iraqi police shift boss there, 45-year-old Najee Hamed, who was a former artilleryman in Saddam's army and was wounded in the leg from an Iranian rocket, said, "Two years ago, we could not cross this bridge without getting shot at. Today, my men liked being here. To be policeman is good job."

Nearby, Sergeant First Class José Guzman stood watch from a guardhouse on the south shore with two policemen, each armed with an AK47. In America, policemen don't walk around with assault rifles, but in Iraq, nearly all did. It was the platoon sergeant's fourth deployment to Iraq. "Last time, the Iraqi police knew if something happened and they did nothing, we would come solve the problem," he said. "Sometimes back then, Iraqi police would even leave their posts or fall asleep. Not now." Yet he was certain that some of the cops at the bridge were active or former Jaysh al-Mahdi, or JAM, militants, foot soldiers of the radical Shia cleric Moqtada al Sadr, when they were home on leave in Baghdad. "Every mission you do, you have to help the people, but there's good people and there's bad people," he said. "Even though I'm helping them, I never turn my back on them. I'm not willing to give my life. I'd give my life for my Joes, but not for them."

As an American, I was proud of men like Guzman, who in spite of great personal cost, did the right thing nearly all of the time. Neither politico, mercenary, nor vigilante, he was a professional soldier.

A day after I talked to Guzman, a prominent Imam in nearby Saqlawiya was assassinated by a magnetic IED attached to his vehicle, and the day after that, an IED tore through a crowd of mourners at his funeral. It wasn't known whether local police had anything to do with the violence.

In addition to the bridge project, our paratroopers helped facilitate Ramadi's first international trade fair for business, helped to stem the flow of weapons and fighters along insurgent "ratlines" in eastern Anbar, fortified voting stations for the March 2010 presidential election and escorted United Nations polling monitors on Election Day, and provided medical and other humanitarian aid to rural communities via temporary medical clinics.

That's day after day of pre-dawn equipment checks, mission briefs, and detail-filled but tedious missions in the sweltering, miasmatic heat and dust while wearing a hundred pounds of body-breaking armor, ammo, commo, and weaponry, followed by refueling, oiling, and cleaning, work details, and a few hours of sleep before the next of three hundred seemingly identical days is upon you.

All of these operations were performed in close association with Iraqi security forces and without major injury to the soldiers or civilians. That's not to say there was no violence. I remember listening to the Iraqi provincial governor deliver his keynote address at the trade fair in downtown Ramadi as multiple suicide blasts drew ever closer, our building shaking with each concussive wave. Occasionally our convoys were targeted by grenades, small-arms fire, or IED strikes.

The most meaningful measure of progress was the 2010 presidential election. Across Iraq, a couple dozen people were killed as insurgents struggled to intimidate voters, but in Anbar, the elections passed almost entirely without violence. In the meantime, life on the FOB became a routine existence, punctuated not by weekends, but by the occasional car bomb or suicide-vest explosion outside the walls. A few times, insurgent rockets hit the FOB, but caused no damage. Around Christmas, insurgents tried to blow up the governor with two suicide bombers that appeared on the FOB as twin puffs of smoke.

For many soldiers on Camp Ramadi, the beat of life was PT, chow, work, chow, work, chow, work, gym, bed. Most quickly mastered their little slice of the war, and with that done, it was as if everyone suddenly realized that there were a whole lot of men on the FOB and just a handful of women, and that wasn't going to change for nearly a year.

Rumors swirled of naval personnel from the SEAL compound vying to see who could sleep with the most army women, this infantry sergeant major sleeping with that admin captain, boyfriends, girlfriends, affairs. What happens on the FOB stays on the FOB. It wasn't long before our public affairs shop had our own gender-related problems.

CHAPTER 4:
GI JANE

TC always said the army's greatest failure was its attempt to integrate women into its ranks. Is that any surprise? Except in the movies, haven't armies and soldiers traditionally been about protecting "the women and children" and only incorporating their betters under the direst of circumstances, such as the siege of Stalingrad? Well, times are changing. In fact, with the relentless emphasis on individual rights, i.e., promotions, "self-actualization," and personal fulfillment over virtually all other considerations, it seems only a matter of time before most if not all combat roles are opened to women. Generals will no longer send in infantrymen, only infantry. It won't be the same army, but it will still be a good one.

During airborne operations, women do everything their male counterparts do, though sometimes smaller bladders and diminished ability to keep warm makes for more discomfort during the long, cold waits that often accompany the airborne timeline before and after jumps. (They still manage because, like all paratroopers, they have no choice.) Also, being in support roles, women don't jump with the same oppressive weight that infantrymen do, but then, neither do males in support roles. Sexes are not the issue, but rather, sex is.

So long as armies train to kill people, they will be male-dominated and male-oriented organizations in which many females will likely be hyper-conscious of their femininity. Female soldiers often report feeling pressured to keep a lid on that part of themselves and behave more like men, while others embrace their femininity, fully understanding that there is no force more powerful among men than a woman. Likely, for most women in today's army, it's a day-to-day balancing act.

My first notable experience with women on the battlefield came during pre-deployment war games at JRTC. I was on a rooftop embedded with infantrymen at a combat outpost, and our building was under siege by insurgents. Suddenly, a small convoy of Humvees rolled in through the gates, a resupply of food, water and ammo by one of our forward support companies. Great timing. While direct ground combat roles were not open to women, jobs such as medic, truck driver, and supply often brought them into a type of combat anyway. That's what was happening three stories below us. "Dude, there's a chick," somebody shouted. The entire roof security element collapsed to gawk over the side.

I doubt it would have happened had the battle been real (we were in the "magic circle" of play). The men might still have looked, but instead of leaving their posts to peek at a chick, their motives would likely have been paternal. One sees that every day in the army, and I've even seen it on the battlefield in Afghanistan. Grossman, the author of *On Killing*, reports that male Israeli soldiers reacted with uncontrollable protectiveness and aggression after seeing a woman wounded. It's natural for male soldiers, warranted or not, to regard their female peers as little sisters in need of protection. But it's obviously more complicated than that.

When our company first arrived in Iraq, we spent several days at the western transportation hub of Al Asad Air Base. Our public affairs shop at that time consisted of Malone, a female officer, me, and another combat correspondent who was a twenty-year-old private I'll call Jane. Jane was a talented journalist, whip smart, and dedicated to her craft. She was also good-hearted and the kind of young woman any parent would be proud of.

With her soft Carolina drawl, blond hair, dark lashes, always-sweet fragrance, and girl-next-door cuteness, Jane would have blended in at any shopping mall back home, but as we walked into a chow hall full of marines, she was suddenly the center of the universe. All eyes were on us, or rather, on her, as we moved along the serving line. A marine lieutenant broke into line next to me, leaned in, and whispered sternly, "Specialist, you keep an eye on that private. Someone will hit her on the head with a two-by-four and drag her into a tent." He was serious.

The sergeant of the fire support cell traveling with us warned his own soldiers, "If you so much as look in her direction, I will smoke the ever-loving dog shit out of you." He maintained that threat for the duration of our twelve-month deployment.

Now imagine being Jane. The army actively recruits you. You excel at your job and deploy to a war zone. Once there, people on your side want to abduct you. Fellow soldiers are not allowed to look at you, and the ones who hit on you dream up ridiculous stories about you because you said no. You just want to do your job. Everyone is hyperaware of your presence, because of your sex. You are halfway around the world in a country that treats your gender as second-class citizens (especially conservative Anbar). Iraqi men, who consider all American women "loose," will ask your peers whether you are a virgin, sometimes while you are in the room. They will insist on taking a photo with you.

On patrol with the infantry near the Syrian border, I was making small talk with an Iraqi border police sergeant, a pleasant fellow who had given many years of service to his country. Kasim was of Yzidi ethnicity from up north near the town of Sinjar. Kasim said that he was busy planning a wedding. "Isn't that women's work?" I chided him.

"No, you don't understand," he replied. "The girl and the family are not willing, so I am forced to kidnap her."

Iraqi men hold Iraqi women to an impossible standard of purity from which they implicitly exempt themselves. They see it not as a double standard, but as a different standard. For instance, an Iraqi woman was translating for marines searching house-to-house for weapons in Al Qaim near the Syrian border during the height of conflict in western Anbar. At one house, the old patriarch surrendered his one AK47, allowed under the current Iraqi law. Conspicuously, the weapon lacked a magazine and ammunition. A marine major bellowed, "Ask him, 'Where is the fucking magazine?'"

Translating the request as best she could, the woman asked, "Sir, the major wants to know, where are your porno magazines?"

The old man took a step back, aghast that he should be found out, and in front of a woman. Did these Americans have no class? "Young lady, be kind to an old man. Do not embarrass me," he begged. "But how did they know?"

"Sir," she said. "They are Americans. They have the Internet. They know everything."

We learned to prohibit Iraqis from taking photos with female American soldiers because it gave the impression that we had no respect for "our" women, so why should Iraqis? That was especially true for female officers, who were apt to have their authority undermined in the humiliating process.

Halting at a police checkpoint near Ramadi one night during a route-clearance patrol with our combat engineers, I snapped a photo of the engineers posing with the Iraqi policemen who manned the checkpoint. In the morning when I downloaded the images, I noticed the flash had caught the Iraqi police commander with his arm around an American female lieutenant, his hand cupping her left breast. She had not said a word, presumably because she was a soldier and soldiers are taught to endure for the greater good.

At Camp Ramadi, one of our young Iraqi media officers would routinely accuse Jane of a litany of bizarre moral offenses. "Your eyebrows are too thick," he scolded. "A woman's eyebrows should be thin or not at all. And why you drinking the caffeine? If a woman need the energy, she should go to the chow hall, not drink the caffeine." It was hard not to laugh at it all. Jane did. She told him where to stick his opinions, but the constant attention to her every move by seemingly every male began to take a toll. It was a perverse environment for her, complicated by how desperately so many of us missed intimacy and social interation with the opposite sex.

America has always tried to slake that thirst, most notably through the USO. Bikini-clad NFL cheerleaders, sassy country-music singers, and a buxom woman named Lee Ann Tweedon visited Camp Ramadi and the other Anbar FOBs, curiously drawing only meager crowds, but when the boys were out on patrol, talk of women never ceased. In fact, it was better then, because in the back of an MRAP in a war zone, every Joe has a shot at any woman.

Tracking across the desert south of Al Taqaddum Air Base, I listened to a conversation between a sergeant, driver, and gunner. The going was slow and tedious over baked, peeling, and blown-up asphalt, with nothing to see but windswept wasteland. The only sign of "civilization" was the aptly named Pancake Village, a wreck of concrete rooftops lying in the dust. The driver and TC (truck commander) were peppering the gunner, McKay, with hypotheticals. The TC had just asked McKay if he'd rather push an old woman in a wheelchair off a cliff or drown a homeless man in gasoline, but the conversation took on an edge when he added, "I want to hear your answer, McKay, because I know you're fucking against killing."

After some awkward back-and-forth, the sergeant wisely turned the conversation to women. "Megan Fox or Sarah Jessica Parker?"

"Dude, she's so old."

"But she's still hot."

"These girls are too skinny," chided the chunky Iraqi terp riding with us. His Americanized name was David.

"That's some bullshit, David, you fucking camel jockey."

"No, man, listen to me. These pretty girls, they get too much attention. They do not know how to take care of a man. I tell you what. I meet this girl tomorrow night who . . ."

"What?" asked the TC. "Dude, you can't meet a girl tomorrow night. You met her last night."

"Okay, so last night I meet this girl. She is big girl, two hundred pounds at least, but she has like two hundred pound heart for girl. She take care of you, the fat girls. You will see, come with me tonight to the hookah bar, she will do the belly-dancing."

"David, who wants to see a two-hundred-pound chick belly dance?" asked the driver.

"You will like, just try it. I call her my 'up-armored girlfriend.'"

Unless they know them very well, most soldiers have enough sense not to talk like misogynistic knuckle-draggers when female soldiers are present. For one, the magic bubble in which everyone in the vehicle actually has a chance with Megan Fox ceases to exist when clearly nobody even has a shot with Private First Class Jessica Jones in combat boots, a two-day stink, and grimy ACUs. Two, soldiers have mothers, sisters, and daughters, and generally want to show women respect when they are around. Three, and perhaps most importantly, there can be a steep penalty for behavior that even appears inappropriate.

But a year is a long time, and like so many deployed women, Jane seemed to experience some form of unvarnished sexism daily. For instance, because Jane was at the police station the day I was almost shot in the face, she was eligible for the Combat Action Badge. When she reported to the Bravo Company tent to fill out the required paperwork for the coveted badge, the platoon sergeant she had traveled with had his back to her. He was watching two of his Joes compete in a videogame. Jane walked up to him and cleared her throat, but the sergeant did not notice her. But he did smell her.

"Something smells like hot bitch in here," he said.

A soldier glanced from the monitor and nodded to Jane, "It's a girl, sergeant."

The sergeant dog-sniffed the air again and asked, "Which one of you perverts smells like a chick?"

"No sergeant, it's really a female, behind you."

The senior NCO turned to Jane and went pale, begging for his life. Jane might have ended his career that day, but she didn't even report the incident. Some soldiers questioned the "fairness" of allowing female soldiers to wear makeup in a war zone (or even while stateside), but that's simplistic and juvenile, in my opinion. What makes a woman isn't just a set of gonads; she's the manifestation of female genes which, for women the world over, includes the behavior of adornment. Blaming a woman for being a woman is as disingenuous as blaming Joe for wanting to look at her.

Before missions, Jane would chew her fingernails to nubs, not from anxiety over war but because of what some soldier on the mission might say or do. For instance, when Jane traveled to a remote FOB for a story, a captain handed her two TV dinners, with a note between the boxes that said, "I scratch your back, you scratch mine."

"Have you ever heard of an EO complaint?" she asked.

He said he was only joking. She said she was too. Neither one was, but they were, but they weren't. Back on Camp Ramadi, Jane received over twenty amorous emails from troopers she had met during her short, two-week trip. In the chow hall, a marine staff sergeant bumped into her as she was rising to leave. Later that day, he emailed her, "Are you interested?" Outside the chow hall, a young contractor left a note on the windshield of the truck she had arrived in with a friend who was picking up supplies. Jane stopped eating at the chow hall, living off of snacks from care packages and the PX.

Because she had no female companions and males of her rank and age were too eager for boyfriend status, she began hanging out with older male soldiers whom she trusted more. That created jealousy and rumors that she was having sex with them, and before long, everywhere I went, Joes would ask me if I had seen "the sex tape." Everyone knew of this video, but nobody could produce it. For a short time when Jane did have a female coworker to socialize with (in lieu of males), the rumors quickly died down. Unfortunately, the coworker left. Stories continued to spread. Jane was in a war zone and her nightmares were about the terrible things being said about her.

Company commanders at some of the smaller combat outposts disallowed female reporters altogether, not wanting the attention or the trouble. To be fair, accommodating female hygiene, safety, and privacy at the filthy outposts while cohabitating with Iraqi soldiers or policeman, or living communally in one tent, with no showers, and urinating in PVC pipes, or "piss tubes," would have come at great cost to limited time and resources.

One of the most capable combat correspondents I worked with in Iraq, Sergeant Katie Summerhill, was able to meet the challenges of being a deployed female soldier quite well, even leveraging her femininity without attracting the label of slut or bitch. Attached to the 366th Mobile Public Affairs Detachment at Liberty Base Complex in Baghdad, Summerhill made occasional trips out to Anbar to help our small shop.

An outgoing dynamo in any group of people, Katie said that, while being a woman occasionally precluded her from going to certain bases, her gender was a net positive. As a blonde American woman, she was a novelty to Iraqi policemen, so they would talk to her freely and do whatever she asked of them. Unlike male soldiers, Summerhill had access to Iraqi women, and children never felt threatened by her. American soldiers tended to be overly helpful much of the time, which could be good or bad, yet she was able to get many interviews that her male counterparts were unable to. She attributed that to "female charm."

"I don't overuse it, I don't make it a sexual thing, and I don't try to seduce. I just treat them like a male and make them feel like a woman is in the room, not a woman trying to be a man," she said. She has found that, in the army, most men are so scared of getting a sexual harassment complaint against them that they won't often speak around women, especially in line units, which can be problematic for a female reporter.

"That was a hard barrier to get through sometimes, but I learned that, if I let them say some inappropriate comments and feel like a man and in control, they work with me more, so I do. I know that, at the end of the day, I can walk away from it."

The big difference between Jane and Summerhill, both very smart and exceptional at their jobs, was that every story Summerhill did was with a different unit. In a very real sense, she did walk away from every situation. Most jobs that women hold in the army don't allow such leeway.

Particularly on long, tedious deployments in mixed-gender environments with the same people, pushing the boundaries of what's appropriate for group conversation is a time-honored tradition akin to a game of verbal roulette, with onlookers, participants, and the occasional loser. Soldiers of both genders do this, occasionally with disastrous results.

A friend who had made some inappropriate comments in a conversation full of inappropriate comments, more than half of which came from women, nearly watched his career end when, weeks later, he was forced to discipline one of the female soldiers for an unrelated offense. Her exact words were, "If I get in trouble for this, then he is getting in trouble for that." And she did. And he did. Male soldiers get angry at how a mere accusation from a female soldier can end a career. We're not used to being the victims of sexism. I'm not sure there are many female soldiers ready to shed tears for us.

For Jane, there was no walking away. She was assigned to the brigade. By the end of our deployment, there was a full-blown investigation over whether a friendship she had with an officer who worked nearby had become "inappropriate." He was married and much older. In the Army, perception is reality, and both knew that a private first class and a major had no business socializing as much as they did. Likely, Jane felt safe conversing with an officer old enough to be her father. It's also difficult to overemphasize the clout that a "field grade" major has in a brigade combat team as compared to a private.

After nearly a year as the central figure in dozens of gossip threads, perhaps the private had lost the distinction between false stories that people tell and false stories that people believe. Acquiescence can look like brazenness. I wish, as I would wish for my own daughter who was just a few years younger at the time, that Jane would have made herself less available, but then, she was only a private. Were they having sex? I really didn't think so. She had a young enlisted boyfriend by then, an infantryman. Jane and the major were eventually cleared.

In spite of the unending challenges invited by bringing sex into the ranks, the army is a diverse service that has benefitted greatly from the inclusion of women. That's the point, isn't it? I'm proud to have served alongside Black Hawk pilot Catherine Omodt, military police officer Shanne Dill, physician assistant Jessica Larson, field medic Tiari Ventura, human resource officer Maira Patino, female engagement team officer Elizabeth Trobaugh, public affairs officer Ginny McCabe, and many others. Each was an airborne-qualified paratrooper who brought excellence and dedication to the job.

Larson left a lucrative career in the aviation industry to find a meaningful life of service in the medical field. During a clinical rotation at Brooke Army Medical Center while working with severely wounded warriors, the Chicago native was inspired to join the army. "They were still proud to be in the army, and they were working really hard to rehabilitate themselves and to do the best they could with what they had," she said. "'This is what life dealt me; this is what I am working with, and now it's time for me to move on. There is no feeling sorry for yourself here.' That was the attitude that all the soldiers had," Larson said. "It was really inspiring."

She recalled trying to internalize the feelings of loss that a young soldier and his wife were grappling with after he had lost his genitals and the chance to father children. "If these guys could give up multiple limbs for their country, the least I could do was to give three years of my life," Larson said.

Like men, women join to serve. Today, the roles of women in the Armed Forces are expanding rapidly, with infantry, Rangers, and Special Forces within sight. Soldiers will do as they're told. In the 82nd Airborne Division, I often heard brigade and battalion commanders actively counsel their paratroopers to always remember the inherent dignity of fellow soldiers, regardless of gender.

It's important to point out that most American soldiers consider service by *anyone* as an automatic guarantor of respect. It's common knowledge that only 1 percent of Americans have served during a decade of two wars, and outside military towns, there is scant evidence that we're still a nation at war. Our soldiers are keenly aware of both facts. In the service, no value is held as high as service.

For instance, in spite of the controversy from the repeal of "Don't ask, don't tell," when members of the Westboro Baptist Church picketed the funeral of a military policewoman killed by a suicide bomber in Afghanistan in early October 2012, thousands of Fort Bragg-area troops turned out to shield the mourners. Hundreds of infantrymen from our line companies attended to support a soldier whom they considered their fallen comrade, in spite of the fact that Staff Sergeant Donna Johnson of the 514th Military Police Company, North Carolina National Guard, was both female and gay. I have my own gender-related story from Iraq, one for which I am still deeply ashamed. In fact, it has to do with how we, as Americans, bring our ideals abroad without fully appreciating the human cost that others may pay for our great expectations.

When 1/82 first arrived at Camp Ramadi, our civil affairs and psyops sergeants got wind of an Iraqi program to train women police, right outside our back gate. Americans had tried to push a similar program just after Saddam's fall, but cultural resistance to women in traditionally male roles was too durable. The program crumbled, and many of its participants were ostracized. But with a national election just months away and a desperate insurgency coercing women to become suicide bombers, there was immediate need for female police to search women, a task culturally taboo for male cops.

Sergeants First Class Dave Lowry and Jeff McFarland thought the training program would make a great news story. I did too. Dave Lowry was a bald, veiny, tattooed, ex-infantryman. At the crack of automatic weapons fire outside the FOB walls one day, he asked me if I knew what the sound was. I thought it was a weapons question. "That is the sound of freedom," he replied. Jeff McFarland was a bullshit-proof soldier's soldier who once put an annoying private on a "speaking profile," meaning the kid wasn't allowed to talk. At all. "Feelings are like weeds," he liked to say. "They always grow back."

Another Dave, an American police trainer working at the Iraqi facility, gave us a tour of the Ramadi Training Center. In its heyday, the RTC had employed over two hundred trainers, pushing through nine thousand recruits a year. Shifting political priorities had reduced the program to twenty-eight hundred in 2009, trained by a reduced staff of twenty-four that was mentored by retired American lawmen.

The female training program was just beginning. In fact, there was a bit of a two-step going on. While the course would fully qualify women for police work, most of the enrollees had already signed on as contractors with the police force specifically for searching. A few women had bona-fide hiring orders from police sub-districts, but not many.

The dean of the training center, Brigadier General Mohamad Khalifa Nazar, was a typical edgy, chain-smoking, patrician officer. In a short conversation, the general granted me permission to interview participants, but only a female soldier would be allowed to take pictures. That was a common request and easily satisfied since Summerhill was on Camp Ramadi at that time.

I met with the program's headmistress, Reem Abdac Rahman, a matronly powerhouse who gave off a kind of pure, kind energy like light reflecting in pools of rainwater. "Many of these ladies are sole breadwinners," she said through a translator. "Some have up to nine children to feed, but they still put their earnings into a tribal pot. The younger ones, the single girls, see this as a way to better themselves."

The women were selfless heroes—this was going to be a great story. We agreed to meet the following day for the interview and photos. However, we were never allowed back on the Iraqi base. The order had come directly from the Anbar chief of police, General Tariq. Months later, we learned that the entire program had been canceled because our "unapproved visit" had "violated Iraqi sovereignty."

Welcome to the graveyard of good intentions. A challenge that soldiers face as they try to "do good" in the countries to which they deploy includes a sobering valuation of what can and should be accomplished. Americans regard freedom as one freedom for all, so when the goal is to bring freedom, where does one stop? Had I been able to get the story out, perhaps I would have drawn the attention of the civilian media, who might have brought the story to major markets. I'm guessing that is the eventuality that General Tariq was trying to avoid, thereby retaining the support of a conservative populace against radically conservative extremists by not calling attention to a necessary but unseemly elevation of women to the level of men. It's just a guess.

What difficulties I had created for the courageous women who had volunteered to search for bombs so they could feed their kids, I can only guess at. Like Twain's lightning and lightning bug, there is only one little word of difference between righteous and self-righteous.

There were plenty of other good news stories to tell in Anbar, but few were able to draw the attention of the international media. They seemed to be interested in telling only one story—how violence was returning to once-peaceful Anbar, and how the area was going to hell fast.

CHAPTER 5:
VIOLENCE RETURNS
TO ANBAR

Operation Proper Exit was conceived as a way for severely wounded soldiers and marines to bring closure to the psychological wounds sustained during the heavy urban conflict of the Iraq War. A soldier might be blown up in an IED strike only to awake in Ramstein Air Base in Germany, or Walter Reed Medical Center in Maryland, far removed from his unit and battle buddies.

Soldiers had lost multiple limbs, square feet of skin, yards of gut, eyes, internal organs, a sense of who they were. One marine regiment alone suffered over 90 amputations during a six-month deployment to Anbar. It can be difficult for unharmed soldiers to rotate off a battlefield before a battle is won. For the severely wounded, there is added guilt for leaving one's friends still in harm's way, and questions of what was gained for the cost. Was it worth wrecking his life for? His wife's life? His children's?

Civilian-funded and supported logistically by the military, Proper Exit brought small groups of wounded warriors back to the battlefields of Iraq where their lives were so violently disrupted. They came to grieve and they came to leave, if not on their own two feet, at least of their own volition.

A big part of the program was allowing the returning warriors to share their experiences with soldiers currently in the fight. In the Camp Ramadi chapel, young paratroopers who had yet to fire a shot listened spellbound to accounts of what the war had been like just a few years earlier in Anbar, and what the fallout had been for some of those wrecked by warfare. It was hard to believe the wounded wanted to come back to Iraq.

Wounded in action. People reading news reports of a battle want to know how many were killed, because wounded is just *wounded*, a supposed trivial inconvenience as compared with death. In Iraq, for every soldier killed, eight were wounded. Fix them up and send them back into battle. Sometimes that works, as it did for Sergeant Kevin Novak, the forward observer who caught the sniper's bullet that was intended for me. After several months of rehab in the States, Novak returned to Ramadi to finish the deployment.

For others, like Sergeant Martin May, a Colorado National Guard gunner who was shot in the face in downtown Ramadi six days after I was targeted, the wounds were life altering. The sniper's bullet struck May below the right eye and exited through the left eye, which he lost. Same goes for the female Navy corpsman who was wounded in the head by a sniper in downtown Ramadi a few months later.

Battle wrecks with intent, distinct from, say, a car crash. Cars are designed to protect bodies—injuries are the design's failure; weapons of war are designed to destroy bodies—injuries are success. Welcome, then, to "life-altering wounds."

Corporal Craig Chavez was serving with the 1st Cavalry Division south of Baghdad in the so-called "Triangle of Death" in 2006 when he was upended by an IED that erupted directly beneath his feet. Insurgents had buried it too deep. Dirt spared his legs, but the blast destroyed his left eye and left the right eye severely damaged. He had so little sight left in the center of the right eye that, when he looked at people, they appeared like ghosts, bodies without faces—no smiles, winks, or tears. The face of humanity had gone gray. For the balance of his days, he would see the world through the lens of the Iraq War.

Retired Sergeant Ethan Payton lost his left arm to an RPG in Baghdad in 2004. The first time he walked the dog after his amputation, the dog ran off with his prosthetic hand. A friend lost his prosthetic hand to a shopping cart. Cry or laugh, the choice is yours, he said.

Sometimes when retired Sergeant Noah Galloway hopped around the house because he didn't want to strap on his prosthetic leg, his three children would hop along behind him. (Incidentally, this is the same Galloway who in 2015 would appear on the television show, *Dancing with the Stars*.)

Retired Sergeant First Class Mike Schlitz lost both hands and nearly all of his skin to burns from a roadside bomb in 2007. The hands came off not from the blast but from burns and infections. What was left of Schlitz was an earless, porcine head and face, two hooks for hands, and an uncaged sense of humor. Schlitz told a crowd of our paratroopers gathered in the Camp Ramadi chapel, "The thing about us people with prosthetics is we try to do things the same way as we did before we had prosthetics. Take something simple, like going to the bathroom, right? So I unzip, reach in, and grab, but I tensed up the wrong way. You've got to realize I can crush a can with these things," he said, brandishing stainless steel hooks from his sleeves. "What happens when you grab and you tense up? You tense up, it grabs it harder. Whoever invented these must have already known that because they make a manual release, and that manual release is the best thing in the world." Our challenges were quickly trivialized by the visiting warriors; our service would never be enough.

Specialist Brent Hendrix, a giant man cobbled back together after sixty-six surgeries and a partial leg amputation following a massive IED blast to his Stryker in Rawah in 2006, said that anything less than amputation above the knee was "weak sauce."

"Schlitz here ain't got no more than a paper cut," he said to the crowd. He made the soldiers in the audience laugh, and helped to bridge the gap between our experiences and theirs. The Forest City, North Carolina native related a story of "messing with Barbara and Jenna Bush" during one of his visits to the White House while he recovered at nearby Walter Reed. The next day he was accosted by the girls' father, President George W. Bush.

"He asked me, 'So, Hoss, what did you say to my wife and daughter yesterday?' and I said, 'Oh shit,' and I cussed right there in the Oval Office," he said. The welded, grafted, splinted soldier had said *Oh shit* before his Commander in Chief, the man who sent in boots-on-the-ground, and tanks, and planes, and helicopters, and Strykers, and was playing the protective father game with this broken soldier over his wife and two pretty daughters.

Hendrix laughed and addressed our paratroopers directly. "So we pretty much run a lot of Al Qaeda out of here, huh?" he asked. He hadn't really come here to tell stories. He wanted to know if his wounds had paid dividends of success. To see with his own eyes, was perhaps the prime reason each traveled halfway around the world to revisit the site of the worst day of his life. They had all to come to Anbar to see the "good news stories" because reporters were not reporting them. It was that way when they were fighting, and it was the same way in 2009. So many had sacrificed so much for so much good, and reporters only reported the fuck-ups, or worse, sensationalized the enemy's successes. This is why soldiers hate reporters.

For instance, several months after our arrival in Anbar, the army flew in Baghdad-based reporters with the *Los Angeles Times*, *New York*

Times, and the *Washington Post,* ostensibly to let them report on the progress of the army's first full-fledged advise-and-assist brigade.

Colonel Stammer, our brigade commander, offered them his assessment of the AAB's progress. Most of the problems in Anbar did not have straight military solutions, Stammer told them, which is why the brigade was working so closely with two ongoing features of the post-insurgency landscape—the Anbar Provincial Reconstruction Team and an array of military training teams. PRTs were State Department organizations that assisted in rebuilding civil government and commerce, and MiTT teams closely advised police and army units.

Violence in Anbar remained relatively low, with about a dozen incidents per week province-wide. Since August, there had been only two attacks on US forces (both involved snipers). Numerous US and Iraqi security assets continued to whittle away at the extremist networks that supplied and deployed car bombs and suicide vests.

After fewer than three hours "on the ground," the reporters flew back to Baghdad to write their stories. It turned out, the situation in Anbar was much worse than we had imagined. The scoop from our intrepid, boots-on-the-ground reporters sensationalized what violence they could muster from the edges of the present time and suggested that the upcoming national elections were sure to be disastrous. A reporter for the *New York Times* began his piece, "Attacks Threaten Fragile Security Gains in Cradle of Iraq Insurgency," with the dramatic lead, "Maj. Gen. Tariq al-Youssef caught a fleeting glimpse of the man who wanted him dead." Tariq was the provincial chief of police, the grizzled old cop who had nixed the female police training program.

Come on, now. In post-insurgency Iraq, was it really that difficult to imagine a whole lot of people wanting a whole lot of other people dead? Cradle of insurgency? Ramadi was also the first deathbed of the insurgency following the Awakening, so why not call it that? The article went on, "The attack in June, from which [Tariq] walked away unscathed, marked the beginning of what Iraqi and American officials say has been a concerted effort by Sunni insurgents to reassert themselves in a part of the country that was once their stronghold."

The *Times* writer marched through a list of violent acts occurring recently in Anbar, the "dozens of attacks on checkpoints and . . . assassinations of influential tribal leaders and the destruction of vital infrastructure," but he failed to mention that this type of harassing violence had been going on since 2003 and even *after* the Awakening crushed AQI in 2007. Only deep in the article's bowels was there a reference to the drama-canceling "vast difference in the level of violence from two years ago."

Reporting from a war zone is difficult, no doubt about it. When Governor Qasim was targeted by back-to-back blasts just after Christmas that year (a car bomb followed 48 minutes later by a suicide vest), the BBC immediately reported that the governor was killed along with thirty bystanders even as he was being medevaced by Black Hawk to Camp Ramadi and then on to Baghdad. Death tolls and other "facts" were careening out of the blast sites with every website reporting dramatically different numbers. That's understandable. It has always been that way in war zones. But why do Al Qaeda's bidding with the constant doomsday proselytizing that the facts don't support?

"Ramadi attacks: Is Iraq heading for more sectarian bloodshed?" asked the *Christian Science Monitor*. The BBC followed up with an article titled, "Deadly double blast hits street in Iraq city of Ramadi."

Despite the blood and treasure sunk into the sands of Anbar and the ongoing sacrifices of our wounded warriors, the press was determined to have its quagmire continue. In March, Iraq held its second national elections since the fall of Saddam. Contrary to widespread media projections of calamity, voter turnout in Anbar reached 60 percent. Unlike the elections of 2005, there was no Sunni boycott in 2010, making it the country's first legitimate election. Across the province, twenty-eight IEDs were discovered and cleared by Iraqi forces. There was only one injury and no deaths. Yet the media hardly mentioned the high turnout or lack of violence in Anbar, the "cradle of the insurgency." Instead, they granted the insurgents victory for killing thirty-eight people elsewhere in Iraq on Election Day, half of whom died in a single explosion in Baghdad. While these deaths were tragic, by Iraq War standards, the elections should have been reported as a victory against the extremists.

The victories of American soldiers and their Iraqi partners continued to go unreported or underreported, while the enemies' efforts always grabbed headlines, and misleading ones at that. The whole point of their spectacular, yet limited, attacks was to manipulate the media into fanning fear and sectarian violence through one-sided reporting, and the media rarely failed to play their part. Where were the stories of the newly erected Saqlawiyah Bridge and how its economic impact would foster peace in an area troubled by poverty, or the Husaybah cops who thwarted the suicide bombers from blowing up schools full of kids, or the schools, waterworks, and power projects that were opening up Karmah, Anbar's last worst place?

Bad news is good news in every newsroom around the world. That didn't make the media's negative reporting on Iraq less frustrating to American service personnel. Soldiers get it: the media never liked George W. Bush or "Bush's War." They only ask that the media stop covering Bush's War and start covering the one that they gave their lives to. It didn't take place in D.C. or New York. It happened in the streets of Iraq.

As bad as the media/military relationship was in our country, it was much worse in Iraq, where the press was locked out of access to the post-dictator military, and the military often regarded the press as near co-conspirators of the insurgents. With our Iraqi media officer, Mo, we compiled a list of legitimate Arab journalists, vetted them, and invited them to Camp Ramadi to meet with top Iraqi security officials on several occasions. There was shouting and acrimony, but the project appeared to be accomplishing its goal.

Near the end of our year in-country, Iraqi generals asked for help clearing insurgents from Hit, a city of about a hundred thousand on the

Euphrates River between Ramadi and Al Asad. Significantly, the commander of all Iraqi forces in Anbar, General Aziz, had directed the 7th Iraqi Division to exploit any success in Hit using its newly established relationship with the local Arab media.

The clearing of Hit would be old-fashioned door-kicking stuff that would draw directly from the shoot-move-communicate native arts of paratroopers. Companies of heavily-armed infantry would secure blocks at a time with support from gun trucks, helicopter gunships, and even Navy SEAL sniper teams prepositioned on rooftops for an unknown duration of time.

Hit was the town where Lieutenant Colonel Waleed of the anti-terrorism police unit was almost assassinated and where a US convoy was recently attacked by rocket-propelled grenades. We were finally going to war.

CHAPTER 6:
THE CLEARING OF HIT

When Iraqi security forces asked our paratroopers to help clear insurgents from the town of Hit in the spring of 2010, Lieutenant Colonel José Thompson, a battalion commander of airborne artillerymen who had been cross-trained as infantry, put together a fully-supported assault force. Besides door-kickers, it included dozens of "enablers," including civil affairs teams, dog handlers, electronic warfare and psychological operations specialists, and more, and staged them all before daylight one morning at a walled police compound just outside the city.

As the sun rose, Iraqi soldiers and policemen packed into the beds of unarmored pickups and rolled out of the battered, dusty compound. Held in reserve, our paratroopers cooled their heels beside a dozen humming MRAPs, waiting for the call.

Inside the police headquarters, Thompson sat at a table with the top Iraqi officers. In the last four weeks, violent extremists in Hit had killed seventeen citizens in thirty-six attacks. Province-wide, there had been 157 incidents over the same period, not a lot by past measures, but enough to warrant some action. Iraqi security forces had made twenty arrests in the past week. There was sure to be reason to bring the might of the 82nd Airborne Division down on the heads of these extremists today.

I stood with the assault team that morning, waiting and wanting to go to war. We listened for gunfire or explosions. Our helicopters were in the air above the town, little Kiowa Warrior two-seaters. There were Navy SEAL teams prepositioned on several rooftops. We heard nothing.

At 10:39 a.m., the Iraqi commanding general reported that his forces had detained twelve suspects with standing warrants and confiscated four AK47s. At 1 p.m., he announced that all operations were complete.

Thompson knew that sixteen Iraqi companies could not have cleared a town of over a hundred thousand in a single day, let alone a morning. The operation was a farce, at most a show of force for the citizens of Hit. Thompson's paratroopers were disgusted. Ten months of "bullshit" advise-and-assist missions, and now this charade.

Thompson reminded his paratroopers that their job was to advise and assist, not to bust down doors. Those days were over. Everyone knew it, even skeptical Iraqis who were now seeing with their very eyes the ever-growing Kuwait-bound river of armored vehicles and matériel draining the country of American warfighting capacity.

Like most of the paratroopers standing there all kitted up for war, I was very disappointed. We weren't sadists mourning the lack of violence, but rather, firemen who rushed to a fire only to find cold ashes and a construction crew. America was leaving. The Iraq War was over. It was over when we got there. That was good news—I guess.

PART III:

The Garrison Life

CHAPTER 1:
TIME

"Five-second fuses only last three seconds."

–Anonymous

Seven words never held so much painful truth about how it goes when the army makes a promise of time. The soldier who is sure about his future—whether it's the next five years or five seconds—is bound for a nasty surprise.

Our civilian widebody jetliner overheated on the runway at Al Asad, pushing our arrival time in the States "to the right," as we say in the army. The deployment may have been light on combat, but we still cheered when the aircraft left Iraqi airspace. We stopped in Germany several hours later to refuel before the ocean crossing. Stepping from the plane into a fresh breeze, I was overcome with memories of my former life when I smelled that sure sign of civilization—a lawn.

I've never experienced a more glorious sensation than coming home to my family from a deployment to a war zone. The only human touch I'd had in over a year was a handshake, the limp-fish Arab version and the vice-grip, American-soldier version. Returning to the intimacy of a marriage seemed too fantastical to be true. My children seemed to be perfect humans, with each hair on their heads a veritable miracle. Food no longer came in just bland and salty, Walmart stores were unbelievable troves of possibilities, and the 98-degree, 90-percent-humidity August of the Carolina sandhills was downright pleasant. In my car again, I peeled out of the parking lot just because I could. I can still remember the feel of the steering wheel in my hands and the lack of the *clickity-clack* of a gun turret panning for targets. I was free in the US of A.

At the military-sponsored Family Readiness Group meeting, my wife and the other military spouses were assured that "nothing can touch your soldiers' thirty days of block leave." However, because of the way the Army tabulates time off, I ended up with four. There were other "new" soldiers sharing my lot. Instead of enjoying our families after twelve long months of separation, we mowed grass at Fort Bragg. When lack of rain kept the grass from growing, the sergeant major ordered us to put lawnmower tracks in the brown grass so that it looked freshly mowed. I am not making this up.

Typically these things happen because an officer makes a promise that the army can't keep and still be in accord with its own regulation. The sergeant major, who has to square the discrepancy, doesn't care if life sucks for soldiers because life has always sucked for soldiers. It's supposed to suck. It sucked for him. Yours will suck too.

Expectation management is the only path to sanity. It can always suck worse. In 2003–04, our company's first sergeant, Bobby Lieske, deployed to the notorious slums of Iraq's Sadr City, and the day before his unit was scheduled to return, they were extended for two additional months. The unit's advance party was turned around on the runway just after landing in Louisiana and sent back to Iraq. With their families outside the windows, they were never even let off the plane.

Recruiters make the two-and-a-half accrued days of leave per month sound like a windfall, but what they don't say is that, during wartime, accrued time off can only be used during tightly regulated "block leave" immediately before or after a deployment, or at Christmas. And what if a soldier spends every weekend of the month in the field for training? Big deal. He still only accrues two-and-a-half days of leave for that month. It's true that sometimes "long weekends" are added to the schedule, but these can be revoked up to the very last minute.

There is another reason so much of a soldier's time is wasted, and it has to do with the gross inefficiencies generated by the steep part of the learning curve. The "system" is not a business, with the goal of achieving high efficiency. It's an army with the goal of winning wars. To do that, it must amass an inventory of replicable and interchangeable parts, i.e., soldiers with a width and depth of cross-training, to withstand the chaotic and unpredictable damage of warfare. That's why, as soon as a soldier becomes efficient at his job, he is moved to another.

The result is inefficiency at every turn. One week, I wasted thirteen hours on a "weapons detail" to count 239 weapons, send them through an hour-long refurbishing process, and then verify that we still had all 239. I spent five hours trying to mail a small package for official army business. I made four trips to the brigade personnel office just to sign my Servicemembers Group Life Insurance. And my favorite—I stood in line outside the dentist office for ninety minutes in a cold rain at 6 a.m., to stand in another line inside the dentist office for an hour, to make an appointment to meet with the woman who made appointments. That's right. I made an appointment to make an appointment.

Inefficiency is compounded by the fact that there often exists only a vague correlation between a soldier's aptitude and education for a job and his assignment to that job. For instance, in Iraq, I met a reserve lieutenant in command of a chemical company that was re-missioned just prior to deployment as a civil affairs outfit. Civil affairs are those people who "win hearts and minds." In the army, no matter how poorly trained or ill-suited someone is for a job, all that's needed is the right PowerPoint presentation to prepare him, or so the thinking goes.

The system is difficult for soldiers to bear, especially for redeploying soldiers. Yet bear it they do. As a result, soldiers hold nothing as dear as time. Soldiers and recent veterans value time spent with friends, family, and doing what they love in a fundamentally different way than their civilian peers.

CHAPTER 2: TRAINING

In garrison, soldiers spend the majority of their time training for war. After one "mass-tactical" night jump onto Fort Bragg's Sicily Drop Zone that began a two-week field exercise, I linked up with the *Huffington Post*'s senior military reporter, David Wood. A massive summertime thunderstorm swept in and pinned down the entire brigade in the dark on the treeless, slight rise of the DZ. Lightning shattered the blackness with wallop after wallop of seething electricity so that nobody dared to move from wherever they were hunkered down. I held my M4 gingerly as I realized what an excellent lightning rod it would make.

After two hours of drenching rain that followed, a fellow soldier and I borrowed a Humvee and returned Mr. Wood to his hotel room off post where he dried off and found a good night's sleep. We returned to the DZ and the rain. It was joyously miserable paratrooper weather. As the saying goes, if it ain't raining, it ain't training.

I admire soldiers because they endure long days and nights of tedium, discomfort, and danger in spite of a system that often does not serve them. They provide essential defense for a country that, in spite of its shortcomings, is still the greatest force of good in the world. Why do they do it? Civilians often obsess over why soldiers serve, but in combat, all the many reasons are meaningless. What matters is shooting, moving, and communicating, and that's it. It's what forms the bonds of brotherhood—a common goal with common tasks coalescing around a greater good. It no longer matters *why* you're doing it, only *that* you're doing it.

Service begins by training to do one's job. Following redeployment, many officers and NCOs change jobs, moving to other bases or other billets on the same base. It is not uncommon for 25 percent of a unit to change over within three months of returning home. Companies, battalions, brigades, and even divisions change commanders roughly at pace with redeployments.

Thus, after a month of block leave, soldiers immediately begin training for the next deployment. There is little time for rest. For paratroopers, training falls into three broad categories: field training, airborne operations, and mandatory quarterly training.

Mandatory quarterly training, required by Big Army, includes lectures on sexual harassment, equal opportunity, suicide prevention and those types of soft subjects designed to decrease internal friction within the force. It ensures that no soldier can say he never learned that his actions could be considered sexual harassment. He did. Four times a year he did.

The army's equal opportunity program celebrates the heritages of select minorities with African-American History Month, Women's History Month, Asian Pacific Heritage Month, Hispanic Heritage Month, and National Native American Heritage Month, but it reaches the pinnacle of appreciation with All Inclusive Heritage Day. No soldier left behind.

Airborne training includes refresher courses for paratroopers who haven't jumped within the last ninety days (such as those returning from combat), jumpmaster training, regularly scheduled "currency jumps" that allow paratroopers to retain their jump status and $150 monthly hazardous duty pay, and mass-tactical airborne operations that are often paired with extended field-training exercises to mimic the kind of combat that the 82nd was designed to execute.

Regaining airborne proficiency after a year of no jumping was an immediate concern for our brigade of paratroopers. Train-up followed the usual crawl, walk, run schema, culminating in a Joint Operational Access Exercise, or JOAX, that begins when nearly the entire brigade and much of its equipment parachutes en masse into a drop zone at night with immediate and follow-on missions that might last several days to a week or more. During a JOAX, formations of C17s and smaller C130s can deliver several thousand paratroopers onto the drop zone in minutes, all in complete darkness.

What is it like? Imagine strapping two large suitcases and a shovel to one's body and jumping from a fast-moving train into the dark of night. That's what combat-equipment jumps are like. Sometimes the landing is rough, other times it's a train wreck. When we jumped in Iraq, the landing was so hard that three paratroopers developed intracranial hemorrhages. However, it's usually not anywhere near that bad. On a normal jump, the injury rate is about 4 percent. In fact, the most painful part for a paratrooper is the so-called airborne timeline, the time-padded schedule of tasks that must be completed prior to paratroopers exiting the aircraft. It's not uncommon for paratroopers to dedicate twelve hours to a thirty-second parachute jump.

Beyond the tedium of the timeline, for a paratrooper, there is nothing better than jumping, especially with combat equipment at night. Paratroopers are not skydivers. We jump from eight hundred feet, not twelve thousand. Our parachutes are partially attached to the aircraft via static line, which pulls the chute open immediately after we jump. Upon exiting, we count to five. If the main parachute has not deployed by then, we activate the reserve parachute or we will hit the ground in three more seconds. Whereas skydivers try to maximize time in the air, paratroopers try to minimize it.

Paratroopers enjoy a special fraternity within the Armed Forces that extends to foreign paratroop units, due to the social leveling effect of airborne operations. Lieutenant Colonel Phillip Sounia, commander of our cavalry scout squadron in 2013, put it this way: "When you are in line at manifest, no one cares what rank you are: You are a paratrooper. The jumpmaster in charge might be a sergeant, a major, or a colonel. It doesn't matter. He's a jumpmaster and that's who you are listening to. You look to your right and left to see who the junior guy is, and that's who you are going to take care of. To me, that's beautiful."

It is beautiful. Even more beautiful is a bright green canopy snapping open above your head following the jumpmaster countdown and your vigorous huck from the aircraft:

"Ten minutes!"

"Outdoor personnel, stand up!"

"Indoor personnel, stand up!"

"Hook up!"

"Check static lines!"

"Check equipment!"

"Sound off for equipment check!"

"Okay! Okay!" Okay thirty-one times, and then a final, "All okay, Jumpmaster" by the lead parachutist, who extends his open hand.

The jumpmaster slaps the lead jumper's hand and takes control of the door from the air force, sweeping it one last time for obstructions. He leans out the door into the wind to check his location and look for more hazards. He then rotates back in, looks the number one jumper in the eyes and yells, "Stand by!"

With that command, the lead jumper moves into the open jump door, waiting for the light to turn green and the jumpmaster to slap him on the butt. No matter how many jumps one has, that sequence of events keys an automatic physical response. Every action is recorded in muscle memory, so all a paratrooper must consciously do is follow the paratrooper in front of him toward that bright, howling hole at the back of the aircraft.

Shuffling with chute, reserve, ruck, and weapon, it's all automatic . . .

. . . looks the jumpmaster in the eye as he hands off his static line . . .

. . . turns into the jump door, hands on the side of his reserve, fingers spread . . .

. . . *vigorous* exit, feet and knees together, chin on chest and *wham!*

. . . *PROP BLAST* . . .

". . . one thousand, two thousand, three thousand . . ."

The main chute billows open, yanking the paratrooper like a ragdoll.

"Huugh!"

Checks canopy, gains canopy control by grabbing the risers in his bare hands. Lower jumpers have the right-of-way. Slips right to avoid other jumpers. Already the aircraft's grumbling engines are out of earshot. Quiet peaceful floating. Two hundred feet from the ground, he releases the ruck buckled to his waist. It slides down a fifteen-foot leash, followed by his M4 carbine in its padded green case. One hundred feet from the ground—assuming he can see the ground—he gauges the direction of drift and pulls a "slip" by yanking the opposite risers into his chest. That changes the shape of his canopy and slows his horizontal drift.

. . . looks at the horizon, not the ground beneath his feet . . .

. . . prepares to land . . .

Lands. Balls of feet, calf, thigh, buttocks, push-up muscle. Rolls and flips to absorb impact. Hand to shoulder, unbuckles a riser to collapse the chute and prevent being dragged. "Riser!" he shouts.

Whips out cell phone; calls wife.

It's a magnificent way to enter the battlefield, but sometimes landings are painful. Feet, ass, head. Sometimes there is no landing, as when a paratrooper drifts over the forest and snags in one of Bragg's longleaf pines. Occasionally the weather does not cooperate. Wind is a big deal. Jumps are often canceled when ground winds blow in excess of thirteen knots. Parachutes work fine in rain and they tell us that paratroopers do too (an unfortunate reality). My friend Brian Hamilton once became a "towed jumper" when his static line didn't separate from his parachute harness. As he bounced against the plane's rear fuselage, six more exiting paratroopers crashed into him before he passed out. He was lucky he wasn't torn in half when his reserve chute deployed, and again that he didn't drown when he landed, unconscious, in a ditch with his head just above the water. Hamilton is a chaplain's assistant.

When I arrived at Bragg from Airborne School still a "five-jump chump," for me parachuting was death-defying derring-do, and with the brigade's intensive train-up for Iraq, I had little time to learn to enjoy that part of being a paratrooper. That changed when we returned from Anbar. One of our first airborne exercises was several days of "Hollywood" jumps from Black Hawk and Chinook helicopters (a Hollywood jump is a jump without combat equipment, usually in daylight). Without any discernable prop blast to help open the chutes, the freefall from a helicopter is nearly twice as long as from an airplane. When we returned from Afghanistan in the fall of 2012, our "fun jump" was parachuting from helicopters into a lake. I grew to love the silky smell of the T10 Delta parachute, the tough texture of its green canvas enclosure, and most of all, the avian tug of suspension straps when the canopy blossomed above me. I loved the violence of slipping into the sky behind giant turboprops and jet engines and the fullness and quietude of floating above the earth's wide dome.

As noted, the army emphasizes adaptability more than efficiency, and for good reason. For instance, when the 82nd's 1st Battalion, 505th PIR parachuted into Normandy during the invasion of northern France, the battalion's top three officers—the commander, executive officer, and operations officer—were all killed within the first forty-eight hours. The beauty of the army's rank system is that, in every group of soldiers, even those accidentally thrown together on a battlefield or in a simple garrison detail, everyone knows who's in charge. Leadership is crucial because the worst action on a battlefield is inaction, or individual action.

As the saying goes, "After the demise of the best Airborne plan, a most terrifying effect occurs on the battlefield. This effect is known as the rule of the [Little Group of Paratroopers, or] LGOPs. This is, in its purest form, a small group of pissed-off 19-year-old American paratroopers. They are well-trained, armed to the teeth, and lack serious adult supervision. They collectively remember the Commander's intent as 'March to the sound of the guns and kill anyone who is not dressed like you . . .' or something like that. Happily they go about the day's work . . ."

Soldiers do two things: They go to war, and they train to go to war. There's a crude saying that succinctly explains the nature of field training in the army: "Hey private, why don't you hold the chicken and let me fuck it." That little profanity holds three important truths: That we are a team; there is a proper order and method; and only one of us can be in charge at a time. It implies a certain unpleasantness and contempt for the training but a collective understanding that it will occur regardless.

The rule of thumb is that a soldier should be able to do the next job up and be familiar with the one above that. For instance, a fire team leader should be able to do his squad leader's job and be familiar with a platoon sergeant's job.

Most army training consists of building muscle memory for simple tasks. Even when rocket science is involved, such as firing an AT-4 anti-tank round, it's still just about training your hands to flick this lever, depress that one, look here, fire. Most of the unpleasantness in training comes from time wasted or misspent as those in charge learn to lead at everyone else's expense. For a private, that includes almost everyone who outranks him, which seems like almost everyone.

Training begins with soldiers learning individual tasks that build into collective tasks with other soldiers. Soldiers learn individual skills through schools such as Ranger, Pathfinder, and Air Assault Schools, but also through locally held competitions such as the Expert Infantryman Badge and Expert Field Medical Badge. Traditional rites of passage such as the Prop Blast for airborne officers and the Spur Ride for scout officers and NCOs test basic soldier skills and endurance in a more collegial, hazing-like manner that typically includes obstacle courses, mud, road marches, sleep deprivation, and lots of push-ups and sit-ups.

Infantry learn advanced marksmanship skills from teams of traveling military instructors. Cooks compete in post-wide cook-offs. Military police and unmanned aerial vehicle (drone) operators get recertified. Troops learn combat first aid and how to survive a dunking in full battle gear. Military intelligence specialists get cultural training and practice questioning foreign nationals, logisticians learn the latest software, and forward observers spend days in video simulators. Many compete for "Soldier of the Year" and "NCO of the Year" in contests designed to test basic skills such as marksmanship, orienteering, and general army knowledge, things they will need to know to advance in rank.

Collective training brings infantrymen together into fire teams, squads, and platoons, and allows teams of mortarmen and artillerymen to certify on their weapons systems. Combat engineers practice detonating claymore anti-personnel mines, Bangalore torpedoes, and cratering charges. Command-and-control jockeys in tactical operations centers learn to integrate computer systems networked by commo soldiers.

Much of the field training is dangerous—the mortars, artillery shells, and explosive charges are all real, and accidents do happen. During field training the year after we returned from Iraq, the Humvee I was riding in collided with another Humvee during a mounted-machine-gun, live-fire exercise under blackout conditions (we were using night-vision devices). At the same range a few weeks later, shrapnel from an errant 105mm howitzer shell hit my parked Humvee (I was between it and the target). That same summer, eight visiting marine artillerymen and two navy sailors training at Fort Bragg were injured when a round exploded in the chamber of their 155mm howitzer.

As training becomes more complex, it also gets more deadly. Imagine the potential for injury during training for airborne field artillery batteries. "Gun bunnies" drop two-ton howitzers and Humvees from aircraft at night under clusters of giant parachutes, then parachute in behind them on the next wave of aircraft. On the ground, the artillerymen rush to fire high-explosive rounds at a target within 25 minutes. To move the howitzers quickly around the battlefield, artillerymen practice slinging the big guns beneath Black Hawk helicopters from a massive double-ended loop referred to informally as a "Q-tip." A soldier on the ground who accidentally touches the hovering craft can be electrocuted by static charge.

Officers are responsible for overall safety. The howitzers fire thirty-three-pound rounds that must fall within a narrowly defined zone. One errant shell can end an artillery officer's career. The "short round" that nicked my Humvee was fired during an exercise called a "walk and shoot" wherein young officers and fire-support specialists call in live artillery and mortar rounds on rusting old tanks as they advance across a gun range. The faulted gun crew chief became a supply sergeant tracking sticky pads rather than artillery rounds.

One of the more dangerous events for infantry is the squad live-fire range. Nine-man squads maneuver through a wooded weapons range, attacking pop-up targets along the way using M4 carbines and M249 squad automatic weapons with live rounds (the M249 "SAW" is considered a light machine gun because its linked 5.56mm ammunition is almost identical to what we fired in our M4s). At the end, the squad enters a concrete "shoot house" to "kill" targets inside, mimicking urban warfare. What makes the range dangerous in a different way from combat is that, when troops are deployed, they become accustomed to having loaded weapons with them around the clock.

Once training reaches company and battalion level, field exercises last from many days to several weeks due to the logistics necessary to support quality training. Role-players must be equipped, shuttled, fed, and housed; headquarters elements erected and networked to the rear; and weapons ranges reserved and manned for large blocks of time. There is also value in staging multi-day missions against which a platoon or company can test its various capabilities over time, with each stage dependent on its antecedent. It can be so consuming that, even when a soldier is home for the night, his mind is still in the "notional" fight.

Complex scenarios give combat veterans like First Sergeant Jerry Tucker a chance to share deployed experiences, for instance, what they know of Afghan cultural norms within some kind of context. He explains to junior soldiers the different roles that *maliks* (leaders, often of ruling lineage such as a prince), elders, and *mullahs* (the local Islamic mosque leaders) play in Afghan village life, and what Afghan men are likely to think of Afghan National Security Forces and the Afghan government. It was a male-dominated society, particularly outside the capital city of Kabul. "The women? Don't even fucking think about looking at them," he warns.

Sometimes the role-playing is borderline ridiculous. During a two-week field exercise in the summer of 2011, the new brigade operations sergeant major was furious that our gear was piling up in his operations tent. "Put it in the sleep tent!" he growled.

Carrying loads of computer and camera gear, Sergeant K and I stumbled around in the dark woods between patches of poison ivy and bands of triple-strand concertina wire, asking every passing paratrooper where the sleep tent was. Nobody knew. Finally we found two soldiers racked out in a patch of red clay and pine needles encircled by white surveyor's tape.

"This is it, dude," one of the bleary-eyed soldiers moaned. "It's a *notional* tent."

Alas, it was outside the foxholes and c-wire perimeter of the base defenses. Well played. We drove away from the headquarters, found a secluded spot in the woods, and slept on the metal roofs of our Humvees.

CHAPTER 3:
POMP

It seems that nothing of significance can happen in the army without cakes and parades. Junior soldiers hate parades. There are good reasons for that. Marching is the first skill a soldier learns in basic training. Marching troops is a convenient way to move many troops quickly and neatly. Marching troops is fun. Getting marched is not.

As a matter of tradition, soldiers march when battalions, brigades, and divisions change commanders, as happens following deployments. Soldiers march onto a parade field, stand in formations at the uncomfortable position of attention, then at the uncomfortable position of parade rest, then at attention, then at parade rest, and so on until it is time to march off the parade field in front of the reviewing stand, where they are admired by dignitaries and pitied by soldiers not part of the parade. It has always been this way.

What the dignitaries don't see but the soldiers all know is the enormous ass-pain that the marching soldiers must endure for thirty minutes of parading. Ass-pain is a type of pain only found in the military. It involves those long, by now familiar, physically uncomfortable periods of waiting to accomplish simple tasks, as when a soldier must arrive at the arms room at 0500 to draw a weapon and a bayonet, stand in a company formation at 0600 for a battalion formation at 0700 to march down to the parade field by 0800 where one will stand waiting until 0945 to march out on the field. If it rains, the plan is the same, with the same amount of ass but more pain. If it's cold and rainy, the plan does not change. When the ceremony is complete and the cake is cut, marching soldiers do not get a piece. The cake is for the dignitaries to celebrate the existence of such magnificent soldiers. The soldiers march back to the arms room to scrub the new rust from their weapons. Then all 130 soldiers stand in line to turn in the weapons, one at a time. If it only takes 90 seconds per soldier, the line lasts three hours.

Were that all there was to it. The army never celebrates pageantry but where it hasn't practiced it to death beforehand. The day prior to the big event, the timeline begins in the same fashion, but when the soldiers arrive at the parade field, they practice marching onto the field, standing at attention, standing at parade rest, marching off the field, etc., three, four, maybe five times, however many times it takes to satisfy the command sergeant major in charge.

(The esteem an 82nd Airborne Division command sergeant major holds for himself and the division cannot be plumbed by nonmilitary people. For instance, two weeks before hosting a dinner for all 82nd Air- borne Division command sergeants major past and present, the reigning division CSM ordered his minions to make sure that Tiger Woods was there. He wasn't joking. The champion golfer had no connection with the 82nd other than the fact that the sergeant major enjoyed golf. Woods' people reportedly declined, citing the need for at least six months' lead time.)

That said, formations of paratroopers are impressive to behold. They line up with the tallest in the front rows, shortest in the back. It's not about seeing faces. It's about seeing stature. Paratroopers are light infantry. They don't drive around parade grounds in tanks or Bradley

Fighting Vehicles or Strykers. It's just them and their rifles and machine guns, marching in step, turning in step, standing together unmoving. The standing together part is important. When people unfamiliar with military heraldry first learn that units are routinely deactivated, reflagged, and reassigned as the defense needs of the nation shift, they may cry foul at the army's notion of legacy, as does author Jim Frederick in *Black Hearts: One Platoon's Descent into Madness in Iraq's Triangle of Death* (Broadway Books). (Frederick, 2011) He writes:

> Except in rare cases, regiments are an obsolete organizational unit in the US Army, but to preserve a sense of history, tradition, and esprit de corps, certain groupings of battalions carry on the names of particularly illustrious regiments. This continuum is entirely bogus, since so few Army units have been continuously active since their inception. The 101st itself, for example, has disbanded and reactivated no fewer than four times since World War II. When a new Army battle group is created, it often simply assumes the colors, crest, and regalia of some illustrious yet dormant unit from the past, even if it is based in a wildly different location or carries a vastly different purpose. Presto, instant history. And yet, this system of perpetuating noble lineages works: soldiers do not take much prodding to adopt a sense of pride and custodianship in the purported legacy and history of their unit. Modern warriors clearly long for a link between themselves and heroes of old. (15)

Frederick is correct in that the regimental system is a legacy organizational unit useful mainly to harken back to a unit's roots. That's certainly true of the Devil Brigade, which is as likely to self-identify as the 504th Parachute Infantry Regiment, even though only two of its six battalions are flagged as the 504th.

As a non-military person, what the author fails to understand (as did I when I first enlisted) is that lack of an uninterrupted bloodline does not make a unit's lineage "entirely bogus." I started to understand why when I began helping to bury soldiers lost in combat. Military units are not organisms. A regiment's DNA does not require a warm blood-stream to persist because its DNA exists and is transmitted through standards, culture, and tradition. The 504th is not a crest, flag, or list of accomplishments. It's a group of soldiers who honor those who served and sacrificed before them by upholding a common ethos. Regimental heraldry is also a way to keep the sacrifices of earlier generations from being forgotten, for when they are forgotten, they are a step closer to being wasted. As the ancient Greek poet, Pindar, said over twenty-four centuries ago, "Unsung, the noblest deed will die."

First Sergeant Steven Noonan, who served in the 82nd's 505th PIR from 1990–93 and the 504th PIR from 2009–13, always struck me as the embodiment of the All-American tradition. Surely one of the origi-nal Apostles of Hard Love, he didn't grow soldiers, he chiseled them. Noonan describes the 82nd this way: "The pride and esprit de corps in an airborne unit isn't found anywhere else in the army. The airborne units have a very short history (World War II to the present), but our obsession with upholding the honor and reputation of the Regiment and always trying to add to its glory is unmatched anywhere else in the army. I was in the 505th [PIR] for Desert Storm, and our obsession with General Gavin was almost cult-like back then. His leadership principles still set the standard, 'A leader in this outfit is the first one out the door of the airplane and the last one in the chow line.'"

The 82nd is but one fork of many in the river of people that has comprised the fighting men and women who have stood for the country. Today's soldiers marching behind a certain regiment's colors are no more bogus to point to the veterans of D-Day as their forebears as the Greatest Generation would be for calling the veterans of Afghanistan's infamous

Korengal Valley campaign their heirs. There are heroes in both camps, and everywhere in between.

Thankfully, there is blessed little marching to be had at military balls, but there is almost always a cake. Balls are usually held at the battalion level because a company ball would be too small and a brigade ball too large. Balls often occur after a deployment, before soldiers ship off to other units. Balls provide a final chance for bands of brothers to celebrate accomplishments and mourn losses before they scatter across the army. (A unit hardly looks like "itself" just a few short months after redeploying because of the army's regular reshuffling of personnel. Again, what makes a unit is its culture, traditions, and ethos.)

For military balls, soldiers add to their dress uniforms newly awarded medals—sometimes Purple Hearts or decorations for valor on the battlefield—and get to wear them among their peers. For married couples, balls can be a public affirmation of what was risked and won. Balls give even the wives of the most junior privates a chance to be Cinderella for the evening. Every ball has a table set for one, with a single rose, upturned chair and empty plate but for a single slice of lemon that symbolizes the bitter fate of those lost in battle. And always, there is a recounting of the unit's history.

In June of 2011, I accompanied a delegation of about twenty paratroopers selected from across the division, to Normandy, France, to participate in a parachute jump commemorating the drop of thirteen thousand Allied paratroopers behind the Omaha and Utah beachheads before sunrise on D-Day sixty-seven years earlier. In the village of Sainte-Mère-Église, we were greeted as delegate heroes because of the "AA" patches we wore on our shoulders.

I wasn't even alive in 1944. My father was nine years old. The 504th, which was regrouping in England after an extended bloody campaign in the mountains of Italy, didn't even make the jump. Over sixty-four hundred other paratroopers with the 82nd did parachute into France, with more landing by glider and boat. Of a total strength of just over 11,000, at least 5,245 were killed, wounded, or missing in action.

Why bring this up? There are 39,224 Allied graves in Normandy. Each has a unit, a tradition, and a flag. We marched under the maroon beret of the airborne with other American paratroopers who had come to northern France for the 67th commemoration of the invasion, and though we were not the liberators of Sainte-Mère-Église, we damn sure felt the responsibility of representing them well. Virtually every marching soldier, male and female, enlisted and officer, was a veteran of multiple combat tours. I think the airborne liberators of Normandy would have approved.

What a soldier thinks when he sees soldiers marching is very different from what a civilian thinks. Sometimes, I think about my childhood friend, Bobby. Instead of college, Bobby had enlisted in the army right out of high school and jumped into Panama with the Rangers to oust Noriega in 1989. In the mid-90s, he earned an engineering degree and became a naval officer with the Seabees. By 2005, he was back at war, this time, in Baghdad.

"How selfish is that?" I remarked to my wife at the time. "He has a family now, with kids." How remarkably short-sighted I had been. Over half of the soldiers in today's all-volunteer army are married. Just under half have children. All have mothers and fathers, and many have siblings.

When a civilian sees a formation of soldiers marching, he sees soldiers marching. When a soldier sees soldiers marching, he sees the sacrifices of spouses, fathers, mothers, brothers, sisters, children, and other invested hearts as soldiers train for, fight, and return from mortal combat that might turn out very badly for any of them.

Tracy Brown, the aunt of a paratrooper we would lose in Afghanistan, said of her nephew Dustin, "We watched him grow from a baby with white-blond hair with a cute little smile, to a boy full of fun and mischief, to a stubborn and strong-willed young man who would do anything for friends and family, and those memories are what carry us on. He is truly the best part of each of us."

CHAPTER 4:
GARRISON LOSSES

In the eighteen months between our return from Iraq and departure to a violent tour in Afghanistan, four paratroopers died in garrison. Of those, two committed suicide and two died while exercising during morning PT.

Master Sergeant Eldridge Jackson, an artilleryman from Dothan, Alabama, died while running on Ardennes Street the day before Thanksgiving 2011. He was forty-three.

Sergeant Joshua Mann, twenty-two, died July 30, 2011, a day after collapsing during a company run up Cooliconch Hill. Cooliconch is a long, straight slog through loose sand and red clay. An uphill gulch more than a mountain, its parabolic interior receives enfilading light from the sun at sunrise, and tall pines on both sides block any breeze. It can be an oven, which is much the point for running it. Sergeant Mann's death was a tragic loss, yet, stay in the Army long enough, and everyone eventually finds themselves within the radius of some unfortunate incident.

As an institution, the army takes suicide prevention seriously. Every trooper is required to have on his person an "ACE" card that reminds him to Ask, Care, and Escort. Regular quarterly training reminds soldiers how to identify suicide warning signs in one's self and others and emphasizes every soldier's responsibility to help prevent suicide.

In spite of the army's efforts, the number of suicides only increased during the years of the wars in Iraq and Afghanistan. Anecdotal evidence blames post-traumatic stress disorder, the stress of multiple deployments, and prevention measures that fall short of the mark. Paradoxically, statistics show that half of all suicides are by soldiers who have never deployed.

While any number of factors may be important in individual cases, if one is going to point to systemic causes of a systemic problem, then one must consider what else has changed since 9/11. Those lords of discipline, the perennially angry sergeants major, are the logical observers to ask about the causes of increased suicides because they have been in the enlisted trenches the longest. When I asked the best sergeants major I knew for their unvarnished opinions, they unanimously attributed the rising rate of suicides to lower recruiting standards and replacement of the old BDUs by ACUs. In other words, the uniform and who gets to wear it.

According to a study by the Heritage Foundation, the overall quality of the American soldier has only risen during the last decade of war. However, a higher average can represent higher highs and lower lows. The increase in the number of waivers for crimes (including felonies) and health issues granted to recruits by the services to meet their enlistment quotas during the unpopular Iraq War has also been well documented. The less restrictive the pool of recruits, the more it should look like the civilian world, so is it any surprise that military suicide rates, formerly below civilian rates, are now rising to meet them? Increasingly, studies are finding that the negative effects of combat are greatly amplified in soldiers with previously existing social issues. It's not hard to fathom how people who were previously unable to cope with difficult situations might show the same propensity in service.

As interesting to me was how the senior sergeants major blamed the uniform change. The old battlewagons could have just grumbled about a general decline of discipline in the most recent crop of soldiers, and while they did that too, when pressed, most dimed out the uniform switch as a major factor. First sergeants and platoon sergeants often said the same thing.

Prior to the wash-and-wear "universal camouflage" Army Combat Uniform with its accompanying, no-care, rough-out leather desert combat boots, a soldier's everyday uniform was the woodland-patterned Battle Dress Uniform, or BDU. BDUs were not wash and wear. Of a different type of fabric and cut than ACUs, BDUs had to be washed, ironed and starched prior to the week's first formation every Monday morning. Black leather boots had to be shined to a mirrored surface.

"Soldiers used to take pride in the uniform, and as a result, in themselves," a sergeant major told me. "These things we wear today are like pajamas. After the first time you wash them, they look terrible. The [soldiers] don't care. Why should they? We used to have to *do* something to get our uniforms ready. Now it's: Take it out of the wash. Now they walk around like homeless people with their pockets open because the Velcro wears out. If they don't take pride in their appearance, how are they going to take pride in who they are or what they do?"

From its inception, the ACU uniform was widely reviled for its almost universal use of Velcro in place of buttons, for the easily torn fabric, and for the hot mess it became after just a few washings. Most of all, soldiers hated ACUs because the "universal" bluish-greenish-gray camouflage only blended with gravel roads and ugly couches. Not Iraq. Not Afghanistan. Not the jungle, woodlands, cities, or suburbs. Prior to its rollout, most troops deploying to Iraq wore the DCU, a suitable desert variant of the BDU. In both Iraq and Afghanistan, our troops wearing ACUs were easily spotted. Adoption of one uniform to blend anywhere was purportedly a budgetary issue, but even the cash-strapped marines, who still flew Vietnam-era Hueys, had two different uniforms with one specifically designed for the desert.

By the time the Devil Brigade deployed to Afghanistan, MultiCam uniforms were standard issue for incoming troops. MultiCams didn't look like pajamas. In fact, they looked like a uniform the world's most sophisticated, powerful army might wear. The blend of browns and greens was ideal for Ghazni Province, where we would meet the Taliban in dozens of small-unit, direct-action engagements.

They weren't perfect. Infantrymen were always busting seams, their crotches torn and flapping like a harlot's tent. Still, MultiCams were worn with substantially more pride than the anemic ACUs, and when we finally returned from Afghanistan and switched back to ACUs, it was like changing back into pajamas. To those of us fresh off the battlefield, ACUs were a symbol of mediocrity, a lazybones jumpsuit for garrison soldiers. We took pride in our accomplishments in Afghanistan, and we wanted a uniform that made us feel like soldiers.

It's always amusing when a civilian slaps some patches and badges on a uniform and goes about in public trying to pass as a soldier, in an attempt at what my fellow paratroopers and I would call "stolen valor." What civilians don't understand is that every piece of a soldier's uniform has an exact place, down to an eighth of an inch (we have measuring tools specifically for this). One soldier can make a pretty good guess at even intimate details of another soldier's life with just a quick glance at his uniform. It's not just dress; it's an active communication tool with its own language. It's that important.

Over 2.4 million Americans have deployed to Iraq and Afghanistan since 2001, probably at least half in ACUs. How many soldiers had the poor camouflage failed to hide? How many soldiers had died there because of a shitty uniform?

How many here at home?

CHAPTER 5:
PREPARING FOR WAR

The week after we lost Sergeant Mann, our brigade took block leave for three weeks before diving headlong into what we suspected might be a very long time without any time off. The plan was to spend all of August in Louisiana at JRTC training in "full spectrum operations," i.e., classic airborne infantry maneuvers, followed by a yearlong on-call status as we assumed the Global Response Force duty.

On July 20, the morning we returned from leave, news came that the brigade had been re-missioned. JRTC was postponed. First Brigade was heading to Kandahar, Afghanistan, the birthplace of the Taliban. There we would fight alongside the 4th Brigade Combat Team under the 82nd division headquarters. We would relieve 2nd Brigade, 4th Infantry Division, from Fort Carson, Colorado. As a heavy brigade combat team, 2/4 had tanks and other mechanized weapons that the 82nd lacked. First Sergeant Jerry Tucker, who had fought in Fallujah in 2003 in soft-skinned Humvees, remarked once that, "We make a lot of the spirit and aggressiveness of paratroopers, and all that's true, but the way these heavy guys roll, well, they just knock the shit out of everything."

It wasn't but a few weeks before we heard that 1st Brigade had been replaced on the patch chart by an armored Stryker unit. Apparently Tucker wasn't the only one who saw the benefits of armor in an urban fight. Instead, our infantry battalions would be pieced out to different areas of Afghanistan. One would leave within the month.

By Christmas, with containers of equipment being trucked to the Bragg railhead for a January rotation at JRTC, the brigade received new orders yet again. No battalion would be sliced off. The entire brigade was going to be the main effort in the last major clearing operation of the War in Afghanistan, in a province nobody had heard of.

Ghazni. It sounded Polish. It wasn't, but there were Polish troops stationed there. Ghazni Province was located halfway between Afghanistan's two major cities, Kabul and Kandahar. Through its arid landscape ran the country's most important road and most dangerous paved road, Highway 1. The Taliban, Haqqani Network, and other extremist groups had gained nearly unfettered movement in the province since the distraction of Iraq pulled the focus from Afghanistan. Many rural villagers in Ghazni had not seen Europeans since the Russians pulled out in the late 1980s. Many times, we would be mistaken for Russians.

High, dry, rugged, and poor—that was Ghazni—a shriveled shell of the one-time capital of the 10th-century Ghazanvid Empire from which Muslim conquests were launched into India, bringing back untold wealth. The word *Ghazni* comes from the Sanskrit *Ghzank*, meaning "treasure." A thousand years of Muslim rule was followed by war with the Brits, war with the Soviets, war with the Taliban, and now us. Our brigade would occupy the nearly 100 percent Pashtun region of southern Ghazni Province.

Lead elements would ship out in February 2012, followed by a major push in March just prior to the onset of the spring fighting season. To abide quotas for "troops on the ground," the brigade commander, Colonel Mark Stock, was only allowed to deploy 2,500 of our 3,500 paratroopers, and we all had to be out of Afghanistan by

September 1. The deployment sounded short and sweet, not unlike the marine deployments that typically lasted only seven months as compared to the army's twelve months or more.

Intel reported that insurgents were funneling weapons, explosives, and foreign fighters up from Pakistan through Ghazni's depopulated southeast district of Nawah, a word that literally means "sewer" in Pashto. Once across the Tarnak River, weapons and fighters were moved north and south on Highway 1 to the urban centers of Kabul and Kandahar.

"It's like the Wild West over there, with dudes still throwing grenades over the FOB walls," Sergeant First Class Jeff McFarland warned one morning at PT. McFarland was one of the NCOs who had inadvertently helped me torpedo the Iraqi female police training program in Ramadi. In twelve years of service, he had been deployed for sixty months. With a five-year-old son and a marriage teetering on the brink, he was not looking forward to another combat deployment.

I began seeking news of Ghazni Province online.

November 1, 2010, Taliban overrun a district center, torching government buildings, and capturing police officers after an intense gunfight.

June 18, 2011, three private security contractors killed by bombs.

June 22, suicide bomb kills seven police officers.

June 27, seven civilians killed by roadside bombs.

October 18, Haqqani Network boosts influence.

December 21, five Polish troops killed by massive IED just outside their base.

In the autumn of 2011, with the Poles mostly confined to a few FOBs, insurgents planted and wired hundreds of IEDs before winter snows froze the ground solid in anticipation of the next fighting season. The Taliban's ruling council, the Quetta Shura, drew up plans to mobilize weapons, IEDs, and foreign fighters to meet whatever new force was going to occupy the NATO bases that American engineers were suddenly expanding along Highway 1 in southern Ghazni. In early January 2012, seven thousand pounds of homemade explosives, or HME, were confiscated from insurgent forces there. It takes a couple hundred pounds to blow apart an MRAP. The Taliban didn't know who was coming, but they knew somebody was.

Just two years from the end of my enlistment, I knew this was my last chance to see combat. I regarded the report of each new act of violence with equal parts of trepidation and excitement, like watching a radar image of a hurricane, knowing it would soon hit. I was thankful to have had Iraq as a dry run. I wanted to do my job as it's done in combat, as did most everyone.

Before Afghanistan, however, we had to contend with south-central Louisiana. I have a favorite photo that succinctly encapsulates my feelings toward JRTC. I'm in the back of an ancient soft-skinned Humvee in a downpour, and water is gushing through the porous canvas top that has seen too many pre-deployment troops. A Joe in the front passenger seat is using a drip pan to catch a waterfall of rainwater that's pouring in between the cab and bed (just before it spills on him). There's a tornado ripping through a swamp less than a mile away. We are soaked to the skin. Miserable. Just miserable.

Yet the training there was hands-down the best preparation that we received before deploying. The army continually seeded the training advisors there with officers and senior NCOs fresh off the battlefields, complementing them with civilian experts whose focus was to train soldiers on ways to gain advantage over the most current threats using the latest technology, most of which soldiers would see for the first time at JRTC.

The mission change for the Devil Brigade also changed the nature of our JRTC experience. What was originally planned to be a return to the full-spectrum training of the pre-9/11 era to include an airborne assault on an airfield became an Afghanistan-specific train-up. It tested the brigade's strength in combat power; "nonlethal effects" such as information operations, key-leader engagements, civilian outreach programs, and public relations; and partnering abilities, all of which were difficult to hone on a brigade scale at Fort Bragg. For the logistics soldiers, moving the brigade to Louisiana wasn't much different from moving it to Afghanistan.

"It's the one chance we have to get the entire brigade combat team in the field to test and stress all its systems, and to make sure we have identified any shortfalls and reinforce any strengths that are out there," said Colonel Mark Stock, the brigade commander who would lead us in Afghanistan.

JRTC began with a week of classroom learning that introduced soldiers to techniques for surviving IEDs, using handheld mine hounds and other bomb-finding equipment, specialized optics and other surveillance technology, battlefield forensics, interrogation and more. Hands-on, problem-based training scenarios came next, followed by the climactic "force-on-force" war gaming that pitted our paratroopers against a large opposing force.

During the entire rotation, troops were sequestered on a half-dozen mini-FOBs in the piney woods of JRTC's expansive "box." Cell phone reception was abysmal for most carriers, which for most soldiers meant no contact with home for about a month. Ever present were the types of bureaucratic headaches that made army training so much fun to bitch about later. Like JRTC instructors requiring vehicles *they* provided to be checked out and dispatched by our motor pool before our motor pool was set up. Like equipping zero of its mighty fleet of vans with jumper cables, begetting the following exchange between an artillery major and a senior NCO.

"What do you mean it's dead?" he asked. "Nobody has any fucking jumper cables?"

"It's not in the SOP, sir," said Persell. He and I had already checked every civilian vehicle in the lot for jumper cables. As a senior NCO with nineteen years of service, he knew how to exhaust a list of solutions before reporting the problem to his superiors, and yet, at the end of the day, all his superior could do was have a fit.

"Let me break it down Barney-style," said the major. "You need a pair of jumper cables."

"Roger, sir."

"You want to play by Big-boy rules?"

"Yessir."

"This is why we don't get to have nice things in the army," the major said dismissively with a head-wag, and with that, he walked off.

"He's a major?" somebody asked from the rear of the van.

"Uh huh," Persell replied.

"Sounds more like Captain Obvious."

Barney-style, Captain Obvious, they're all just sparks of hot metal-on-metal as the separation of powers between officers and NCOs continually works itself out. When that doesn't work, there is always rank, paper, scissors.

During the force-on-force war games, I rode out of an FOB with an infantry platoon that was searching for a "notional" enemy mortar position. Unfortunately, real rain had fallen, making a muddy field through which our Humvees, outfitted with notional tow straps, were traveling. Lieutenant Dare O'Ravitz, a tall, bespectacled platoon leader from Scottsdale, Arizona, who was more the intellectual surfer and less the mechanically-inclined farm boy, suggested his men use a JRTC-provided fifteen-ton MRAP to free the mired Humvee. So his men drove the monstrous, top-heavy MRAP into the mud. Once the vehicle was in place, his soldiers discovered that the MRAP's winch, while real, did not work. The MRAP was now bogged down as well, and threatening to tip. When O'Ravitz radioed battalion for help, battalion told him that no recovery assets were available. Also, a real tornado was on its way.

At this point, a very frustrated JRTC trainer unholstered his blue "god gun" that was used to either kill or reactivate the laser-tag equipment mounted to our weapons and vehicles, and threatened to start shooting people.

"Why? I'll tell you why," said Sergeant First Class Durden. "Because nobody hates the army like the army hates the army. I just got to the 101st [Airborne Division], and being the FNG, they immediately sent me to Fort Polk for thirty days." FNG means fucking new guy. Durden waved his god gun at the darkening sky and added, "Now *you* are making *my* life miserable."

Finally a wrecker arrived. The driver maneuvered the giant eight-wheeled behemoth through the stump-choked field and positioned it to retrieve the MRAP. The wrecker got stuck. The sky was gravid, with clouds boiling toward us. Staff Sergeants James Miller and Theodore Bird, both big fellas, threaded a tow cable underneath the wrecker's belly, attached it to a low, rotted stump, and to everyone's surprise but theirs, freed the fifteen-ton wrecker using its own cable. Racing the weather, Miller and Bird freed the MRAP, one Humvee, and then the other just as funnel clouds spun out of the sky to the north and south of us. Sheets of lightning electrified the sky as torrential rains pelted our soft-skinned Humvees.

In my Humvee, every ground hit set off the hood-mounted "combat kill" police-like strobing light. Unable to turn it off without a god gun, the driver stepped out into the rain to cover it with a cardboard box. Our canvas roof began leaking. We kept the cameras and weapons dry, but soon our bodies were all as soaked as the driver's. I took a picture of it all. Later when photos of the vehicle retrieval were published on the army's main email website, the battalion command sergeant major, Billy Chaney, swore at me, "Dammit, Mac, don't take any more pictures of my fat guys, only skinny ones."

Another day, I was waiting for some 101st medevac birds to spin up so that I could fly with them to photograph their medics in action on our notional wounded. When the lead medic finally showed up—also a sergeant like myself—I explained that I wanted to stick close to him when the helicopter picked up our notionally wounded paratroopers from the battlefield.

"No, I don't think that's possible," he groused.

I asked him why.

"Just stay out of my ass," he replied, tossing an aid bag into the passenger cabin. I had dealt with young NCOs like him before. I considered his disdain for POGs like me a possible learning experience for him, because my photos would likely end up on the Department of Defense homepage, where he would represent his entire unit, including the officers who were flying the Black Hawk. I climbed aboard and strapped myself in. Just before liftoff, with a smirk he suddenly ordered me off the bird, lifting his hands to feign ignorance as to why. He was kicking me off. Little did either of us know that that he was flying off to Karmageddon. When his Black Hawk landed on a simulated battlefield to pick up our wounded, it was "blown up" by Durden's god gun.

With our rotation wrapping up, thoughts turned away from JRTC to the war that awaited us. A battalion commander, Lieutenant Colonel Kevin Brown, counseled his troops: You are as great as the Greatest Generation. Be an All AmeriCan. We will be fighting uneducated people. Illiteracy does not mean stupidity. You are the best person to take care of the family you leave behind. Prepare your family, and then stay in touch. I was struck by how different and nuanced the reality of soldiering is from media and Hollywood stereotypes. Not all army leaders were good, but many were very good.

In the hooch that I shared with fifty other soldiers, I overheard three young buck sergeants talking about saving some sperm in case they died. "Dude, I know this guy who put sperm in a sperm bank just before he deployed," said one. "Six months later, a mortar hit the TOC and the tail fin cut his head clean off."

Said the second, "I knew a guy who knocked up his wife, then deployed. He was helping out this Iraqi dude whose vehicle had rolled over and was leaking gasoline and then blew up. Dude, he was obliterated. Never got to meet his son. So if the wife asks, 'You want to have a kid before you deploy?' Hell no."

There was silence as each considered his own actions on contact with the wife back home, just a day away.

Said the third, "That's wrath of God shit."

"I know," said the first. Dear God. You can't make this shit up.

What I was looking forward to in Afghanistan was finally having toilet paper in a military setting. For whatever reason, the army seems to think that soldiers only need it downrange. We always had plenty in Iraq. Never at Fort Bragg. Never at JRTC. I don't know why.

Just before deploying, the infantry plussed up on gear specific to the Afghan campaign, including GPS-guided mortar rounds to limit collateral damage, several new sniper rifles with long barrels and superior optics to compensate for long-range engagements we would encounter, and the 84mm Carl Gustav, a shoulder-fired recoilless rifle that loosely resembled a high-tech version of the old World War II bazooka.

Each infantry battalion was also assigned a FET, or Female Engagement Team. A FET is a pair of female soldiers who accompany infantry patrols into Afghan villages to meet with local women and girls to learn of their concerns. Provide for those concerns, so the thinking goes, and win their hearts and minds. FETs were required of units deploying to Afghanistan.

Injecting females directly into the all-male infantry combat operations outside the wire was bound to create resentment, and it did. While infantrymen had to pass through arduous training and live every day in a grunt's dog-eat-dog world, the only qualification that the female soldiers had to possess was the correct anatomy. Many were "legs," the pejorative term for non-airborne-qualified personnel. Resistance and some derision came at nearly every level. I overheard a private remark to his platoon sergeant after a FET lieutenant passed by, "Sergeant, there goes FET. Do you want me to have her make us some *sammiches*?"

The addition of female soldiers was probably hardest on the company first sergeants since they are, ironically, the mother hens of a company. Whereas "doing great things" is an officer's lot, "not getting the men killed" is a first sergeant's lot. Add to his list of concerns sexual harassment, pregnancy, female hygiene, and privacy issues, whether his new troops should be allowed to wear perfume and makeup, and the question of whether they carry a load into battle.

What do you say to a female soldier who has no energy during a three-day clearing operation because, to avoid getting fat, she has only eaten two bites of a Snickers bar and six Jelly Beans? You can't get fat if you're dead? This happened. Above all, a first sergeant wants to bring all of his soldiers home, and because he is a paratrooper in the 82nd Airborne Division, he will do his best to do the right thing with his new circumstances. Doesn't mean he has to like it.

Not without some guilt toward our loved ones, most paratroopers, myself included, were anxious to get to war, if only to escape the endless games the army invents for garrisoned soldiers. We all wanted to feel once again the ordination into professional soldiering, lethally armed and missioned for real-world problems. Where the sergeant major's supremacy is shrunk back to normal limits of mortal men, because he can die as easily as you. Where polishing your weapon toothbrush-clean at night may save your life by mid-morning. Where bombs underneath roads blow up soldiers if engineers don't do their jobs, infantrymen die if artillerymen don't do their jobs, nobody eats, drinks, moves, shoots, or returns fire if support troops don't do their jobs, and the deployment is a waste of everything if the infantry doesn't do theirs.

It's not about being in danger for soldiers. It's about *doing* in danger. People die in garrison, it's true. In combat, mortality walks in your boots.

PART IV:

Warfare

CHAPTER 1:
AFGHANISTAN

As spring arrived in Fayetteville, the news out of Afghanistan was not good. Amputations for combat-wounded soldiers had reached a wartime high of 240 in 2011, as compared to 205 during the violent Iraq Surge. In 2010, nearly half of all amputees had lost multiple limbs, most from IEDs.

Soldiers at Bagram Airfield had burned Qurans that Taliban prisoners had used to share secret messages, sparking protests and riots across the country. At least thirty people were killed, including four Americans.

Only three weeks later on March 11, Army Staff Sergeant Robert Bales left his base alone after dark and murdered sixteen Afghans in two villages in Panjwai District of Kandahar Province, the spiritual birthplace of the Taliban. Nine of the victims were children. As a result, Afghan President Hamid Karzai insisted that US troops be restricted to their bases and focus only on reconstruction. Had the threat been more than political jousting, our mission would have been neutered from the get-go, and a single American soldier might have accomplished what the insurgency had been unable to do.

I was more aware this go-round of the people I was deploying with, their families and relationships. Rank, that always present mark of the army caste system, impressed me much less coming into my fourth year in service. Rank was a role, not a worth.

It helped that most of our sergeants major, that bane of the enlisted soldier, were quite good at eliciting teamwork, and some, like Chuck Gregory and Kurt Reid, were even inspiring.

As an army journalist, I served soldiers. We had 3,500 paratroopers in the Devil Brigade, each with a compelling story. Yet some stories were more compelling than others. Take my friend, Dan Loeffler, for instance. His life reads like the marketing blurbs of an energy drink. A gregarious southern Baptist from Texas, Lieutenant Dan quit college in his senior year and enlisted the day after terrorists attacked his country on 9/11.

I met Dan in Iraq on his fourth deployment. He was already the famous face of an iconic photo of 82nd paratroopers in dark BDUs, assault rifles and maroon berets patrolling the flooded streets of New Orleans after Hurricane Katrina. He had survived an AK47 shot to the chest (saved by body armor), being blown up by multiple IEDs, and losing his best friends in bomb blasts. Promising his wife, Dorothy, that he was done with the grunt's world, he became an officer and pursued a litany of safer jobs. Yet here he was, heading back to Afghanistan as an infantry officer in 1st Battalion, 504th Parachute Infantry Regiment, soon to be assigned a platoon of scout snipers to hunt and kill Taliban roadside bomb emplacers.

On his first deployment to Afghanistan in 2003, Dan had met another infantryman, Specialist Matt Madison of Decatur, Alabama. Nearly a decade later, Madison was also assigned to 1/504, but as its chaplain. "I decided to enlist in the infantry because I was joining the army to do what my grandfather had done during World War II," the captain told me. "I thought I would join, serve for a few years and then return to civilian ministry. But God had a different plan." Chaplain Madison and his wife, Janet, celebrated their sixteenth wedding anniversary shortly before we deployed to Ghazni. His children were eleven and eight. Loeffler and his wife, Dorothy, had been married eight years. Their daughters were six and eighteen months.

Forty-year-old Private Steve Bastean, an infantry mortarman, enlisted for his 19-year-old son, Jordan, a marine who was killed in Afghanistan's Helmand Province, Oct. 23, 2011. "He inspired me," Bastean told a reporter for the hometown Illinois newspaper. "Fathers are supposed to inspire their kids to look up to them. Well, my son is my hero and what I look up to."

Another "old-timer" by army standards, Sergeant Kenneth Jones also enlisted just before the clock ran out at forty-one. A carpenter of twenty-five years from central Florida, the wiry black grandfather joined the army in part to help pay the bills accumulated from his wife's medical condition. He was a truck driver for 2-504's forward support company, on his second deployment. His grandfather served in the Korean War, and his father in Vietnam. Jones had always wanted to be like his father, and military service was the one thing he lacked. "When I told him I joined the military, he was tickled to death," Jones said. "That's all he wants to [do] when he sees me is to compare Afghanistan to Vietnam." He hoped that his daughter, also in the military, would get to deploy so she would have a foreign war under her belt too.

Sergeant Colton Hurley, a solemn, twenty-two-year-old infantry-man from Hannibal, Missouri, enlisted to honor the memory of his mother, Krystal Hurley, an army medic who died during the invasion of Panama. Hurley was an infant at the time, but he was determined to "do my twenty because she was going to do her twenty."

First Lieutenant Elizabeth Trobaugh from the Bay area was the daughter of classic West Coast hippies (both were Vietnam-era vets). A passionate liberal redhead, Trobaugh joined the army to pay for her education at the ultra-liberal Mills College, a female-only school that touts its commitment to "sustainability, social justice, and diversity." She wasn't wearing shoes regularly on campus when she joined ROTC.

Not exactly a pedigree for military service. After commissioning, she was stationed at Fort Bragg managing an Army post office when she heard that the 82nd was hiring officers to lead Female Engagement Teams in Afghanistan.

"Joining the army was the hardest decision I ever made; nothing felt more right *and* more wrong. Everyone who spoke truth into my life knew this was going to be monumentally important for me. However, it took a few years to come to terms with what it really meant to be a soldier," she said. Always-smiling Trobaugh said she sometimes felt like a quasi-biblical character, "kind of a fuck-up, continually blessed, and trusted with bigger and bigger responsibilities," as she described it. At other times, she simply felt in over her head. "What am I doing in this organization as a liberal? I didn't particularly agree with the war in Iraq, what was I doing?! But at every step, I've been blessed and keep hearing something or someone whispering in my ear, 'Keep going, you were made for so much more.'"

Roughly 2,500 of our 3,500 paratroopers deployed to Ghazni just before spring 2012. While each had entered service for his or her own reason, they shared one major impetus for deploying: Temporary Change of Station orders from the Department of the Army.

MACLEOD, MICHAEL JOSEPH XXXXXXXXX SGT 0082
AB BDE 01 HQ ABN DIV (WABAAA)
12 January 2012
You are deployed in a Temporary Change of Station (TCS) status as shown below and are to return to your permanent station upon completion of your tour in support of this operation.
Assigned to: 0082 AB BDE 01 HQ ABN DIV (WABAAA)
Purpose: Deployment will be in support of **OPERATION ENDURING FREEDOM** AFGHANISTAN
Number of days: Not to exceed 215 days.
Will proceed on or about: 29 February 2012

In groups or "chalks" of about three hundred, we traveled from Fort Bragg's Pope Army Airfield in commercial widebody jets contracted by the DOD to shuttle troops to and from military staging areas halfway around the world. In Manas, Kyrgyzstan, we passed through the old Soviet membrane. Kyrgyz soldiers with their ridiculously oversized parade caps, Mongol features, and high leather boots fulfilled the prophecies of a score of *National Geographic* issues from my childhood. On the US base in Manas, we walked past war-weary troops in our fresh MultiCams. We tried to imagine what their deployments had been like. Were they shell-shocked? Serially bored fobbits? There were bins where soldiers could safely toss out threadbare uniforms, and other bins for recycling. No bullets or grenades, they said.

We boarded military jets that can also carry tanks—vacuous C17 Globemasters—for the flight into Afghanistan. There, our chalk stayed at Bagram Airfield north of Kabul only long enough to complete training required of all incoming troops and to zero our weapons before pushing out by C130 transport to a forward operating base just north of Ghazni Province. As a paratrooper, I felt it quaintly odd to actually land in a military aircraft.

Whereas BAF was an expansive base with paved streets, multi-story buildings, and circus-sized housing tents, the next base, Sharana, was a more typical war zone FOB, with pods of low-slung troop tents buttressed against haphazardly built windowless plywood buildings, mazes of concrete blast barriers and dirt-filled Hesco barriers, gravel roads and few signs. We arrived by C-130 at 2:45 a.m. It was cold and dark on the blacked-out FOB, and it felt as if we were the only souls on a windswept moonscape even though there were hundreds of troops sleeping nearby. We bedded down for a few hours in twenty-man "transient" tents. Our next hit time was 5:45 a.m., for helicopters leaving at 7:15 a.m. for our destination, FOB Warrior in southern Ghazni province.

A salty chicken MRE for "breakfast" on top of no sleep, a caffeine hangover, and one of the ugliest FOBs I'd ever seen . . . scratch that.

There are no pleasant-looking FOBs. One just grows familiar with an FOB and appreciative of its concealed pleasantries—the chow hall, MWR Internet portal and gym, the containerized showers and chemical toilets known to grunts as "porta-shitters." In a war zone, familiarity breeds more comfort than contempt, for these things form the physical redoubt of the inertia of life versus no life.

Our flight was delayed until 9:40 a.m., then weather-delayed until further notice. With a day to kill, I tried to touch base with home via the MWR (Moral, Welfare, and Recreation facility) Internet portal, but the FOB was under "River City," the mandatory twenty-four-hour communications blackout that follows the death of a soldier to keep the family from learning of it accidentally via Facebook or email. The night we arrived, an Afghan had opened fire on a group of soldiers who were returning from a patrol. The soldiers had just finished emptying their weapons at the Sharana gates. One soldier was killed, and three were critically injured.

It might have been the lack of caffeine, but I was getting the pre-mission jitters like I had had before landing in Ramadi three years earlier. The place was like a stripped-down dinghy of America shipwrecked on a random elevated plain of nothingness, surrounded by treeless Asian badlands. Yet I wasn't some hapless victim of cataclysmic forces. I had signed up for it, volunteered three times. The comforting familiarity of routine was being ripped from our lives again, that was all. I hoped that Sharana was but a hinterland truck stop, an ugly waypoint on the way to someplace nicer.

Many soldiers slept. I caught up on some reading. At 10 p.m., a sergeant poked his head into the tent and said there were no flights for the next two days, so relax. At 10:30 p.m., I closed my book and fell asleep. At 11:00 p.m., the sergeant woke us and said it was "go time." Just after 1 a.m., seventy of us boarded two Chinooks packed to the gills with gear and kitted-up bodies and left FOB Sharana for Ghazni.

Riding in a blacked-out Chinook at night is like riding inside and outside a bus at once. The side windows aft of the cockpit act as gills, pulling fresh, cold air down the length of the craft over troops and equipment and out the tail ramp. Gear and bodies prevent movement except at the two ends. It's not a place for the claustrophobic.

At 2:30 a.m., our thundering CH-47 banked hard and flared. As it settled into the blacked-out HLZ of FOB Warrior, its giant popping rotors lit with a corona of a million pieceless stars. Never having witnessed the pyrophoric collision of the abrasion-resistant helicopter rotors with Afghan dust at night, I thought we were under attack by small-arms fire. Yet nobody seemed alarmed, so I put my worry on hold. Nobody wants to look like the FNG.

We unloaded by red light and dragged our equipment to what felt like the edge of the helicopter landing zone. Sergeant First Class Garcia, the soldier in charge of the Warrior HLZ, immediately warned us that two local nationals hired to haul trash off the FOB were just that week caught pacing off distances for a mortar attack. The FOB had taken a 107mm rocket the previous evening. Keep the white lights off, he ordered.

Soldiers find themselves in some of the most peculiar situations on combat bases. What happened next was one of those moments. After our Chinooks churned back into the dark, two more came in as shadows across the stars, again landing in pitch-darkness. "Gimme ten," Garcia yelled. Ten volunteers, he meant. Both Chinooks were completely full of brand-new twin mattresses, still wrapped in plastic. Since we'd left Fort Bragg, we'd not slept on real mattresses, yet like army toilet paper, here they were in abundance in Afghanistan. After unloading them a short distance from the tail ramps, a dozen of us draped ourselves like human cargo nets around the mattresses while the big Chinooks beat us with rotor wash and thundered back toward civilization.

By now my eyes were accustomed to the dark. The sky sparkled with our own brilliant galaxy above a murky, clay-brown terrestria bordered by high peaks that cut flat shapes into the starfield. Garcia was talking. There was a significant insider threat on this FOB. Don't walk down Rape Alley, especially on "man-love Thursday." Don't drink from DNA Creek. Chow opens at zero six.

By the time we downloaded all of our equipment from the baggage truck and moved into a brick hovel recently vacated by Polish soldiers, it was nearly five in the morning. I stayed awake until 0600 to visit the chow tent, then sacked out on an Army cot until one in the afternoon when First Sergeant Lieske came through to inventory who was bunking where. Lieske had that "I'm about to retire so I can play this game as long as I need to" attitude. Bobby Lieske had one helluva long nose, a Ranger tab, and a dangerously dry sense of humor. From Louisiana, he loved to fish. To his friends, his nickname was Catfish. I always liked First Sergeant Lieske.

Outside, the sun was bright and warm, and the mountains in every direction raised violent-looking peaks, crenelated as if they had been snapped off rather than worn down. I had seen fluted peaks like these in parts of the Montana Rockies. Though treeless and nearly barren, they still reminded me of home. The Afghanistan sky was nearly as clean a sapphire as the Big Sky back home. It was late March, well before the season of daily dust storms.

In flipflops and PTs, I poked around outside the rows of dilapidated brick-and-mortar buildings, troop tents, and sandbag revetments, looking for the shower tent that was rumored to exist somewhere near DNA Creek. Passing through a narrow band of smooth-barked, white trees that resembled the aspens of home, I heard someone call out, "Hey Mac!" I turned, and there was Lieutenant Dan.

CHAPTER 2:
GHAZNI

Loeffler had been assigned a platoon of 1-504 infantry back at Bragg, but as the deployment approached, he was tapped to be the officer in charge of his battalion's rear-detachment, meaning that he would not deploy. Just before we left, he was switched to battalion S4, the logistics officer. Suddenly and with no prior experience, he was in charge of moving all of the battalion's equipment to Afghanistan. Just like that.

When he arrived in Ghazni with the battalion's first deployers, the "torch party," there were two feet of snow on the ground with nighttime temperatures as low as minus 16 degrees. The Afghan civilian trucking system that stocked the FOB with fuel and other necessities had withered substantially under the care of the Polish troops we were relieving. Not only was Highway 1 a nightmare corridor with its constant threat of IED, craters from past IEDs, Taliban shakedowns, private Afghan security contractors that would shoot at anything and often nothing, but the Poles treated the truckers poorly, often requiring them to wait in the cool-down yards for days before offloading supplies. Several times, fuel tankers would arrive at FOB Warrior, and faced with days of unpaid waiting, the drivers would decide to push on to Kandahar or some other US base.

Of water, food, fuel, and ammo, fuel was most important to a FOB's operation. Without fuel, nobody shoots, moves, or communicates for very long. Fuel powered the generators that ran the lights and pumped the water, and when fuel ran low, as it did a few days after my chalk arrived, showers and lights in the living quarters were first to go.

Since Loeffler's arrival, nearly all of the materials the FOB had received had been slingloaded from the bellies of helicopters, both military CH-47 Chinooks and the smaller CH-46 "red and whites" that civilian contractors operated. Development of the base had proceeded, but, he said, Afghanistan was not Iraq. There was no equivalent to the massive Iraqi supply hub of Taji or nearby Kuwait. The sixty-five additional concrete T-wall barriers that brigade had requested to beef up security? They might arrive eighteen months after the brigade left, if at all.

FOB Warrior was the southernmost base in Ghazni. It was the main NATO presence in Gilan District, just west of Nawah, the district through which all bad things flowed. Nawah was so lawless that during the 2009 elections, there was not a single polling station there. The hub for Devil Brigade operations at the north of our area of operation, or AO, was FOB Arian. Until recently, Arian was so insignificant that the Poles closed the front gate at night by parking a gun truck in it. Like Warrior, it sat practically astride Highway 1. Through the intense Ghazni winter, heavy equipment engineers with the Louisiana National Guard had more than doubled the size of Arian to make room for nearly all of 2-504's infantry, a trucking depot, mechanics and medics of our 307th Brigade Support Battalion, and a company of our combat engineers whose job was to keep a section of Highway 1 free of IEDs.

In addition to FOBs Warrior and Arian, the brigade would man three smaller combat outposts, or COPs. COP Ab Band lay just a few klicks south of Arian and was headquarters to our cavalry scouts, 3rd

Squadron, 73rd Cavalry Regiment. Between Ab Band and Warrior in the economic and political hub of restive Muqor District lay COP Muqor, a congested little base built around an old British mansion, with a World War II era Soviet T34 tank rusting outside. Two infantry companies with 1-504 were stationed there along with a battalion of Afghan soldiers. Finally, east of Arian in the heart of "Indian Country" was COP Giro, a tiny post manned by a single company of CAV paratroopers, Charlie Troop.

"Muqor just got showers this week, and the Taliban already blew them up with a rocket," Loeffler said with a sardonic chuckle. He laughed because he was infantry, and it's an infantryman's lot to embrace the suck. One of the most dedicated and competent officers I met during my time in the Army, Loeffler was kept on battalion staff until midway through the deployment. At the height of violence in southern Ghazni, he was given command of the battalion's Scout Platoon and sent to hunt IED emplacers near Nawah District.

Eventually I located the showers in a sagging green tent next to the laundry drop-off point beside narrow but quick DNA Creek at the head of Rape Alley. A handful of Polish soldiers in T-shirts were fishing in the three-foot-wide creek as it gurgled through a ribbon of aspen-like poplars that skirted a narrow lane. They were lazing about as if this were a normal way to spend a day in a combat zone. Perhaps for them it was. Distilling moonshine was another, we discovered. One learns to appreciate end-states in military life, and rinsing away a week of travel grime in a crappy plastic shower with a lock pliers-controlled water valve in a dank grimy tent next to a filthy creek in a place called Rape Alley was just such an instance. It could always be worse. The Taliban could rocket *this* shower.

That night out on Highway 1, one of our logistics convoys was hit by an IED. Insurgents prematurely detonated the command-wire bomb between the last two trucks, blowing an eight-foot pit in the road. The trail vehicle, an MRAP with battalion Sergeant Major Billy Chaney aboard, braked hard but slid into the hole nonetheless. Luckily, there were only a few minor injuries.

The highway through Ghazni had a history of more than roadside bombs. In 2007, the Taliban kidnapped twenty-three South Korean missionaries passing through on a bus. Two males of the mostly female group were executed before the Taliban successfully extorted a reported $20 million from the South Korean government and the promise to withdraw its forces by the year's end, which it did. It was largely an act of road piracy in a province that was not unlike a sea of dust, a lawless hinterland. Ghazni had not always been so. Long ago, Ghazni City was the most important city in Asia and a cradle of culture for two centuries before it was repeatedly overrun and destroyed by advancing empires, including that of Genghis Khan. Now with just fifty thousand residents, Ghazni City was Afghanistan's smallest city.

Outside the provincial seat, Ghazni Province was arid farmland set against barren slopes and hardscrabble peaks, its "farmland" irrigated by an ancient yet ingenious system of hand-excavated, aquifer-tapping shafts and pipes that our infantry and route-clearance engineers would come to hate. Not only were the *karezes* easily damaged by the thirty-thousand-pound MRAPs, but they also provided a tunnel system from which insurgents could operate undetected, somewhat like the Vietcong had in Vietnam. Our engineers were finding copper trigger-wires for IEDs up to two kilometers long threaded through the *karezes* from the highway to hiding places.

Most of Ghazni's residents were Pashtuns, classic Afghans with dark skin and hair, heavy eyes, and prominent noses. This was a land of beards. Like Al Qaeda and the Taliban, Pashtuns were mostly Sunni Muslims. Hazaras, a more oriental-featured people descended from the Mongol armies, were lowest on the social ladder, and the Kuchi, nomadic herdsmen who migrated with the seasons, were off the social ladder altogether. Overwhelmingly illiterate and Sunni, many of the Kuchi were recruited by the Taliban.

Charlie Company of the 82nd Airborne Division's 1st Battalion, 504th Parachute Infantry Regiment, poses for a photo backed by a 19th Century British mansion and a World War II era Russian T-34 tank on Combat Outpost Muqor, Ghazni Province, Afghanistan. In the spring and summer of 2012, the airborne infantry company took part in the last major clearing operation of the war in Afghanistan.

US and German jumpmasters identify terrain features along the approach to a drop zone prior to dropping paratroopers there during a bilateral training event October 5, 2010 at Fort Bragg, North Carolina.

An 82nd Airborne Division paratrooper jumps from a UH60 Black Hawk helicopter during an airborne training operation over Fort Bragg, North Carolina, in late 2010. Paratroopers train to jump from a number of aircraft.

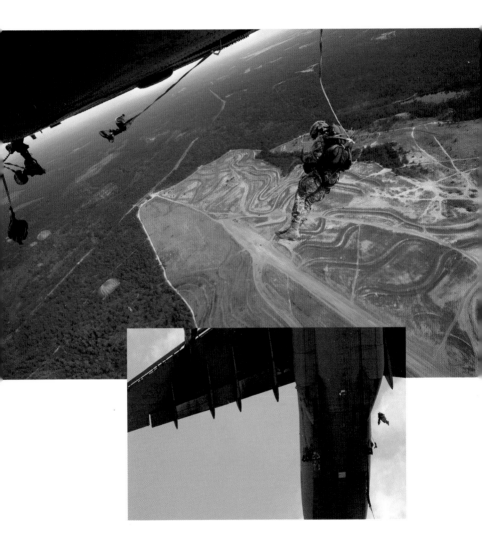

Paratroopers exit from a C-17 Globemaster cargo jet as part of regularly scheduled training at Fort Bragg, North Carolina.

A US Army paratrooper gives the signal to cease fire during a firefight with the Taliban near Combat Outpost Giro in Afghanistan's Ghazni Province, May 17, 2012. The paratroopers belong to Charlie Troop, 3-73 Cavalry, part of the 82nd Airborne Division's 1st Brigade Combat Team.

A Charlie Company paratrooper trips and rolls during a firefight touched off by a Taliban ambush June 30, 2012, in Afghanistan's Ghazni Province.

Devil Brigade paratroopers practice battlefield first aid on roleplaying detainees at the Joint Readiness Training Center at Fort Polk, Louisiana, in the spring of 2009 prior to deploying to Iraq.

Delta Company, 1-504th Parachute Infantry Regiment (PIR) paratroopers fight off a Taliban ambush during a patrol, June 15, 2012, at Spedar, Afghanistan.

Second Lieutenant Nicholas Prieto, a Charlie Company platoon leader, uses an armored vehicle for cover while communicating with his company commander during a Taliban ambush June 30, 2012, outside of Muqor, Afghanistan. At left is his radioman, Private First Class Blaze Glocar.

Sergeant David Pickard fires his M4 carbine from the partial cover of a MaxxPro MRAP when attacked by Taliban forces, June 30, 2012, near Muqor, Afghanistan.

Devil Brigade platoon leaders and forward observers practice calling in artillery rounds during a live-fire exercise at Fort Bragg, North Carolina, in June 2009 prior to deploying to Iraq.

An airborne infantryman armed with an M249 squad automatic weapon pulls security on the corner of a building that he and his team have just cleared of threats during war games at the Joint Readiness Training Center. His team has employed a smoke grenade to cover their movements from nearby opposing forces.

An Iraqi army medic applies a tourniquet to a patient with a simulated arm amputation during a mass-casualty training exercise orchestrated by US Army medics of the 82nd Airborne Division's 1st Brigade Combat Team, June 3, 2010, near Al Asad Air Base, Iraq.

Dust sparks against the rotors of a CH-47 Chinook helicopter as Afghan soldiers and 82nd Airborne Division paratroopers load for an air assault mission near Combat Outpost Ab Band in Afghanistan's Ghazni Province May 23, 2012.

Devil Brigade paratroopers and Afghan soldiers with the 6th Kandak, 203rd Corps, prepare to exit a CH-47 Chinook helicopter moments before touchdown during a nighttime air assault, May 4, 2012, in Ghazni Province, Afghanistan.

Private First Class Michael Trevino, an 82nd Airborne Division combat medic, accompanies an injured Afghan soldier to a makeshift helicopter landing zone in between firefights in the village of Spedar, Afghanistan.

Private First Class Michael Trevino treats an injured toe of a boy whose family lives near Joint Security Station Hasan in southern Ghazni Province, Afghanistan, where US and Afghan troops were attacked multiple times a day during the summer of 2012. US Army medics often treat civilians, even for non-combat-related health issues.

A US Army paratrooper shows his ball-handling skills to local Afghan boys in the town of Muqor, Afghanistan, during a patrol there in June 2012.

Major Jason Glemser, Lieutenant Colonel Robert Salome, and Lieutenant Colonel Daniel Mouton, enjoy the stars and a quiet evening at Joint Security Station Hasan June 11, 2012, in southern Ghazni Province, Afghanistan. Erected just weeks earlier in southern Gilan District, the rural post was attacked by the Taliban multiple times a day until the Muslim fast of Ramadan.

Private First Class Kristina Batty, a medic with the 82nd Airborne Division's 1st Brigade Combat Team, dons a headscarf to meet with female Afghan villagers May 5, 2012, in Ghazni Province, Afghanistan. She is part of a female engagement team.

Sergeant Joshua Smith chats with an Afghan boy during an operation to clear several villages of Taliban, April 28, 2012, in Ghazni Province, Afghanistan. Smith studied the Pashto language prior to deployment.

One family cheers, another mourns as Devil Brigade paratroopers return home from the war in Afghanistan in the fall of 2012. At right is Deanna Howard, whose son, Private First Class Christian Sannicolas, was killed by an improvised explosive device, April 28, 2012, in Ghazni Province, Afghanistan. Howard is greeting the soldiers of her son's returning infantry company.

While land ownership in Ghazni was high, sharecropping was still the most common arrangement. Tractors were common, but shovels more so. The average farmer earned less than a dollar a day. Wheat was a major crop, but it was the raisin industry that shaped the landscape. Afghan grape farmers didn't use trellisworks. Instead they constructed furrows, but deep ones, sometimes four or five feet high, that severely constricted foot travel. Grapes were dried in "grape huts," elongated mud-brick structures perforated with regularly spaced holes to allow even airflow over the drying fruit. Grape fields and huts presented an ideal landscape for insurgents to lay ambushes and quickly escape.

The people of Ghazni had cell phones, and service was adequate during daylight hours, but not at night when the Taliban came into the villages demanding food and quarters. Their threat to blow up cell towers—occasionally made good—was enough to bend mobile companies to their demands to cut off service at sunset. In neighboring Pakistan, the government had threatened to shut down all cell towers unless companies stopped ceding to the demands of the Taliban. Not here in Afghanistan.

The insurgent fighters our troops would face were mostly imported Arabs, Chechens, and Punjabi fighters from Pakistan, 19–25 years old, many with military training. As foreigners and self-righteous holy warriors, Taliban fighters cared far less about collateral damage than even the "infidel" American troops who came from halfway around the world.

According to one senior officer on his third deployment, he had never seen so many civilians willing to come in with tips on insurgent activities. The people of Ghazni were weary of their blowhard Islamist neighbors from Pakistan and their violent cruelty. Recently, insurgents had forced the mayor of Ab Band to watch as they executed his father, mother, brother, and son. In another instance, two teenage girls who offended the Taliban's extreme views on purity had their faces burned off with acid. They died, of course. These barbarisms fueled a localized yet growing revolt in Ghazni that would only be fanned by the presence of US Army paratroopers during the summer of 2012, not unlike a small-scaled Anbar Uprising of 2007 in Iraq.

Even before the Poles officially transferred authority of southern Ghazni to the Devil Brigade, the Taliban was learning of the aggressive nature of paratroopers. On March 30, a gang of motorcycle-mounted insurgents opened fire on a passing AH64 Apache attack helicopter belonging to the division's Combat Aviation Brigade. Insurgents often fired on Polish Hind helicopters because they rarely fired back. The Apache quickly killed three of the attackers with its 30mm electrically operated chain gun. Another insurgent, critically maimed by the exploding rounds, crawled off and died.

Our first casualty came on April 6. A team of Arian-based engineers on its first solo sweep of Highway 1 was ambushed near the village of Mushaki. "They were about 150 meters off the road sweeping for command wires when they were ambushed," recalled Sergeant First Class Bryan Butler, the engineers' platoon sergeant. An armor-piercing round sliced through Corporal Antonio Burnside.

"I'm hit," the Montana native yelled to his team leader, Sergeant Ryan Fry. Then Burnside took a fatal blow to the head. Fry was also grazed in the head.

The insurgents retreated into a courtyard in the town. When Apache gunships arrived, the pilots spotted the insurgents, who were making no attempt to hide. One was holding an RPG in one hand and a child in the other. They knew our rules of engagement. "They continued to surround themselves with children until the Apaches left for fuel," said Bulter. "We decided not to chase after the enemy because the situation could have been worse and our mission was to clear the road for IEDs. Those mud walls turn into mazes pretty quick, you know."

Burnside's death was an early gut check for the brigade and a blow to fellow engineers. He was well liked, and at thirty-one, an older corporal. He and I shared a common past. He grew up in Browning, Montana on the Blackfeet Indian Reservation abutting Glacier National Park and the Bob Marshall Wilderness. In my early 20s, I used to fish for trout nearby and backpacked in the Badger Two-Medicine Wilderness, just south of the reservation. The dominion of his childhood was not unlike parts of Afghanistan, for the Blackfeet lived at the abutment of the Northern Rocky Mountains with the Northern Great Plains, as raw and demanding a country as exists in the Lower 48 states, where grizzly bears, mountain lions, wolves, and wolverines still haunt the aspen and fir hollows, and deer meat is still a staple in every home. I knew we loved many of the same things.

Tony "Many Hides" Burnside had been born into a warrior culture, once among the most feared of the Northern Plains. He had told his mom Annie that the military was just a big extended family, and for that as much as anything, he had recently decided to reenlist. He was the second of his tribe to be killed in Afghanistan. Burnside left behind wife Christine, daughters Ariana, Heartlynn, and Angel, and son Tony Jr.

I was in the brigade TOC when the attack occurred. Colonel Stock rushed down a narrow plywood hallway with desperation on his face. Military commanders deployed to Afghanistan know they will lose soldiers. Stock must have been expecting it. Yet I saw no sign of surrender or even acquiescence to that fact. I was moved by the degree of his concern for a single fallen soldier.

That night in the chow tent, I sat with Master Sergeant Pablo Michel, our Puerto Rican retention NCO. Michel was a humble, dignified man, and somewhat old school. Once the chaplain, a major, asked him to whisper when talking in the large office space that several staff sections shared. "I do not whisper," Michel replied. "I am a man." At dinner, Michel told me that in 2005 he had helped build the original FOB Warrior. "Man, it was a different place around here then," he said. "No IEDs during the entire deployment. Our terp was killed by a Soviet-era mine, and that's it. No other injuries."

The IEDs seemed to be everywhere now. The next day, one of our infantry patrols discovered three daisy-chained IEDs five kilometers west of Warrior, and to the north, a 2-504 convoy was hit by an IED. One troop suffered a head injury.

Sergeant First Class Jeff McFarland, the information operations NCO roped into one last deployment with the 82nd, warned me, "Mac, listen. This ain't Hajji out here. They're mountain people. They're tough as fuck, and they know how to shoot. When you go out, be super careful." Jeff always spoke really fast, as if every word was in the throes of its own anxiety attack.

"Well, I'm mountain people too," I replied. I didn't mean it as bravado. It was more of an appreciation, really. Punjabi zealots I could do without, but the Pashtun intrigued me. Decades earlier as a young wildlife biologist, I had met my share of armed, crusty old bastards who lived among the bears and wildcats of Montana's remote North Fork of the Flathead River Valley, just over the divide from Burnside's people.

In truth, I was rather fond of the breed and recognized them as the tough, bitter milk of an unforgiving yet beautiful landscape. I was anxious to meet the Pashtun. I didn't have to wait long.

CHAPTER 3:
FIRST CONTACT

"After Burnside died, we totally changed the way we did things, and it probably saved lives," Burnside's platoon sergeant told me. Butler was on his fourth deployment, but his first to Afghanistan. "Iraq was all about mounted patrols. Here we get out in the dirt," he said. The RCPs, or route-clearance patrols, began partnering with our military police for additional security during bomb sweeps of Highway 1. More often than not, as their high-tech trucks scoured the asphalt, dismounted engineers with handheld detection equipment walked for miles in ankle-deep dust, just off the highway shoulders, looking for buried bombs and the thin copper wires that often triggered them.

After Burnside's death, the new SOP was to have a platoon of mounted infantry lagging just in the distance for added firepower. Surveillance was nearly always provided by the hi-res cameras slung under a big white aerostat blimp, officially called a Persistent Threat Detection System or PTIDS, tethered high above Warrior and Arian and monitored by TOC personnel. Sweeping the highway for mines morphed from a daily service to a standing assault, a tack so successful that it would eventually bring in Big Army analysts to learn and propagate the technique.

As far as living conditions on FOB Warrior, it appeared that the Poles had simply hunkered down. The troop tents, chow hall, and office buildings that surrounded the eroded mud-brick ramparts of a 19th-century British fort were largely unimproved. The only industry that our Polish brothers seemed to have applied to their own comfort was a pair of moonshine stills.

The army, and particularly the 82nd, always improves the standard of living at its forward bases and combat outposts. Perhaps it's an American thing (though one wouldn't know it from living with marines in Anbar). For weeks, every paratrooper on Warrior pitched in, building partition walls and doors, filling and erecting sandbag walls, running wires, and moving supplies around. Force protection within the base, i.e., structures such as concrete blast walls, Hescoes, and sandbags, were doubled and tripled, to limit the potential of mass casualties from explosive devices such as mortars, recoilless rifle rounds, and suicide bombers.

I had one of those odd army moments one night when Sergeant K and I found ourselves driving a pile of "requisitioned" lumber balanced on a "gator" ATV across the FOB beneath a pulsing Milky Way, blowing up a cloud of dust in our tracks as we struggled to balance the heavy load. We had only K's dying amber headlamp for illumination while I sped along too fast for conditions, trying to make it to the TOC before the batteries gave out or someone of higher rank spotted us.

The third enlisted soldier of our public affairs shop was a young ex-infantry sergeant from the Sacramento area named Jonathan Shaw. Sergeant Shaw, or "Shawsome" as we called him, was on his third deployment in six years, but his first as a public affairs practitioner. He had never published a piece of journalism when the army placed him in charge of our shop. We were all sergeants, but Shawsome outranked us by "date of rank." That was a win for K and me because that left Shawsome "in charge" with our public affairs officer at a desk on Warrior while K and I traveled around southern Ghazni providing news coverage of our paratroopers.

For the most part, we worked well together in spite of great differences in age and experiences. Shawsome, K, and I built a floor for the FOB post office down by the HLZ so that it could be certified to ship as well as receive. Prior to that, the shed was just walls and a roof constructed over egg-sized gravel. We also built the world's sturdiest map table and a number of interior walls and doors for the brigade TOC.

One day, I was returning a number of tools I'd borrowed from a company across the FOB, when one of the busiest officers in the brigade, Major Michael Labrecque, happened to see me with my cumbersome load. Labrecque was the brigade staff's top logistics advisor to the colonel. Ultimately, getting the 2,500 paratroopers mobilized, deployed, fed, watered, fueled, equipped, and eventually returned to the United States was his responsibility. I didn't ask for his help and even tried to brush him off, but Labrecque, a ranger-tabbed, red-headed former infantry officer, who bears a striking resemblance to the actor who plays Dick Winters in the *Band of Brothers* series, wouldn't have it. It wasn't a big deal to him; it was just part of the "Rule of LGOPs," little group of paratroopers. He saw one paratrooper doing a job requiring two, so the major pitched in and helped me walk the tools a quarter mile. After our deployment, Labrecque would go on to become the brigade executive officer, and even then, he led by example, eschewing the privilege of rank and always working for the greater good of the force.

In Ghazni, Labrecque had a massive job. The army was spending $65 million before fuel costs to prep the FOBs of southern Ghazni for the arrival of Task Force 1/82, and while every porta-john had toilet paper, door hinges were hard to come by. Wood screws were rationed and bartered over. Having the right tools to lend out could nearly get a guy laid. By anybody.

One of the advantages of my job as an army journalist was that, unlike your average Joe, I got to see the strategic along with the tactical. During a respite in construction, I accompanied Colonel Stock and a few other staffers on a helicopter trip to Ghazni City to meet the provincial governor, Musa Khan. It was a first chance to meet Afghans and to see the countryside in daylight. From the altitude of our Black Hawk, in early April, Ghazni was staggering bleakness from end to end. Apocalyptic mountains, dusty plain, more barren mountains. Large expanses of the landscape were void of anything but the regularly spaced moraines of dirt and open holes of *karez* shafts that from the air resembled needle tracks in the arm of a heroin addict. Mud-brick villages scattered here and there were like the nests of mud-dauber wasps, constructed of little more than earth, water, and the hardening sun. Every yard had a mud-brick wall, every home a comely castle of mud-brick battlements, parapets, curtain walls, courtyards, and keeps. As yet, there was nothing green anywhere. Highway 1, a lone thread of access to a world beyond, was drawn taut over the land in long, efficient straightaways. Buses, semis, vans, and scooters vied for open road along the two-lane asphalt.

Musa Khan, the governor, was a concrete businessman and former general in the mujahedeen in the war against the Soviets. One of his sons was studying in South Korea, and his wife and another son resided in Pakistan. He was a master of conversation and a reminder that politicians are not accidental tourists wherever one finds them. During the security meeting, Colonel Stock agreed with the governor that the best way to expand the reach of provincial governance was by strengthening the security and services of its district centers and encouraging the district subgovernors to actually live there rather than in the safer Ghazni City. That was no small request since the Taliban often killed them when they tried to, and life outside of Ghazni City was significantly more seventh century.

The provincial police chief told Stock and other Afghan officials that the Taliban was recruiting fighters in Pakistan ages nineteen to twenty-five, and suicide bombers ages nine to fifteen. Their goal was to attack the district centers with IEDs, targeting important government officials. Much of the insurgents' Intel on US and Afghan forces was coming from shakedowns of Afghan truck drivers who supplied the American FOBs. A tall Afghan army general with Hazara-like features told Stock that he would like to begin partnered operations within a few weeks. "They have only propaganda and mines," he said, with dismissive bravado, of the Taliban.

In fact, the Taliban had much more than that. Some fighters in certain areas of Ghazni were among the best light infantry in the world. Experienced, well-armed, and highly mobile on their motorbikes, they coerced support from the local population through fear and intimidation and remained unencumbered by any of the laws of warfare that bound our troops. At least to American eyes, they also looked like the locals.

Back on FOB Warrior later that day, for a human-interest piece, I interviewed thirty-year-old Warrant Officer Weldon Malbrough Jr., an affable intelligence officer who I learned was the oldest brother of three siblings concurrently deployed to Afghanistan. Brother Jordan was a grunt with the 25th Infantry Division at FOB Apache in Khowst Province, and sister Jessica was a medic in Kandahar with the 4th Infantry Division.

When their father died of a heart attack, Weldon was only eighteen. He became the surrogate father of his siblings. They had followed him into service, and now, they were also in Afghanistan. It was humbling how much some families contributed.

Using a DSN phone, I called Weldon's mom Windy at her home in New Orleans. "It's something they chose to do," Windy said like a dissenting partner. "To keep peace with my mind, I try to think happy thoughts." Philip, her fourth child, worked on an offshore oil rig, another dangerous occupation. "There is no worry-free time for mom," she said. "My kids are my heroes."

Jessica Malbrough sent me a photo of the four Malbrough children posed in the family driveway in the late 80s, clustered like chicks, leading with smiles and bellies, Weldon a head higher than the rest. With every reason not to, Windy's children all went on to do brave things.

As our intelligence cell spun up, they uncovered a plot by the local Taliban commander to destroy the Warrior surveillance blimp, or PTIDS, when the aerostat was lowered for periodic maintenance. They were going to hit it with an RPG fired from a *kalat*, or mud-brick compound, just a hundred meters from the FOB's northwest perimeter wall. As a result, Operation Goodyear was drawn up, the first named operation for 1-504 to execute.

"Hey, anybody got a hookup on forty-mike-mike?" It was an ignominious way to begin a mission brief, even for a casual company commander like Columbia, South Carolina native, Captain Joseph Driskell, or "Joey D" to his friends. The battalion was on the eve of executing its first planned mission, and his infantrymen were short on 40mm explosive rounds for their rifle-mounted M320 grenade launchers, the standard M67 hand grenades, and even 5.56mm ammunition for the M4 carbines that everyone carried.

The officer in charge of Afghan police partnering with Driskell's paratroopers, a handsomely bearded Pashtun in his mid-twenties, shrugged. His name was Noor Allah, meaning "light of God." He had no forty-mike-mike, and in fact, his own weapon, a battered AK47, was held together with clear packing tape.

In the Alpha Company headquarters at a tabletop model of the target compound, one of Driskell's lieutenants was explaining to Noor Allah that once the compound was cleared, he and his men should come out.

"No," the Afghan policeman replied in pretty good English. "We come out, you shoot us. You think we bad guy." He was saying, to Americans, all Afghans look alike, even ones wearing uniforms. To be fair, Afghan army and police uniforms were rarely standardized, and some insurgents wore camo pants and/or tops.

The lieutenant tried to reassure Noor Allah that his policemen would not get shot at by the American paratroopers who would be covering them, but the chiseled Afghan knew better. He had worked with Americans new to the country. Driskell waved off his lieutenant, "It's okay, man, we'll be in there with him." With a hand on Noor Allah's shoulder, Driskell repeated, "We'll be in there with you."

Just before midnight, mission participants met under starlight next to the HLZ to rehearse. There were eighty-two total, including ten Afghan policemen. In addition to Driskell's infantrymen, there was a FET team, a psychological operations team, civil affairs, combat photographer, police mentor, Security Force Assistance Team (SFAT) officer, scout snipers, a mortar team, and me, a journalist.

"My God," said Driskell. "There's more enablers here than trigger pullers."

We staged for the actual mission at 3 a.m. near the front gate. It was customary during the final brief for the leader to share the latest significant actions, or SIGACTS, that might affect the mission. "Hey, listen up," said Driskell. "Charlie Company took out twelve Taliban up at Muqor yesterday with the SF. They know the new guys are in town, and they're probably ready for us." SF is short for Special Forces.

At 4:30 a.m., two lines of paratroopers in a "tactical column" walked out the gate through the poor roadside village of Janda in a meager blue light. Janda sat astride Highway 1, and at the hardball, or pavement, we hooked right through little shops of sundry goods, open-air meat markets, motorcycle and tractor garages, and yards of construction supplies. In the pre-dawn, many locals were already up and about. Several stood in doorways watching us pass, cell phones to their ears. "Hey Mustafa, the Americans are coming." Or the equivalent.

What followed was a harmless little clusterfuck. Our column moved several hundred meters southwest on Highway 1 before striking north across the open desert behind several giant MRAP gun trucks. We walked over a thousand meters along the perimeter of FOB Warrior, all in the open. We were still in the open as dawn lit the sky. Outside the target *kalat*, I overheard Driskell's men trying to verify that we were at the right place.

"Does it have double red doors?"

"No, they're blue."

"It's at the right grid."

"I know."

Dr. Nicole Lassiter, an academic researcher who came along to interview Afghan women, crouched pensively in her oversized helmet behind a slim tree near the *kalat* wall. Her blonde ponytail stuck out from the rear, and though she was dressed just like the paratroopers setting up security around her, she was unarmed.

Everyone was waiting to get attacked, but no attack happened. The Afghan police entered first through the rusting blue steel doors, followed by several paratroopers, and then a whole gaggle of paratroopers and policemen. Thick smoke billowed through the wooden slats of a door to the living quarters. A sergeant yelled, "They're burning something. What are they burning? Go find what they're burning!"

A couple of paratroopers slipped into the main living quarters of the compound with Noor Allah. In less than a minute, they piled back out, gasping for breath.

"They're just cooking, sar'nt."

"Well, who the fuck cooks like that?"

The only males present were a few Afghan teenagers and old men. If we were in the right compound, our targets had already fled. As terps questioned the males, FET soldiers began searching the females. "No, no, not here," scolded Noor Allah. "Not in front of the males." We were all FNGs.

The FET ushered a half-dozen women and girls into a small room off the courtyard. Outside, paratroopers and police continued to search for weapons and explosives in the mud-brick animal mangers, on rooftops, in piles of drying silage. Strewn about the baked mud "yard" was a broken pickax head, rotting shoes, an aluminum teapot, old tires worn of tread, and lots of trash. The smoke smelled pungently of hashish.

As our soldiers used a camera-like HIIDES to scan the iris and take fingerprints of the young man who seemed to be left in charge, he was trembling with fear. Nobody there knew anything about the Taliban, he said. "Then why are you shaking?" the terp asked.

The young man shrugged and said, "You are soldiers."

A locked door prevented a grape hut from being searched, but instead of breaching the door, one of Driskell's sergeants requested the policemen ask the young man for a key, which he procured. The grape hut was empty. There were no signs of Taliban or weaponry anywhere. After an hour and a half, Driskell pulled his men off the objective.

On the march out, I asked Dr. Lassiter what she had learned from the women. "They are very poor," she replied. "Life is hard for them. The mother's fourteen-year-old daughter recently miscarried from being beaten. They didn't want to talk because they are afraid the Taliban will cut off their heads. And when I asked them if they knew who the head of the government was, the mother asked me what a government was."

I had no doubt the women feared for their lives, but the old woman not knowing what a government was seemed more like self-preservation rather than ignorance. What were the Taliban demanding if not abstinence from supporting the government?

Walking back through Janda, I smelled Kuchi gypsies before I saw them. They traveled in overloaded wagons pulled by ancient farm tractors. The men rode on the tractor, while the women and children, dressed in rags, were balanced high on the chattel behind them. Though I knew it was taboo, I briefly locked eyes with one of the women. Unblinking, she stared back from what seemed like another century.

Janda was less than a kilometer long. Highway 1 was its Main Street. On either side, men in pairs and threes tinkered on humble motorcycles, field-worn tractors, and unadorned generator blocks. Slabs of raw meat hung in the doorways of small markets, and caged wild birds resembling our meadowlarks were displayed for sale. A lumberyard stocked only doors and debarked poplar poles used as floor joists in the construction of mud-brick houses. Except for the Kuchi, only men, boys, and young girls were out of doors. They watched us pass out of their morning back into the FOB.

At the after-action review, Noor Allah was fired up. He told Driskell to make sure he had better information in the future because sometimes Afghans just finger the neighbor they don't like. He also said if the Americans were serious about killing Taliban, he could get six guys together anytime to go attack them. "I can show you the car, the home, the exact spot where IEDs are made," he said.

Driskell conceded the mission was a tactical flop, but perhaps it was a strategic win in the long run. The operation had been based on Intel from a single source—always risky—but one that the local Special Forces team swore by. Had the insurgents been tipped off? They could have been warned by any one of the villagers. In fact, the PTIDs had spotted several men on motorcycles fleeing the area before we arrived. With over a dozen Afghan policemen on the raid and every one of them with a cell phone, a tip-off could have also been an inside job, and ultimately, Driskell believed it was. From then on during partnered operations, Driskell's men avoided divulging a mission's target to their Afghan counterparts until they were practically on the objective.

I had my own dustup with the enemy later in the day, but that enemy was called "division." In a deployed environment, the word *division* is often spoken with derision typically reserved for drunken oil tanker captains. For our public affairs shop, "division" referred to the Regional Command—East public affairs headquarters, operated in a modern brick building at Bagram, manned at that time by a division public affairs department that was not ours from Bragg (in the modularized army, any division-level PAO will do, regardless of what subordinate units are operating under it). Thus, we were as new to them as they were to us.

One might reasonably expect a rise in competency at ever-increasing levels of organization, i.e., from battalion to brigade to division, but that's not always the case. When Shawsome emailed my first two articles to division for them to review and clear for public release, division returned them "fixed," with my leads so dull that even all-caps and Spanish exclamation points wouldn't have pumped life back into them. Changes their editor made to one story gave it four grammatical errors and two errors in fact. One of my leads now read:

FORWARD OPERATING BASE WARRIOR, AFGHANISTAN – The governor of Ghazni Province promised the partnership he has shared with Polish forces to an incoming American airborne unit here today.

Say again? A sentence in my Malbrough story read, "While her brothers pushing her hard to 'drop a packet' . . ."

Then there was this pronoun grammatricide: "It's something they chose to do. To keep peace with my mind, I try to think happy thoughts," she said, who [sic] still lives in metropolitan New Orleans where she raised her children."

When Shawsome called to get the errors fixed, the shop boss, a Master Sergeant Connor, shut him down before he could get a word in. "You can call here and ask about anything except those two articles," said Connor. "We are your superiors. You are our subordinates. You will do it our way. Are you tracking, Sergeant Shaw?" And that was that. My articles were published with leads that were dead on arrival and texts that were gut-shot with six known errors. Hooah. *Fucking* division. (Blame always goes to the unit one level higher, as in, "fucking battalion," or "fucking brigade.")

When our officer, a captain, emailed Connor's boss to avoid embarrassing the army, he received this grammatically incontinent reply from the major: "This should have been resolved at a [sic] NCO level and if the two would have spoke [sic] directly this probably would have been avoided. It is too early in the rotation to have this kind of conflict over verbiage." Grammar is now "verbiage," like a kind of cabbage that goes with anything. I am satisfied.

On the brighter side, while I sat in the office, cursing division, a platoon with Captain Caleb Ling's Charlie Company based at COP Moqur turned what was almost a disastrous patrol into success. Just after 9 a.m., the company's Third Platoon, an undermanned anti-armor platoon consisting of a single rifle squad and headquarters element, was heading north from Moqur on Highway 1 to conduct a mounted reconnaissance patrol. Led by Ranger-tabbed First Lieutenant Shane Joyce, it was the first patrol of the deployment by paratroopers in his battalion. Captain Ling and his fire support officer, Second Lieutenant Jorge Jimenez, also tagged along, adding a fifth gun truck to Joyce's four MRAPs and two Afghan National Army Humvees.

The target villages were Jomjomeh and Monak Kheyl, small enclaves of ethnic Pashtuns just off the hardball to the east. Joyce had only a map of the area and the ANA's insistence they not go into either of these "bad" villages. Only two of Joyce's sixteen paratroopers had ever seen combat, and he wasn't one of them.

At the turnoff to Manak Kheyl, Ling decided the platoon would head east, directly toward the village of Khamat Kheyl, two klicks (kilometers) distant. "We were still working out how we would be structured if we dismounted," said Joyce. In the sparse open country, the gun trucks might be their only cover and their turret-mounted machine guns, the soldiers' only support by fire, so the platoon leader dismounted with eight paratroopers and pushed two trucks to the front to lead the way. His platoon sergeant, Sergeant First Class Carl Felton, stayed aboard and commanded the vehicles.

"There couldn't be two more different people on the planet, but he was hands-down the best platoon sergeant in battalion, and not only did we work incredibly well together, he also quickly became a true friend of mine," Joyce said of Felton, a sinewy black man and career soldier from Chicago.

Off the hardball, it was typical Ghazni landscape: maze-like *kalats*, courtyards, and small farm plots demarcated by chest-high mudbrick walls (what the Afghans use as fences); stone-hard alleyways that reeked of animal dander and human waste; the occasional shade trees that lined whatever creek had become the village sewer; as yet fallow fields, furrowed and sunbaked to a thin crust, and in between, expanses of foreboding open country, blanketed with ankle-deep moondust and no cover but the occasional shallow, dry wadi and your own imprint in the earth. Distances were measured by the effective ranges of the weapons carried, and those of the enemy. The M4 carbine, five hundred to six hundred meters, useless until we are halfway across. Squad automatic weapon, eight hundred meters (a half mile), a little better and more threatening-sounding. The enemy's AK47, much bigger bullet, more powerful, less accurate. Russian-made Dragunov sniper rifle, a half mile. PKM machine gun with its 7.62mm ammunition, a mile, can pin you down anywhere that you can be seen. Enemy 82mm mortars can hit you even behind cover at several miles.

Just five hundred meters off the highway, the patrol started taking small-arms fire from the southeast. Joyce estimated two to four enemy, well within a winning ratio for sixteen paratroopers. So far out in the open, they had little choice but to locate the enemy, return fire, and maneuver on him. They began shooting back, but while the country looked flat from a distance, up close, it was a morass of small-scale terrain features.

"We got one truck on a goat trail and sprinted alongside it in full kit for a thousand meters," Joyce recalled. When Specialist Brandon Barker crumpled into the moondust, Joyce thought he'd been hit, but it was only a twisted ankle. Barker swapped places with Specialist Mark Harris in the truck. Reaching a ruin, the winded men set up a supporting firing position, which allowed Felton to get his five trucks in line and push through the enemy position. The enemy broke contact. It was 10 a.m.

Riding high on their first contact and the assurance for all of the coveted Combat Infantry Badge, the men looked for evidence of the enemy—shell casings, blood, etc.—who had fled into a tree line a thousand meters to the east. CPT Ling directed Joyce to pursue, Joyce gave the order, and his paratroopers sprinted across the open ground. Unable to navigate the impossibly fickle stability of the soil, their trucks stayed behind.

At the end of the open void, they found several terrified locals. Joyce questioned them, but the locals divulged nothing on the enemy. Meanwhile, Ling and the gun trucks moved into Khomar Kheyl a kilometer to the southwest to investigate a suspicious building. The platoon of sixteen was effectively cut in half and separated.

Joyce and his men pushed into the tree line where the enemy had fled. Suddenly, an Afghan man popped out of the poplars, with jerky body language and a startled expression. "He looked at us, looked over his shoulder, made a distinct arm signal to someone behind him, and then I heard that familiar *whoomp* of a mortar round leaving the tube," said Joyce. The shell exploded a dozen feet in front of the forward-most paratroopers. Fortunately, the powdery soil that the men had been cursing all morning dissipated the blast energy and shrapnel so effectively that not a single man was hit.

"Everything opened up on us at once," said the lieutenant. Hives of single rounds snapped overhead, machine guns rat-tattled, mortars cracked and shook as fast as the enemy could feed the tube, and RPGs fired, hissed, and snaked in with spidering shrapnel. Trees came down. They were being attacked by twenty to twenty-five Taliban fighters in at least four elements, including two groups of four to five fighters, two PKM machine gun teams, and a mortar team, spread out over 120 degrees of the paratroopers' position.

The enemy mortar team's forward observer—the guy who had given the signal—turned to run. Sergeant John (Cody) Williams gave the order to open up, and he and Joyce fired. The man toppled, sandals kicking high in the air. "That's when a slew of mortars and bullets really started," Joyce recalled.

Fortunately, the patrol had made the tree line and a slight rise, providing cover and observation of the battlefield. "It turned into a fight for everything we had," said Joyce. "We were all laying on the backside of the berm trying to get into a good fighting position and trying not to catch one of the thousands of rounds pouring on us."

More trees were coming down. Everyone was behind their weapons firing away, including squad leader Staff Sergeant Patrick Percefull and his team leaders, Sergeants Ortega and Buhl. To keep every rifle in the fight, the lieutenant took up their roles of adjusting sectors and rates of fire.

"Considering we were almost all new at this, it was amazing," Joyce said. "Nobody froze. Everyone was fighting and maneuvering." That was the upside, Joyce knew. The big downside was, they were pinned and in danger of being wiped out. The enemy had them trapped by two machine guns with interlocking sectors of fire, and mortars were zeroing in on their little redoubt. If they tried to fall back or maneuver, they would be quickly cut down. It was only a matter of time until the Russian-made mortars hit home. "If the mortarman would've pushed the tube another millimeter forward, or the wind had blown an infinitesimal amount harder, everyone would've been hit."

Even more worrisome, the young liuetenant could not get through on the radio to coordinate support from the vast array of firepower he believed was at his fingertips, including artillery from FOB Warrior, mortars from COP Muqor, Apache gunships from Sharana, and even his own gun trucks, stuck behind them. The problem was that, so early in the deployment, none of the companies had established separate radio networks for each of their platoons, so everyone was trying to talk on the same frequency.

The Taliban had implemented a textbook defense. The purpose of the initial contact was to pin down Joyce's paratroopers while Taliban forces, paralleling his patrol since Muqor, set up a proper ambush. Once ready, the initial contact was broken off, and the fleeing fighters lured Joyce's men into a trap.

"We had no reason to believe the enemy in our area was either capable or prepared to conduct such a highly organized, massed attack against us," he said. "All intelligence reports indicated that they only operated in small, two-to-five-man teams armed with merely rifles, or a PKM [machine gun] at worst. They told us that the most dangerous action would be an ambush initiated by an IED, followed with small-arms fire."

Fortunately, Ling and Jimenez finally made it to the berm, and Jimenez immediately went to work bringing in air assets. To the north at Khamat Kheyl, platoon sergeant Felton was trying to figure out how to maneuver the top-heavy gun trucks through the snaking wadis and restricting mud-brick walls to Joyce's isolated squad of paratroopers. It was then that the two untested paratroopers Joyce had left in his truck—the driver, Specialist Rich Rogalinski, and gunner, Specialist Terrance Crosby—recognized the dire straits that their platoon-mates were in and reacted by driving there in spite of the loose soil. Other trucks followed, though the terrain kept the drivers in crisis mode the entire way. Such decisive action by junior enlisted in the absence of orders is almost uniquely an American characteristic.

Twenty minutes into the fight, Staff Sergeant Percefull, a crusty old smoker from Fort Worth, Texas, spotted a Taliban fighter with binoculars five hundred meters off to the southeast, bobbing up every time a mortar round struck. He was clearly acting as a forward observer, helping the mortar team walk their rounds into the American position. "Sir, I see a spotter," Percefull said in his rough smoker's hack.

"Well, shoot him!" Joyce replied.

Percefull fired one shot and hit the spotter in the head. "Sir, spotter down," he deadpanned. The mortar rounds became less accurate.

Sergeant Jeffery Buhl was armed with an M14 EBR (Enhanced Battle Rifle). Prior to the patrol, SGT Buhl hadn't the opportunity to sight in the highly accurate rifle. Buhl improvised. He used the heads of the enemy as his zeroing targets. He would fire, watch for the impact of the bullet and make the adjustments on his scope, all while under heavy, accurate, direct, and indirect fire. He repeated this process until he finally saw one of his targets burst into a pink mist.

Popping up over the berm to get a shot at one of the PKM teams, Joyce suddenly felt as if he were punched in the eye. He fell back and felt for blood, but there was none. Later, he learned the pain had been from the overpressure of a bullet passing close to his face.

Thirty minutes into the fight, while the paratroopers still had ammo thanks to judicious pacing, they were black on water, which means they were out. All of the extra water was in the trucks. When Jimenez finally got through to Warrior, the news was not good. The battery of giant M777 155mm howitzers emplaced there had not yet been registered. Same with the 81mm and 120mm mortars at Muqor. Sharana might be able to send a pair of Apaches, but it was going to take a minute.

Felton finally maneuvered two gun trucks to within five hundred meters of Joyce's position. Armed with an M2 .50-caliber heavy machine gun and a MK19 automatic grenade launcher, the trucks were a game changer. (Many US fighter planes in World War II shot the same giant, five-inch-long .50-caliber machine gun rounds, and the "Mark 19" could fire sixty half-pound high-explosive rounds with an effective range of up to a mile in under a minute.) Yet the MK19, operated by Specialist Christian Contreras, was not firing because the rules of engagement required Joyce, the platoon leader, to sign off on its use.

"I was desperately trying to break through the constant radio traffic to tell him to get the Mark 19 into action," said Joyce. "It pissed me off beyond belief that I had the fire power to kill these bastards, but

I couldn't communicate on my own damn freq to use it." In disgust, Joyce threw the handset of his radio at his RTO, Specialist Springob.

Suddenly, he heard the thump, thump, thump of serial grenades. Contreras was firing off an entire thirty-round can of explosive 40 mike-mike at the Taliban positions. Cheers and laughter erupted in the tree line.

Yet the fight was not over. To get the trucks close enough, Felton had traversed terrain so rough that one of the trucks broke a front axle. He was outside the vehicle trying to help get the broken rig unstuck when the Taliban mortarmen began dropping rounds at his position. "I watched Sergeant Felton walking around the truck as mortars impacted within mere feet of him, and bullets splashed all around him as he fever-ishly tried to free the stuck truck," said Joyce.

In the turrets, Contreras and Barker (at the .50-cal) never let up even as mortar shrapnel was hitting the tires of their MRAPs and bul-lets were snapping by their heads. Contreras fired over 80 grenades. Simultaneously, Jimenez talked the gunships in. Over the next twenty minutes, Apaches made several gun runs with their 30mm cannons, destroying one of the mortar crews and the tube.

"Jorge saved our asses out there," recalled Joyce. While he and his riflemen were on their faces going blow for blow, Jimenez was standing up, running from tree to tree so he could get eyes on enemy positions and talk the Apaches on target. "I don't know how he didn't get shot. He got [the gunships] to smoke the mortar that was hemming us up, which allowed us to really pour it on and finally gain fire superiority." The fight was over.

The troops reconsolidated. Joyce's men pushed forward to assess the battle damage and clear the dead enemy under the watchful eyes of the Apache pilots circling overhead. Just ten feet in front of the berm lying dead in the dust was the first casualty, the original forward observer who queued the mortar attack. Wearing trousers rather than "manjams" and a zippered sweat suit top, except for a beard, the dead man looked and dressed nothing like the local Afghans. The paratroopers gazed at the face of war in Ghazni—foreign fighters—this one, from neighboring Pakistan.

The men pushed on to the closest insurgent position. Joyce had seen Specialist Joshua Locke-Thompson cut a man in half there with his M249 squad automatic weapon, but all they found was blood and drag marks. They pushed to the second enemy position, where Sergeant Buhl had shot an enemy fighter with his M14. Again there were only drag marks. The pattern repeated as the platoon continued south toward the village of Rabow Khyel, from which the enemy mortars had emanated. By the time they reached the village, the paratroopers of Third Platoon were distraught. Had they killed only one Taliban with that enormous expenditure of munitions?

In Rabow Kheyl, the ANA led searches of several houses where the Apache pilots had seen wounded Taliban take refuge. In the courtyard of the compound where the mortar tube was destroyed, they found pools of blood, chunks of scalp, and great swaths of shrapnel damage to the *kalat* walls from the Apache's devastating gun.

Joyce knocked on the door. A tall Afghan woman in her twenties opened it. He noticed that moondust had been scraped into the door threshold to hide a trough of blood. Oddly, the woman's face was not concealed, and she looked Joyce in the eye as she answered his questions through the terp, breaking cultural taboo. Her presence was more formidable than Joyce had expected, and she left him unnerved. Yet her story seemed to square with the evidence. Several Taliban had come to her door demanding entry and medical attention, she said. Before the American and Afghan soldiers arrived, the insurgents left with their wounded and dead. That is all.

The ANA and Americans then cleared over thirty *kalats* but found little trace of the enemy. After recovering one of the MRAPs that busted through a bridge over the village creek, Third Platoon mounted up and headed for home. To the north, headlights bobbed in the desert dusk, in the vicinity of the berm, now but an anemic wrinkle in the landscape from the vantage of Rabow Kheyl. It was the ironically named Quick Reaction Force, or QRF, from Muqor. Well. At eighteen hours, the four-hour patrol was over.

Over the next few days, Joyce caught hell from the company first sergeant and battalion command sergeant major for expending so much ammunition with only a single dead Taliban to show for it. "I couldn't believe it," said Joyce. "Contreras alone had to have killed a half dozen, Locke smoked at least one, Willy another, Percefull another couple . . . Buhl, Crosby, me, the Apaches . . . I know we hooked up more than just one."

A week later, an officer shared fresh Intel on the gun battle. Multiple sources confirmed the platoon killed fourteen and wounded eight. Among the dead was a man who had made the Joint Prioritized Effects List to be killed or captured, one of the three top Taliban commanders in southern Ghazni. Another top commander, Naim Saboor, was also killed. "The cool thing about it was, we had zero friendly casualties and we didn't piss off any of the locals," said Joyce. In fact, as they left, villagers had lined up to cheer.

Two weeks later, several of Joyce's men were called into the battalion TAC, or command post, to give sworn statements. Concerned how the rules of engagement might be applied to the two forward observers he and his paratroopers had killed during the battle, the young lieutenant feared the worst. "I thought, well shit, I'm going to jail," he said. He was wrong. Based on accounts offered by his own men, First Lieutenant Shane Joyce was awarded the Bronze Star Medal with Valor Device for his actions on the battlefield that day—the day *before* combat operations were to officially begin.

That same day, April 6, Afghan soldiers came into Combat Outpost Muqor with information on a secret Taliban prison in a newly constructed *kalat* near the hamlet of Isa Kheyl. That night, Charlie

Company, 1-504, conducted a mission rehearsal, and in the morning, they assaulted the *kalat* with a company of Afghan soldiers stationed at Muqor with them. In spite of mortar attacks and small-arms fire, the combined force captured five Taliban insurgents and their commander and freed six prisoners who had been detained for up to two months. They also found weapons, switches for IEDs, and US military uniforms.

CHAPTER 4:
FOB ARIAN AND
MASSIVE IEDS

The best place to get the latest scuttlebutt was breakfast chow. One had to be careful of what was said because third-country nationals, Afghan soldiers and police, interpreters, and American contractors all ate there. Without doubt, there were ears that shouldn't hear. Breakfast chow was sparsely attended very early in the morning, when I preferred to eat. It was also when many of the busiest TOC staffers ate.

Around five one morning, I was taking advantage of the open bandwidth and vacant computer stations at the MWR, updating the brigade Facebook page with recent photos of soldiers, when the building began to tremble from outgoing 155mm howitzer rounds. I wanted to know what our artillerymen were shooting at, so I went to the chow hall. Sitting at a table were the deputy and sheriff of the good-ol'-boy network, brigade combat engineer Staff Sergeant Joel Watts and Cory Kroll, a retired sergeant major who was the brigade's safety officer (a civilian position). If something was dangerous and on a FOB, Cory knew about it and Watts was probably involved. I sat down with my tray.

"They were just registering their guns, Mac," said Cory.

Like most sergeants major, Kroll was a bottom-line guy, but as a civilian, a friendly one who was always there to give a guy a hand anytime, day or night. Plus, he was from Billings, Montana, just down the road from my town of Bozeman. He and Watts were discussing the feral dog problem at the FOB dump. Rabies was a real threat in Afghanistan, so the order went out to eliminate all the dogs and cats on the FOB. Watts, a man of the woods from Georgia, had already killed two dogs with his M4 carbine, using a water bottle as a silencer. Both dogs tested positive for rabies.

In other news, Kroll said another vehicle had been struck by an IED up north by FOB Arian. The recovery vehicle got stuck in the mud, and when they called the Quick Reaction Force, the QRF was hit by an IED. No major injuries.

"Them boys have to deal with some serious IEDs up there," Kroll said.

I remarked on how fortunate our brigade had been through so many IED strikes with no major injuries.

Cory shook his head, "You heard about the fellow up at Muqor? Now that fellow was lucky."

I hadn't. Charlie Company's Second Platoon had been working their way down Nawah Road to clear the village of Hasti. A Bravo Company platoon was conducting an unrelated patrol nearby when its mineroller (an MRAP that pushes a multi-wheeled attachment to trigger mines) became stuck in a drainage canal paralleling the road. On QRF that day, Charlie Company's Lieutenant Joyce came to the rescue with Third Platoon and a MaxxPro wrecker. The wrecker was twenty meters in front of Joyce's vehicle when it suddenly lurched into the air.

From the passenger seat of his own MaxxPro, Joyce watched the fifteen-ton vehicle ripped apart by a massive IED. In his periphery, the lieutenant caught movement. It was one of the MaxxPro's five-hundred-pound tires careening through the air three hundred meters across open ground. The entire front end of the vehicle was amputated in the powerful blast, and when Joyce opened its armored door, he expected to find human soup. Miraculously, the wrecker operators were dazed but okay. The armor and V-shaped hull had done their job.

Platoon sergeant Carl Felton pushed up from the rear to transfer the two blast survivors into his truck as Joyce ordered his paratroopers into action. After visually checking the ground around the truck before exiting, the paratroopers followed the unit's standard TTP, or tactics, techniques, and procedures, and dismounted a security element around the blast site to provide cover for casualty evacuation. Joyce and his RTO, Specialist Nicholas Springob, moved onto a head-high berm just off the south shoulder for a better view of the security situation. It was early spring, so the surrounding wheat fields were beds of dust. With two disabled vehicles, no cover, and only the IED-laced road for egress, the American position wasn't exactly robust. Springob and Joyce were checking security positions on the crest of the berm not far from the Bravo company commander when Springob stopped.

"Sir," he said, "there's some radio traffic for you." As Joyce reached for the handmike, Springob stepped forward onto a Russian-made PMN anti-personnel mine placed upside down on top of a seventy-pound plastic jug of HME buried in the rocks. (HME, or homemade explosives, are the explosive propellant used in most IEDs in Afghanistan. Insurgents smuggled basic chemicals into the country and then combined them in "HME factories" which were often little more than repurposed, out-of-the-way mudbrick compounds. HME is a catchall phrase for a variety of chemical compositions employed by insurgent bombmakers.)

Springob fell forward over a muffled explosion. Joyce thought somebody had accidently shot off a grenade round from an M320. But fate had smiled. The main charge had failed to detonate, and his RTO was only lightly wounded.

Not so lucky were two ANA soldiers who triggered a duplicate of Springob's mine later that night as the immobilized convoy waited for another wrecker to arrive. The IED was identically-spaced off the road but on the north side, as if the insurgents knew the soldiers' SOP.

Joyce was scanning the horizon with his heat-reading night-vision optics when a sheet of white blinded his view. The blast of the IED left only the torso of the Afghan soldier who stepped on it. The other's guts were spilling from his abdomen, and gray matter leaked from his skull. Joyce's medic tried to stabilize the severely injured Afghan, but he needed to be evacuated immediately. Unfortunately, the remaining ANA soldiers became hysterical and would not leave without finding the dead soldier's AK47. One waved a severed foot he'd found in Joyce's face while yelling in Dari. The only terp was farther down that daunting road with the Second Platoon. Eventually, Springob, the wounded ANA, and the wrecker crew were all evacuated to FOB Warrior.

EOD arrived in the dead of night to blow in place the main charge of Springob's mine. "The explosion shook our truck," said Joyce. "It was really eerie." If Springob's mine had detonated, Joyce and Springob would have been dead, along with four other paratroopers. The company commander would have been killed or severely wounded. After hitting five IEDs and finding a sixth, the patrol finally returned to COP Muqor early the next morning.

With few restrictions on where they traveled, our troops were getting outside the wire daily. On FOB Warrior, as the construction projects began piling up, I decided to take my leave. Like Watts, I had handyman skills from years of building, but he was the engineer, not me.

The official "main effort" of the brigade was up north at FOB Arian, where our troops were de-mining roads leading into the Qara Bagh District Center, clearing insurgent safe havens, and building a new district center from which the Qara Bagh subgovernor could operate safely. Most of those missions fell to 2nd Battalion, 504th Parachute Infantry Regiment, commanded by Lieutenant Colonel Praxiteles Vamvakias.

On Tax Day, April 15, Sergeant K and I packed up and caught one of the "blue bird" civilian helicopters that ran daily routes to many of the military FOBs in Afghanistan. In twenty minutes, we landed at FOB Arian. It was a Sunday, the day that insurgents launched their spring offensive across Afghanistan. In Kabul, militants kicked off an eighteen-hour attack on the US, German, British, and Iranian embassies. Military bases and government buildings in several provinces were hit by small-arms fire and suicide bombers. Though at least eight Afghan soldiers and four civilians were killed, Afghan and NATO forces crushed the attackers, killing all forty.

Arian was a dense, rectangular base that sat on the west side of Highway 1 across from a mostly-vacant collection of rundown *kalats*. The big white PTIDS aerostat hundreds of feet above Arian was its most prominent feature. Everything else was Hescoes, concrete, plywood, and canvas. Afghan soldiers of the 6th Kandak, 3rd Brigade, 203rd Corps, occupied the front third of the FOB nearest the highway. Between them and the American holdings was a large cooling yard where Afghan truckers waited to offload their rigs, most of which were garishly decorated, multi-axle "jingle trucks," so named for the jingling chains often hung from their bumpers. The American base began with a giant PTIDS pen of double-stacked Hescoes and several headquarters buildings, followed by rows of low-slung troop tents, motor pools, a supply yard, the artillery "gun line" and finally the HLZ. Spring rains began almost as soon as we stepped off the bird, turning the interior of the FOB into a quagmire of sucking mud and lagoons of standing runoff up to three feet deep. Hundreds of empty water bottles floated along their leeward margins like flocks of ducks.

The name "Arian" refers to a hardy people, the Ariani, who lived in the vicinity of Ghazni Province and much of central Asia in pre-Islamic times. They are unrelated to the Germanic people, as are the swastikas that have adorned houses in central Asia for the past forty centuries. The FOB was surrounded by grazing lands and low-yield agricultural crops, stepped and traversed by mud-brick walls and meandering villages. Several kilometers to the west at the foot of a tooth-shaped mountain was the village of Andar, where the Taliban operated a madrassa, or religious school, for boys. In the summer, FOB Arian was like a reverse zoo, with herds of Kuchi camels, sheep and goats roving the plains outside the Hesco basket and concertina-wire perimeter along with the predatory Taliban. Inside the troop tents, living space was cramped. Containerized showers worked some of the time, laundry service was an issue, the MWR was a tiny tent with underpowered bandwidth, and the adjacent "gym" was a tent with pieces of broken, infomercial-type equipment usually dominated by a cabal of scrawny Afghan interpreters. Many infantry platoons had made their own gym equipment out of whatever scrap materials they could find—boxes of MREs, sandbags, heavy chains and lumber. If all they had was pipe cleaners and feather dusters, American soldiers would find a way to get buff.

To get a sense of what was going on, I attended a security meeting with the FOB commander, Vamvakias, at the Security Force Assistance Team headquarters. He and several American officers were meeting with local Afghan police and army officers. The mayor of Qara Bagh—the first elected in twenty years—was also considering attending.

Vamvakias was a serious soldier who also enjoyed the human events of life, for really, what else was there? With graying hair well beyond his early forties and professorial bushy eyebrows, the lieutenant colonel's demeanor suggested a wisdom that probably worked to his advantage in Afghanistan, where age was still venerated.

Accompanying Vamvakias was his operations officer, Major Jason Condrey, a sandy-blond field grade who had deployed to Afghanistan for a year as part of the International Security Assistance Force planning cell, only to be reassigned to our brigade and sent right back to Afghanistan. "It's my fault we're here," said Condrey, who had been part of the team that had called for the clearing of Ghazni during the summer of 2012. "I just didn't know I'd be here too."

While we waited on the Afghans to arrive, I talked with Vamvakias' head interpreter, a handsome young Afghan and naturalized American citizen who went by the name of "Zack." Zack had been with the marines in Helmand Province in 2012 when 1st Battalion, 2nd Marines lost ninety-three troops to IEDs. It was a very difficult assignment, he said, with no showers for up to a month, daily patrols in eighteen inches of moon dust, and defecating in "wag bags." The sun was so intense that he burned his lips drinking from his water bladder. Zack saw his first dead bodies in Helmand, twelve truckers executed and set on fire by the Taliban. The smell of blood and sight of exposed, broken bones kept him awake for two days straight.

"But now is better," Zack said. This job was safer except for the IEDs. Zack was engaged to an Afghan woman who had lived in the United States for twelve years.

"Has she changed much?" I asked. Having been married over twenty years, I never lost interest in learning something new and useful about human nature, especially in male/female relationships.

"She talks nonstop now, and she will no longer get me tea," he replied, shrugging in a way that could have indicated dismay or dismissal.

The security meeting was postponed. Shortly after leaving the Qara Bagh District Center, the Afghans had found an IED blocking their path and engaged insurgents in a thirty-minute running firefight on their way back to the district center. That was a bad sign.

The following afternoon, the security meeting did happen. This time on the way to FOB Arian, the officials found three IEDs south of Qara Bagh on the infamous "D Loop," a business route shaped like an upside-down "D" that forked off of Highway 1 for about ten kilometers, passed through the busy district center market, and rejoined the highway to the north near Mushaki, where Burnside was killed.

It was a typical meeting with Afghan leaders—American coffee and Afghan tea, a poster of Karzai on the wall, and fake flowers in the corner. Around a plain conference table in a drab paneled room, the allies planned how they would wrest Qara Bagh from the Taliban.

The commander of the Afghan army's 6th Kandak was Colonel Mosafer, a middle-aged man with a leathery russet face and uniform of brown and green digital camouflage. He appeared to be Uzbeki. The colonel was dismissive of Taliban fighters in the area, but said they would become more daring as the trees leaved out and the land greened up. "Now with the Americans here, all of my soldiers are volunteering for missions," Mosafer said. "They are like, 'I, I, I.' In 2010 we operated seventeen checkpoints. All of them got hit. When the Polish came, it got better. Now you just arrived and it is even better." This all came through Zack the interpreter of course.

The police chief was a scrappy young Afghan in a slate blue uniform named Lieutenant Abdul Roulf. A native Pashtun, Roulf had narrow sunken eyes, erect ears, a hook nose, thick black hair with bangs, and a thin beard. He spoke with passionate animation and was quite friendly. The IEDs were bad, but worse a year ago, he said. With the arrival of the American paratroopers, the villagers were saying the enemy were scared and didn't know what to do. But the Taliban knew the rules of engagement. He saw at least forty of them every day in the bazaar, but because they were unarmed, he could do nothing. He knew who they were and where they lived. "We need night ops and foot patrols. Night ops can catch them with their explosives." Roulf wagged his fist regularly while talking. In spite of the political upheaval from night operations in Afghanistan, Afghan security forces everywhere were telling our planners to conduct more night operations, not fewer.

"Let me tell you this," Roulf continued. "The Taliban meet in the mosques in the mornings, and when they see the Apaches flying around, they dare not leave for fear of attack," he said. "The enemy can hit your MRAPs during the day because you are on the roads. We can do daylight raids with your choppers."

Roulf set out his bona-fides with information relating directly to the Burnside slaying. "I know a guy named Hamid who shot a Coalition Forces soldier recently. Satar, the leader of that cell, said he saw two Coalition Forces hit the ground. They used a Russian-made weapon. That's how much information I have." He had Vamvakias' attention. "I am ready for a combined operation, and I will be the first on the line," continued Roulf, shaking his fist. "I know where the Taliban commanders live, and I know where to ambush them. Give me a month to train with your forces." Roulf said that he was beefing up his force with trustworthy, college-aged men that he had known since childhood, and though Taliban were pressuring their parents to force them from the police, they weren't having it. Like our enlisted, they would return to college when the fighting was done, they told their parents.

"In the last ten years, there have been no foot patrols in Mushaki," Roulf said. "We must kill the Taliban commanders now, because someday the Coalition Forces will leave and the ANA commander will go back to Mazar-i-Sharif, but I have a house here."

As in Anbar, the police were key to rooting out the insurgency because they were part of the fabric of the community. They knew who belonged there and who didn't, but they were also more likely to have competing interests. Some of their best friends might be Taliban.

As the security meeting wrapped up, I learned that 2-504's Alpha Company was planning to clear Mushaki within a week or two. I knew many of the soldiers in Alpha, so I thought I might persuade the company commander to let me tag along on that mission.

It was tough. Sergeant K and I hadn't had any success getting on a patrol since we'd arrived at Arian. Nearly all were mounted, with every MRAP seat assigned to someone more essential to the mission. Of the battalion's four rifle companies, Alpha was manning the FOB towers and gate, Bravo was pushed out to COP Qara Bagh, a tiny outpost on Highway 1 a few klicks north (it was separate from the village of Qara Bagh by two kilometers of open country), and Delta was providing extra security for logistics convoys to and from Ghazni City. That left only Charlie Company, commanded by a tall, seemingly humorless Texan named Captain Robert "Trey" Gacke III. Gacke, who as a lieutenant had deployed to east Baghdad to fight Muqtada al-Sadr's Mahdi militia during the Iraq troop surge, wasn't about to give up a rifleman's seat for a cameraman.

Fortunately I had made a great many contacts over my years with the Devils, and eventually I was able to get Sergeant K on a patrol with Burnside's route-clearance platoon. I linked up with Sergeant First Class Scott Shepro, platoon sergeant of Second Platoon, Charlie Company, to tag along with them. At the time, his platoon was attached to Delta Company and designated "AT5," as in "Anti-tank Platoon Five." (Delta Company trained with special tank-killing weapons.) That put them effectively out of Gacke's reach. AT5 was providing extra security for the engineers as they swept Highway 1 north of Arian for IEDs.

Shepro was a methodical leader. He was a tall, slow-speaking, health-conscious runner from California who joined the army right after high school. Already he had served in Fallujah, Baghdad, and Kandahar. His last post was with 4th Brigade, 25th Infantry Division, out of Anchorage, Alaska, and since then, he liked to call Alaska home. Any day now, he and his wife Saskia were expecting the birth of a daughter, the couple's first child. (I felt bad that he would never smell the lilac skin of his newborn daughter's head and tiny gripping fingers, but even bringing it up seemed cruel.)

In the morning, the platoon's MRAPs were staged by 6 a.m. in a roux-like mud. As a fine drizzle fell, Shepro and the platoon's officer, Second Lieutenant Anthony Pappas of Milledgeville, Maryland, briefed the men. The engineers would roll out first and work north toward the turnaround point, Mushaki. AT5 would follow thirty minutes behind, stopping at a few villages and Afghan checkpoints to converse with the locals. According to the latest Intel, Taliban had warned the people of Mushaki to stay indoors that day because they were planning to attack

Coalition Forces. Unfazed, Shepro and Pappas ordered their paratroopers to mount up.

As truck commander of our rig, Shepro rode in the passenger seat. Driving the MRAP was Private First Class Thomas Almodovar, or "Almo." From Long Island, New York, Almo was the smallest and youngest of the bunch. Riding next to me in back was the platoon's combat medic, Specialist Ramiro Bojorquez, or "Doc." Doc was Hispanic and hailed from Arizona. Across from Doc, seated at the controls of the vehicle's top-mounted, remote machine gun was a lanky Indiana farm boy, Specialist Ryan Robinson, or "Rob." Since our truck was the last in a combined patrol of US and Afghan soldiers, Rob would watch the convoy's "six" in his monitor.

Before we pulled onto Highway 1 behind the Afghan soldiers in their little green unarmored Ford pickups, Shepro quizzed his men: How do they react to contact or a rollover? What if they hit a mine?

"There's a lot of fear involved with IEDs," Shepro explained to me later during a stop. "I try to take emotion out of it whenever possible. We train constantly, and we tell them our own stories. I was wounded in an IED attack about five years ago in Iraq. I tell my soldiers exactly what happened, exactly what I saw, exactly what I dealt with." In the four weeks since the platoon had been operating out of Arian, they had yet to encounter their first IED, though every roadside village had its own crater at one end or the other, or both.

Just past the first village, our truck skirted a ragged blast hole ripped in the pavement three weeks earlier. AT5 had been on QRF when the night insurgents tried to repack the same hole with more HME, homemade explosives. "We wanted to mortar them, but they were too close to the village," said Shepro. Instead, EOD was called in.

Now moving up the highway, Shepro worked to keep his paratroopers relaxed but vigilant. "Since there's not a huge tactical risk or big movement piece for our platoon, my focus is to ensure the guys are looking out the windows, pulling security with their eyes open for that unknown enemy that might be out there," he said. In the meantime, light banter kept the guys calm.

"Almo, after this deployment, you'll be qualified to drive a garbage truck," Shepro said over the intercom. The joke was a nod to the fact that their MaxxPro was built on a dump truck chassis. Almo laughed and replied that he'd rather be the guy on the back of the garbage truck.

Rob the gunner said he wanted to be a crane operator because they made upwards of $80 an hour. "That's as much as the Afghans are getting to fill sandbags all day," he said. Doc shot him the look that said, Did you really just use the Afghan day laborers as your base unit of measure?

"I want to discover oil," Almo said.

"I don't know," said Shepro, looking out the window at the muddy world. "Oil is dirty."

Traffic was heavy with jingle trucks, the commerce of an emerging nation. Every now and then, another bomb crater appeared in the asphalt, forcing traffic in both directions to slow and thread a narrow path around it. Each time, the pucker factor rose a few notches. "Making sure Highway 1 stays open is the lynchpin of this whole operation," Shepro said. "There's been a big deal made about it being the most dangerous route in the area, but with us running up and down it and the remote sensing capabilities we have, I don't see it being a huge risk. We drive up and down it every day, and there's tons of Afghan army and police along it. Now that we're here and setting the tone that we're not going to put up with that stuff, I think the threat is going to go down. That will play into the goals of the higher echelons of command when they talk about this being a 'clearing operation' [in Ghazni] leading to our withdrawal." He added prophetically, "But I think as soon as you move off the pavement, it's a whole nuther ballgame."

Just after 8 a.m., the engineers stopped to check out a blast hole to the north of a roadside bazaar. Our trucks were backed up on the highway inside the village. Shepro was telling Rob about a favorite herbal tea that the Aztecs once drank.

"Do you swallow the seeds?" asked Rob.

"Absolutely," Shepro replied. "Energy boost, incredibly high in omega 3s and fiber." He was watching a father and three grown sons pass on a tractor. Shepro tapped on the windshield with his gloved fingers. "I'll bet these farmers love the rain. You know, it's sort of a strange existence," Shepro said to nobody in particular. "Every day we leave this FOB, there are people out here who are trying to kill us." Just like that, he changed gears. "We're dismounting," he said. "LT wants to talk to the elders."

While the platoon sergeant and a dozen dismounts pulled security, Pappas arranged a quick meeting outside a mud-brick shop to speak with the white-bearded village elders about how best to keep the Taliban from planting bombs in the road. A boy brought out chai tea. The Afghan soldiers who were part of our patrol spread across the bazaar. Some were pulling security while others talked to locals or searched motorcycles and other vehicles for weapons and explosives. Two soldiers sat on a curb and shared an MRE, tossing the wrapper aside to be disposed of by the wind.

"We've all been amazed at the progress that the Afghans have shown since the last time most of us have been here," said Shepro. "We are pleasantly surprised, and we want to keep the momentum going in their growth as an organization, and for individual soldiers and policemen." The last bit was a very NCO thing to say, for it recognized that impacting the institution and the individual were not at all the same.

The goal was to move from creating an environment where the Afghans were seen as the good guys and bringing peace to their country to where they actually *were*, without help from Coalition Forces, he said. The two are not unconnected, as Joe knows. His life is a crawl, walk, run experience, repeated in endless waves of training and doing. This was no different. Welcome to crawl. Let the politicians and media types grind teeth over what is "real."

Farther up the road, the convoy halted again so that Pappas could meet with an ANA commander at a checkpoint manned by a ragtag roadside garrison. While we waited, Shepro barked into his handset,

"Hey, tell those ANA to stop and search all the motorcycles, and not just the saddlebags." Two weeks earlier, paratroopers had found a motorcycle frame packed with HME.

I joined Pappas inside the meager Hesco-walled ANA checkpoint. A dozen American and Afghan soldiers squeezed into a tiny, unadorned sleeping quarters with blankets arranged neatly on the floor around its open center. Across from a set of bunkbeds was a single set of marbled windows letting in diffused light. It was humbling to see how our "partners" lived, with no air conditioning or refrigeration, no mattresses, and only a one-burner stove for cooking meals. Possessions were minimal. They were within range in multiple directions of whatever malevolent device the Taliban chose to hurl at them.

In comparison, we lived large on the FOBs and COPs and seemed to be ponying up relatively little sacrifice. Pay-wise, we made more in a month than they did in a year. Yet it was their country, their freedom and liberty at stake. The threat of an Afghan-based Al Qaeda attack on the United States had long been neutralized. Our soldiers didn't have to be there.

The Afghans gave us chai with sugar cubes as we chitchatted. Their lieutenant, a broad-faced Hazara with rabbit-like front teeth and narrow eyes, said that he had twenty-two men. The Taliban attacked their bantam fortification from every direction in RPG hit-and-runs off motorcycles. "Most are from other countries," he said. "They cannot attack American Forces directly, only use IEDs."

These were interesting observations, considering we'd only been in-country a few weeks. Was the Taliban testing our reactions? Gathering for a fight? At that point, it was anybody's guess.

We compared war experiences. The Afghan lieutenant showed a scar on his arm from a rocket in Kunar Province. Staff Sergeant Andrew Williamson spoke of violent firefights in mountainous Nuristan. The Afghan lieutenant told Pappas that his son was a boxer and lived with his mom in Kabul.

"I have a soldier who dances and fights," Pappas replied. "Seriously, it's called *capoeira* or something like that, a Brazilian martial art."

"Yes, we have lots of guys like him," said the Afghan drily.

"I'm so sorry," Pappas said with a laugh. He asked if the Afghans played volleyball.

"Of course," said the Afghan LT.

"Do you think you can beat us?"

"Yes, you cannot shoot."

The soldiers all laughed. Shepro called in like a girlfriend calling a girlfriend to help end an awkward date. It was time to go.

Driving north again, we were closing in on Mushaki. With the rising tension in the truck, conversation got more risqué.

"Where's the neatest place you've had sex, Almo?"

Almo admitted that it was with his future wife a few hours before he proposed, when he lost his virginity.

"You just had sex and then saw the light?"

"I had a plan, sar'nt."

"Almo, I just don't know what to think of you anymore."

"Thief!" hollered Doc.

The drizzle turned to rain. "Red air," Shepro said into the intercom. Medevac helicopters would not fly with such a low ceiling, which increased the risk of any casualty dying on the battlefield. He listened to more radio chatter and then announced, "RCP is turning around before Mushaki."

"Yes!"

"Sweet."

"Awesome."

I wasn't sure if the relief was from our not going to Mushaki or the prospect of getting back in time for hot chow, or the double-win. Pappas came over the radio. He wanted to clear the upper end of the D Loop. You could have heard a pin drop in that truck.

Shepro cleared his voice and keyed the mic. "If something happens, they'll want to know why we were screwing around up there." *If something happens* and *screwing around* formed a couplet that any young lieutenant could understand. We turned around.

Passing some farm stock in a field, Shepro said, "Watching horses and cows get back up is one of the scariest things I've ever seen."

That night, I borrowed a satellite phone from the Air Force JTACs I was tenting with to call my wife, Barbara, back in Fayetteville, our "army" home two thousand miles from Montana. She had been worrying over news of a helicopter going down in Afghanistan, killing all four aboard. To make matters worse, the army community at Fort Bragg was hot with controversy because the wife of a soldier had just learned of her husband's death on Facebook (that soldier belonged to another brigade).

My wife was nonplussed. "In every picture you publish, I look for your hands, your boots, or even your reflection in the sunglasses of people," she said. It was sobering detail that made me realize just how difficult deployments really were for loved ones back home and how necessary and humane regular contact was. I took great satisfaction in publishing photos of our paratroopers online so their families could see them being soldiers, feel proud, and be sustained through the long nights and nagging fears of black sedans pulling into the drive. Photos of Shepro's men were published on the army email login page, the most coveted real estate for army photographers because the page is viewed millions of times a week.

My wife's comments also triggered a memory of a photo I had published of high-fiving a dirty-faced Iraqi farm boy. My left hand is in the photo, and my wedding ring is clearly visible. She was so excited to see that, she had told me. Not long after that, a fellow paratrooper lost his ring finger when his wedding band hung up in the door of the MRAP he fell out of. After that, we were told not to wear rings of any sort. In Afghanistan, I was glad not to wear mine because it reminded me too often of what I risked.

Late in the afternoon two days later I was returning to FOB Arian with the battalion commander. He and several staff officers had met with

Afghan military officials at the far northern end of Vamvakias' battlespace, and I had joined him to take pictures. At the FOB entrance, we passed another group of belching diesel gun trucks heading out. It was the Alpha Company QRF led by First Lieutenant Jonathan Walsh. Nearly thirty, Walsh was an older lieutenant. After college, he had spent several years in the finance world, settling down in Kennesaw, Georgia, with his wife Debbra and son Austin before joining the army. Walsh was a big man, an accomplished bodybuilder, and according to his fellow lieutenants, a colorful yet loyal friend. I was scheduled to go on patrol with him the following morning. Older than most platoon leaders, he was well-liked by his NCOs for his willingness to leverage their combat experience.

Twenty-two-year-old Private First Class Michael Metcalf was driving for Walsh. "Cowboy Mike" of Boynton Beach, Florida, was a bull rider who loved driving the big army vehicles. He was covered in tattoos, many of which he had inked himself. Passionate and loud, like most "eleven bravos" (the MOS of infantrymen), he enlisted to find adventure. When the call came in that AT5 had been hit by an IED, Metcalf had raced through ankle-deep mud to his MRAP while playing the air guitar. Help was on the way.

Over the intercom, I heard bits and pieces of a conversation that I didn't like. AT5. Off the hardball. IED. Shepro's platoon had traveled off the main highway for the first time, to meet with some village elders. One of his trucks had just been hit by a massive IED. The date was April 22, 2012.

CHAPTER 5:
MORE IEDS

Shepro and Pappas' AT5 had left the FOB just after the sun climbed over the mountains to the east on a bluebird day. They had the FET along and Delta Company's Vietnamese-born First Sergeant Thinh Huynh (pronounced "When"), a stocky, powerful man who, as a child, escaped from Vietnam in a small fishing vessel with relatives and was afloat for days in the South China Sea before being rescued. The goal was to meet with the elders of three villages a half-dozen kilometers to the northeast of Arian during impromptu visits.

As the convoy traveled east off the highway, each successive village was less hospitable than the last. The people who did offer information said that none of the villages in the area had *imams*, *mullahs*, or elders, because when they did, the Taliban would kill them.

At Akhtar Kheyl, Pappas was invited into the village, but locals said their mullah was at the mosque praying. Shepro thought it odd because it wasn't prayer time. The Taliban seemed to have a tight grip on the village. After a futile hour in Akhtar Kheyl, the patrol prepared to head east through the grape-growing country toward the village of

Bagi Kheyl. Oddly, the lead ANA vehicle moved back behind Pappas' MaxxPro, now the second vehicle in the order of march. The first vic, piloted by Staff Sergeant Brian Boyt, was one of the relatively light-weight MATVs with a mineroller attached.

In retrospect, Shepro is certain that the Taliban knew exactly which vehicle his lieutenant was riding in when the patrol rolled north out of Akhtar Kheyl. Not only were the ANA likely aware of what lay immediately ahead, but Boyt's MATV would have been much easier to destroy than Pappas' MaxxPro. Except for one, every vehicle that the Taliban would hit over the next seventy-two hours was an officer's vehicle. (After months of partnered patrols, Shepro and Pappas were certain some ANA were colluding with the Taliban, and even shooting at them unless the Afghan company commander was present.)

The sun-hardened mud road was wide open to Bagi Kheyl, and Boyt, being a country boy, ordered his driver to hit the rainwater puddles for maximum splash. Near the village of Ghanday, the mudbrick walls of farm fields closed in on the roadway and then, a crushing explosion. Shepro saw tires flying from a cloud of black smoke.

"I was in the second to last vic, but from my experiences in Iraq, I'd seen a couple of trucks blown up," he recalled. "I called 'IED, IED,' over the net." Shepro jumped out of his truck with Doc Johnson as First Sergeant Huynh ran past and yelled for Shepro to get ahold of battalion while he managed the rescue.

The IED was made of several hundred pounds of HME, buried in the center of the road. The initiator had triggered it a little early, blowing off the front end of the MRAP and sending the two front tires flying hundreds of meters in either direction. Sergeant Walter Feller, the driver, was bleeding and appeared to have a busted nose. Pappas was bleeding from his wrist and he had his bell rung. The turret gunner, Specialist Timothy Petersen, was knocked unconscious. He'd broken the buttstock of his brand new M240L—the medium machine gun mounted in his turret—with his face and had a cut above one eyebrow. He also had a severely sprained ankle. It was a lucky day for the passengers, including FET officer, First Lieutenant Nalise Gaither of Stephenville, Texas.

Gaither had joined the army because she loved what it stood for. Upon graduating from Tarleton State University, she was commissioned as a quartermaster officer and was serving as the executive officer of a sustainment company when she heard about the need for FET officers. "I knew it was a definite possibility to encounter an IED or an attack but never thought it would happen on my first time outside the wire," she said later.

She remembers that Pappas and Sergeant Feller had noticed there were sheep in the field but no sheep herder, and just as she was about to correct them that the word was "shepherd," the IED exploded. "There was dust and Easter M&Ms flying all over the place," she recalls. Everyone appeared to be okay except Petersen, who was crumpled inside the gunner's turret. Gaither used her FET scarf to stanch Petersen's facial wounds, and engaged him in conversation to keep him awake while he was being treated.

Given the destruction to the MaxxPro, Shepro knew there would be no self-recovery. He tried to radio battalion headquarters, but he could raise no FM comms. As Huynh and other soldiers searched for secondary IEDs, rifle rounds began snapping over the heads of the soldiers standing at the front of the column. ANA soldiers ran to the front to return fire with their AK47s and PKM machine guns pitched wildly into the air.

Shepro worried about Petersen's head injury going downhill in a hurry. His men backboarded the injured paratrooper and carried him back to Shepro's truck since it was already configured to carry casualties. Still without comms, Shepro used the Blue Force Tracker (a GPS satellite-based system that displays the positions of all US forces) to text in a medevac request. The response from the 82nd Combat Aviation Brigade in Sharana was that the air was red. Clouds had moved in since the morning, but as a civilian pilot, Shepro knew the ceiling was nowhere near the three hundred feet Sharana was claiming, which infuriated him. Finally after some time, two Black Hawks circled and settled into a makeshift HLZ.

Shepro insisted that his LT also climb aboard. Pappas seemed woozy, and getting knocked unconscious was an indicator of traumatic brain injury, or TBI. Shepro knew it was going to be a while before they got the damaged MRAP out of there. After some arguing, the lieutenant begrudgingly obeyed his platoon sergeant.

It was almost 5 p.m. at that point, and the Alpha Company QRF was on its way. As several paratroopers began conducting a preliminary post-blast analysis, a farmer opened an irrigation ditch that flooded the blast crater and prevented further inspection. Right after that, Huynh found another command-wire. It seemed as though the convoy was surrounded by Taliban sympathizers.

"We were in a comms hole, and I still couldn't talk to battalion," Shepro said. Over the duration of their predicament, he would send and receive nearly 450 text messages over the BFT. As my own convoy passed the Alpha Company QRF at the Arian gate, Sergeant K was with 2-504's forward support company, Fox, at COP Qara Bagh, which included the battalion's mechanics and vehicle recovery assets. He overheard Shepro calling Fox Company for a lowboy flatbed and a wrecker.

Walsh's QRF drove north on Highway 1 a short way, then veered east on a dirt road to link up with Shepro's platoon. At 5:16 p.m., as it passed through a narrow gap between high mudbrick walls, Walsh's MRAP was rocked by an IED that was embedded in the wall. Walsh and Metcalf were blown out of the MRAP, and Walsh was killed instantly. Metcalf was airlifted to FOB Sharana, where he died of massive spinal injuries on the operating table.

Above Arian, evening clouds were lit from below by a low-slung sun as Apache gunships raced through light showers to give Shepro's platoon top cover. A Cold War B1-B bomber made an eerie low-pass, like a great white shark suddenly there and suddenly not. Alpha Company's First Sergeant, William Anger, a balding, wiry soldier's soldier and perhaps the oldest NCO in brigade, gathered his remaining paratroopers together outside the company command post. At that time, Metcalf was still clinging to life. K and I, together again, listened to the crusty old paratrooper brief his men.

"Sometimes part of being a soldier is dying," said Anger. "Lieutenant Walsh died the right way, the best way. You don't want to die like a fucking pussy. Lieutenant Walsh didn't die like a pussy." Anger was no warrior-poet, but his words seemed to strike a chord in the hearts of Alpha Company paratroopers.

Walsh was a soldier. He died soldiering.

Life for the living would not be simple, but his death was that simple. Anger believed what he said, but more to the point, he knew that he could not coddle the fear of death so early in this deployment. Nearing retirement years later, he said of that day, "The memories of those men I knew and loved hurt more as I get older and as I also prepare to leave Big Army. I have never served in a finer organization than the '04, and it is the soldiers that serve so selflessly that make all the pain and misery worthwhile in the end. I only wish that I could have taken the place of any one of the soldiers that have given their all." An old soldier, especially one with a family of his own, does not make that claim lightly.

In the battalion TOC, all eyes were on the infrared PTIDS video feed, including mine. It was dark. Four armed insurgents were spotted at a *kalat* a few kilometers from Shepro's stranded platoon. At least one had an RPG, and another appeared to have a night vision device. The Apache gunships had closed in, and the lead pilot was asking permission to shoot.

As the ground commander, it was Vamvakias' call. Over the radio, he asked the pilot if he could fire without damaging what appeared to be an isolated wall of a nearby *kalat*. This was the battalion's first use of AWT, or air weapons team, and he was being extra cautious about damaging a civilian structure because his soldiers were not in immediate harm's way. Somebody whispered "it's fucking mud," but Vamvakias was going to do this on his own terms.

"I remember very clearly the soldier saying [that], and that irritated me because in my mind, he didn't see the bigger picture," said Vamvakias years after the incident. "But I didn't let it influence my decisions . . . I've seen people make poor decisions in the heat of the moment and the influence of group think in a TOC, and it usually doesn't end well." Beyond a Taliban propaganda win, if private property or an innocent person were hit, the rules of engagement were stringent and Vamvakias did not want to bring unnecessary scrutiny that might inhibit future engagements. "Everyone wants you to kill bad guys and whoever is seen as a bad guy, but until you are the one responsible for the decision, you don't really understand the long term impacts," he said.

When the lieutenant colonel was convinced there would be no collateral damage, he gave the go-ahead. One of the insurgents, shouldering an RPG, was standing alone in the open. He was an easy target. Around that horseshoe of desks in the TOC, I think we were all holding our breaths as we were about to witness a man shredded by cannon fire. Just as the Apache pilot announced that he was firing, the massive white tail of the PTIDS aerostat lazily swung in front of the video feed. When it passed, there were only chunks of body on the ground. The pilot reported that thirty rounds of 30mm machine gun fire hit the mud, ten hit the insurgent, and two hit a nearby flatbed trailer. When the gunship landed to refuel, Major Condrey went out to the HLZ to personally review the gun tape just to be sure that was all the Apache had hit.

Over the next thirty minutes, another insurgent was killed and two others were wounded. The following day, a patrol picked up the two wounded and found an HME lab and more weapons, but tellingly, only women in the nearby compounds. "Luckily, it worked out and it was a Taliban leader they killed," said Vamvakias. The patrol also recovered an M16 that belonged to an Afghan soldier killed before our arrival, and the NODs, which were traced to another American unit on an earlier deployment.

In the battalion human resources department, personnel specialists organized, cataloged, and packed the belongings of Walsh and Metcalf. Risqué items posed the obvious dilemma, but in the end, they were artifacts of lives that the cataloging soldiers were not there to judge. The next hands on them would be family.

Twelve hours later, AT5 was still stranded. It was morning, and "Rock," the Afghan interpreter, was trying to engage the few farmers who would venture out to their fields for even short durations. A grandfather with a limp said that, even if he had information on the roadside bomb, he would not share it because the Taliban would come at night and kill him. The Taliban had already shot him in the leg. "I realized then that all of the people who might stand up to the Taliban were already dead or gone," Shepro recounted. "For the rest of our time that we were in Afghanistan, we never got anything useful out of the people in that AO. All our Intel was signal Intel, or from the blimp."

The ANA did as the ANA always do. They subsumed into the fabric of the village and soon came back with fresh rounds of footbread and hot tea. A child began talking to the Afghan soldiers at the head of the convoy and told them that the Taliban were going to kill them all if they were not gone by the next day.

In the afternoon, a Delta Company patrol from Arian approaching via a northerly route was only three hundred meters from the disabled convoy when it hit another IED. The bomb detonated underneath the rear axle of Lieutenant Steven Blum's MRAP and flipped it completely over onto its roof of antennas and gunner's turret, pinning the gunner, Specialist Justin Lansford, underneath. The blast crushed Lansford's right ankle, broke both femurs, ruptured his spleen, collapsed both lungs, fractured his nose, and all but amputated his left leg.

When the dust settled, Lansford saw his left foot next to his face. "Well, this is shitty," he thought. "That's not a place where my foot should be under any circumstance." Lansford's immediate concern, however, was for his best friend and squad leader, Sergeant Anthony Guadagnini. Guad had been dismounted, and Lansford feared that he'd been hit by the explosion. "Guad!" Lansford yelled. "Guad!"

First Sergeant Huynh, now with his soldiers of D Co., dug his way under the roof of the MRAP, and in Vietnamese-accented broken English, yelled, "Lansford, shut up! Guad okay, you not." Huynh reached to hold the gunner's hand to comfort him. "Lansford, what you need?"

"I need a cigarette, first sergeant."

The engine of the MRAP was on fire.

"No, you can't have that, Lansford. What else you need?"

"Doc" Jace Dennison, the medic, applied tourniquets to both of Lansford's legs to stop the arterial bleeding. He patched a nasty gash on Lansford's head. A few rounds cooked off from the engine fire, causing the soldiers who had crawled under the overturned hood of the MRAP to jump.

The convoy's recovery vehicles were themselves bogged in the mud, and there was no way Lansford was going to be freed without them. With both lungs collapsed, he was having trouble breathing. He was spitting up blood. "Everyone who spits up blood in the movies dies," he thought. "I must be dying." Doc Dennison struggled to keep the gunner conscious. He could see Lansford had been peppered with shrapnel from the blast, and he continued to lose blood.

After fifteen agonizing minutes, Sergeant James Hayes and three other mechanics finally arrived with a wrecker and lifted the MRAP high enough for Lansford to be extricated. In ten minutes, the rasping, battered paratrooper was aboard a medevac helicopter bound for the emergency field hospital on FOB Warrior. Nobody who saw Lansford's pale, mangled body expected to see him alive again. (Delta Company would themselves spend the night mired in a muddy field.)

Back at battalion, Intel came that insurgents were planning to bring to bear a Soviet heavy machine gun called a Dushka on Shepro's immobilized patrol. Firing a 12.7×108mm cartridge, the Dushka is roughly equivalent to the US M2 .50-caliber machine gun. The weapon posed a grave danger.

Shepro and Huynh decided to move all but the stricken MRAP to higher ground northeast of Ghanday where they had much better vantage of the surrounding area. They stripped the wreck and arranged the others in a loose perimeter on a hillside, which only by light of the next morning did they realize was a graveyard.

On FOB Arian, plans were laid to airlift two Charlie Company platoons to their rescue, but roving thunderstorms kept the big Chinooks grounded. (Later, one was able to resupply AT5 with food and water.) Vamvakias ordered Captain Gacke's Charlie Company to walk in on foot. Just before dark the second evening, a hundred paratroopers marched out the front gate into a light rain. Flash floods that night destroyed over eight hundred homes across Afghanistan, killing sixteen civilians. FOB Warrior flooded, shutting down the DFAC and most of the base functions for several days. Heavy spring snows draped the high peaks to the west of Arian, creating stunning vistas against emergent greens of leaving poplars and crops of wheat.

Through the night, Gacke's troops slogged through the supersaturated soil, hampered by the ANA who had insisted on bringing a few light pickups and a Humvee with extra supplies and firepower. "Between the mud and the mazelike topography of intersecting walls, roads, and ditches, it was a nightmare," he said later. In the dead of night under a light rain and only halfway to their objective, Gacke sent his First Platoon led by First Lieutenant Josh Hughes on ahead. Unfortunately, a resupply helicopter mistook Hughes' platoon for Shepro's and dropped off several bodybags of food and water that First Platoon had to then drag all the way to Shepro. As the sky began to lighten in the east, Gacke's main element arrived just after First Platoon and set up additional security around Shepro's position.

That same night, another convoy had pushed up from our cavalry squadron to the south at COP Ab Band. At 3 a.m., they hit two IEDs.

The first was a pressure-plate mine that blew the mine roller off the lead vehicle. The second was detonated by a command wire that led over a thousand meters to a centralized lair where other wires terminated and where the initiator had apparently operated from. There were no serious injuries in either explosion. That brought the total to eleven IEDs with five detonations in three days.

Perhaps because of Charlie Company's arrival, in the morning the Dushka attack failed to materialize. Word came from battalion that yet another recovery element was moving to Shepro's position, and before long, route-clearance engineers with Sergeant First Class Butler's platoon—Burnside's guys—climbed up the hillside. They had walked the entire distance, leading recovery vehicles. "I was extremely thankful," Shepro said. Incredulously, Butler's engineers found one more IED—right where Huynh's truck had been parked.

It wasn't until midnight that night that AT5 and the rest of 2-504 were safely back on FOB Arian. The cost: eight recovery efforts, twelve wounded, and two killed in action. Doc Dennison called up the aid station at Warrior to check on Lansford. From the medevac, he had gone into immediate surgery and required six units of blood. The physician assistant at Warrior gave him a 50/50 chance of making it before putting him on the bird for Bagram and eventually Landstuhl, Germany.

The following evening while photographing artillerymen stacking sandbags against alpenglow washing over the snowy peaks, I ran into a friend, Sergeant Vincent Gonzalez, a truck driver. He was one of those soldiers who seemed to be everywhere at once, always involved with whatever critical task was going on. His unit, the 307th Brigade Support Battalion, had recovered Walsh's vehicle, and he described in detail the damaged caused by the IED. Walsh had been ejected so forcefully that one of his legs had been flayed to the bone from ankle to hip. I knew that his family had requested the details of how their son had died. I tried to imagine myself in their shoes—knowing or unknowing the physical trauma of their son's demise—in order to give some kind of weight to that knowledge. It was their right to know, and as a parent myself, I could understand wanting to scrape together every last detail of a life so quickly and unexpectedly gone.

War is a fickle god of cold blessings. Walsh, who brought his first child into the world just before deploying, died trying to help Shepro, whose wife was expecting their first child any day. Walsh had joined the army because he wanted his life to make a difference. His family had served in every war since the Civil War.

The bereaved parents that I would speak with after the deployment often wanted to know what the objective was for the mission their son died on. "What has the army traded for my son's life?" Yet war rarely affords a fair value, or even any value, to the individual life. Soldiers who have tasted the brine of combat understand this, which is why they get so angry when someone disrespects the flag. *This country* is the value, what we value is the value, and often, that's as specific as one can get. First Sergeant Anger was right. Walsh died a warrior's death. So had Metcalf.

By April 26, Alpha Company was making preparations for a memorial ceremony set against snowcapped Afghan peaks. I tried to call home, but the FOB was on River City because three Special Forces soldiers, a Navy EOD technician, and his dog were killed in Nawah District that day, most likely by an IED.

For Alpha Company, the memorial was a chance for some kind of closure before they left on a seventy-two-hour mission north of Mushaki, during which contact with the enemy was expected. Colonel Stock flew in from FOB Warrior, an army general arrived from Bagram, and hundreds of paratroopers were able to pay their respects following a brief ceremony, a twenty-one-gun salute and a bugler playing "Taps." Toward the end, a serendipitous rainbow appeared through a faraway rainsquall, creating what soldiers call "a significant emotional event" for many in attendance.

Before leaving on the mission with A Co, I posted dozens of memorial pictures on the brigade Facebook page for the benefit of families back in the States. By the time I arrived at the Alpha CP, the squad leaders—guys I had known for years—were livid. They calmed down after I explained the official process of DOD next-of-kin notification, the 82nd Airborne Division's policy of holding downrange memorials within a week so that soldiers can find closure, and the commander's intent to let families back home share in that closure via a Facebook photo album.

The staff sergeants—all squad leaders—were finding that some of the younger army wives were wallowing in the grief depicted in the memorial photos as a means to draw sympathy from friends and family, and that wasn't helping their soldiers in Afghanistan move forward. With a mission in the morning, they had to move forward, time now. Welcome to war in the era of social media.

On the other hand, the NCOs conceded that sharing the photos on Facebook was the right thing to do to honor the sacrifices of Walsh and Metcalf and their families.

For me, trying to occupy the headspace of soldier at war and civilian at home was at times challenging, especially since I had to imagine the latter. Later in the deployment, I posted a photo of a medevac helicopter picking up two of our wounded soldiers. I was thinking that the families of the helicopter crew might like to see how their soldiers were saving lives. What I would describe as a "righteous shitstorm" blew up immediately, and the photo was removed. Via Facebook, I received this message from the wife of one of the wounded soldiers:

"You have to have this weird sense of denial to be a soldier's wife . . . and suddenly that was ripped right out from under me. I no longer have that denial that has gotten me through three deployments and that's ok because I still have my husband but at the moment I was mad. I have this sense of ownership over my husband and what happens to him, like it's nobody else's business. Which is just weird and I don't even know how to explain it."

I thought she explained it quite well, and I was shocked that I'd become so estranged from the sensibilities of those on the homefront.

I immediately thought of Mike, the terp in Iraq who had sent graphic photos of combat to his sister in Michigan, and only later, realized the inappropriateness of what he had done. And now I had done it too, but as the public interface of our brigade combat team. I wasn't necessarily bothered by the fact that I was becoming desensitized to the violence—that actually struck me as a useful adaptation to the battlefield—only that it was becoming challenging to see the war as our families were seeing it whenever my journalism job required it. The instantaneousness of social media made it a useful but dangerous tool.

I don't think that was why the NCOs of Alpha Company seated me in a so-called bomb magnet for the three-day mission. The MATV, a scaled-down MRAP that was less tippy and more maneuverable offroad than the larger MaxxPro, had a reputation for being nearly worthless against large IEDs. There were a limited number of seats on the convoy and four other soldiers riding in the tightly packed vehicle with me, I reminded myself. It was a purely selfish thought. My life was worth no more than their lives. Their families would miss them as much as mine would miss me. The fact that I could even wonder about it to myself is why infantrymen distain POGs.

The photography that I brought back from the seventy-two-hour mission was rich with advancing lines of paratroopers beneath ragged clouds and dramatic peaks, fuelers filling gun trucks in the indigo nocturne by red light, sweeps of seemingly desolate landscapes punctuated by like-colored, busy little villages, riflemen patrolling past the totem flags marking Soviet-era mass graves, and Afghan kids running around at twilight with chem-lights given them by American paratroopers. As with most early missions, the operation also provided plenty of frustration and learning, in that order.

By the end of the first day, Captain Tyler Vest's Alpha Company had cleared the day's target village and the next day's, so that after forty-eight hours, the company had met every objective except finding Taliban. ISR (aerial surveillance) showed "squirters," insurgents fleeing on motorcycle, every time our paratroopers entered a village, and at night, the Taliban left so-called night letters warning villagers against cooperating with the Afghan government or the Americans.

Because it was a multi-day mission, there was some sleep involved. Let me say a word or two about "camping" with the infantry. The infantry does not camp. When an infantryman must rest, he simply gets as horizontal as possible wherever he happens to be. That's it. There are no campfires or marshmallows, no hot cocoa or burning weenies, no tents or even sleeping bags. Sleeping bags are for POGs. An infantryman might bring his "woobie" or poncho liner along. Outside the wire, when they do sleep, infantrymen sleep in their body armor and helmet, with weapon at hand. Picture a turtle on its back. Like it's going to die there. That's how it looks and feels. That's how infantrymen sleep. Nights got down in the 30s, so I was glad to cram into my seat in the MRAP for a few hours each night and nod off.

On the final day of the operation, Captain Vest wanted to return to the village we had searched the first day, but prevent squirters from escaping by establishing blocking positions at the village exits before first light. Vest's Third Platoon departed camp at 3 a.m., walking south just off the shoulder of Highway 1. Captain Vest was about to lead his Second Platoon on a two-klick hike to the north side of the village when his radio operator stopped him. A Polish drone had just discovered a large group of armed enemy moving south from our position. Vest was sure it was his own paratroopers, but he had lost communication with them. The line-of-sight radios were having difficulty in the hilly terrain. By the time Third Platoon was recalled and sent out again, dawn had broken. The mission went off anyway, but lacked surprise. The company was back at FOB Arian by lunch chow.

During our three-day mission, a route clearance team with the 54th Engineers out of Germany was clearing the D Loop when they struck an IED. One soldier lost both feet, and five others were injured.

Later the same day pulling gate guard on FOB Warrior, Specialists

Corey Deer and Michael Wallace had just been briefed by their first sergeant to be on the lookout for a white station wagon with a yellow stripe that insurgents had rigged as a car bomb, and that a pastor in Florida was telling his church members to burn Qurans so there might be some blowback. "Up in the tower, we saw a flash of light in the distance from Muqor," Deer said, "then two medevac birds flew out. They called all medical personal to [the medical tent], then they started to call for blood-type donors. The medevac birds were back in no time, then we saw multiple airplanes hovering over Muqor, fast movers. It looked like a true war zone."

At COP Muqor, 1-504 had just begun to maneuver for a large operation when one of its gun trucks hit a massive IED placed in a culvert beneath Highway 1. Though the truck had been traveling at least fifty miles per hour, the blast blew it end over end, ejecting gunner Private First Class Christian Sannicolas of Anaheim, California, before skidding to a stop on its roof. Sannicolas, who had been thrown from his harness, was killed on impact.

A few days later, I visited the boneyard of bombed-out MRAPs on a back lot on FOB Arian. For morale's sake they were kept out of the view, and for security's sake, away from nosy local nationals who worked on the FOB, but they had to go somewhere. Looking at the crushed and twisted armor, broken axles, and cracked plate glass, it was hard to believe that the kinetic force needed to generate that degree of destruction had thus far only resulted in three deaths. One MRAP was opened like a tuna can, its back end ripped off.

Yet the HME-based mines in Afghanistan were not like the EFPs our troops had faced in Iraq. One of Captain Gacke's radio operators, Specialist Timothy Rodgers, related how awful those molten copper bombs had been. On a deployment near Baghdad's Sadr City in 2008–09, Rodgers saw a corporal in his MRAP get cut in half by an EFP on the corporal's first time out as truck commander. A major in the back couldn't cock his M9 pistol because there was so much blood and guts in it. The gunner's kneecaps had been sheared off. Rodgers had vomited uncontrollably all over the road, he said.

For the two paratroopers we had lost to IEDs, how many had walked away from those twisted hulks of steel? It seemed that, for the most part, the MRAPs were doing what they were designed to do. The IEDs kept coming. On May 2, a Charlie Company patrol struck a pressure-plate IED on the D Loop that destroyed the mine roller on the lead vehicle. The QRF came to their aid and hit another. There were no major injuries in either case.

On the same day, President Obama made a surprise, six-hour visit to Bagram Airfield. Timed politically to coincide with the first anniversary of Osama bin Laden's dispatch by Navy SEALs, Obama used the anniversary to sign a new strategic agreement with Afghan President Karzai intended to guide relationships after the planned 2014 general troop withdrawal. Just hours after Obama left, the Taliban set off explosions in Kabul, killing six civilians and one security guard.

The very next day, artillerymen and mortarmen on Arian fired six rounds at insurgents spotted burying another IED on the D Loop. Cheers went up in the battalion TOC as the building shook with the concussions of outgoing rounds. It was very satisfying to think that we might finally be dealing some payback for those terrible mines.

The feeling didn't last long. On May 7 at far-flung Combat Outpost Giro operated by our cavalry squadron's Charlie Troop, an MRAP rolled over a pressure plate attached to a large plastic drum of HME, slaying three paratroopers inside and touching off an eight-hour firefight. Killed were Sergeant Jacob Schwallie, Specialist Chase Marta and Private First Class Dustin Gross. The explosion was so powerful that it took searchers over an hour to find one of the MRAP's giant two-hundred-pound tires.

CHAPTER 6:
THE POLICE CHIEF'S
AIR ASSAULTS

In early May, an article in the *Washington Post* reported 1,828 US service members killed in Afghanistan since 2001, with 1,520 of those due to hostile action. The Devil Brigade was losing on average of one a week for the first seven weeks of its tour. We had nineteen weeks to go.

There were many close calls. Warrior and Muqor were receiving regular indirect fire, or IDF, from rockets, mortars, and recoilless rifles. Warrior was so large that the chances of any individual being hit were low, but many troops were still injured. Not two minutes after a company commander stepped out of his office one morning to shave, a mortar crashed through the roof and blew up his desk. Our former company first sergeant, David Robertson, was hit in the foot by rocket shrapnel and evacuated to the States. Another soldier received a serious head injury from rocket shrapnel.

On FOB Arian, the line companies of 2-504 began clearing Taliban safe-havens via helicopter air assault as suggested by the Qara Bagh police chief. Captain Gacke's Charlie Company was first. After midnight on May 6, his infantrymen boarded pairs of throbbing, twin-bladed CH47 Chinooks in two flights. I rode in on the second wave to cover the two-day mission. The target was Ghat Kala, a scenic agrarian hamlet built on the slope of an undulating rocky ridge that ended to the east with a promontory that dropped precipitously into the town of Andar. Andar seemed to be the source of much of the IDF targeting Arian. With caves in the cliffs above the village, plenty of high ground around the landing zones, and a building already identified as an HME factory, enemy engagement seemed likely.

Not since my first airborne jump had I felt so much adrenalin lighting the walls of my arteries as when I boarded that Chinook at 3 a.m. I kept thinking how the peers of these young paratroopers were back home agonizing over college and job applications, acquiring the newest smart phones, and how amidst the malls, games, vacations, and good times at bars to best express this generation's social-media battle cry, *YOLO!* "You only live once" was more burden to the twenty-year-old fire team leaders, soon to charge down the tail ramps of blacked-out Chinooks, leading privates and specialists who just learned to drive a few years earlier. Together they would be dropping into a moonless hive of who knew what, brandishing weapons that could as easily kill Americans and innocent civilians as Taliban. Even with night-vision devices, there might be little time to discern who was who.

While a sergeant is the lowest-ranking NCO (not counting corporal), with this kind of responsibility, there is no such thing as "just a sergeant." One of Gacke's team leaders, Sergeant Steve Brabner, detailed some of his thoughts on air assaults before the tailgate dropped:

"Have I done everything possible to ensure my men know what to do when something happens, something being anything? The answer is almost always no. It takes you back to times where we would be sitting around at JRTC and everyone is tired, but instead of squeezing in some last minute training, you rack out. Or wasting time at the Company instead of [passing to] your soldiers knowledge gained through prior experiences. That leaves a constant worry lingering in your thoughts. I also worried about ensuring my team members were properly equipped to self sustain during operations—ammunition, water, medical aide, MREs, extra batteries. Do they have enough to last through multiple engagements and then some? Prepping for an operation is probably the most stressful time because you always have a lower [ranked] enlisted who tries to get away with packing light, and if I do not constantly check, then it is I who have failed him once we leave the wire. During infil, the thought of hitting an IED is constant. Are we in a vulnerable position for an ambush? Are all the gunners maintaining their assigned sectors of fire? Are all the [radio] jammers operating properly? Who checked all of these systems? Do they know their job? . . . Every person in the helicopter has to trust someone somewhere along the line. All we can do is worry about our piece."

Once airborne, with my camera on a small tripod, I took a slow-exposure shot down the hold of our Chinook—Afghan, American, Afghan, American and so on—all bathed in a thin green light, barrels down, grimacing. It was a photo of soldiers ready to enter battle that, since then, has been published over and over.

We were airborne less than five minutes when the Chinook flared and rocked softly to the ground. In the hold, it was as if a zipper were opening, soldiers picking up, hunching against the thwop-thwop of rotors indifferent to what they hit, scuffling down the tail ramp into a murk of pixilated green sensation. Even the high-tech NODs attached to our helmets required some ambient light to operate, and on that night, there was scant little. A thirty-second exposure shot off a tripod with the ISO jacked up registered stars in my camera but only muddy forms below, blurred against a barren landscape. At least it wasn't raining.

There was no automatic weapons fire, no ring of protective IEDs around the village, nothing at all in the mountainside caverns above Ghat Kala. As we moved into the village awash in the morning golden hour, the people—meaning men of various ages and children—were mostly friendly, the children especially so. No, no Taliban, said the adults, but the children said yes.

The "HME factory," a single mud-brick dwelling set apart from the village against the base of the ridge, contained no HME, only the drug paraphernalia of a heroin addict married to the daughter of the brother of the local Taliban commander. In the cellar was a locked briefcase containing women's lingerie. The home was owned by the brother, a five-feet-nothing, spry, middle-aged fellow with a big gold watch and red-dyed beard. His son-in-law was kicked out of the Taliban because of his drug habit, he said. The son-in-law was not home, of course. He was traveling to Iran.

Behind the house, Staff Sergeant Mick Miller tested soil in a large, shallow pit for traces of explosives using litmus papers and tiny vials in a kit designed for that purpose. "Why can't it be easy like the good old days, an old windup clock attached to some sticks of TNT?" Miller asked his LT while struggling to drip the right amount of reactants into the mix.

Miller's lieutenant, Geoffrey Dean, played along whimsically, pretending to crouch on a plunger. "Come on, come on!" he intoned like Wile E. Coyote. Dean was taking dramatic license here because everyone knows the roadrunner's nemesis never speaks. Meanwhile, the five-feet-nothing owner gestured toward the village. "Taliban live in better houses, not here." Like gangsters with gold chains and molls.

Around Miller, a dozen young boys crouched with eyes squinting, mesmerized by the portable chemistry lab. Such command of the earth's elements strikes a cross-cultural chord in little boy heads. We joke that young men join the Army to "blow shit up," and back home, little boys play with matches, bake garage door openers in the microwave, toss antacid tablets at seagulls, and make bombs of Mentos and Diet Coke, and it's all just a little funny until it's Afghan boys mixing chemicals to blow up our boys.

An elder told Captain Gacke that the Taliban had shuttered the schools, but the headmaster swore that no such closing had occurred. Yet mouse turds littered the top of the school's unused tin stove. On a classroom wall was an illustrated poster of various types of bombs and ammunition, an education to the dangerous munitions they might find in the fields after decades of warfare, or ones they might use as Taliban warriors. Having soldiers of the most powerful army on earth drop into one's dilapidated mudbrick schoolhouse might induce awkwardness in anyone, but it did not seem like the headmaster was telling the truth.

"He was definitely Taliban," said Gacke. Gacke's paratroopers stayed alert and postured for a fight in the streets and alleyways as their commander ducked into yet another compound to break bread with more elders. Meanwhile their partners, the Afghan soldiers, lounged around, chitchatting with the villagers, bartering for flatbread, eggs, and chai. It was breakfast time, after all. Were the Afghans undisciplined soldiers or, as natives of the country, were they responding to the lack of threat from cues that our soldiers could not perceive?

With help from a terp, I interviewed a rugged-looking, square-bearded soldier of Tajik or Hazara descent. His name was Najibolla. A platoon sergeant now, Najibolla was thirteen when the Russians invaded. He showed me a thick scar running the length of his left forearm, acquired from a Soviet slug. I asked him why his company commander, Major Niyazi, spent more time with the children than the adults of the village. Najibolla shrugged as if it were obvious that every parent wants children to feel safe.

"When we came in the morning, the children ran to their parents, screaming, 'The Polish are coming,' because the last time the Polish came, they shot up the hills with their armored vehicles," Najibolla said. With mischief in his eyes, he changed the subject. "I was making fun of you earlier, but I found out you have a wife and children. It is good." At least he wasn't asking if I drank whiskey or had the swine flu. Old Man Rivers, at your service.

Later, I asked our head interpreter Mike if he would help me ask Najibolla a few more questions. "Why you ask him?" Mike asked with a pained brow. "He is retard. Several of them are retards. He makes talk of nothing." It was a fair reminder of the layers of human drama through which actionable information must pass to American troops. In the heart of every Afghan lay starkly different motives, engendered thru infinite personal journeys: the Hazara soldiering in an insular Pashtun village, the Jalalabad farmer's son interpreting in a dangerous province so he can earn money for college, the Pashtun dirt farmer that only knows this field, this mountain, and his toil.

Sometimes the water smelled of petrol and made people sick, an elder told Gacke, but they didn't want filters because the bad guys would ask where they came from and then kill them. "The best thing is for you to make peace with the Afghan Taliban," the elder counseled Gacke. "The Pakistani and Iranian Taliban don't want peace because they don't live here. The Afghan Taliban is better." In some of the villages we visited, the Taliban was clearly considered an oppressive force against the people's will; in others, it seemed like the local Rotary—benign enough compared with the field, the mountain, and the work. This was one of those villages.

Late afternoon on the second day, with its mission complete, Charlie Company staged for helicopters at the edge of a second village, Akhund Khel. We waited for several hours, but a giant dust squall swept in from the west. The order came that we were walking out, which was fine by me. I had no desire to spend another night curled up in the Afghan dust in my body armor "camping" on my back like an upended turtle, shivering and waiting for the warm breath of morning.

The paratroopers walked out across the scrubby desert rangeland, and though much of the perishables we'd carried were consumed by then, the weight digging into our shoulders hadn't changed much. About every fifth troop was a SAW gunner carrying a twenty-two-pound M249 squad automatic weapon with twenty pounds of ammunition, thirty-five pounds of body armor, ten pounds of helmet and NODs, ten pounds of water, his personal effects, and whatever cross-loaded platoon or company equipment he was assigned such as giant rechargeable batteries, mortar rounds, radios, etc. Nearly all that weight bore down on the few square inches of strap that cut across his shoulders. After standing for most of thirty-six hours burdened thus, the infantrymen walked twelve kilometers punching through the lightly crusted desert duff back to FOB Arian, arriving just as the chow hall was shutting down for the night.

For all that effort, the lone detainee the company had apprehended during the mission appeared to be a wash. That was the bad news. The good news was that, while we were out, we had missed a mortar attack on the FOB. One round had landed between the two tents where Shepro's platoon lived, destroying an M2 .50-caliber machine gun. Luckily the platoon had also been out on patrol. One of the comforting facts about life in Afghanistan was that a person could only be killed in one place at a time. Mortars inside the wire are no danger to troops outside the wire.

Truth be told, that kind of random violence on the FOB was almost more disturbing than what the infantry met with on patrols because there was an expectation of a certain level of security on the FOB. For instance, one day Sergeant First Class Ray Ostil, a legal clerk, was paying off some farmers for a *karez* that an MRAP had damaged. We were standing just inside the front gate of Arian wearing no protective gear. I was taking pictures. The money was literally changing hands when an 84mm recoilless rifle round zinged across the highway and skimmed just over our heads, exploding against Hesco baskets in the truck cooldown yard. It was like a drug deal gone bad, jarring yet funny when we realized nobody was injured. It was less funny for the farmers. Clearly the Taliban knew they were taking cash from the Americans.

The air assaults continued. Captain Vest took Alpha Company on a raid to the north. Shortly after debarking from the assault aircraft, Vest saw six insurgents moving tactically from a woodline to a mosque, pulling security and protecting their flanks. "I wish I could get my paratroopers to move like that," Vest joked. They were well-trained foreign fighters, not local cowboys. Before Vest could maneuver on the mosque, ISR showed the group splitting up, squirting out singly and in pairs on motorbikes and on foot. Alpha Company's "high-value target" turned out to be a man with no Taliban connection whatever, just a guy fingered by a disgruntled neighbor. The "target" just walked up to Vest's soldiers and invited them into his house.

As we failed to make contact with a living, breathing Taliban, their bombs kept hitting our trucks. Scouts in overwatch at Ghat Kala had seen two IEDs explode on the D Loop, and during Vest's air assault, Charlie Company's Third Platoon hit an IED at the village of Margaz that destroyed a mine roller. To date, the brigade had suffered 130 injuries, about 80 percent of which were battle related, including seven KIA. We had conducted 270 patrols and five air assaults with only minor gains. Merely finding an enemy to fight presented significant difficultly in this "densely sparsely populated" landscape. To add insult to injury, a ferocious dust storm devastated the PTIDS dock on FOB Arian and took down a nearly complete $1 million vehicle maintenance bay. The same gale popped the aerostat at Warrior, poking the eyes out of both FOBs.

It was time to return to my home base to refit. I caught a morning bird to Warrior, early enough to hit the MWR before the morning rush and Skype my wife, Barbara. My daughter was turning sixteen at the end of the month. She had brought home her first boyfriend. There was more news. The wife of a longtime friend had died from a routine surgery. I was disappointed to miss my daughter's "Sweet Sixteen," but the death of Amy Gehring hit me pretty hard. She and my buddy Tom had each survived earlier marriages and, by all accounts, were divinely happy together. My wife said that I should call Tom. Yet, with the fighting season just warming up in Ghazni, I felt an odd inhibition, as though I might be casting my own wife to his lot by assuming that I would survive this war.

Early the next morning at HLZ with the brigade chaplain and his assistant, I was still debating whether to call Tom. We were waiting for the pair of Black Hawks to ferry us and brigade leaders to COP Giro for a memorial ceremony for Schwallie, Marta, and Gross. My job was to take pictures and write an article in remembrance of the fallen. "So how was FOB Arian?" asked the chaplain.

To the north, I recognized the hollow pop of a recoilless rifle firing. With no cover nearby, we hit the deck with me between the two pious soldiers. The round passed overhead and exploded a hundred meters to the south in an empty field of mud. Shaking the dust from his pants, the chaplain stood up and exclaimed, "Man, that was close. That was kind of scary."

"Not really," I replied. "Look who I was between."

The chaplain laughed. "Somebody needs to get those guys," he said.

If there was a turning point in our little war against the Taliban, it was right around then. Our infantry based at Warrior were on the verge of pushing into the heart of Taliban country. They were erecting a small post to overwatch the only bridge over the Tarnak River that could support heavy trucks the Taliban used to transport weaponry. The Taliban would react violently, as I would see firsthand. In Andar District north of Giro, villagers were revolting against Taliban who had tried to close all of the schools in retaliation for a new government law requiring all motorcycles to be registered. Insurgents didn't want their names tied to the vehicles they used so effectively to maneuver around the battlefield. At Giro where I was headed next, every other patrol was getting hit by automatic weapons fire, mortars, and IEDs. Of the last fourteen patrols, seven had resulted in multiple TICs, or "troops in contact."

When I landed at Giro, I knew my war was about to begin. Before I even found a bunk, they made me re-sight my weapon.

CHAPTER 7:
GIRO

Giro District had no paved roads. To the west lay Qara Bagh District and the asphalt ribbon of Highway 1, IEDs, and FOB Arian; to the north, Andar District, a secluded sub-region of rural dirt-farming communities where a popular uprising against the Taliban was just beginning to catch fire. Giro was Indian Country.

Across an arid plain spotted with scab-like Kuchi tents, lines of evenly-spaced *karez* shafts scarred the landscape like wounds from an addict's needle. Amidst the tracts of tilled dust and lazy hillsides lay a dragonback ridge of crimson rock that rose and fell, south to north, dividing Ghazni from Paktika Province and the lawless reaches of Pakistan's notorious frontier.

Built in a natural bowl of prominent knolls on which Charlie Troop had established a sensory ring of observation posts (OPs), Combat Outpost Giro was an island of NATO power in a sea of Taliban-friendly villages. "Bascially we're surrounded by six villages that hate us," explained Sergeant Brandon Mendes in a husky baritone as I stepped off the bird at Giro for the first time. "Because of the OPs, we rarely take IDF, but our patrols get hit all the time," he said. Well, paratroopers are supposed to be surrounded.

Officially, Mendes was a commo guy. At COP Giro, the broad-shouldered, jack-of-all-trades from San Diego seemed to just follow his passion wherever it led—managing the commo shack and the HLZ, providing comms while patrolling with the infantry, and playing ambassador to the Giro subgovernor, who lived in a plywood shack on the outpost. Mendes was always the loudest non-casual voice in the room. Stuck at a larger FOB with its top-heavy rank superstructure and suffocating regs, men like Mendes just shuffle along like good soldiers, but away from the flagpole, they have room to expand and far outstrip the plenary responsibility the army has apportioned them.

COP Giro was operated by a single company of paratroopers belonging to 3rd Squadron, 73rd Cavalry Regiment. Bastards in every sense, the grunts of Charlie Troop, to include their company commander and first sergeant, preferred to be called Charlie Company. Nearly all were 11B, "eleven bravos," straight-up infantry, not scouts at all.

The grunts of Charlie had TICs the last four times out, during which they killed at least 15 Taliban fighters, Mendes explained.

"And the day Schwallie, Marta, and Gross died?" I asked. The fatal IED initiated a daylong firefight, he said. Schwallie, a short bulldog of a sergeant, had volunteered to command the first truck (most likely to be hit by IED) because he was unmarried, unlike many of the other NCOs. That had surprised nobody since Jake was literally born into army culture at Fort Campbell, Kentucky (his father had been assigned to the 160th Special Operations Aviation Regiment).

The subgovernor was so enraged by the attack that he had led Afghan troops on a six-klick march with RPGs and machine guns across the desert to help the ambushed patrol in the fight against Taliban. "Fazel the subgov is amazing," Mendes said, nodding in the direction of a thin, serious-looking Afghan wearing a blue vest over the traditional white "manjams," sitting on the front row of seats arranged for the memorial. "Dude fought with his pistol and went through two clips."

The weather was hot and dry, the memorial short and poignant. All of the Afghan soldiers, policemen, and other workers on the active little base stopped whatever they were doing to watch admiringly how America honored its war dead. I took about a hundred photos of the ceremony, the last of which was a group shot of Second Platoon of Charlie Company gathered around the boots, weapons, and helmets of their fallen comrades, flanked by giant MRAP gun trucks. There was noticeably less angst among these paratroopers than I had seen in others at earlier memorials. My sense was that they knew they would be closing with the enemy again shortly, and while abiding the laws of war, vengeance would be had. Unlike the atmosphere on larger FOBs, COP Giro felt more like a place where soldiers slept between gunfights.

After the memorial, Colonel Stock awarded combat badges to just about everyone there. For many, it would be the most important moment of their careers as infantrymen, the day they received the Kentucky long rifle on a blue field, the Combat Infantry Badge. The only way to get one is to get shot at and return fire.

I met with the squad leader of the fallen paratroopers, Staff Sergeant Justin Boardman. Another hands-on leader who thrived in limited oversight, Boardman invited me out on patrol with his men. "I promise you won't be disappointed," he said. I didn't expect to be. The paratroopers who moved around Giro were as different from fobbits as the cutting horses back home were from show ponies. What worked tightened up, what didn't sloughed off, and every day, the feed was earned. I wanted to be a part of how it was earned. Every paratrooper did. Boardman's promise would prove good, but my immediate future held more FOB than COP. I flew back to Warrior later that day.

I sat in on an interview of Colonel Stock by *The Economist*'s Ben Farmer. It was the British journalist's first time in Ghazni, though he had lived in the capital city of Kabul for over three years. He professed to be writing a general piece about the 82nd's clearing operation in Ghazni, but with journalists always looking for some unique hook, one never really knew what to expect.

Mark Stock was a bright man and studied commander who believed unapologetically in soldiers and soldiering, understood his brigade's strategic role in the War in Afghanistan, and routinely engaged the press in a warm but always professional manner. At Stock's level, all decisions are in part political decisions. He seemed comfortable carrying that burden. Most everyone who spoke of him commented in some way on his intelligence and breadth of knowledge.

Ghazni's security problems were not unusual for Afghanistan, Stock explained to Farmer. Out here, the reach of GIRoA (Government of the Islamic Republic of Afghanistan) was thin, Taliban ratlines were well established, and the operational reach of Afghan security forces was limited, with many police and army units operating practically independently along the narrow highway corridor. Since our arrival, insurgents were losing impact on the residents there. No more shakedowns, no impediments to travel.

Most insurgent activity was occurring in belts of support zones a few kilometers off the thoroughfare. Stock believed the purpose of IED attacks on the highway was to keep Coalition Forces focused on the road and away from the support areas. Most of the attacks were against American and Afghan military forces, he noted, and they were falling off precipitously the longer we were there.

While the Haqqani Network and other insurgent groups had a presence in Ghazni, most combatants answered to the Qetta Shura, the Taliban based in Pakistan. The people did not like them, and Afghan troops backed by Stock's paratroopers were causing significant disruption to the established order in Ghazni. He described how one partnered patrol had killed twelve insurgents including two local commanders during a pursuit that stretched over six kilometers. One Taliban commander had almost drowned while fleeing across the Tarnak River.

"People, even women, were coming out of the villages to shake the hands of the ANA soldiers," Stock recalled. "It's kind of fun to watch," he said somewhat wistfully.

While the main effort of the brigade's campaign had been 2-504's operations to build up Qara Bagh District Center, most of the kinetic action was occurring elsewhere—on the Tarnak River in Gilan District to the south, at Muqor where paratroopers were challenging the boundaries of Taliban control with daily incursions into support zones, and at COP Giro, where I was headed the next day.

I couldn't sleep that night—a rare problem for me downrange—so I Skyped my wife at the MWR into the wee hours of the morning. Nerves? Probably. I was forty-four and understood the value of life. A life was worth the vacuum created by its absence. My wife of two decades was well past that point in which anything other than a life together just wouldn't do. To my children, she was the nurturing font, but I was the lodestone. I could hear my buddy Leo from Fallujah saying, "If the husband got killed, the wife is done. The family is gone." Now, nothing is so meticulously kept current by the army as a soldier's Servicemembers Group Life Insurance policy beneficiaries. We were always signing the things, in part, to avoid Joe giving the value of his death to the hooker he met just before deployment. Dead I was still worth $450,000 to my wife, Barbara. It would be enough to keep her going until our kids were through college. As a dollar value for my life, I was okay with that.

With the sun finally up, I caught a helicopter out of Warrior. We landed at Giro just before an American general arrived to meet with the top Afghan officers of the local security forces. I wasn't on the ground more than two hours before I was kitted up, locked and loaded, and walking out the front gate with Staff Sergeant Boardman and his platoon. The mission was to clear a small section of the ominous-sounding Route Rattlesnake of several IEDs reported by locals. It wouldn't take long, Boardman said. There were just two IEDs to blow up, and the first was under two klicks from the front gate.

The patrol was led by First Lieutenant Daniel Miller, a pensive young paratrooper who was weighted down by responsibility for the lives of his men every time they left the outpost. In seventeen patrols, his platoon had been engaged on eleven. Currently, they were on a run of eight for eight. The last time out, Private First Class Benjamin Stegemann was shot in the knee and calf while relieving himself on a mountainside.

"We have a pretty good chance of getting into a TIC today," Miller said with what seemed to be misplaced modesty, given his recent success of getting shot at. TIC is short for troops in contact. Miller ordered me to stay with a fire team led by Sergeant Ricky Muenzer of St. Louis. Muenzer's team included Private First Class James Burson of Tyler, Texas, on an M14 sniper rifle, and Private First Class Daniel Attebury of my hometown, Bozeman, Montana. Attebury was born in the same hospital as my son six years earlier. He was a senior at Bozeman High just two years before we met halfway around the world, and now he was on the M249 SAW, a handheld light machine gun capable of firing over seven hundred rounds per minute. If we did get in a TIC, Attebury's main job was to plaster the enemy with 5.56mm bullets, allowing the rest of the team to find tenable fighting positions.

We walked out the front gate in a dissipating sandstorm and skirted vacant mud-brick ruins on the outskirts of Pana Village. Pana was the provincial seat, but so dangerous that the provincial subgovernor lived and worked out of COP Giro. The LT and EOD techs kept to the rutted main road as elements of his platoon pushed left into the village and right into pastureland. Child shepherds herded a ragtag flock of sheep and goats near a broad dry wash that eventually ran under the road. Just short of the wash, Muenzer halted. We lay in behind low rocks in an old shallow bomb crater. Our position was better than no position, but it lacked any real concealment or cover. I was glad to be near Attebury's SAW.

Almost immediately, the *rat-tat-tat* of AK bursts reverberated from within Pana behind the headquarters element, removing any doubt that today was not going to be that ninth day. It was like a trout hitting on first cast. None of the infantrymen in our little pod, nor those tucked into a thin windrow of leafing poplars to our front, nor the child shepherds guarding their flocks, mustered more than a passing interest at the sounds of war. With so much firepower just feet away, I stayed on my Nikon, *click, click, click, click* . . . a deliberate, deep-throated staccato replied to the first bursts, clearly a more serious weapon. Over the radio, Miller told Muenzer that it was "just the ANA." Afghan soldiers in Pana had answered wild shots off the back of a motorcycle with a hail of PKM machine gun fire. No loss, either side.

An Apache gunship appeared in the west above the village. As it made laps overhead, two EOD techs ran wires to an IED buried in the roadbed near the dry wash while other soldiers pulled security.

"Controlled det in 30," the LT said over the radio. A half-minute later, a bicolored explosion ripped into the sky—silvery-black effluvial from combusting explosives and the brown earth it cast. The destroyed bomb had been a relatively small charge like the one Boardman had nearly stepped on a few weeks earlier, designed to kill dismounted troops like us.

Signal spooks with Miller were picking up Taliban chatter over the airwaves. The same insurgent who had shot Stegemann was emplacing a machine gun to ambush the platoon just up the road in Babakur, the next town to the north in our direction of travel. After a second detonation, we picked up and moved. Miller turned us east through Pana toward the village of Giru. Today's mission was to blow up IEDs, not movement to contact.

The men moved through waist-high wheat that grew in "densely sparsely populated" fields of summer green from an ungenerous, crusted soil that was powder before the last rain. Like walking through an old man's thinning hair. From the soil came the wheat, the earthen cookware, the homes, roads, and bridges. In the dust the enemy hid their bombs, left their tracks, and buried their dead. Soldiers climbed chest-high mud-brick walls under a hundred pounds of gear, covered one another crossing roads and alleyways, fanned out across fields. Most of the farmers just toiled in the sun, though others seemed to melt away. Everywhere, children stopped and gawked. Somewhere we passed from Pana into Giru.

Above Giru on a high barren hill was a machine gun team that Miller had directed to sit in overwatch as we entered the village. The hill was a conical bald, with steep barren slopes on three sides and a gentler runoff on its backside, away from the village. It was the hill where Stegemann had been shot. "Goddammit Stegemann," someone mumbled and laughed as we passed through its shadow.

In Giru, villagers were warning the ANA of another IED behind some compounds to the north. Were they baiting us? The effective range of the M240 Bravo on the hilltop was between one and two thousand meters, far enough to reach the backside of the village. Steeply angled shots from high ground can be tricky, I knew from my own experiences hunting elk and mule deer in the mountains. I knew there was no place on Fort Bragg where our gunners could have practiced that kind of shooting. Underestimating the distance could have sent bullets raining down on the wrong heads, villagers or even ours.

Near a simple mosque next to a wellhead of an open *karez* and surrounded by kids and women in light-blue burkas, the platoon halted and set up security. The women scurried off, but the boys and younger girls stayed. Two ANA soldiers descended a short flight of steps to the water and doused their heads to wash off the dust and beat the heat. They laughed with the old men and teenage boys and entertained the children with silly jokes. One Afghan soldier bought a live chicken for dinner.

Boardman asked if I wanted to come with him to investigate the rumored IED, so I left Muenzer's team at the well. The threat turned out to be nothing, but as we were returning, Santiago, a gunner at the OP, radioed in that he had almost stepped on an IED. The Taliban had foreseen our tactics and planted an IED on the top of the hill.

Boardman volunteered to escort EOD up the hill to the mine. We moved swiftly from the village through a broad wheat field between the hill and another to the west, to the back side where the climb was not so fierce and, as importantly, where we would not have our backs to the village as we ascended. "Hit the ground if we take fire," Boardman ordered. There was no cover for a distance of three hundred meters, though the corrugated furrows and waist-high wheat would at least offer some concealment.

"I can do that," I assured him as we fanned out. A photo that I have of us walking through the wheat is classic blue sky and green wheat, soldier . . . soldier . . . soldier.

The EOD team found the IED where Santiago said it was. Wind or a poor packing job had exposed it. The bomb looked to be about eighty pounds of HME, more than enough to completely disassemble Santiago and his assistant gunner.

While we waited for EOD to wire the bomb, Boardman pointed to a high knob many kilometers to the southwest. "That's where we had our first firefight," he said. "Motherfuckers had set up a machine gun on top, trapping us in the saddle below with no way out except across open ground." The engagement had lasted nearly five hours, and it was a miracle that nobody was hit.

"Controlled det in 60 seconds!"

The EOD guys were finding cover. Boardman and I hid behind some large volcanic-looking rocks as EOD blew the mine in place, raining a cascade of rock pellets over our position. After a second blast, we regained our feet.

"Well, now they know we're here," I said. Everyone in the district knew we were on that hilltop.

"Oh, they always know where we are," Boardman replied dismissively.

As Miller led the rest of his platoon through the wheat below us, two white minivans racing into the west end of the village had Boardman's attention. Both vans disappeared near the mosque, fifty meters from the well. The villagers were gone.

A curious aspect of firefights is that, regardless of how many weapons are involved, they always seem to begin with a meager shot or two. One can almost hear the lead "motherfucker" saying in Pashto, "Don't fire until I fire." And that's what happened. A lone Kalashnikov opened up on the EOD techs, who were caught separated from their weapons on the hilltop. Several more AKs chimed in as the soldiers flopped behind low slabs of jagged rock. Boardman sprinted up the hill, with me right behind him, clicking the shutter of my Nikon.

Accurate rifle fire cut us off. We dropped to the ground. A half dozen Afghan soldiers and policemen rushed past, establishing fighting positions in the rocks on either side of EOD. Boardman ran toward them as I framed a photo of an Afghan policeman launching an RPG toward the village. A ball of fire ballooned out the back of the launcher just as I tripped the shutter.

The air around me was snapping and hissing—not the sounds I had expected to hear during a firefight. There was no Hollywood *pyerrrr* or *wwzzzzziiing*. I had no more than a vague notion of where rounds were coming from, and with 360-degree exposure, that was terrifying. I picked up and ran forward, passing right behind the RPG-wielding policeman as he touched off a second round.

At basic training, they taught us to never stand behind the similarly-shaped AT-4 recoilless anti-tank weapon because the backblast could cause severe burns and overpressure injuries. I was only vaguely aware of this as I ran through a bright orange fireball. Was that the smell of burning hair?

I dropped down behind one of the EOD guys, still trying to make sense of the chaos engulfing the hilltop. To the left, right, and rear were Afghan policemen and soldiers firing machine guns and AKs from the hip, pointed at the sky as if they were indirect fire weapons. Bullets snapped overhead and ricocheted off the rocks to our flanks and front. One of the EOD guys saw me taking pictures and asked if he could borrow my M4. His weapon and assault pack were still in no-man's land.

I had nowhere to go. I couldn't see who was shooting at us. I handed him my weapon. I have a photo of him with it. This was not how I had imagined my first firefight going down. True, I was as anxious as the next guy to fire my weapon in combat, but I also didn't like carrying the heavy thing around for nothing. Yet there was my weapon in the hands of another. But my job was to photograph our soldiers fighting. But I was a soldier. This is how it went. For about a second.

To my right, a bearded Afghan soldier and a policemen with his cap on backwards stood up together, both lifting PKM machine guns. They blasted away at the village with heavy bursts of automatic fire. In the photograph, they are gritting their teeth.

From behind me, the other EOD guy yelled that we were being attacked from the rear, but with the noise, nobody heard him. The Afghan policeman with the RPG, who was now slightly to our rear and left, turned to face us and fired. The round sizzled past overhead and seemed to be going toward nothing at all. It exploded high above the village like a burst of ugly fireworks. "Jesus Christ!" somebody yelled.

"They do that on purpose," someone answered. One might call it a show of force, I suppose. While I worried about a few stray machine gun rounds, this guy was air-bursting rocket-propelled grenades over the village.

Private Reid Chitty, a rangy, baby-faced paratrooper with a brand new XM2010 Enhanced Sniper Rifle that fired the flat-trajectory .300 Winchester Magnum cartridge, moved up and began taking well-considered shots into the open window of the mosque where he could see muzzle flashes. I photographed Lieutenant Miller and two other paratroopers charging up toward us, past teams of Afghan and American soldiers firing side-by-side. Miller dropped in next to Chitty to get a read on the situation.

A QRF of gun trucks had departed COP Giro, and as the lumbering MRAPs traveled north on Route Rattlesnake and turned east at Pana, we could see them entering the village. "They're going to get blown the fuck up," said the EOD guy behind me, still flat against the hillside. At least we won't get attacked from the rear, I thought.

Knowing he would never get permission to hit the mosque with artillery, Miller called back to headquarters and asked permission to drop 155mm rounds from the howitzers at COP Giro into the wheat field as a show of force. Negative, they told him. Too close to civilians. Miller couldn't believe it. After wasting time and still under fire, he ran back down the mountain to organize a ground assault. I got my M4 back and followed him halfway down the ridge and stopped where I had a better angle for photographs.

Above me, Chitty was still sniping. With my long lens, I could see faint puffs of dust kick up from the front of the mosque and the *kalat* wall that extended from its left side along a roadside grove of trees. AK fire was still echoing off another higher mountain to the east that was now casting shadows across the wheat field. It occurred to me that insurgents climbing the backside of that hill might get above us. Behind our position to the south was an even higher ridgeline that led west to the knob of the platoon's first firefight. Our position was riddled with liabilities that time and more insurgents might make good on.

I looked through the ACOG 4X scope of my rifle. How far was the insurgent position, four-hundred? Six-hundred meters? I aimed at the puffs of dust along the *kalat* wall and pulled the trigger. The little M4 carbine popped in my hands, a runt for the distance. It always felt like such a toy compared with the .30 '06 that I used to hunt deer and elk. There was nothing but rooftops and mud above and below the wall, so I pumped out a half-dozen rounds at the spot the AK fire was emanating from. First shots. There, that was over.

To my left, one of our machine guns stopped firing. Miller's assault force was entering the village. The Afghan soldier with the chicken nonchalantly walked past, still holding the live hen upside down by its feet.

The firing suddenly ceased. ANA and ANP came down from the hilltop to smoke cigarettes. Binoculars and riflescopes scanned the leading lines of walls, roofs and windows around the mosque, along the field margins, tree lines, and ridges. The sun was setting in the west, casting a pastoral peace over the village and our craggy hillside.

A slow-moving A10 Warthog appeared overhead and flew laps around our position. We waited. I photographed the buttery light as it lapped along the slanted shadows of the hills. We still waited. Miller returned an hour later. His men had found a handful of AK shells near a hole in the *kalat* wall and took biometrics on some of the bystanders, and that was all. With the A10 overhead, we walked cross-country under NODs back to Giro.

We arrived after hours, but the chow tent was lit up inside. The cooks had prepared for our return—one third of the fighting force of the little COP. That would never have happened on a larger FOB. For Miller, the day was ending the way every day should, with happy, dirty faces eating burnt oriental chicken and rice.

For me, I was glad to lose my cherry. I had engaged in my first firefight, as ridiculous as my own shots had been. Four years after enlisting, I had photographs in my camera of paratroopers engaging the enemy in combat. None had even been wounded, including me, the old man. It was a good day. I cleaned my camera, my weapon, and then slept.

Life on Giro was Spartan. The chow hall put out two hots a day, each ration more fit for a wrestler trying to make weight than a soldier in daily combat. Piss tubes and soldiers burning barrels of human waste marked the latrines. Lacking contractors and left to its own devices, the army of course provided no toilet paper. Since even water had to be sling-loaded in by helicopter, the ever-calm Charlie Company First Sergeant Ogbonna Kenyatta enforced a strict regimen of one shower per trooper per week. The laundry rotation was similar.

I spent the morning processing photos. At noon, I linked up with a newly arrived team from the *Fayetteville Observer*, our hometown newspaper. They were ending a month-long excursion to report on Bragg-based troops scattered across the southern and eastern part of the country. Captain Cieslak, our public affairs officer, believed the best way to get good press from embedded journalists was to send them to wherever they were most likely to get killed. If they died, they would write nothing. If they survived, they would be hard-pressed to write bad things about the paratroopers who kept them alive. Thus, Giro.

Military writer Drew Brooks and photographer James Robinson seemed glad to see a familiar face at Giro. Brooks was a mildly reticent, pure South Carolina native with an accent to match. Robinson was a thin, garrulous, manic press type with a beard, hook nose, and Irish flat cap to cover his thinning dome. Both men were in their early 30s. We had worked together on stories back at Bragg, so I knew they were both standup journalists. Soon they would be running journalists.

At that point in their journey, they were happy to be far from the flagpole. While reporting on the division's 4th BCT in Kandahar, military police had forced the newsmen to wear PT belts on the congested FOB. "Well, at least we have one. Can we use it around here?" Drew asked facetiously.

They had slept in a helicopter hangar at Sharana while visiting the 82nd's Combat Aviation Brigade, a transient tent on FOB Arian, and in a tiny roofed box on Warrior. By comparison, the ramshackle brick-and-mortar quarters they shared at Giro were deluxe accommodations.

Sergeant Mendes introduced Brooks and Robinson to Fazel Rahman, the pistol-packing district subgovernor who had charged into the fight the day that Schwallie, Chase, and Marta had died. Fazel was a fine-featured, gracious, and introspective man who was once a shopkeeper in Andar District to the north. His father had disappeared during the Russian occupation. After the Taliban came to power, infighting between strongman Hektmatyar, the Haqqani Network, and the Taliban created a web of suspicions that ensnared many a disinterested Afghan. The Taliban accused Fazel of aiding first one, then the other rival organization. They beat him and threatened to kill him. He moved to Pakistan, returning to Kabul once the Taliban was booted from power. He moved to Giro three years ago to serve as subgovernor.

Fazel told Brooks that his district needed more Afghan soldiers and policemen to open commerce and stoke the economy. That was it. The Polish forces were idiots, he said. They were too few, so they made a deal with the Taliban: no IEDs, and the Poles would leave the Taliban alone. In truth, the Poles had a farcical mission, with too few troops and impossible rules of engagement. I could understand Fazel's frustration, but I could also imagine the simple math in the Polish commander's head to bring all of his soldiers home. Risk was the exponent. "People like the Americans," Fazel said. "Americans have been helping Afghanistan since the Russian occupation."

Drew asked Fazel if that was why he ran into the fight that day.

"I was so upset because the Americans left family and children and died over here while these idiots ruin our country," he said.

I asked Fazel if he went out with every patrol.

"Every patrol that I can," he replied. That's what I'd heard.

On the morning of May 19, we left on a patrol southwest to the village of Osmat to sweep it for insurgents and weapons, or as was more likely to happen, to engage the enemy when engaged. It was always safer to travel north than south, according to Sergeant Mendes.

"They all hate us," he said with a shrug.

"The governor said they like Americans," I said.

"They shoot at us," he replied.

I brought my camera along, but my job was to keep Drew and James safe while they got the material for which they had come so far. I would have done the same for any journalist, regardless of who they were or what I thought of them. It just so happened that only the hometown boys were willing to go out on patrol in such a dangerous setting.

We would be traveling with Second Platoon, led by First Lieutenant Gareth Scott and Sergeant First Class Garrett Williams. Schwallie, Gross, and Marta had been their soldiers. Sergeant Mendes was along to provide commo support. The difference between having Apache and artillery support, and not having them, was often commo.

As the platoon sergeant, Williams did not hide his dismay with the civilian journalists in tow. Nothing against them, but as a bottom-line NCO, he saw added distraction and two more liabilities, neither with any combat experience, neither adding combat power to his patrol. He also didn't want to get them killed, a very real possibility.

"Stay with the LT," he ordered. That was often the case. Keep all the eggs in one basket. A platoon's lieutenant is the unit's nerve hub, not the muscle. His job is to gather information on the battlefield, communicate with his squad leaders and company headquarters, and give direction to his air and ground assets, all while keeping himself alive. The platoon leader always has a radio operator at his side and usually a forward observer to call in air and artillery support. Enablers such as FET, civil affairs, and journalists are typically told to stay with the LT because the LT should never be directly in the fight. I have plenty of photos of platoon leaders doing just that, but I have more of them hunkered down in some barely-there oasis of safety, screaming into the radio handset.

As a photographer, I knew my chances of getting photos of paratroopers going toe-to-toe with the Taliban were diminished if I stayed near the LT. The same would apply to the photographer, James, one of my two charges for the day. I had learned over time to make a point of *telling* army leaders what I intended to do rather than waiting for them to tell me. Leaders respect a plan. I told Williams that I would keep an eye on Drew and James, and he let it go at that.

The day was a scorcher. We didn't leave until mid-morning, with a shimmering heat already melting ground-level objects on the horizon. Just two klicks west of Giro, with the COP at our backs and barren, rocky knobs to our left, right, and front, we halted. Soldiers who had climbed the hill in front to establish an OP found another gift from the Taliban. Once EOD had blown the IED, we marched south through a saddle between two hills and dropped into a dry wash that skirted the walled village of Adini.

Skirting the village, Brooks, Robinson, and I climbed halfway up a high hill on the far side, along with the signal spooks and some scouts armed with sniper rifles. Big Chitty was there with his XM2010. In Afghanistan, all hills are rocky hills, but this one was especially so. Good news—plenty to hide behind in case of gunfire. Below us, three Afghan villagers in man-dresses were watching us from a high-walled, triangular compound. Not a wise move on their part. When an infantryman wants a better look at something—or somebody—he uses his rifle scope. They must have thought better of their half-concealed peeking, because they moved outside of the compound into the open. Just like that, one turned his back to us, squatted, and shat on the edge of a narrow road. "Well, okay, is that for us?" one of the snipers asked.

On an open plain in the distance, a white minivan scuttled along the road from Pana heading south. "Company says it's a wedding party," the radio operator, or RTO, told Lieutenant Scott. I hadn't realized he was with us. His terp said sardonically, "The road is clear, no IEDs." The soldiers laughed.

"Thanks to the route clearance guys," somebody added.

Acting on a tip passed over the radio, Scott decided to search Adini for a Taliban commander. Our group moved to another hillside that offered better vantage for the snipers. "What was wrong with our other hill?" Brooks asked, playing the role of Fat Boy. We were all sucking wind in the heavy body armor as we climbed the second hill.

In a nest of jagged boulders, Chitty and the other snipers set up firing positions while the rest of us drank water and caught our breath.

The perch was much better for seeing into Adini. The village was not unlike a Pac-Man maze set to an 11th-century theme. Big walls and half walls; tiny fruit orchards; water traps, crap drying in rows, kids playing in the dusty narrow streets. There were also bad guys. As Afghan police moved into the village, we watched Taliban spotters retreating ahead of them, jumping *kalat* walls and staying just out of reach. They weren't shooting. It didn't even look like they were armed. They knew better. Be armed, get shot. The Intel soldiers listening to Taliban radio chatter said the Taliban was waiting for us in nearby Asmat, not here.

Drew and James wanted to move into the action, so we picked our way down the hillside and joined up with the LT as he entered the village. So far as Ghazni villages go, there was nothing remarkable about Adini. A creek ran through its center into which villagers shat regularly. There was a well with an oversized handpump for teasing water from the aquifer. Courtyards were covered by plate-sized discs of fuel dung spread for drying, and grapevines grew in ragged green masses in deep furrows, a vineyard for every home. Dirty-faced kids begged soldiers for pens and candy and were rewarded here and there. Americans back home send pens and candy in care packages, and soldiers load them like ammo before missions, even when the parents of the kids shoot at them. Pens and candy somehow translated in a soldier's heart into education and wealth, or for a time, a dream of both.

Williams, the platoon sergeant, had flanked the village with a squad of paratroopers and barely missed capturing the Taliban commander. In the village center, the LT's terp, a gritty old Afghan who kept up by sucking on cigarettes and Rippits (small, army-purchased, hyper-caffienated "energy" drinks), questioned the Taliban commander's brother. Following the terp, a uniformed Afghan National Directorate of Security officer who had come with us had his turn. The NDS is similar to our CIA.

"He's a bad-ass motherfucker," Mendes said. "People know him. They know he doesn't fuck around. Watch people when he walks past them." The NDS officer was just a short, thick man with sunglasses kicked back on his head, dressed in a simple tan uniform, but villagers gave him berth.

Williams' soldiers cataloged a dozen male villagers using the HIIDES and searched two motorcycles while Afghan soldiers combed through houses and adjacent buildings. Nothing.

After some time, the platoon left the walled village and continued its mission toward Asmat. Out of Adini, we traveled along a road in the flats below a kilometer-long ridgeline that terminated in a long spur that descended to the valley floor. The spur shielded Asmat from our view. The Afghan soldiers asked Scott to halt so they could clear the village themselves. The police would climb the spur in overwatch. We could just sit back and relax. It was their country. We waited. With the Taliban supposedly lying in wait in Asmat, we cooled our heels a klick away, chewing on "Scooby snacks" and "pogey bait" and listening for the sound of gunfire.

A fast-moving dust storm was closing from the south, soon to limit air support or medevac, should we need them. Scott was nervous. The ANA finally returned, but as the sandstorm overtook us, the police had not yet descended from the spur ridge. Mendes climbed into the storm, returning ten minutes later with the police. We turned for home.

The storm was a mean little sinus-clogging squall that coated everything with atomized orange dust, temporarily removing all terrain features. We kept walking, though, and it passed over by the time we reached a chokepoint between two high hills leading back into Adini. Drew recognized both hills as the ones we had previously climbed.

Suddenly the Taliban opened fire from the very place the police had just vacated.

Machine gun fire snapped overhead, sending us scurrying for the nearest rocks. Some of our soldiers began climbing the hill we were closest to, which happened to be that very first hill we had climbed above Adini.

Drew was a hundred feet up the hill already and James was maybe thirty feet higher than me. Paratroopers and Afghans were firing thousands of rounds back toward Azmat. I braced against a large rock and fired at the ridgeline. The enemy was well out of range for my little M4, but what else to do? "Where are they at?" I yelled to the paratrooper closest to me, trying to get a better fix on them.

"They're on the ridgeline," he yelled back and pointed.

I popped off a few rounds, again feeling very ineffectual with my weapon. The ridge was at least a kilometer out, three times the distance at which I could reliably hit a target with my M4. Drew was still climbing, so I turned to catch up to him just as an Afghan soldier fired an RPG twenty feet in front of James. For some reason, even though I wasn't in the fireball this time, the concussion was so much worse than the one I ran through, and louder. James was bowled over by the blast. "Holy crap, did you see that?" he yelled. I did, and immediately I wished I'd taken a picture of it.

Below us, behind a low ripple in the flats, a machine gun team was hammering back with steady bursts of 7.62mm rounds. To their right, Chitty was engaging with his sniper rifle. Next to him, another marksman, Gonzales, was firing the formidable .50 caliber Barrett sniper rifle. To control the blinding dust caused by muzzle blast, they were synchronizing their shots.

Mendes charged into the field between the two firing positions and dropped behind the machine gun team. He kept the radio handset pressed to his ear as PKM fire continued to dig up the dirt around them. An Afghan soldier suddenly walked into the clearing like some fighting Scotsman ready to lift his kilt at the enemy. He hoisted a heavy machine gun to his chest and rattled through over a hundred rounds.

Robinson and I caught up with Drew just before he reached the crest. I suggested staying away from the summit in case of IED. The LT was trying to call in a fire mission for the 155s but could not get permission. Williams was leading paratroopers across the ridgeline to attack the enemy fighting positions. We ran after them. It may have been more like a shuffle.

Ten minutes later, gasping as we climbed the last few feet to Williams at the abandoned Taliban gun position, we heard Williams yell,

"Where's my terp?" The platoon sergeant regarded us expectantly, but when he realized who we were—and who we weren't—he threw up his hands and said, "Seriously? None of our terps made it up here, but the newspaper guys did?" At that moment, Drew and James knew they'd measured up to the task. They had been accepted by the infantry, and they hadn't even been killed.

Lieutenant Miller's platoon went out the next day, but I stayed on the COP with Drew and James to process photos. I hadn't taken nearly as many photos as James Robinson's fifteen hundred, but it still took hours to edit, caption, and send them out over the outpost's slow Internet connection.

Early in the morning, the 155s fired two rounds. Not a good sign. At 11:20 a.m., two Air Force jets started making laps up and down the valley, and just after 12:30 p.m., a pair of Black Hawk medevacs with an Apache escort passed overhead and landed several kilometers to the north just long enough to pick someone up. I hoped it wasn't one of ours, but who else could it be?

When the patrol finally returned late in the day, Miller recounted the mission. The platoon had walked out of Giro at 7 a.m., heading north along Route Rattlesnake to investigate a possible cache site for a Dushka heavy machine gun used during Miller's last engagement, the one I was in. When the patrol reached the village of Safarwal, the ANA and NDS searched but found nothing. As the ANA were finishing, the Taliban began hitting them from two positions. The Afghans returned fire. Simultaneously, Miller's scouts on a hilltop to the west were engaged by another Taliban element. With the LT were two infantry squads, some Afghan police and soldiers, and the subgovernor. They began receiving ineffective gunfire, followed by more accurate sniper fire, and finally the Dushka. Having three elements engaged in three locations at once severely limited Miller's ability to maneuver. That's when he called in the fire mission for the 155s. He put the massive shells into an empty field between the villages of Musakhel and Mosalli. That brought an immediate end to the small-arms fire.

The patrol resumed their search and was engaged by four insurgents from a tall building. To prevent squirters from escaping, Miller sent gun trucks around back. As he tried to maneuver closer to the fighting, one of the gun trucks intercepted a farm tractor with a trailer transporting a wounded boy of 15. Oddly, the boy had an IV tapped into his arm, and his head was professionally bandaged. As Miller tried to piece together what had transpired, his medic checked the boy out. Brain matter was coming out of a head wound, so Miller immediately called in the medevac.

The man driving the tractor professed to be the boy's teacher. The boy was shot while in school, he said. The building they were in was the same one from which Taliban were firing. Miller suspected that the boy had been firing too. Regardless, the LT put him on the medevac to Sharana, sending Staff Sergeant Boardman as his escort.

At that point, Miller received new Intel that six vehicles were gathering along a tree line in nearby Musakhel. Men were seen exchanging some type of equipment.

When the vehicles departed Musakhel, the first three passed Miller's gun trucks without seeing them, but when the last three passed a few minutes later, a white van suddenly stopped, someone moved inside, then opened fire on nearby Afghan soldiers. The van sped off. Miller alerted paratroopers with his first squad, who were staged down the road. First Squad reported more fire from the van and engaged it until it stopped.

At that time, the medevac was just landing to pick up the boy. A black car (one of the last three) sped to the HLZ with another civilian casualty inside, a male. Boardman didn't know if the man was "good" or "bad," but he loaded him on the helicopter anyway because that's what Americans do. More soldiers were searching the other vehicles and found numerous shell casings. On the ground was a man in a woman's burka, dead.

Villagers would not let anyone near him, and oddly, several women removed their veils, allowing the paratroopers to see their faces. It was as if they were showing a little skin to be distracting. The subgovernor found it very suspicious, as did Miller.

Returning to base, the platoon was moving through an open area when the signal spooks overheard a Taliban asking his commander for permission to fire on the Americans. Less than a minute later, machine guns and AKs raked Miller's column.

Luckily, a B1-B bomber was nearby and made a low-pass "show of force." That was enough for the insurgents to leave the Americans alone. It was a good day not to be on patrol with them, Miller said.

It also sounded like a good day for journalists not to be along. Not that he or we had anything to hide. War is war. Was the boy a fighter or just an unlucky teenager? Was the man in the burka a Taliban disguised as a woman? Some villagers were probably complicit in the attack; some were probably not. The ones with guns get shot, and sometimes so do those nearby. Did every person in the school know that insurgent fighters were about to unleash hell on the infidels? Of course.

For young soldiers still itching for a world that turned on black and white themes, the day was a bewildering slurry of humanity at its worst, and best. One can talk about what "happened" by limiting the conversation to observable facts, yet even the most scrupulous observation includes a physical viewpoint. In other words, what went unseen? What was seen but perceived incorrectly? What happened yesterday or five years ago that caused today to happen? What of expectations for tomorrow?

What happened? Two genetically dissimilar races engaged in resource partitioning in eastern Afghanistan. Or, a Taliban was martyred while conducting jihad against infidel invaders. Or, a patrol of US Army paratroopers engaged insurgent forces, with one confirmed enemy KIA.

Or, someone shot a schoolboy in the head and killed a man in a dress. Such is progress in Afghanistan.

With the departure of Brooks and Robinson, another embed arrived. David Gilkey was the first photographer I'd ever met who had the thousand-yard stare. Either that or he smoked a lot of weed. At the time, he was shooting for National Public Radio. Who knew there were prestigious photography jobs at radio stations?

Gilkey was tall, bearded, and bald. His photography relied heavily on stylistic interpretation achieved through a combination of heavy vignetting, the use of specialized "tilt-shift" lenses that allow for Photoshop-type blurring by mechanical means, and of course, careful selection and composition of his subject matter. Thus I shouldn't have been too surprised that the first question he asked me when he arrived at Giro was whether I had made any art yet. Well, no. I had made my bed.

We passed by the company CP where, on the concrete stoop, Miller was talking quietly to his squad leaders. Gilkey nodded. "Those are soldiers who have seen combat. I can see it in their faces. They're not FOB soldiers." Unlike the ANA soldiers who were constantly high on hashish, our soldiers hadn't been smoking weed.

My boss Cieslak had told me that Gilkey would want to come directly to the front lines. Well, here he was. In the chow hall, I quizzed him about his photography, with perhaps a little sport intended, to get under his skin. He did work for the liberal-left NPR news organization after all, so he was fair game and an easy target. From his bio and online portfolios, I knew Gilkey had seen as much conflict as many of our most experienced soldiers, and his photography had earned him many prestigious awards.

His images, depicting the brittle sour of life that soldiers feel, deployed to a foreign land to kill strange people for the best of causes or no cause at all—pick one—are top notch. Yet as a soldier myself, they struck me as one-sided and from a very narrow point of view. Civilian writers and photographers—outsiders all—transpose their own insular feelings onto combat and interpret everything through that color cast. Wearing a ring of etched skulls doesn't make a soldier a stone-cold killer with a devalued respect for life any more than wearing a Disney T-shirt makes him a Mousketeer. We, as soldiers, entertain ourselves with the outlandish to make the task of war more bearable. Alienation and despair may be part of a soldier's story, but only a part. In between those moods, many of these guys were having the times of their lives. Many Iraq War vets felt the same way, I told him. Gilkey only shrugged.

I was going to press him, but he changed the subject. "You know what worries me?" he asked. "With the troops pulling out, the fighting in Afghanistan is being taken over by the SF [Special Forces], and the press is not allowed to see it. There's no accountability."

Well, I was going to get a sporting chance after all. "No account-ability?" I asked. "And the press is going to provide that?" I had seen press accountability in Iraq, I told him. "Who is going to hold the press accountable, the SF?"

He shook his head. "Seriously. I've been embedded with ODA here twice and I didn't get to see hardly anything either time."

"That's because you're the press."

He sat back and considered me. I wasn't SF. I was just another soldier in the chow hall. I could tell that he wanted to close the dis-tance. "Listen, here's a funny story. I'm in Iraq with these marines. Guy says, 'My wife hasn't sent me a single care package.' I tell him I haven't received any either. He says, 'You're not supposed to. You're a journalist. You're a faggot. I gave that woman three non-retarded kids and she can't send me a single care package? If it was raining pussy, I'd be the only one to get hit by a dick.'"

We laughed the laugh of two guys sharing an adolescent joke, but we both knew that wasn't the point of his story. Though the marine's sentiment was cloaked in grunt vulgarity to match the unexplainable violence one finds in war, we each understood it really as a poignant lament: That he was not at home helping to raise the children he helped create with the woman he loved. That he felt genuine guilt for not being more of a father (it was not happening the way he had imagined). That he hoped she would forgive him someday, perhaps when these constant deployments were past. That he felt a certain helplessness in the face of the irrevocable loss of these many years.

Some of Miller's soldiers that night might lie down and dream of brain matter leaking from a boy's head, some of being shot dead by a teenager, and others simply of home and what their absence might mean for those loyal hearts left behind. But when they awake, they will still be in Afghanistan and still at war.

Gilkey might only photograph the part of our soldiers' lives that his employer or the market were interested in seeing—I could hardly blame him for repeating what has worked. At least I knew he understood them.

CHAPTER 8:
OPERATION
NO LEAF CLOVER

Lieutenant Shane Joyce began Operation No Leaf Clover in the familiar company of his men, by now one of the most combat-hardened platoons in the Devil Brigade.

"I'm supposed to inspire my men as a leader, but I think most of the time, it is the other way around," he said.

Still recovering from shrapnel wounds from the Russian toe-popper on Nawah Road, Springob had been replaced as Joyce's RTO by Specialist Christian Contreras, the enthusiastic MK19 gunner. A very young-looking paratrooper with dark Mediterranean features, Contreras already had one kinetic deployment to Afghanistan with the 173rd "Sky Soldiers" before this tour. "Contreras was a badass," said Joyce. "He could answer 90 percent of the radio traffic himself, and I loved having such a skilled rifleman by my side."

Sergeant Jeffrey Buhl had become leader of Second Squad, and Sergeant Wesley Hatfield directed Weapons Squad, which, due to the limited personnel that currently made up Third Platoon, was just a single machine gun team of Specialist Richard Rogalinski and Specialist Raul Bermudez. Sergeant First Class Felton was along as usual. The backbone of Joyce's fighting element, First Squad's crusty Staff Sergeant Percefull, rounded out the leadership.

"Percefull reminded me of an old cowboy," said Joyce. "Nothing scared the man. He bred in everyone the feeling that you have to be tough as nails to be good at this job. Having a booboo lip about bad days or combat losses didn't help. He was a role model to Buhl and the most dependable guy to get a job done." Joyce had outfitted Percefull with an M14 sniper rifle after witnessing him kill an insurgent with a five-hundred-meter head shot on April 6.

Because No Leaf Clover was a company-level mission, senior fire support NCO, Staff Sergeant Jerry Hubbard, was attached to the platoon to coordinate air assets.

A month earlier during Operation Thunder Eagle, Joyce's platoon had uncovered an IED factory containing a thousand pounds of raw materials in Lalkhan Kheyl, the eastern-most village in their AO. The find was significant for many Charlie Company paratroopers since Sannicolas had been killed by an IED on the first day of that operation. (For that operation, Captain Ling had identified potential objectives by compiling historical data to determine the average distance from a mosque to a cache, mosque to a bed-down location, creek to a cache, and a major road to a cache. According to the brigade commander, Stock, the operation produced more tangible results than any other mission. The triggerman of the three-hundred-pound IED that killed Sannicolas was also captured.)

The goal of the forty-eight-hour No Leaf Clover was simple: helicopter into Lalkhan Kheyl, raid the factory a second time, and find a nearby IED storage facility, then helicopter out. "We had been making contact virtually every patrol," said Joyce. "We were confident, but this was our first air assault."

Just before 3 a.m. on May 21, two CH47 heavy lift Chinooks with Apache escorts ferried Charlie Company's Second and Third Platoons and a headquarters element under the leadership of Captain Caleb Ling to a barren open of packed clay just outside of Lalkhan Kheyl (the birds had been delayed ninety minutes due to maintenance issues). At first light, Second Platoon, led by Second Lieutenant Erik McCaffrey, infilled on a second flight and, with Captain Ling, searched a number of pre-planned objectives on the west side of Lalkhan Kheyl. Meanwhile, Joyce's Third Platoon set up blocking positions on the east side to catch any Taliban trying to escape Second Platoon. Once villagers were about and it was apparent that nobody was trying to flee, Third Platoon broke from its position to search a suspected weapons cache. The kalat was empty, but a local told them they weren't far off.

The muddy dawn had yet to give up the sun, and since the kalat was in the direction of a possible mortar cell known as Objective Sandman, the paratroopers set off. "We got down there, and it was exactly as the informant described," said Joyce. "The kalat was horseshoe-shaped, abandoned, but with fresh vegetation piled up in the middle, which is how the tipper said it would be." Underneath the vegetation, the paratroopers found twenty-five hundred rounds of Dushka ammunition, which EOD techs destroyed with twenty pounds of C4. "That was a big score for us," said Joyce. "There's not much you can hide behind when that big [Dushka] starts throwing six-hundred-grain rounds at you."

The heat was already oppressive, so the paratroopers stopped to rehydrate and eat.

Just after noon, Second Platoon worked north toward the village of Chahar Kalay. Third Platoon pushed south toward Sandman. The problem was, there was nothing in between them and the lone kalat. Unless they maneuvered an additional four kilometers up a circuitous wadi, the paratroopers would be exposed for the entire approach.

By now, everyone knew how company-level missions went down. Original objectives got buried under a moraine of follow-on objectives wrought by an avalanche of "good ideas" turned loose from the head shed just as soon as the first boot hit the ground. No matter how they reached Sandman, the day promised to be long and exhausting. They took a vote. Frontal assault won.

Joyce had his men spread far apart to limit the effectiveness of area weapons. They moved quickly across the open plain in traveling over-watch, an infantry movement tactic that balances speed with security when contact with the enemy is uncertain. Spread over four hundred meters in echelons of wedges, the lead squad maintained a steady pace, while the trail squad paused periodically to glass the horizon for threats.

After only a few hundred meters, several paratroopers heard some kind of racket emanating from a tree line a thousand meters to the west. The platoon seemed to automatically drift toward the noise. All at once, enemy machine gun and rifle fire laced through their formation.

Lacking cover, the paratroopers charged directly at the raking fire. Rogalinski, Hatfield's exceptional 240 gunner, quickly found the only elevation around and returned fire with his twenty-seven-pound machine gun—up to a thousand .308-caliber rounds per minute reaching the insurgent redoubt in about a second.

Still nine hundred meters out and finding themselves even more exposed on the downhill face of a shallow hill, Joyce called a halt and the platoon fell back. He and Contreras had been zigging and zagging, and when they finally hit the dirt shoulder to shoulder, an enemy bullet zinged between their heads. After a moment, the lieutenant stood up to run back to the mortar team to get them shooting. Staff Sergeant Hubbard, who was moving with the 60mm mortar team, yelled at him to get down. Joyce dropped just as PKM fire streamed over his position.

The mortarmen began lobbing three-pound charges at the tree line as fast as they could load the tube, but the barrage had no noticeable effect on the enemy rate of fire.

Ling and McCaffrey had mobilized part of Second Platoon and headquarters to flank from the north, and they began a 1.5 kilometer run down a creek line to help. On the radio, Hubbard reached the Air Force JTAC with Ling, who contacted the pilot of an F18 in the area. Cleared to engage, the jet came in straight out of the clouds.

"It looked like he was going to fly straight into the ground," recalled Joyce. The pilot pulled up without firing his 20mm cannon or dropping a bomb. He said he needed to make a better approach.

"Tell him to make that tree line disappear," Joyce radioed Hubbard. The second pass was also a dry run. Rogalinski was running low on ammo, and the platoon was still getting shot at. Joyce was seething. On a third pass, the pilot let loose a burst from his 20mm cannon that missed the tree line, but it was enough for the enemy to break contact.

Ling ordered Second Platoon to sweep the tree line, but the enemy was gone with no trace of injury. He then sent them back to their last patrol base to gather rucksacks while his headquarters element moved with Third Platoon to a landing zone for aerial resupply.

As they moved through an open field of kids playing soccer, the game occasionally spilled into the line of paratroopers who, even after a day of heavy patrolling, were not above trapping the ball and returning it with a swift kick.

Suddenly the kids scattered. Staff Sergeant Percefull's First Squad took first contact, AK fire from the north and west of the designated patrol base. Ling's headquarters element was immediately pinned down from a machine gun and rifle fire to the east. This time, however, Percefull's squad made it to a tree line, where they were able to establish effective fighting positions. Buhl's squad was still moving into the fight.

Joyce peered out of the wadi just in time to see a man peeking around a nearby kalat. "Peekers are always guilty," he said. The lieutenant rested his M4's ACOG sight on the corner where he had seen the man and waited. When the peeker reappeared with an AK47, Joyce pumped the trigger of his carbine, hitting the insurgent twice in the pelvis.

Looking to his right, he caught a glimpse of Buhl standing on a berm, giving hand and arm signals to his fire team leaders. "I couldn't believe he was just standing there under fire," said Joyce. "Some would call him foolhardy, but more often than not, on the battlefield, the difference between bravery and stupidity is whether or not you got shot."

Buhl's squad was pouring on the fire, forcing the enemy machine gunner to break contact. Joyce gave the signal, and the headquarters element sprinted for the patrol base.

Within the safety of the walls but still sucking wind, one of Joyce's privates addressed him, "Sir, you can go fuck yourself. I'm never bounding with you again." Hard love from Joe.

Hubbard called in a roving B1-B Lancer for a show of force. The swept-wing bomber came in like a silent missile just five hundred feet off the ground but rumbled overhead like an apartment complex fitted with afterburners. That was enough for the Taliban fighters. The Americans were left alone for the evening.

After dark, the platoons prepared to receive a resupply of food, water, and ammo from a pair of Black Hawks. Incredulously, the four green duffel bags were dropped five hundred meters from the patrol base in a waist-high field of green wheat. The platoons drew straws to see who would retrieve the supplies but settled on each forking up a squad. Many hours later, the hapless squads returned from the fields, bags in tow, for a few hours' rest before moving out again.

As soldiers shivered awake inside the patrol base, rumor was that Captain Ling received orders from battalion: clear every kalat in every village all the way to Rabow Kheyl. In fact, battalion commander Lieutenant Colonel Salome wanted Charlie Company to search the kalats surrounding the compound of Fazilhuddin, a reputed expert mortarman who often targeted their base.

They left before first light, clearing several villages on the way to Salim Kheyl where Fazilhuddin lived. In Mina Kheyl, a local who was detained agreed to lead Ling to the mortarman's house if he could be disguised as an ANA. Ling complied. Ling radioed Joyce and Third Platoon made a beeline for the compound. When the Taliban realized where the Americans were headed, they opened fire from the west, still within the village—a rare occurrence.

Inside a village, rifle reports echoed off buildings, complicating the task of locating the enemy. The paratroopers had to watch impacting rounds to judge where they were coming from. To expedite searching, Joyce had split the platoon into two sections. The first section led by Felton and Percefull had moved to the north when the Taliban hit Joyce and Buhl's section.

"Everyone fell into four-man fire teams just like we had practiced at JRTC," said Joyce. His paratroopers moved quickly through the village, alternately bounding and covering each other.

At the edge of a field, the paratroopers saw muzzle flashes opposite them. They fired back as Buhl maneuvered his teams. An armed insurgent popped out of a grape hut. "Put a round in there!" Buhl hollered to his grenadier. Private First Class Yamil Salas fired his M320 from the hip directly into the doorway and smoked the insurgent.

Specialist Caleb Heinzig, one of Buhl's SAW gunners, slunk around the corner of a kalat to meet face-to-face with a Taliban machine gunner who had just done the same thing. They locked eyes, raised their weapons and fired simultaneously. Each fell away, neither injured. The Taliban gunner ran for cover. Heinzig found himself in the dirt next to an ANA soldier firing a Dragunov sniper rifle. The Afghan ripped through the magazine so close to the American paratrooper's head that Heinzig was deaf for the remainder of the mission.

Now established on higher ground, one of Buhl's fire teams had gained fire superiority over the enemy, and they finally broke contact, but not before Fazilhuddin was able to escape.

Ling passed the ten-digit grid to the insurgent's home to Joyce, who led his platoon there. The compound was one of the plushest any of them had seen, with a ten-room living quarters, carpeting and buffed concrete floors, and farmland completely walled in. The barn was enormous, with multiple stories. Only women were home, of course. The compound was split into a residence and a farm, connected only by a little hobbit door in a dividing wall. On the other side, Joyce's paratroopers were confronted by a very agitated cow tethered to the wall.

"That cow was pissed," said Joyce. In the commotion of searching soldiers, the animal pulled loose and charged Specialist Joshua Locke-Thompson, who ran. "The best paratroopers in the world were screaming like little girls from a cow. It was hilarious."

Locke-Thompson tripped and fell, and the mad cow dashed off toward another screaming paratrooper. The same Dragunov gunner who had deafened Heinzig walked forward like a Spanish matador, stood on a tall pile of dirt, and squared off with the cow. The cow stopped, lowered its head, scraped the dirt as if it were a bull, and charged. With his sniper rifle, the ANA muzzle-thumped the cow in the forehead, sending the bovine rolling on its back in a seizure.

It was a kind of violence that might be shocking back in America but was commonplace in Afghanistan. In graduate school, I had trapped, darted, and tranquilized wild animals in the name of science, and as a lifelong hunter, I regularly killed game for food. Yet much of the violence to animals that I saw or heard about in Afghanistan seemed gratuitous, or at the very least, not recognized as violence at all. I guess it's no surprise that where human suffering is underappreciated, animal suffering is more so.

Incidentally, Ling's informant led the headquarters element and Second Platoon to the very house that Third Platoon was searching. Inside the living quarters, the Americans found multiple IDs for the same man, travel papers to Pakistan, rifles, a shotgun, and empty 82mm mortar round boxes.

"At that point, everyone was smoked," recalled Joyce. The mission intent had been satisfied, but Captain Ling wanted to push on through Rabow Kheyl and walk all the way back to Muqor rather than wait for the safety of nightfall. Without another resupply planned for the mission, he and his first sergeant were concerned about running out of radio batteries and water. Several paratroopers had dysentery and were crapping their pants, furthering their dehydration. What came next developed into a heated argument between the platoon leaders, platoon sergeants, and Captain Ling.

"We were all smoked, and getting ambushed again was hardly in our best interest nor within the intent of the mission," said Joyce. "Lieutenant McCaffrey, the platoon sergeants Morrison and Felton, and I pleaded with Captain Ling and First Sergeant Brashears to wait just one more hour so that we could travel under limited visibility, almost guaranteeing that we wouldn't be engaged."

The mission was over. All they had to do was get home, so what was the rush? "Move out" was the answer.

"In his defense, Captain Ling said we had dedicated air assets to cover our movement, which normally worked to keep the Taliban off of us," said Joyce. "However, we all knew that 'dedicated' air always had to leave for some reason or another, and that would leave us flapping out in the open."

From Ling's perspective, the A-10s would allow the company to move expeditiously across the open danger area to the cover of a tree line near Rabow Kheyl, and the three hours of coverage would have been more than enough to get them all the way back to base.

Charlie Company stepped off for Rabow Kheyl. Under cover of low-flying A-10 Warthogs that made several show-of-force low passes, the platoons made it through the first open area without incident. Unfortunately, the attack jets were being pulled off to support paratroopers with 2-504 engaged in a big firefight to the north at Qara Bagh.

At the same time, an EOD tech found an IED command wire leading to a road the paratroopers were skirting. It was too obvious, as if it were planted to slow the Americans down.

To the northeast and south, white vans and motorcycles began circling the formation. "We all knew they were maneuvering on us but

ROE restricted us from killing them since we couldn't see any weapons on them. All we could do was hope to have some cover when the attack commenced." The paratroopers picked up speed in a race to make the village walls.

Second Platoon, the company headquarters, and Joyce's lead element with Buhl reached the village. As Percefull's First Squad moved through rows of grapes still nearly two hundred meters out, insurgents began peppering them with rifle fire. Hatfield pushed his one machine gun team past the incoming squad and set up on the far corner of the grape field just as the Taliban pulled the trigger on a three-sided ambush.

From a tree line to the north, multiple machine guns, RPGs, and rifles opened up on Percefull's squad, pinning it in the grape rows. From the northeast, east, and southeast came more automatic weapons fire from multiple prepared fighting positions, and from the south, more machine gun fire from a kalat.

Ling had Second Platoon reposition a squad to provide covering fire for Third Platoon to move. As the machine guns fired from the north, he spied two men on the roof of a kalat twenty meters northeast of his headquarters element. Nearly surrounded, it was much worse than their initial contact on April 6.

At first, machine guns bore down on Felton and the medic, Private First Class Dylan Wells. Over the radio, Joyce tried to get Buhl's squad to maneuver north to suppress the worst of the enemy fire emanating from the tree line, but Buhl had already pushed his men southeast into an L-shaped creek to hit aggressors arrayed among the grape fields ahead of them. Behind the lone 240 Bravo, Rogalinski was hitting money with carefully-aimed bursts, and soon, most of the enemy fire was concentrating on Hatfield's tiny redoubt.

"There was so much dirt erupting and tracers pouring all over their position, I was sure they were all smoked," said Joyce. Then he saw Hatfield roll over and light a cigarette. They were still alive, but pinned flat to the earth, and the platoon's lone machine gun was effectively out of the fight.

Comms were chaotic, and desperate to bring his platoon to effective use against the ambush, Second Platoon's leader, Second Lieutenant Erik McCaffrey also began working south, thinking that Joyce was attacking north. Just then, the first call for a medic came over the radio: "Three-six, this is Three-one. I need a medic at my position." There was no mistaking Staff Sergeant Percefull's husky voice.

"Three-one, this is Three-six. Roger, who's hit and how bad?" Joyce asked.

"For me," Percefull replied.

The platoon's venerable old squad leader had been shot by machine gun fire in the neck just off center of the throat and in the shoulder. A bullet had ripped a hole lengthwise in the carotid artery that should have been feeding his brain with oxygenated blood, but instead, blood was arcing from the side of his neck. He used one hand to stanch the fountain and the other to grip his M14 even as he called for a medic.

By the time Doc Wells was able to dash up the grape rows to Percefull, Private First Class Jason Denton was already there with both hands in a chokehold around his squad leader's neck. Wells took over and slowed Percefull's blood loss with a field dressing, but he was going to die if not evacuated soon. With Percefull bleeding out, senior team leader Sergeant Michael Welcheck took command of the pinned squad.

Ling and Rob Tubbe, an American law enforcement expert and former enlisted paratrooper there to help tactically question detainees, engaged men on a rooftop firing RPGs, but the explosive rockets continued to streak from the northern wood line. One detonated a few feet behind Specialist Mark Harris, sending hot fragments into his right arm. Nevertheless, the grenadier kept fighting.

From the south, a new terror entered the battlescape. The unmistakable thump of six-hundred-grain Dushka bullets designed to take down aircraft was being turned against their frail earthworks, ceramic plates, flesh, and bone. From Percefull's position, Hubbard was screaming, "Get a machine gun up here!" That was too much for Joyce. "When I was a kid, I was a little wild bastard," he explained. "My mom said, 'You won't understand until you have kids of your own.' I knew exactly what she was talking about. I had twenty-eight lives that I was responsible for. That changes a human being." Joyce was about to make a dash for Rogalinski's 240, the most effective weapon nearby. He handed his M4 to Contreras and ordered him to stay put, but just as he stepped out, the young RTO tackled him.

Across the battlefield came a long rip off an M249 squad automatic weapon. Joyce had told Buhl to "kill everyone down there" to the south, so Buhl's SAW gunner, Heinzig, climbed a berm and single-handedly killed a whole team of insurgents.

Heinzig had neutralized the Taliban's southern pincer, allowing the paratroopers pinned in the grape rows to stand up and effectively return fire on the northern tree line. As the paratroopers gained fire superiority, the enemy broke contact in stages.

With the medevac birds inbound, Second Platoon's platoon sergeant, Sergeant First Class Dave Morrison, took it upon himself to talk in the Black Hawks, pop smoke, and help the wounded to the choppers, all under fire. There was Harris being helped onto a bird and then Percefull—walking. "That crusty old fuck wouldn't let anyone carry him onto the helicopter," said Joyce.

Just before liftoff, Sergeant Welcheck reported that he was hit as well. He had taken RPG shrapnel behind the patella but had only just noticed. He boarded one of the two aircraft, leaving Specialist Lock-Thompson as the squad leader. Despite the loss of his two most immediate senior leaders, he knew what to do. It wasn't "hang your head" time. He was now a leader of a little group of pissed-off paratroopers. Not even a noncommissioned officer, the young specialist immediately reconsolidated the squad and pushed into the tree line.

Signal intelligence suggested that, though the Taliban had quit firing, they were ready to reengage. Ling quickly moved the company into the cover of one tree line after another to the safety of Muqor.

The mission had confirmed the area was an insurgent support zone, but the complexity of the attacks suggested capable leadership. In fact, they were coordinated by Fazilhuddin himself and another Taliban commander, Mohammed Noor. Ling estimated that, over the four firefights, the enemy fired fifteen to twenty thousand rounds of 7.62mm ammunition, suggesting a healthy supply of small arms ammunition in northern Muqor.

For actions that day, Locke-Thompson was awarded an Army Commendation with Valor, as were Denton and Wells. Morrison was awarded a Bronze Star Medal with Valor.

Staff Sergeant Patrick Percefull was flown to Warrior, but despite their best attempts, the surgeons could not get anything inside the carotid artery to patch it. He died there, then was brought back to life. He died and was revived again at BAF (Bagram Airfield). In Germany, surgeons spliced a section of Gore-Tex onto the lacerated artery to repair it. Decorated in Iraq and now Afghanistan for valorous actions under fire, Percefull's combat was over. He was alive, and he was going home.

Losing the senior squad leader was a blow to the platoon. Percefull's departure left a leadership void at the platoon's most lethal node. Joyce had to find a suitable replacement quickly—not an easy task since all able noncoms were already gainfully employed. That left the washouts and dirtbags.

Recognizing that the platoon needed a break in combat, they were given a week of "R&R" gate-guard duty at FOB Warrior, during which Joyce and Felton searched for a new squad leader. They were given Staff Sergeant Kent. The man's reputation was not good. He had been a mortician before the army and once bragged that he had cremated his own brother. Joyce struggled to find anyone else, but no dice.

"I tell you this because I want you to know how wrong I was proven," Joyce said. "Staff Sergeant Kent's reputation was anything but desirable, and I let that taint my impression of him. It wasn't long before I learned otherwise, and he quickly became just another one of us redheaded stepchildren, albeit one of the weirdest motherfuckers I've ever met. He was a really good squad leader."

It was Third Platoon's lucky day. They received more than a new squad leader. The platoon was plussed up by six, to twenty-eight paratroopers, which gave Joyce enough for two machine gun teams. That would be a game-changer.

CHAPTER 9:
DEATH FROM ABOVE

Blood loss is the primary killer on the battlefield, always has been, but bleeding out doesn't haunt a soldier's dreams. Like young women trying the last names of men they might marry, soldiers try on different ways they might die.

For instance, few worry about getting shot as much as they worry about getting shot in the face. Soldiers commonly exposed to the threat of IEDs sometimes barter with their fears by consciously accepting a certain amount of loss beforehand—perhaps a leg or an arm, but not two legs. Expectation management. Everybody knows somebody who has it much worse, and in a way, that is comforting.

Naturally there is little recovery from getting "blown the fuck up." There's not even time to consider how irrecoverable pieces will be, even for miracle surgeons. Around May 18, a friend of a friend in Helmand province walked behind a steel shipping container to relieve himself and stepped on an IED packing ten pounds of HME. Married, with a one-year-old, he became a triple amputee. Mutilation is part of the reason that IEDs are such an effective weapon of terror, particularly for those not terribly concerned with collateral damage.

A news report in late May implicated a NATO airstrike in the deaths of eight civilians in Paktia Province. Yet even as the author blamed NATO, he admitted that nearly 80 percent of civilian casualties were caused by insurgents. Around that time, I saw classified photos of Taliban fighters in the wake of a NATO airstrike in a Paktia forest. Modern military munitions are as cruel to flesh and bone as HME. Hunks of meat lay in the duff like hastily butchered brisket and drying jerky, strewn about timbers snapped chest high, bodies were fractioned off in generous ragged chunks, limbs were disarticulated at alien angles, and faces were smashed inside out or blown off with most but not all of the head. As our soldiers do not see the IED until it is too late, the insurgents had not seen the airstrike. Airstrikes must haunt Taliban dreams. I was glad of that.

The Taliban were cavalier about collateral damage because they could afford to be. In much of Ghazni and the rest of Afghanistan—certainly most of the rural areas—they controlled the public conversation. IEDs and propaganda were both cheap and easy to manufacture. Propaganda became more difficult when crowds of people with cell phones were involved, as they were during a series of missteps by Taliban IED emplacers near FOB Arian in late May.

On May 22, a pressure plate IED exploded beneath a civilian vehicle on Highway 1 near Ab Band, killing all aboard. Then on the 24th, a bus was hit, killing eight civilians and injuring sixteen. A day later, a commercial truck was hit north of FOB Arian. There was probably little coincidence that only two days later on May 27, just up the road in Andar province, the Taliban school-closing situation boiled over. Armed citizens attacked Taliban forces, killing twelve of them. As much as the Taliban's ability to move freely among the populace was a strength, it became a game-ender if the people rebelled.

Before sundown May 27, a Taliban commander named Mullah Kamran set up a Russian-made, 82mm mortar tube on the edge of Andar, a half-dozen klicks west of FOB Arian. The mortar tube was probably the same one used to hit the Arian chow hall tent a few days earlier, the same one that sent me scurrying away from my chicken enchiladas a day after that. In the 2-504 battalion TOC, Mullah Kamran was on a big-screen TV. As he sighted the mortar tube on Arian, villagers gathered around as we would in the States for fireworks.

I was in the chow hall, about to be separated from my hot meal for the second night in a row. I loved being a fobbit, especially on Ice Cream Night. At 6:30 p.m., the sirens went off. I dashed with the rest of the chow hall into one of several above-ground concrete bunkers and waited, wishing I had brought my chow along this time.

Inside the bunker, a female specialist who had been at the chow hall entrance checking IDs asked, "Was that for incoming or outgoing?"

"I dunno," said a mechanic from Fox Company.

Boom. Boom, boom, boom.

"Pretty sure that was outgoing," said an infantry private first class.

Sweet.

In the PTIDS screen, villagers around Kamran were seen running when they heard the FOB guns fire—155 howitzers and 120mm mortars. While the 155 is the larger munition, because of the angle of impact, the 120mm mortar actually has a larger kill radius, seventy meters as compared to fifty. The person nearest the mortar tube, presumably Kamran, shied away but quickly returned.

A man passing by on a moped appeared to catch the first round in his lap, an unfortunate bit of luck for him. Who rides casually past an insurgent commander about to attack the US Army with noisy, trackable bombs? In the TOC, wild cheers went up as the artillery rounds pulverized the mortar site. A patrol was sent out to recover the mortar tube. By the time the paratroopers arrived, however, there was little evidence that the attack had even occurred.

A few days later, I accompanied Shepro's platoon as they investigated another "POO site," or point of origin for a mortar attack. This one was on the opposite side of the highway, several klicks to the east underneath a high bridge that carried irrigation water across a ravine. Finding nothing, Shepro's platoon moved into the nearest village, where he confronted the village elders. He told them that, so long as they continued to harbor the Taliban, his men would continue to search their homes.

An elder with a snow-white beard squatted beneath the broad branches of a shade tree with his arms stretched across his knees and listened to Shepro speak. When the platoon sergeant had said his piece, the old man told Shepro that he and the other elders would never rat out the Taliban. "We are not afraid of you," he said without boast or belligerence. "We know you will not hurt us. If we tell on the Taliban, they will kill us." Particularly for the more vulnerable civilians, the women, children, and old men, that's the way it was, he said.

Two days after the Kamran incident, I patrolled out to Andar with Second Lieutenant Kirk Shoemaker's First Platoon. My friend Najibolla, armed this time with an RPG launcher, came along with a dozen Afghan soldiers. Shoemaker was checking in on a Taliban madrassa where young boys were boarded and indoctrinated. It was his second visit to the school and third to Andar.

Andar village lay at the foot of a mostly barren lopsided mountain that literally backed insurgents into a wall. One of the rules of warfare is that, if the enemy has nowhere to run, he's more likely to fight viciously. On the other hand, when the enemy blends with the populace—or is the populace—he may not fight at all. It could go either way.

As we moved into the village from the open plain between Arian and Andar, Taliban radio chatter picked up.

"There are lots of soldiers here today."

"Don't do anything stupid."

Najibolla stopped and questioned several villagers who were riding bicycles to another village. A young man informed him that our mortars had severely injured Mullah Kamran but had not killed him. Others said they hadn't even heard the mortars land. "They can't hear their wives either," Najibolla said with a smug grin.

We moved on to the Taliban school. After questioning a dozen boys—the instructors were never there when Shoemaker visited—our patrol moved deeper into the village. There was a tension among the villagers, and for long stretches, there were no children about. Every avenue seemed a perfect avenue for attack, and since we didn't know how to navigate the maze of walls, pathways, irrigation ditches, and high-walled compounds, we were in for a shellacking. The signal spooks reported that the Taliban was still trying to fix our location so they could send us a "special guest."

"What is that? Mortars? A suicide vest?" Shoemaker asked rhetorically. "I'll tell you, this is my third time in this village. The first time, they were pretty friendly. They are not friendly at all this time."

As always, Najibolla attracted the youngsters. Today it was boys old enough to ogle the RPG he carried. In a market, he put the war on hold and plopped down in the shade for a rest. Soon he was talking in serious tones to a gaggle of boys who should have been in school.

"What is he telling them?" I asked our terp.

"He is say, the Taliban is bad," he said in his broken English. "You should love your country and be strong for your country."

I wondered at the likelihood of one of their fathers having been killed by our artillery barrage? For all we knew, Kamran's son could have been sitting there with Najib.

When we reached the edge of Andar, we saw that the desert had absorbed all traces of the nine rounds of high explosives cast by our artillery tubes. It was as if the barrage had never happened. How long would the villagers be angry? The code they lived by, *Pashtunwali*, demanded retaliation for even the threat of an attack.

As we fanned into the rising wheat fields that formed the apron of the village, Shoemaker warned, "This is probably where we're going to get hit if we do." He pointed to a long *kalat* wall on our right flank."Grazing machine gun fire from over there."

At least we weren't trapped inside the village. Out here, there were only so many pieces of the puzzle. And room to bring in artillery or Apaches, so-called death from above. I looked to the south. Shoemaker had prepositioned his scouts for counterattack on our flank just in case, a strong offense being the best defense. But nothing happened. We walked back to Arian in time for hot chow.

I had come to Arian to cover Captain Vest's air assault against Mushaki, and after several delays, the mission was finally green-lighted. Before the midnight departure, an emergency situation developed called a DUSTWUN, short for "duty status, whereabouts unknown." In other words, there was a potential hostage situation involving American troops somewhere in our AO.

Specialist Kedith Jacobs Jr. and Private First Class Leroy Deronde III, both operating out of Wardak Province with 3rd Brigade Combat Team, 1st Armored Division, were believed to be abducted by insurgents and moved to Ghazni Province. A Special Operations task force was gearing up for the rescue. Every military asset in Ghazni was being brought to bear in the operation. The army's response to a DUSTWUN was unequivocally Leave No Man Behind. It made me proud. Suddenly the emergency was called off. Jacobs and Deronde were "found," incinerated when their fuel tanker had struck an IED. Unfortunately, the helicopters pulled off of Vest's mission could not be redirected in time for the air assault, and it was postponed until further notice.

With the local Taliban commander possibly wounded and in hiding, Vamvakias was taking 2-504 on a manhunt for Mullah Kamran. His intelligence analysts believed they knew where he was. Just after one in the morning of June 1, a half-dozen Chinooks and Black Hawks raced westward from FOB Arian, passing low over Andar and other villages dotting the rim of an ancient fluvial fan that grew only thistle and goats, now glowing softly with starlight. At eight thousand feet above sea level, the helicopters touched down long enough to disgorge chalks of paratroopers, and beat back into the sky.

On the ground, there was barely any breeze. Starlight reflected softly off of fantastical landforms worn smooth and curvy by the primal elements. Voids of black to the immediate north and south indicated steep peaks blocking the stars. There were no trees, or vegetation to dampen the sound. Without care, a whisper could become an echo.

Some three hundred paratroopers filtered down the starlit slopes as if deposited there by the Milky Way. By NODs they moved through the high-altitude badlands, where wind and water had near-universal command over the soft sandstones. Gullies fed ravines that dropped into a basin of deep dust bordered by steep slopes. At the end of the basin was the highest reach of the habitable part of the mountain valley. There sat the village of Barlah. The first compound to the left belonged to Mullah Kamran.

Vamvakias and his staff climbed high above, establishing a battalion tactical assault command, or TAC, on the northern wall of the valley to overwatch western Barlah and Kamran's compound. Captain Gacke's Charlie Company halted inside a basin just short of the compound, while Captain Jared Larpenteur's Delta Company maneuvered on to the next village downslope.

Dogs were barking. Dogs were always barking in Afghanistan. With the pink and lavenders of dawn tinting the sky, it became clear why Kamran had chosen this place. Barlah was breathtakingly beautiful. Castle-like sandstone formations surrounded broad, green tasseled fields of wheat, with bands of leafy poplar trees abiding the margins of cold-water creeks. The mountains were stark, barren, and substantial. Were the valley in the States, it would have been a national park.

But we weren't in the States. Najibolla was wielding his RPG launcher while helping paratroopers search a *kalat* next to the *kalat* of a Taliban commander. Najib found an old breech-action shotgun and a bucket of Dushka shells, and when he questioned the old man of the compound, the pepper-bearded farmer just smirked and threw up his hands. "I am just a farmer."

Najib's face contorted with anger, and he grabbed the old crank by the throat. I thought he was going to crush the man's face with the buttstock of the shotgun, but the old farmer offered no resistance and kept talking as if he didn't even need a face to farm.

"He just found them, he says," the terp translated.

With disgust, Najib released the old goat-like man.

Sergeant Jeffrey Wiley collected the farmer's biometrics as others continued to search the sprawling compound. Over the radio, First Lieutenant Jamal Stevens learned that Mullah Kamrah's compound had been thoroughly searched, with no detainees. The mullah was not home. Only women and children.

Captain Gacke arranged to have tea with a neighbor of the mullah's, an elder with a downy beard, burnt olive skin, and no teeth, who lived in a tidy, two-story building accented with pygmy goats, chickens, fruit trees, and a small vegetable garden. The view from the porch where they sat for chai was postcard-worthy—a pastoral reach to high, folding mountains and deep blue sky. Several neighbors joined in the tea.

The Taliban came here often. He might even get a reprisal for having tea with the Americans, the elder said. While Gacke chatted, a lieutenant interrupted to say that D Co. had found a weapons cache in the lower village and were about to blow it up. Sure enough, in five minutes, we saw then heard the explosion down the valley.

On a red rug set with flatbread and crystal tumblers of chai tea, the old man said he was pretty sure that he was around seventy-three years old. He had been a soldier before the Russians invaded. Some of his children still lived with him, but he was building a house in Muqor for two sons. He cursed the corruptness of the government, pointing out that it had taken him three years and a bribe to obtain a national ID card.

"This is our government," he said. It was a statement and a query.

Gacke offered the man a hand-cranked radio that would also run on solar power. The staid Texan was growing on me, and I felt his embarrassment when the first radio failed to work. The LT handed him a second. "Do you listen to the radio much?" Gacke asked, as he demonstrated the crank.

"No," replied the old man. "It's all bad news." Nonetheless, he seemed delighted by the radio.

By noon, Charlie had cleared to their second objective, an imaginary predetermined "phase line" drawn on a map to pace the operation and to communicate progress to higher headquarters. One platoon had found a bag with nine remote control devices, nine wristwatches, and a spool of angel-hair copper wire (triggering components for IEDS) hastily tossed in a field. An old man in a tiny house was complaining to Gacke that all the trouble in the village came from Mullah Kamran. The village women were scared all night from the noise of the helicopters. They hated Kamran. Even Kamran's brother, who lived up the hill, was feuding with the mullah. Yet even as the old man griped about Kamran, radio transmissions indicated that the Taliban knew which house Gacke was at.

But nothing happened. Nothing happened the entire seventy-two hours we were on the ground in Barlah. If the area was a Taliban safe haven, the insurgents had felt so safe that none of the assumed defenses—rings of IEDs, suicide vests and car bombs, and fortified fighting positions—were ever deployed to defend the mountain sanctuary.

We slept in the town square that night and returned to Mullah Kamran's compound in the morning for a second sweep. The wife of the mullah's brother was very angry to have her home ransacked again, her words. She was arguing with an Afghan soldier when Najibolla thrust a hand in her direction, pretending to have a cell phone in his other hand. Speaking into his pinky, he said, "Kamran? Kamran?" A goat walked by him and he held out the phone to it, asking, "Kamran?"

Other women in the compound told our terp that no males lived there at all, and that Kamran hadn't been there in a year. Their husbands were away at Muqor, Qara Bagh, and Iran.

"They are Taliban," the terp said with a nod.

Meanwhile, another of Gacke's platoons found a large cache of weapons near a town well, and Lieutenant Shoemaker's platoon discovered several AK47s and magazines stashed in an adjacent wheat field. By evening, there were enough weapons and ammo for another controlled detonation. At dusk, Gacke led the company several kilometers out of Barlah to a secluded fruit grove, where we rested a few hours until dawn.

The following day was a prolonged wait for the ride back to Arian. It was hot, dry, and tedious with our sleepy eyes tugging at our faces all day. As evening approached, the action picked up. Delta Company made one last controlled detonation. Some of Gacke's soldiers paid a farmer sixty dollars for a goat, and an ANA sergeant slaughtered it at the edge of the trees where we waited. Over a fire, they cooked and ate it.

Over three hundred paratroopers had dropped out of the sky into the unsuspecting valley and combed it for nearly three days. No soldier got more than four hours of sleep in that time. For the effort, they had destroyed maybe two hundred pounds of weapons and ammunition. So much for "death from above." Sometimes missions end that way. I think for Vamvakias and his captains, it was a frustrating time. The battalion's human intelligence workers believed that the air assaults were compromised by the Qara Bagh police chief's new chai boy, a suspected Taliban informant who was hired after he began partnering with Vamvakias' paratroopers.

Back on FOB Arian, I stayed up all night to process nearly a thousand digital images. I caught an early helicopter and was back at FOB Warrior by 6:30 a.m. One of Ben Farmer's articles had finally been published in *The Economist*. After all those interviews with our paratroopers, his piece was about Taliban leaders in Ghazni who were captured and then paid a bribe to Afghan officials to be freed.

In other news, locals in Andar province continued to fight the Taliban, defiantly reopening all but two of eighty-three schools the foreign fighters had closed. We wanted to believe that a tribal revolt could happen in Ghazni as it had in Anbar Province, but the pushback against the Taliban just seemed to simmer.

On June 8, brigade actually assigned me a mission, something that had not happened since my arrival in Afghanistan. It involved a cake.

With enlisted representatives of each of our six battalions, I flew to the big NATO base at Bagram to take part in an official cake-cutting ceremony to celebrate the US Army's 237th birthday. The cake had been made by the celebrity *Cake Boss*, Buddy Valastro, and flown in from the States. We would prerecord our boys cutting the cake with the commanding general of the 1st Infantry Division (who was, at that time, also the commanding general of the entire area), to be aired as if it were live when a sister cake was cut in New York City's Times Square on June 14, the US Army's actual birthday.

It was all very "gay" in an army way that has nothing to do with sexuality or homophobia. In army-speak, gay simply means putting a ridiculous amount of energy into a task of little perceived significance when there are more important things needing attention. Wearing a PT belt when operating a lawnmower is gay because nearby people can already hear the thing. When Sergeant Mann died during PT, there was a post-wide ban against any soldier running more than four miles during morning PT. For paratroopers training for war, *that* was gay.

The excess of super-FOB Bagram was enough in its own right for our paratroopers, who hadn't even seen a PX for months, let alone a Pizza Hut, Burger King, or Green Beans Coffeehouse. The greatest army in the world may not subdue the Taliban, but we can put a Pizza Hut in their backyard.

Now all of our soldiers were paratroopers, but the 1st Infantry Division is a "leg" unit. More specifically, paratroopers call non-airborne soldiers "dirty, stinking, nasty legs." Now *there* is a proper pejorative. Paratroopers are not known for their humility. To the general's chagrin, buttered in the frosting of the army's birthday cake was a beautiful, red-and-blue All American "AA" logo of the 82nd Airborne Division.

The general's command sergeant major panicked and ordered our paratroopers to don 1st Infantry Division ball caps, which he provided surprisingly fast. He was going to let us paratroopers know who was inferior to whom. He handed the first ball cap to Private First Class Jeffrey Liu, a young SAW gunner from southern California who had just come off the line at the new Tarnak River outpost where insurgents had been hitting his platoon daily with everything they had. Liu held the cap like it had herpes and said, "That's gay."

The general laughed good-naturedly and said, "No, we're not going to do this to these young paratroopers."

Not the sergeant major. He grimaced and said, "Well, general, I'm sure you and I have more jumps than all of these guys combined."

It was that gay.

I'm not much for cake or cake cuttings. I still don't understand the army's infatuation with cakes. Nevertheless, I did enjoy how at ease I felt those two days on Bagram knowing for sure that I wasn't going to be shot, mortared, rocketed, or blown up. I don't even eat cake, but I ate a piece of the Cake Boss' cake. It was that good. And it was Airborne. Death by chocolate.

Later that night, I read that Al Qaeda's number two had just been killed in Waziristan, the mountainous region of Pakistan's lawless northwest that borders Afghanistan and feeds the ratlines of Ghazni's Nawah District. He had been obliterated by a drone strike.

CHAPTER 10:
JSS HASAN

On Friday, June 1, Ateequllah, Muhammad Naeem, Muhammad Ya'qub, Ibraheemi, and Kareemullah joined six other suicide bombers and assaulted FOB Salerno in Khost Province, breeching the perimeter with a massive truck bomb and rushing the grounds with RPGs, AK47s, and suicide vests. Two US troops and five Afghan civilians were killed, with over a hundred troops suffering minor wounds. All of the attackers were slain within sixty meters of the breech.

The five men above were all from Gilan District, the heart of Taliban country in Ghazni Province. Gilan was the place where 1-504 had only a week earlier constructed Joint Security Station Hasan to overwatch the Tarnak River Bridge. At the cake cutting, Liu explained to me that JSS Hasan had been built in a compound abandoned by an ostracized family. It had taken ninety men over a dozen days to fortify the burned-out *kalat* for occupation. Now manned by paratroopers of Delta or "Demon" Company, 1-504, and an ANA company out of Muqor, the base had been attacked nearly every day since its occupation.

Two paratroopers had been shot in the head, but in both cases, their helmets had saved them. For base defense, the paratroopers used strategically positioned gun trucks and a few 60mm mortars (hand-held tubes that infantry carry on patrol). The ANA had one 82mm mortar, worn so thin that the Americans worried the rather talented mortarman was going to blow himself up.

The Poles rarely dared to travel as far as Hasan or nearby Karwaddin, the home of locally grown Taliban commander, Faruk. It was Faruk who had harbored the suicide bombers who attacked Salerno and who orchestrated most of the arms and explosives flow through this part of Gilan. Many locals had not seen white-skinned people since the Russians pulled out. The novelty may have been responsible in part for a young child telling American paratroopers, "My dad shoots at Americans all the time."

Returning from Bagram, I asked the 1-504 operations officer, Major Jason Glemser, to hook me up with a ride to Hasan. I was on my way later the same afternoon.

At times, the army felt rather small, as it did on the trip to Hasan with Staff Sergeant James Ozsomer. "Oz" had been the team leader of a night patrol that I had accompanied in Iraq along the Syrian border three years earlier. I could still hear him scolding me in the dark, "Hey PAO, you're too fucking noisy with that tripod. Quiet the fuck down!"

Oz was now part of the battalion commander's personal security detail, or PSD. The 1-504 battalion commander, Lieutenant Colonel Rob Salome, and Command Sergeant Major Billy Chaney were convoying to JSS Hasan to plan operations with the Afghan military leaders there.

Our small convoy left Warrior later than planned because Hasan was reporting substantial contact. On the way in, we listened to a lieutenant's repeated call for artillery from Warrior's 155mm howitzers to neutralize Taliban forces that had his paratroopers pinned down in a grape field beneath withering machine gun fire. The LT was calling for "danger close" artillery fire, so close that his own troops could be hit by shrapnel from incoming rounds.

Four kilometers out of Warrior and still six klicks from Hasan, Oz dismounted with a squad and some Afghan soldiers to check out a culvert on the far side of the sleepy little village of Latif. The culvert was clear, but the road ahead had not been checked in some time. There were sure to be IEDs. Delta Company's tank-like Hispanic first sergeant, Trey Corrales, led one squad through the scrubby desert on one side of the road, while the platoon sergeant, Staff Sergeant Francisco Ruiz, led a squad on the other side. The gun trucks traveled overland just off the roadbed. Oz and two other soldiers bearing mine detectors stayed on the road for a while and finally moved off it altogether. It was a wise choice. Days later it would take combat engineers the better part of a day to safely detonate all the IEDs they found in that section of road.

The closer we came to Hasan, the more gunfire we heard. Between moderate interludes of single shots came dramatic clashes of machine gun fire and explosions. The Taliban had rearmed. It was a battle. Just before six in the evening, a farmer approached the patrol and warned Ruiz and Corrales that the Taliban had planted an IED in an orchard wall along the road three hundred meters ahead, and they were waiting there in ambush. On the horizon at our 2 o'clock, the battle was peaking, with uninterrupted high-low staccato of small arms, machine gun fire, and burst after burst of RPGs. The lieutenant there was calling again for 155s. With Taliban lying in wait, giddy ANA soldiers armed with old Russian-made weapons ran ahead. Soldiering skills aside, many of the ANA cherished a good fight.

Corrales and Ruiz deployed their troops in a sort of bounding overwatch up to the wall, giving wide berth to the danger zone. Nothing happened. Either the Taliban fighters had pulled out, or there never had been an ambush. Our soldiers sometimes believed that passersby reported IEDs and ambushes just to make the Americans slow down so they *could* organize a proper ambush.

The convoy finally reached the outskirts of Hasan, a typical poor, if sprawling, agrarian hamlet. The road narrowed as it passed through a patchwork of *kalats*, some inhabited, some abandoned. Shoulder-high walls forced all traffic onto the road. The gunfire had finally ceased.

"I wouldn't walk there," Oz said to me, pointing at my feet. He was pushed tight against the wall on our right. "We hit an IED there last week." I remember Oz saying that his LT's gun truck had been hit twice by IEDs.

"Like right here?" I pointed at my feet.

"Like right there," he said. It felt like splitting hairs, but not one to argue with experience, I tiptoed to the right and followed in his steps until we reached the security station. We arrived just before dark.

Inside thick fifteen-foot-high mud-brick walls was an Alamo-looking edifice ringed by sandbags and flagged with the blue company guidon of Company D, 1-504th PIR. That was the company CP. Next to it was a gun truck partially concealed by a large camouflaged net. The truck was the communications center for the company. In the CP were three dirt-walled rooms—an aid station, a map room, and sleeping quarters for the company commander, Captain Philip Schneider. There was no roof other than a couple of haphazardly placed flattened Hesco baskets, draped gingerly from burned logs jutting from the mud walls. The north wall of the little fort was formed by the ramshackle remains of a long, narrow building. Schneider's paratroopers were using its many roofless rooms as quarters, some sleeping on army cots, others on sleeping bags laid in the dirt. The station's several guard towers went mostly unmanned due to the sniper threat.

Outside an internal gate, across a creek and jutting east toward the Tarnak River was a pleasant grove of trees under which the rest of Schneider's men slept in shallow, body-length foxholes known as "Ranger graves." Incoming mortars had blown off most of the upper branches of the fruit trees in the grove. Just outside the trees was the ANA mortar pit with its single ancient mortar tube. Several MRAPs were parked between it and a simple barrier of concertina wire, facing outward toward the Tarnak River bridge. Insurgents regularly hit "The Grove" with mortars and RPGs, the paratroopers said. Pieces of spent munitions—tail stems of spent grenades, rockets, and mortars—littered the grounds.

The outpost had a single computer for the mortar-detecting radar equipment, no showers or running water, and only a hole in the ground for a latrine. It was little more than four walls protecting a stash of MREs, water, ammo, and ground to sleep on. The engineers who built the base had left the powdery, ankle-deep moondust in place, believing that it would help impede shrapnel from IDF. By all accounts, it did. Hasan was hit by some kind of projectile multiple times a day every day that I was there, and nobody was injured.

That night, to plan for a morning *shura* with elders from the surrounding villages, US and Afghan leaders gathered at the Afghan compound. The Afghan compound was adjacent to the American compound, rented from a local man with US taxpayers footing the bill. There were roofs at least, and a well.

In a modest low-ceiling room lit by oil lamp and accented by gold wainscoting, white-scalloped wallpaper, and a dirt floor, Lieutenant Colonel Salome and Captain Schneider sat on the floor with their Afghan counterparts, Colonel Wazeel from Muqor and his operations officer, Major Aktar, and the Hasan-based Afghan company commander, Captain Jawid Ramin. The American and Afghan company first sergeants were also present, as was the Afghan's most ferocious fighter, a heavily bearded, wiry Pashtun clutching a worn AK47. His name was Arabkhan.

"The guy is like a damn Rambo," Captain Schneider had told me earlier. "He will go right through a wall of fire to get to the enemy." Arabkhan had flinty yet thoughtfully deep eyes, tobacco-colored skin, and a warlike Pashtun nose. He sat quietly in the flickering yellow light, holding his battered AK upright between his knees. I had noticed since joining the army that many soldiers, even gym rats, had small, undeveloped hands compared to the carpenters that I worked with. Arabkhan had thick, muscular workingman hands.

The leaders agreed that the key to breaking the Taliban's grip in southern Gilan was standing up to a local police force, drawn from area citizenry. The trouble was, no village wanted to be the first to make a stand and invite Taliban reprisal. Furthermore, Hasan was a central hub to the villages of Jabbar, Reza, and Ghazi Kheyl, and without army checkpoints in the outlying villages of Patishi and Karwaddin, the elders knew the Taliban would keep coming in.

Colonel Wazeel, the Afghan battalion commander, said the problem was not in Gilan, but in Pakistan. Obama should bomb Pakistan, he insisted.

Salome, a stout, bald man who always reminded me of the Tin Man from the original 1939 movie, *The Wizard of Oz*, said no, we're not going to Pakistan. Let's stay in the here and now.

Major Aktar complained that his battalion was almost out of ammunition, and they needed more radios from the Americans. The Afghan company first sergeant backed up Aktar's request for ammo. The Taliban around Hasan were not like other Taliban who fight for ten minutes and leave, he said. These Taliban fight all day.

Through all the talking, the warrior Arabkhan just sat stoically in the lamplight. He knew some English but not much, whereas his young captain, who grew up in an educated family in Kabul, spoke army English well enough to refer to the Taliban as "cocksuckers."

Afghanistan was a complex country. Within two weeks, Wazeel and Aktar would be arrested for corruption, an event that Salome knew was coming even then. In fact, the fighters at Hasan did not have enough ammunition because Wazeel was selling it on the black market just outside his base in downtown Muqor.

The meeting adjourned.

I knew that Schneider's Second Platoon was walking out on patrol before daylight to create a distraction for the Taliban as village elders came in for the *shura*, so I wasn't too surprised to hear gunfire by 8:30 a.m. Lots of gunfire. Outside the company CP, Staff Sergeant Johnny Davis, a Ranger-tabbed veteran of four deployments, was busy inventorying a stockpile of MREs and bottled water. When he lost count, he yelled, "Fuck!"

Sitting in the doorway of the CP was Staff Sergeant Jacob Hurndon, as blond as Davis was not. With him was a female medic brought to Hasan to check an ailing woman villager, and the medic's required female companion, a tiny soldier who normally worked in the chow hall. "Echo company just dropped off a fuck-ton of water and a fuck-ton of MREs," said Hurndon to the women. "When you have a half fuck-ton, we need more. I know he's trying to do the right thing, but watching him count water every day is comical."

At 9:30 a.m., the platoon leader of Second Platoon requested four rounds of airburst artillery, which came ripping through the air within minutes, exploding in rapid succession a few kilometers out. By 10:45, two dozen elders from the surrounding villages gathered in the ANA compound. Most wore the traditional *salwar kameez,* white manjams with a blue or gray suit vest, and white *lungee*, or turban. Some wore open-toed shoes, others sandals, and all had beards. Many wore gold watches. Because showing the bottom of one's feet insults a Muslim, they either squatted or sat cross-legged. Many kept a string of worry beads in hand.

The first order of business was to quell their anger over an incident that occurred two days earlier. The ANA had dragged a dead Taliban fighter through Hasan behind a motorcycle captured from the insurgents. For a few days, the Americans had been down to only one platoon, not enough to guard the JSS and patrol. The ANA wanted to go kill Taliban. When the paratroopers refused to patrol, the Afghans said, fine, we will go kill Taliban and bring them to you. And that is what they did, dumping the body at the gate of the American compound.

"You have the right to kill him, not to drag him," said one elder. The Afghan and American officers agreed it was disrespectful to treat even a Taliban that way. What the area really needed, they said, was a local police force. They had brought this up at the last *shura*, and they were bringing it up again.

Salome pointed out that villagers in Andar and Dayak districts had stood up to local police, and they were driving the Taliban out.

An elder fired back in Pashto, "The Taliban has Pakistan. Who do we have?"

That really pissed Salome off. He stood up and shook with anger. He raised his voice, "Do you see Pakistan coming here? You have the backing of the United States of America." Salome recited the names of several villagers injured by Taliban mortars who were right then being treated in American hospitals. "Ask if the Taliban cares for wounded like that."

Most of the elders conceded the point. (In southern Gilan, locals called the other side of the river Pakistan even though Pakistan was over sixty miles away. Taliban, weapons, explosives—they all came from "Pakistan" across that bridge. It was easy to blame their problems on Pakistan.) "You need to stand up for yourselves," Salome said. "We treat your sons and daughters like our own sons and daughters."

"That is true," said another elder, "But we need to get the higher ups in Pakistan."

Captain Schneider, a square-jawed, muscular Citadel graduate who was sporting a dust-encrusted pompadour from days without a shower, told the elders emphatically that they had called the meeting for solutions, not complaining. "Yes, Pakistan sends fighters and weapons. Yes, there should be no civilian deaths. We all agree we need checkpoints. No village will stand up to a police force by itself, I know. I don't want to hear more complaining from anyone. I want to hear solutions."

An elder said they needed to have a bigger *shura* with more tribes before they confront the Taliban, but Schneider replied that they didn't need another meeting. They needed to make a pledge to contribute their young men to a police force now. "At least agree on a neighborhood watch to keep the fighting out of town," he pleaded.

The elders were standing now, arguing among themselves. An American officer nodded and shrugged. "This is what success looks like here," he said. "If they are arguing, they're figuring things out on their own." The meeting broke up quickly after that.

Just after noon, three mortar rounds slammed into the JSS. The entire footprint of the base was less than the size of a football field, so while one could dive for cover if there was time, one could also just get lucky. But not too many times.

In late afternoon, Second Platoon returned with a dead Taliban strapped to the back of one of their LATVs, a side-by-side four-wheeler mounted with a passenger-side machine gun. Part of the Taliban's trademark was a ghost-like presence on the battlefield, quickly cleaning their brass and leaving no trace, so when the Americans took the body of one of their dead, they retaliated violently.

The dead Taliban was in his mid-30s. He had a large head, bare feet, and yellow skin. He was a little chubby. I wondered if someone had removed his shoes. Many Taliban wore western-style sneakers on the battlefield. At first, he appeared to be yet another Punjabi fighter from Pakistan, but Arabkhan believed he was a local boy, trained in Pakistan. In the dead man's shirt pocket was a little notebook and a similar-sized prayer book. As Intel, soldiers began taking his fingerprints, two RPGs streaked in over the front wall at low angles and exploded. Whoever had fired them was very close. Everyone dove for cover, leaving the dead Taliban alone in the dust. Later in the day, the body was handed over to the village elders.

Salome and his PSD returned to Warrior that evening. I stayed behind with the men of Delta Company. As a combat correspondent, I belonged where the combat was happening. I found a piece of relatively clean plywood and made a bed in the billowy dust inside an empty sandbagged bunker that I had discovered when the RPGs came in. At least it was flat and had a roof. As I bedded down, the last thing that I heard that night was small arms fire, followed by an explosion, and then the monotonous "waaaaaaaah" of a small unmanned aerial vehicle droning in the cloudless sky.

The next morning began the same way: small arms fire, explosion. At 9:30 a.m., there was another explosion. Nobody got too worked up over any of it. There were no patrols going out, so I used the day to learn more about the fight in southern Gilan District. I found Captain Schneider with his soldiers in the grove.

Schneider was a Captain America. Originally from Falmouth, Massachusetts, he was a Citadel graduate who was assigned to armor but spent most of his career with infantrymen. As a lieutenant, he led an infantry platoon on targeted raids in Baghdad through most of the 2007 Surge.

"There were only a few areas in Iraq where the enemy would fire and maneuver on you, but here in Hasan, they are legit fighters," said Schneider. With grape fields five feet deep, hilly terrain, and tunneling *karezes* that the enemy can pop in and out of at will, the battlefield terrain was a major challenge around Hasan.

Southern Gilan had been under Taliban rule since the war began. They pushed the women around, prohibited clinics and girls' schools, and many of the boys' schools were closed. The women especially were tired of the tyranny. "We ask permission to come in and search their homes. The Taliban comes in at night and strong-arms them. They lock villagers in their homes and take stuff while they stay. The locals hate the Taliban fighters but are also intimidated by them," he said. Most of the Taliban were paid mercenaries, well-equipped Punjabi fighters from Pakistan, Schneider believed. Many were ex-Pak army. They were equipped with Japanese handheld Icom radios, Iranian night-vision devices, and GPS units. "We come in with force and the Taliban leave, but then we leave and the Taliban come right back in."

The Punjabi fighters were very effective in the first few moments of a firefight, often using flanking movements, but it was hard for them to sustain. They would stash their weapons and flee on motorcycles. They communicated with cheap, handheld, two-way radios and talked in code, often trying to mislead the Americans listening in.

"The learning curve is very steep down here," the captain said. "We use danger-close artillery extensively. We've called gun runs in with [A-10 Warthog aircraft]. We have had rounds fall within two hundred meters of friendlies."

Schneider could not say enough good things about his Afghan partners, especially Arabkhan and his company commander, Captain Ramin. "I have trouble keeping up with Arabkhan sometimes," Schneider said. "We got in a firefight, and we were flanking around. I'm trying to get everyone up to the front. I turn around, and he's taking a small element and going straight at the enemy, bullets kicking the ground all around him, and he's just charging ahead. He's fearless." Arabkhan was also Schneider's go-to guy when he needed to speak with the locals because the Afghan platoon sergeant was also a preacher. He was a bona-fide warrior poet.

Captain Ramin, the young Afghan company commander, had enough money and family connections that he did not have to be fighting in the dirt if he didn't want to be. Ramin was handsome, athletic, thoughtful, and soft-spoken. His father and mother had died in the Soviet War when he was just three, and his brother was severely injured by the Taliban. He said the Taliban had come in as saviors after civil war had completely destroyed Kabul. "We thought that they were good people, and the first time they said, 'We are the bearers of peace, and would capture all of Afghanistan and unite all of the tribes,' everybody believed them. When they captured many places and started torturing people and beating them, and not just the Tajiks, Usbeks,

Turkmens, and Hazaras but Pashtuns as well, the people realized they were not good people." Under Taliban rule, there was no health care, no school, no power, and no water. The people lived like barbarians in a Stone Age, he said. As if on cue, a large explosion shook the building that we were in.

Schneider radioed the CP. They said it was a controlled det. Combat engineers from Warrior were clearing the road for a visit from Colonel Stock, the brigade commander, the next day.

Ramin continued, "If a person is educated, they are not joining the Taliban. If people are not educated, they can say, 'If you kill yourself, you will go straight to heaven.' Poor, illiterate people are more susceptible."

As the midday heat was dissipated by the long shadows of evening, I hung out inside the company CP to enjoy the colorful exchanges between Staff Sergeants Hurndon and Davis. The room pulsed orange like the inside of a pottery kiln as Davis built a small fire to heat his dinner. The two were talking about the day that the ANA drug the Taliban around Hasan before "shanking him multiple times" and dumping him at the gate.

"I married a Colombian," Hurndon jokingly said. "I've been shanked. She beats me with flip-flops. Don't marry a Colombian."

"The ANA called us pussies because we wouldn't go fight with them," Davis said. "Where was their first sergeant that day? I don't know." A first sergeant is the top disciplinarian of a company, and at least in our military, would have prevented that type of behavior.

A soldier stuck his head in the door looking for something. It was Davis' roommate, Sergeant Nick Fredsti. I recognized the name from training back at Bragg because my father's name is Fred, an unusual name these days. Fredsti was tall, thin, and serious, but with a sturdy quality about him too.

"What do you need?" Davis asked.

Without a word, Fredsti shook his head and backed out of the room.

"Johnny, no way am I going to be one of those bitter old first sergeants," said Hurndon. "I'm going to get out of the Army at twelve years, be a postman or something."

"An angry postman," Davis chided.

"Hell, I'm from Henry County, Georgia, and I don't even like guns. I grew up working on a dairy farm. There's nothing violent about milking a cow."

Long after I returned from Afghanistan, I would think about that night often. Davis, who had lost two of his last three roommates, Hurndon, who didn't like guns, Nick Fredsti, who didn't say a word.

CHAPTER 11:
PATROL

The morning of June 14, I climbed out of my bunker bed at 4 a.m. to crowing roosters and barking dogs, pink clouds, and a cool breeze. High overhead was a big white jet heading south. Civilization at thirty thousand feet. I ate my MRE cold and saved the chemical heater to heat water for shaving. Since I was in the 82nd Airborne Division, I didn't dare set foot in Taliban country with a stubbly chin.

Finally, I was going out on patrol, this morning with Lieutenant Frederick Reier's Third Platoon. Frederick, there you go. Say something is uncommon and it'll bite you in the ass. Reier was a serious young man from Greenville, Ohio, the youngest of a family of four. His features were easy to pick out in a group of soldiers: high cheekbones, sandy hair, tall, and somewhat gangly, O Positive (written on his helmet), not yet Ranger tabbed, call sign "Demon Three Six."

As we waited for the ANA near the gate, shepherd boys passed by pushing flocks of sheep and goats. A young boy plodded by on a miserable little donkey. Specialist Wilfred Hunt bowed to the boy with a flourish and greeted him with the customary Muslim expression, "*As-salamu alaykum.*" Peace be upon you. Ah, yes, infantryman as ambassador. As the Afghan boy nervously spurred his donkey on, Hunt yelled to our terp, "Hey, ask him if I can ride his donkey."

The terp hollered to the boy in Pashto. "The boy says you need money," replied the terp.

"I love these people," Hunt laughed. "Everyone is a hustler." That ended that.

The ANA were slow to arrive, so we didn't leave until 5:30 a.m. The goal of the mission was to walk south through the grape fields and open desert, cross through the Tarnak River gorge to the south bank, and search the hamlet of Hutake. Reier expected to get hit by machine gun fire in the three hundred meters of flat, open space between the river and grape fields two klicks from Hasan.

That didn't happen. In fact, the patrol was just like a dozen others that I had been on: long hot walk, pull security while the LT drinks chai and eats flatbread with the elders, watch the ANA search some homes, long hot walk back. In Hutake, a soldier gave an Afghan boy the peanut butter pouch from his MRE. Instead of eating it, the boy stomped it with his foot, exploding it all over the ground. I couldn't tell if the kid was trying to be spiteful, playful, or just a pain in the ass. Two Afghan soldiers fed fish in an open *karez* until it was time to go, then they shot at them with their AK47s. That was all the excitement until, on the way back, Arabkhan found a large, yellow, plastic container full of white powder. It was the type of container that insurgents used for HME-based IEDs. To see if it was an IED, Arabkhan stood back fifty meters and shot it.

It didn't explode. So then our sniper shot it with his M14. And then the terp had to take a shot with Arabkhan's AK47. See how this works? Just like the peanut butter.

In the afternoon, we had a visit from our brigade commander, Colonel Stock, who rode into Hasan with his PSD for a few hours. While at the security station, he met with Arabkhan. Captain Schneider was seeking to persuade the Afghan battalion commander to give Arabkhan a battlefield commission to lieutenant, and he thought Stock might provide the needed leverage.

Stock's command sergeant major, an artilleryman, didn't want to be left out of the conversation, so he asked Arabkhan if he ever took time to train his men. Training is generally an NCO-run activity, and since the sergeant major and the Afghan were both NCOs, I suppose he thought it a good mentoring question.

Arabkhan politely considered the ridiculous question and calmly answered, "The fighting here is very good training for war." That's about as true a statement as you will read in this book.

The last thing I did that evening was to prepare my kit for another patrol departing the following morning to the village of Spedar. Just in case we ran into more Afghan kids, which seemed likely, I packed a bag of blowpops that my sister had mailed to me for that purpose. Officially, the command was calling it a recon mission, but in reality, it was nothing short of "movement to contact" in the direction of the village where the Taliban leader Faruk was born. In Vietnam they called these missions search and destroy. Movement to contact is the kinder, gentler version.

"Recon mission?" the NCOs mumbled to one another. "We were just there two days ago. We know what's there: PKMs, RPGs, and bad dudes." In fact, the day of the *shura*, Lieutenant Matthew Archuleta's First Platoon had been caught in a U-shaped ambush just outside of Spedar.

"It was a shit-show," said Staff Sergeant Hurndon, who had run ammo between squads separated across many meters of open ground while under fire.

Well after dark, as I was looking for Lieutenant Archuleta to get the mission brief, I found Staff Sergeant Davis in the CP. He didn't know where the LT was but suggested that I ask Sergeant Fredsti for the details. Fredsti was a squad leader in First Platoon. I walked around in the dark to the backside of the Alamo and poked my head inside the tiny chamber where Fredsti was gathered with two of his soldiers around a small fire. "What's up?" he asked.

Feeling a bit intrusive, I asked, "Are you going on the mission tomorrow?"

He nodded.

"I am too," I said.

He looked at me like, okay, congratulations. And?

"What time is SP?" I asked. SP means start of patrol.

Fredsti hesitated. "We're leaving at zero three, but I think Lieutenant Archuleta is leaving at zero four." He paused, analyzing the ass-pain of bringing me along. Finally, he said, "I mean, you can come with us, but the LT probably wants you with him."

I thought about it for a moment. An extra hour of sleep always sounded good. On the other hand, I never wanted to give soldiers, particularly infantrymen, the impression that I wasn't willing to embrace the same suck that they did. Fredsti was right, though. The LT would expect me to at least start off with him. It was good politics.

We left at four. Arabkhan stood in the center of the dusty street in his trademark dark digital camouflage, green beret, and red scarf. Archuleta's men were mixed nearly one for one with Afghan soldiers they knew well through many shared firefights. As soldiers passed in lines to his left and right, he halted one and then the other to achieve the proper spacing to prevent mass casualties from area weapons such as IEDs, grenades, and mortars. In all of my travels, I had never seen an Afghan soldier giving direction to an American soldier like that. Our paratroopers respected him.

From the murk of dead twilight, we passed into a beautiful pastoral sunrise as we stepped up the hard-packed road into the little berg of Ghazi Kheyl, where Third Platoon had been hit hard just weeks earlier. Tiny puffs of pink-tipped clouds gathered like birds at dawn, hanging in the weak indigo sky as night bled away. Villagers passed by, stone-faced from recent sleep. The road was a road, then a dry wash, then a road again. Passing through a field of wheat nearly ripe, I photographed the soldiers around me:

Langan, Jason. Specialist. Humping the 240 Lima. He's a big fella, wears it like a barbell, doing reps.

Watson, Matthew. Private. SAW gunner, olive skin, big smile, helmet-mounted cam ready to record the action.

Deer, Corey. Specialist. A trained drone pilot, but carries a SAW because that's what is needed today. Enlisted at 17.

Leyba, Johnny. Sergeant. The helmet is almost bigger than he is. He's quick, aware, on point.

Chan, Ka. Private First Class. Red scarf and mortar tube.

Hurndon, Jacob. Staff Sergeant. Weapons squad leader, has the fancy new NODs that squad leaders get, controls the big M-240 machine guns, but hates guns.

Shafer, Matthew. Staff Sergeant. First Squad leader. Freckles and aggressiveness. A Taliban was about to fire an RPG into the back of a vehicle when Shafer and another paratrooper, Specialist Brian Roy, shot him dead.

Archuleta, Matthew. First Lieutenant. Broad face, tiny chin, and wild hair that only an LT can get away with.

Nearly all of the paratroopers of First Platoon wore a traditional Afghan *shemagh*, aka "drive-on rag" in military cant, scarves wrapped around the neck against the sun, the dust, and the sweat. In the 82nd, the scarves were strictly verboten, but the boys of Company D saw them as an Afghanization they had earned and one that brought them closer to their Afghan brothers in arms. These paratroopers weren't going on chai patrol, they were going to war and they knew it. There was a pregame intensity in their faces, in their step, in the way they gripped their weapons. How they would climb over the walls that divided fields, and the gravity with which they would cross the barren opens.

Past Ghazi Kheyl, the armed column crossed a large concrete bridge supported by three massive stone pilings above the languid Tarnak River, clouds and sky reflecting in the low flow of mid-summer. Johnny Leyba out front. Hurndon and Arabkahn side by side, Langan on the 240, Chan and his mortar, Deer scanning the horizon. Watson, Shafer, Archuleta. So many more. An Afghan packing what Hurndon would call a "fuck-ton" of RPGs. And each knew that he would only live once.

On the far bank, the road rose and pinched as it passed through the noiseless village of Patishi. Arabkhan and Hurndon stopped to search a tight but clean compound of a suspected Taliban. Nobody was home, but the Afghans found a new motorcycle—big money for a modest villager. Though they commonly requisitioned the bikes of Taliban killed in battle, they left it parked.

Outside Patishi, we continued east into the rising sun. It was 6:15 a.m. The earth beneath our boots was already parched. We crossed through more wheat, then tilled ground, then hard-baked earth, and hit a steep, narrow, forested wadi. The column turned north to make use of an easier crossing and continued east through more open fields. Tiny blue butterflies scattered like magical seed heads as soldiers brushed through green and golden stalks.

We descended into a wadi full of head-high plumegrass and climbed up the far bank. Across a short field where it feathered into yet another wadi of tall white poplars, I noticed several of our soldiers crouched in the grass pulling security. It was Fredsti and the rest of his squad, who had left before us. We had made linkup.

We rested in the shade of the poplars. Archuleta studied a map on his new Army-issued smartphone. Arabkhan kicked back in the grass just beyond the trees, sucking at a green stem in his teeth. Others snacked on MREs, "field stripped" to just the good stuff. I saw Fredsti standing alone at the edge of the grove. He looked ready to go. I wondered how long his team had been waiting for us and what it had been like for them to travel so far from base with so few soldiers. I raised my camera and snapped a photo of him.

I knew the LATVs with more machine guns, ammo, and firepower were trailing us, but I had not yet seen them.

At five after seven, Archuleta gave the word. Back into two staggered lines of a tactical column, the patrol left the cover of the trees and marched up a deep, winding wash that led directly into Spedar. It was exactly the way they had approached the last time, except today, the platoon sergeant would hold Fredsti's team in reserve in a flanking offshoot of the wadi to the left. If Shafer's First Squad did take contact, once they were able to provide a distance, direction, and description of the enemy, Fredsti's Second Squad could be used to maneuver on them, or at the very least, to provide covering fire.

The wash petered out near the ruins of an old grape hut off to our left in the direction of Warrior. I could see the PTIDS in the distant sky. I was walking next to Staff Sergeant Shafer, switching lenses, which was always a challenge in dusty conditions.

"We're going to get hit really soon," Shafer said, as if warning me to get my camera ready. "The Taliban are rushing fighters into Spedar right now."

Ahead I could just make out the low walls that demarked the grape fields at the edge of Spedar. A grape hut two hundred meters to our front rose like a ship's prow above the wavy vineyards. Closer to us, a head-high wall ran the same direction as we traveled, with knee-high grass on the right side and barren ground on the left. The wall ran for about fifty meters before hooking hard left for another hundred meters, forming a long "L."

When the first shots sounded, there were so many RPG trails smoking overhead that my first impression was that somebody was throwing a party, like Fourth of July fireworks. Overcome by sensation, I was vaguely aware of an internal struggle to figure out why someone was celebrating here, now.

Leyba, Watson, and Deer sprinted for the perpendicular arm of the wall that formed a natural fighting position against the incoming fire. Others, including Archuleta and his radioman, dove for the nearest ditch. Bullets snapped overhead like quick strings of ladyfingers. RPG blasts blew great crescendos of cordite and dirt as more and more RPGs sizzled overhead. I lost count at fourteen.

The Taliban had ambushed us out of the sunrise, forcing us to look directly into the sun through eye pro that was sweaty and fogged from two hours of steady marching. The eye pro came off quickly.

This was significant only to me. Our brigade sergeant major would not let me publish any photos of paratroopers missing proscribed protective gear. In fact, at one point, he threatened to arrest any soldier who was seen in a photo without eye pro, gloves, and kneepads (Shawsome provided what is known as "topcover" and informed the sergeant major that all those pictures had been lost due to computer problems). Didn't matter that they were fighting for their lives and the eye pro might have gotten them killed. Well it did, but it mattered more that the entire army might see photos of 82nd soldiers "out of uniform," which would bring shame to the 82nd, to the command, and to him.

I was in the ditch next to Archuleta, who was working the radio, talking to his squad leaders and updating company and battalion. Watson was crouched behind the long wall, wheeling with his SAW over the top of the barrier every thirty seconds to deliver a burst of machine gun fire. Leyba was farther down the line with Deer and a dozen paratroopers. With all the metal in the air and being so far back from the cover of the perpendicular wall, I knew it was only a matter of time before one of us was hit.

We rushed forward, crouching low in the ditch until we reached the main wall and were able to spread out. Watson's eyes were lit wild like a hunting cat's above a shit-eating grin as a crouching ANA soldier ran past him. He locked eyes with Hurndon, who began laughing, which made Watson laugh. Yeah, it was happening again. Ambushed in the same exact spot, two days later. Watson swung up to fire, but his SAW jammed. He ducked as enemy rounds bit chunks of dried mud off the wall above his head.

Taliban bullets were ripping up the rim of the mud wall, ricocheting and snapping overhead in a menacing chaos of cracks and explosions unlike anything I had ever experienced. Combat soldiers talk about the immediacy of battle, of being in the *now* as if it were a choice, and I guess it is. In *Band of Brothers,* Lieutenant Spiers says as much when he tells a private the trouble is that he still thinks there's a chance that he'll live. "We're all dead already," Spiers says.

I think what he means is, to function well under fire, a soldier must relinquish the *love* for his life, the record of which is held in his past memories and future hopes. It's not an easy thing to do the first time because the fear is—logical or not—that even if one survives the fight, once one relinquishes the love of his past and future, he many never get it back again. I learned to do it because I had to, though doing so seems to have long-term implications that I don't quite fully understand yet. My wife says that after I arrived back at Bragg, it took me another year to come home from Afghanistan. When a soldier is deployed, in spite of Facebook, Skype, and Gmail, loved ones really only exist in the past and future. Yet only when a soldier is willing to let his past and future slip away is he fully available to act in the present. Even in that state, the fear of injury and death doesn't completely go away, or it never did for me anyway, but it did become manageable.

I photographed big Langan on the 240 Lima in the apex of the L, standing on a tiny ledge on the tips of his boots, alternately pounding away at a target directly to his front and ducking for cover as PKM fire sliced back at him. Taliban gunners knew they had to take him out and sent hails of bullets raking his position when he wasn't firing.

Chan had settled on a slightly elevated piece of ground not far behind Langan, still under cover of the wall but not by much. He methodically launched mortar after mortar from his hand-held mortar tube.

A baby-faced Afghan soldier on the wall next to me had mounted a 40mm grenade launcher underneath his AK barrel, and every time he fired a grenade, a long metal strip sprung off the weapon. He would go search the grass for it and repeat the process. It seemed only a matter of time before the weapon failed during launch and blew us both up.

I wondered where Arabkhan was.

Hurndon, the dairy farmer who didn't like guns, had already blazed through his ammunition. His ammo bearer was out too, so he took the AK47 from an Afghan soldier crouched next to him in the fetal position and began firing it. That spurred the Afghan soldier to rise with Hurndon's M4 and fire it, but the magazine was empty.

Hurndon was firing over the wall sometimes in blind sprays, sometimes with carefully aimed controlled pairs—bursts of two rounds each. Then the AK jammed, and he was back to his M4.

He and Shafer hollered orders to their men, and the men repositioned along the wall. Behind Shafer, a soldier was pressed flat against the mud-brick, his face gripped with fear. He was not functioning. Another soldier yelled at his face. Suddenly, the two and a third paratrooper, Deer, popped up and opened fire. The worst thing one can do during a firefight is nothing because it quickly leads to feelings of helplessness, and when that happens, the grip of fear can set a man's bones, leaving him incapacitated.

Closer to me, Chan was now behind his M4, taking shots through a drainage hole at the foot of the wall. I was moving past several paratroopers to position better for photos when somebody called out that Sergeant Fredsti had been hit in the chest.

Fifteen minutes earlier when the firefight had kicked off, the men of Second Squad had still been deep in the wadi, so the enemy's fire was also plunging fire.

Specialist Darren Keblish, a SAW gunner, found a small crevice to his left and pressed his body into it. He sat there for a few seconds, bullets cracking in the air around him. "My butt was puckering so hard," he would tell me later, "that I could have made a diamond in there if I slipped in a piece of coal."

Keblish had been raised on Fort Bragg by a father who had once served in our brigade. He had always wanted to be a paratrooper like his father. Well, here he was.

He spotted Sergeant Fredsti, who told him the enemy were in front, to the left, and to the right.

Fredsti yelled, "Keblish, fucking follow me!" and ran straight through a hail of bullets and up the side of the wadi. Keblish followed, laying down a base of fire at Fredsti's direction. Fredsti tapped him on the shoulder, and they fell back into the wadi, where Fredsti told Keblish to grab a group of huddling ANA and set them up to protect the right flank.

Moving up a right fork in the wadi with Keblish were Privates First Class Steven Anderson and Gabriel Paniagua, who were following their team leader, Sergeant Jon Daeuber. Anderson had come to the deployment late so he could be home when his wife, Danyel, gave birth to their third child. The twenty-two-year-old from the Orlando suburbs had been pulling guard all night leading up to the patrol's departure, beginning what he still considers the longest day of his life with no sleep.

Anderson followed Daeuber up the wadi berm and began spreading out to find a good fighting position when he passed behind an ANA firing an RPG. The backblast knocked him back into the wadi. With his bell rung, he climbed back up and found a spot midway on the right flank and started laying down fire. Fredsti and Daueber were in the prone (lying down on their stomachs) to the right. Sergeant Bracey, Wallace, and Keblish were pushed further right. Paniagua, the SAW gunner, was on Anderson's left.

Rounds were hitting so close that Anderson felt the vibrations of their impact in the foot of earth he hid behind. He felt their velocity as they buzzed past his cheeks.

Fredsti told Daueber to sprint to Bracey and warn him to be prepared to push through the ambush. Daueber picked up and sprinted to Bracey. Fredsti was popping up on a knee to shoot, with PKM rounds impacting just feet in front of him. "Do you believe this shit?" he yelled to Anderson. "Oh, these motherfuckers. I think I might have got him."

Suddenly, Anderson heard a smack, like a palm on a tarp. Fredsti stood up. "I think I've been hit," he said, rolling his shoulder as if the socket were sore.

"You're sure?" Anderson called back.

Fredsti buckled to his knees, then fell into a divot. Anderson low-crawled to his squad leader. "Man I can't feel my legs," Fredsti said. The ground shook with explosions of dust as the enemy keyed in on their position with heavy machine gun fire. Anderson pulled Fredsti behind a meager foot of berm and began yelling for a medic.

"I've never yelled that loud in my life," Anderson recalled later.

Paniagua glanced at him, and yelled between bursts of his SAW, "Is he going to be OK?"

"Just keep shooting, or we're all going to get shot," Anderson yelled back.

Paniagua laid out all of his extra and went to work. The incoming fire picked up so high that Anderson laid his head right next to Fredsti's. When the fire died down to controlled bursts, Daueber arrived. He immediately radioed to platoon that Fredsti was hit and then, with Anderson, began removing Fredsti's gear and sweeping him for wounds.

In and out of consciousness, Fredsti noticed that his expensive Oakley sunglasses had slipped off. "Hey, put my sunglasses back on," he chided them. "It's so fucking bright."

The glasses were all bent and smashed, but Anderson played along and did as ordered. He knew Fredsti was trying to keep them calm. The two eventually found the entrance wound of a single machine gun slug—no more than a thorn scrape on his right deltoid. The bullet must have ricocheted or railed on a rib, because the exit wound was in his lower back.

Fredsti complained of breathing difficulty, so they punctured his chest cavity with the large needle in a first aid kit. At first, Anderson thought they had goofed the decompression, but then Fredsti lifted his head to inspect the large needle and said, "Okay, I feel better. That looks right." Immediately, he fell back unconscious from blood loss.

Anderson tapped his face and said, "You can't take a nap right now, we're busy."

Doc Trevino finally arrived. From working in an emergency room, Trevino had more experience treating trauma than any medic in the battalion, and he blew through assessing Fredsti's wounds. He pulled Anderson's helmet band back, shoved a bag of Hextend under it, and said, "Now you and him are connected at the hip." Doc showed him where to apply pressure to the wound.

For the first time, near panic, Anderson feared for Fredsti's life. Welling with raw emotion, he dropped his head in anguish. "I told myself that if I stopped, I wouldn't be helping the situation," he recalled later. Anderson picked his head up and fought to remain present.

Trevino related, "When I got to him, we were under pretty effective fire, still out in the open. We had a SAW, two riflemen, and me and him. He was calm and collected the whole time. He was declining pretty fast when I got to him, but still pretty calm. When I asked him all the normal questions a medic asks, he said, 'Yeah, I can hear you, Doc.' He was telling me he was having trouble breathing, and that he wanted to sit up. After the interventions, a couple times [Fredsti] couldn't hear me and I'd yell. His reply was, 'What, doc?' I'd answer, 'Just making sure you're still there, buddy.' It says a lot about his character, that he was still conscious with the amount of blood he lost, the amount of pain he was in, for how calm he was. You don't normally see that."

On the line with the rest of the platoon, I moved up to Watson and Leyba, stopping suddenly to flatten against the ground. Something had passed by my head that sounded and felt like a fast-moving car. I was scared to move forward and scared to stand still, so inexplicably, I stood up as high as I could, barely peeking over the wall, and blindly fired my M4 in the direction of the nearest grape hut. It was the biggest thing I could see. I fired maybe three or four rounds. I doubt I hit anything of value because I was so short, but when I crouched back down, I felt better. Adrenalin flooded into my feet. I was extremely thirsty.

Then I stood up and repeated the maneuver, but with fewer shots. I felt very exposed with so much metal snaking past my head. I knew it would only take one little fragment to pop open this bag of human blood. Soldiers bleed out, get blown apart, dismembered, disemboweled, lung-punctured, and brain-punched by fragments of metal big and small. Mortal fear was there, but the greater fear was for the family's loss.

Yet this is what soldiers do. This is what they risk every time they expose themselves to fire their weapons at the enemy. Bravery was not easy to show in pictures, but that was the point of me being there with the infantry. I realized that, unless I could clearly see the enemy fighters, I owed it to my fellow paratroopers to do what I did best, to show the world that they were brave and courageous, just as their forefathers had been when they stood against tyranny and fascism.

Hoping that nobody had noticed my pathetic attempt at infantry, I dropped my weapon and lifted my camera, moving along the wall again until I reached Shafer, who, with his soldiers, was laying down a base of fire. I stood up and tried to focus the image, but the viewfinder wouldn't un-blur. Dropping back to my knees, I tried to get the camera to work. The problem appeared to be with the lens. The auto focus no longer functioned, but I could still use the manual focus.

Deer was on his toes to see over the wall, and when that wouldn't work, he laid his SAW sideways and learned by trial where to aim in his scope to hit accurately. Seeing a notch in the wall where he might gain a crucial inch or two, he stepped down. Suddenly the SAW flew from his hands. With no time to consider what had happened, he retrieved the machine gun and continued sending bursts at the enemy. Only later did he notice the bullet impact on the SAW, which could only have come from our right flank. The enemy was trying to surround us.

Next to me, Shafer was hit. A round had penetrated the two-foot-thick mud wall and entered his left side. "Motherfucker!" he yelled. Immediately he rose again and returned fire. It was the aggressive response of a true warrior. Yet when he turned back around, his face was drained of color, and he eased to the ground. "Motherfucker," he repeated.

Specialist Winston Corcino immediately began giving Shafer first aid. Hurndon made his way down the line and peeled the ceramic-plated cummerbund from Shafer's left side, then lifted the uniform top. He found entrance and exit wounds in the meat of Shafer's lat. A single bullet had gone in and out of Shafer's sleeve three times, penetrated, and cauterized the soft tissue of the *latissimus dorsi*, and exited. Hurndon taped it up anyway.

With his eye pro slung from his neck, Shafer turned toward my lens, lifted his middle finger and said, "Fuck you, Taliban."

Click.

About that time, one of the Air Force's giant B1-B bombers came swooping in for a low-pass show of force directly over enemy lines. The Cold-War jet was no more than five hundred feet off the ground. "It was so funny because both Taliban fighters and us stopped shooting to say, 'Yeah, that is badass,' then we resumed shooting," recalled Hurndon. "I'm thinking they will drop a bomb on them motherfuckers, but that didn't happen."

We were too close to the village for bombs or artillery. The enemy picked up again with AK fire. Some of it seemed to be coming in from the right, and by then, Deer was sure of it.

"We've got to get out of here before they flank us," Hurndon hollered. Archuleta agreed, and we scuttled back down the wall to the mouth of the wadi. Standing there was Arabkhan. He wanted to know what was taking so long. The medevac should already have been there for the injured American troop. He knew Fredsti's platoon sergeant would have called in the medevac report.

After consulting with Arabkhan, Archuleta and Hurndon decided the entire force should consolidate several hundred meters back down the wadi, where another deep wash came in from the south. Soldiers had moved up that branch a hundred meters to an open field where the medevac birds would land. Seeing nothing but a type of trench warfare at the wall, I was glad to move away from it. We moved quickly and met up with the rest of the platoon in a matter of minutes.

When we arrived, Hurndon discovered that only a partial medevac request had been radioed into Warrior. He got in the platoon sergeant's face and screamed, "Get on the fucking radio and do your fucking job!" Archuleta was on the radio now, trying to get the birds in. Hurndon asked the platoon sergeant where Fredsti was.

"I think he's up there," he said, pointing east.

Everyone reacts differently under fire. Some do well. Many learn to manage. Others just don't. Another of Delta Company's platoon sergeants went out on patrol one day and got mixed up in a typical Hasan-type firefight, and the next morning, he was knotted up with anxiety and passing blood in his stool. A day later, he was replaced.

"Docs say PTSD is a real thing, and I will take their word for it," Hurndon said. "I've been in quite a few firefights, and it hasn't affected me, but maybe it will later."

In the circumstances at hand, a platoon sergeant's job was to be with his casualty and the medic, and this platoon sergeant was not. "Where's Doc at?" Hurndon asked.

"I think he's with Fredsti," the platoon sergeant replied.

Hurndon found the medic still treating Fredsti at the site of the injury. He enlisted Leyba's fire team to help evacuate the wounded soldier to the pickup zone.

Captain Schneider finally arrived with the LATVs, a Carl Gustav recoilless rifle and more soldiers, including some sharpshooters. From the direction of the battlefield, six paratroopers emerged from the grass carrying Fredsti by his limbs. His torso was naked, and in his lower back was a bleeding hole the size of a silver dollar. Blood was smeared on the boots and uniforms of the brothers carrying him.

"Get me a litter, and get me a fucking Red Bull," Fredsti said calmly. "Don't let me lose my glasses."

Arabkhan helped load Fredsti onto a litter. Fellow paratroopers carried him to the makeshift HLZ as the medevac Black Hawk swooped in for a thirteen-second touch-and-go. Shafer was evacuated as well. To deny the enemy satisfaction, several paratroopers kicked dust on the blood trail.

Arabkhan convinced Schneider to push into Spedar. Apache gunships had just arrived, giving our team a significant advantage. We retraced our steps up the wadi and skirted a minefield on the opposite side of the L-shaped wall where, a few days earlier, Arabkhan had saved Leyba from blowing himself up. From there we sprinted for cover behind the outermost walls of Spedar under light automatic weapons fire. For all the running I had done on Ardennes back at Bragg, I really wished that more of it had been sprints in full kit. From wall to wall, we sprinted two hundred meters.

Our Afghan partners, who were sometimes better brawlers than they were soldiers, moved hastily into the village, firing at retreating insurgents. Our paratroopers split into two elements. They went in more cautiously, and when Apache pilots reported Afghans fleeing to the north and west, nobody was sure if the pilots were seeing Taliban or ANA. Gradually, the assault morphed from high pursuit to methodical search and destroy. The ANA searched nearly every house in the village but found only some camouflaged clothing and a motorcycle that they confiscated.

On the far side of Spedar as Archuleta was questioning a frail old man, insurgents opened fire from a nearby grape hut. Langan immediately laid down a base of fire with the 240 from behind a chest-high wall. I fired a few rounds at the grape hut and then ducked behind a wall to switch lenses to be ready for the attack helicopters that were lining up for a gun run. One of Archuleta's RTOs was on the radio with the Apache pilots.

A paratrooper near Langan was yelling at me. I couldn't hear what he was saying, but I could tell it was urgent. Just then, an ANA soldier directly behind me fired an RPG right past my head. I noticed the concussion more than the sound, but that's just because I couldn't hear anything at all after it went off. Gradually the sensation came back, but I was distracted by the incoming Apaches and forgot that I couldn't hear.

The Apache pilots saw Afghans with AK47s near the mud building and radioed that he had PID and was cleared hot. Archuleta's radioman repeated, "You have PID, and you are cleared hot, roger," meaning that he understood the pilot. However, the pilot took it as affirmation to open fire, which he did. Just before the rip of the chain gun, our soldiers realized that the gunship was taking aim at Afghan and American soldiers that had charged the grape hut and were in the line of fire. It was too late.

"Medic!"

Archuleta called off the second Apache. People were screaming and rushing back up the road. An ANA soldier's forehead was bathed in blood. Leyba motioned for him to squat down under cover of the wall. "Medic!" Leyba yelled, but when none came, he said, "Fuck it. Combat lifesaver," referring to the battlefield first aid techniques taught to soldiers. He retrieved the small aid kit that every American soldier carries, mopped up the blood and wrapped the Afghan's head in gauze.

Another Afghan soldier was standing next to us desperately trying to clear a jam from his PKM machine gun, repeatedly yelling, "Fuck America!"

Leyba and I knew the guy was going to open up on us when he finally got the jam cleared, but I could see that Leyba had already committed himself to the bleeding Afghan. He was going to fix up the soldier's head or die trying. Other ANA were about to fire an RPG at the Apaches. Leyba's resolve seemed to remove the worst of the moral outrage from the gunner's anger, and he stomped off.

Arabkhan was walking among his soldiers, trying to dissipate their rage. Two LATVs sped past carrying two more seriously wounded ANA. We followed the vehicles to an open field, where medevac birds picked up the casualties and whisked them to Warrior. The Afghan soldiers were still furious, and when we reached the grove of trees by the wadi, the Afghan company's first sergeant was waiting there in a pickup truck mounted with a Dushka heavy machine gun. He explained to Schneider that his soldiers were done fighting with the Americans for good.

The ANA struck out on the main road back to Hasan. We traveled cross-country but parallel to the Afghan column. At the first long open space, the menacing Dushka swung in our direction and stayed there, trained on us. The gunner could have had enfilading fire right down our column if he wished. "Oh God, they're going to kill us all," said Hurndon.

Deer's fire team was on point. The young paratrooper had enlisted to see more of the world and to serve his country. He got both. Since he was underage, he had needed his mother's signature and his father's death certificate to enlist. Just before deploying, he learned that his mother had been diagnosed with cancer. Yet here he was.

Just before we entered a wadi, the big gun fired. Deer hit the deck. He was in the open and completely expected death, but then he realized the Afghan soldiers weren't shooting at him. The gunner had swung the gun and was squeezing off bursts at Spedar.

There was only one bridge across the Tarnak, so eventually our forces were bound to come together. We met in the tiny hamlet of Kheyruddin. Individual Afghan and American soldiers greeted one another warmly even though the Afghans knew they weren't supposed to like the Americans just yet. The two groups walked in parallel lines on opposite sides of the same road, pretending the other didn't exist until, at the far end of the village, the Taliban opened up from tree lines on either side of the road. Once again, we fought side-by-side, and then again in Patishi before the river crossing.

From radio intercepts, Archuleta learned that the Taliban were setting up an ambush at the bridge, where there was little cover. He called in another show-of-force from the Air Force, and two fighter jets responded with a low pass.

No ambush followed, but the Taliban had used our delay in Kheyruddin and Patishi to hastily emplace an IED on the bridge. The charge was easily discovered and cleared.

As I walked those last two klicks back through the dry fields of stone and sun-bleached wheat with the battle-hardened paratroopers of First Platoon, the land seemed so much more barren than it had at the promise of dawn. There was no color at all, nor in the mountains or sky, only the dismal tones of dust. Damp dust, dry dust, packed dust, whirling dust, walled dust. A destitute narcissism of small differences. Was the morning we had seen all lit up in lively lilac hues the lie and this the reality, or was this the lie and the other what was real?

I knew one thing for certain. Until we walked through the gates of the security station, there was nothing but the present, and I didn't much care for it. Arabkhan walked next to me, deep in thought. He seemed to be above the petty recriminations of what was obviously a case of mistaken identity. Sensing it wasn't the best time to pepper him with questions but worrying that I might not get another chance, I asked him how the Taliban fighters in southern Gilan compared with those he had fought elsewhere.

Like a good leader, he patiently answered. "Next to Waziristan, the second most dangerous place in Afghanistan is Ghazni because they are good fighters here. But I don't care whether they are good fighters or bad fighters, I still want to fight them."

"Why do you want to fight them so bad?" I asked.

He and another Afghan soldier had stopped at a depression in the road where they had once dug up an IED. He turned to me and said,

"Two of my brothers died during the civil war. My other brother was killed by the Taliban. Now there are twenty-two relatives for me to care for, so I come here to fight but also to earn a living. When the Taliban killed my brother, I decided to spend my life fighting them."

"And you are a preacher?" We started walking again.

"It is not about religion," he said. "When we talk with villagers, I tell them I am a Muslim, you are a Muslim too. I am Afghan. You are also Afghan. Because of that, we should not allow Pakistan to molest our house. Everyone agrees with that."

I sensed that Arabkhan had had enough, so we walked the rest of the way in silence. Entering the village of Hasan, I saw the first children of the day—little Afghan girls and boys gathered near a group of old men talking. I remembered the bag of blowpops stashed in my drop bag. I wanted to smash it at the face of the first kid who asked for candy.

It turned out to be a girl of five, in a pink dress. If I gave her the bag, she'd be mobbed by the boys, and that wouldn't do. My revenge would be cultural. I gave her two and made the boys back off and wait. The next child, a very small boy, I gave two as well, and the next, and so on. When the bag was empty, I looked up. I was alone in the village. Not good. I picked up and moved along.

Inside the walls of the base again, I heaved my body armor and kit over my head and set it against the Alamo wall in the dust. I tucked my M4, still loaded, into the neck, barrel first. I popped my kneepads off and wrapped them around the stock of the M4. I looked at my watch. 1:30 p.m., June 15, 2012.

I thought of my wife, daughter, and son.

A bearded Special Forces officer stopped in to speak with Schneider. Feruk, who was born in Spedar and lived in Karwaddin, would be just a kilometer away in Ghazi Kheyl that night to meet with the mullah there, he said. His Afghan terp had a blue aluminum baseball bat slung over his back on parachute cord. I doubted it was for playing pickup games.

Before leaving Hasan later that afternoon, I ran into Lieutenant Dan, who had just arrived with his newly acquired Scout Platoon. The battalion commander, Salome, had ordered them to Hasan for an indefinite period to hunt and kill IED planters.

Loeffler and his men had had little time to prepare. When I got back to Warrior, he asked, would I mind emailing his wife Dorothy that it might be a while until she hears from him?

No, not at all, I said. I'll have time.

CHAPTER 12:
MUQOR

Sergeant Nicholas Fredsti was promoted to Staff Sergeant posthumously. In the wake of his death, First Sergeant Corrales briefed the platoon when they rotated back to Warrior. In nineteen years and seven deployments, Corrales had lost twenty soldiers, and once, nearly half of his platoon. Like so many soldiers he had known, before dying, Fredsti had apologized for getting shot. "He's in a better place," Corrales said to his paratroopers. I believed he believed that.

Originally from San Diego, Nick Fredsti arrived at the 82nd Airborne Division as a newly minted infantryman six months prior to 9/11. He deployed to Iraq and Afghanistan three times each, for a total of fifty-one months overseas, before he was killed. His roommate, Staff Sergeant Johnny Davis, said that Fredsti's reserved personality sometimes gave people the impression that he was an outcast, but that was a misread on who he was. "When I was little, my dad used to tell me, the true measure of a man is the ability to do what you know in your heart to be right no matter the cost, and I think that's something everyone strives for, but for Nick, it was easy," Davis said. "He was always the nicest, most dependable, most trustworthy person you could count on. He was a great, great friend. That's the real Nick." Davis and Fredsti shared a tiny room on Warrior. Over the last four deployments, Davis had now lost three roommates.

Hurndon said, "I don't got no problem with dudes dying, because this is what we do. Fredsti wasn't the best at developing the leaders below him, but so far as himself, he was a phenomenal warfighter. This is going to sound really fucked up, but the bullet couldn't have taken a fuckin' idiot out instead?"

Among the 539 photos that I kept from that day, I have one of Nick Fredsti standing outside that grove of trees on the outskirts of Spedar. He is alone in the sun, radio at his right, GPS on the wrist, spare tourniquet fastened to his kit, M4 in his left hand, finger resting over the trigger guard. He has a black-and-tan *shemagh* wrapped around his neck, and he's wearing dark eye pro. The photo was taken at 7:03 a.m., less than fifteen minutes from when he was mortally wounded while laying down fire for Shafer's squad.

He stands there waiting, and I can't read him. I have a photo of Mike Metcalf all kitted up with his buddies, taken five days before he was killed. Each is a man about to embark on the greatest mystery of human life, that of human death. Knowing that makes me look again and again at the photos, as if I might be missing some clue—a wink, a slight smile, or nothing at all. I can never look at them enough.

When Delta Company walked off the plane at Fort Bragg in late August, Fredsti's mother Sherrie and sister Sarah were there to welcome home the men who had fought and bled with Nick. Sarah and Nick had been best friends. When he enlisted, she was hurt that he was leaving and angry because soldiering was so dangerous. As the older sibling, she had always been able to protect him, but no more. "But I could never stay mad at him long," she says.

They once carried on an hour-long phone conversation when Nick's parachute snagged high in a pine tree and he had to wait for help, and when she worked for Verizon Wireless, he would call her from random locations and ask, "Can you hear me now?"

One of Sarah's favorite phone calls was during Nick's first tour in Iraq. She could hear gunfire in the background, so she asked what was going on. He said calmly, "The fuckers are shooting at me." He was standing on a roof so the satellite phone would work. He yelled to somebody, "HEY! Shoot back at those fuckers already! I'm on the phone and I don't have my weapon!" Sarah told him to sit down. He replied, "Oh yeah, that might be a good idea."

When his two best friends Dayton and Nixon were killed, Nick made Sarah promise that if he was killed, she would do everything she could to talk to the guys and make sure that they all knew that she was there for them no matter what. That's what she was doing. I took a photograph of Sarah and her mother at Green Ramp, the main aircraft terminal for paratrooper use at Fort Bragg. They honored Nick with their courage. They honor us all. I hope that I always remember that. Staff Sergeant Nicholas Fredsti was buried at the Miramar National Cemetery in San Diego. It's not Arlington, but it's close enough for Sherrie and Sarah to spend any old afternoon with Nick.

The day after Fredsti died at the Warrior Aid Station, another paratrooper was flown in with a gunshot wound to the chest. He was Staff Sergeant Paul Hadley, a squad leader with Company C, 1-504, based at COP Muqor.

Hadley had been shot in the upper chest by a sniper. He was one of four soldiers hit that day in The Playground, a semi-rural area just off Highway 1. The others had been spared by the ceramic armor plates they wore. That night as Hadley lost blood, the call went out over FOB loudspeakers for military personnel with AB blood, then O-, then civilians with the same, then a by-name list of potential donors. Miraculously, Hadley lived.

Hadley had been assigned to the same Muqor-based unit as Sannicolas, First Platoon of Charlie Company, as were the other soldiers hit that day—Batcher, Shore, and Himes, all names I would come to know. Muqor was the only base that I had not yet visited, but it would produce some of the best combat photos I would take. It was time to find my way there.

A funny thing happens during the accumulation of rank on the officer side of the house. With their single gold bar (a.k.a. "butter bar"), second lieutenants arrive at their first duty station from college—Clemson, West Point, Whatever U—quite impressed with themselves. The burnish on their little gold bar doesn't last long. Particularly in the 82nd, lieutenants are "rode hard and put up wet," and even privates understand the lack of karat power in a second lieutenant's rank.

As a captain, most officers will serve some time as a company commander, where they are legally responsible for up to two hundred soldiers or more at a time.

Then comes major. The gold is back. Majors plan and direct day-to-day military operations for battalions, the level of organizational unit primarily responsible for waging the wars in Iraq and Afghanistan. Yet, in most army units, majors command nothing. They are staff officers who organize, plan, and manage but are rarely held accountable for soldiers' day-to-day welfare, as is a commander.

Yet they have substantial authority. Some of the hardest working officers in the Army are the so-called "iron majors"—brigade and battalion planning, operations and logistics officers who work nearly around the clock for months at a time. For others, the rank of major is like a second puberty. With more rank than responsibility, they are free to indulge in the good life they associate with the elevated status of "field-grade officer," and they often do. Majors rarely stand in lines like Joes, even majors who are not terribly busy, whereas captains, even terribly busy captains, often do.

All that changes again at the next promotion when they become lieutenant colonel. Lieutenant colonels command battalions of eight hundred soldiers or more. Downrange, they own major portions of battlespace. A "light colonel" gets his own command sergeant major, battalion colors, and traditions to uphold (that often predate his birth). Lieutenant colonels hold major responsibility.

In Afghanistan, Lieutenant Colonel Paul Narowski told me that he finally understood why rank had its privileges. As the commander of our sustainment battalion, 307th BSB, he was struggling with the combat injuries to the troops he led. "It's difficult," he said. "You find yourself second-guessing your decisions. These are lives forever changed, and you gave the order."

Not all lieutenant colonels are battalion commanders. Some never command battalions. However, whether it's a simple issue of maturity, or because the rank is the first of those that can be spectacularly political, lieutenant colonels typically comport themselves much differently than majors. They can be significant power brokers in the army.

Attached to our brigade were a number of small Security Force Assistance Teams, or SFATs, that acted as trainers and liaisons to the Afghan security forces with whom our infantry battalions were partnered. The SFATs were each headed by a lieutenant colonel.

A lieutenant colonel leading a battalion of eight hundred airborne infantry can radically alter the conditions of his battlespace, yet over the same period of time, a lieutenant colonel exerting his rank, experience, and influence on an indigenous security force can alter the nature of the battlespace. It can be a beautiful thing to watch.

A case in point is the story of Lieutenant Colonel Daniel Mouton, the SFAT leader who worked with the Afghan 2nd Kandak, 3rd Brigade, 203rd Corps, based at Combat Outpost Muqor ten miles north of Warrior. COP Muqor was more like an "inpost," nestled in the center of Muqor, a market town teaming with economic activity. Its main gate opened directly into a bustling bazaar. Mouton worked directly with the kandak (battalion) commander, Colonel Wazeel, his operations officer, Major Aktar, and Sergeant Major Saiful Rahman.

Mouton cut a striking figure as a soldier and paratrooper. He was

Eastwood tall, rangy and all jaw, an energetic presence in any group. He also possessed a poet's gift of saying much with few words, and a charm of one who can lay the bare bones of the human condition, particularly the Afghan human condition, out to dry, and to smile a genuine smile while doing so, and for all the best reasons. Mouton fought the good fight even while wading through the hip-deep excretia of a thousand years of Afghan corruption and intrigue.

Wazeel was stockpiling arms and ammunition in the basement of the old British mansion and selling it to insurgents in the bazaar, who were using it to attack the American paratroopers that shared Wazeel's base with his 2nd Kandak. Wazeel didn't hate Americans. In fact, he rather appreciated them for the economic opportunity. When Mouton asked what the kandak needed to become more combat effective, at the top of Wazeel's short list was always more weapons and ammo.

Over several months, Mouton, his NCO, Master Sergeant Anthony Gilbert, and Rob Tubbe unraveled the trail of Wazeel's corruption that included grossly over-reporting the manning of his kandak to pocket extra wages, shaking down local contractors hired to build a new head-quarters with US money, and taking leave in the heart of the fighting season. By judicious use of rank, influence, and networking, Mouton's team had Wazeel arrested by the Afghan higher command in Ghazni City.

When Wazeel was finally detained, he asked his captors, "Is this that big of a deal? I can give the money back."

With Wazeel's departure, Aktar was the kandak's nominal leader. "He's a manhole cover," Mouton said poetically. Luckily, in the person of Sergeant Major Saiful Rahman, the Americans had an incorruptible partner and the Afghans a competent leader.

Mouton acknowledges that the conditions at COP Muqor were radically different than from past deployments, where advise-and-assist teams were seen as something that might contribute solely to a kill/capture and/or clear/hold approach. Had the SFAT been limited to that, the team would have focused more on getting guns and ammunition to

Wazeel (pouring gas on the fire) without attacking some of the deeper problems. "At least with Rob Salome," Mouton said, "the SFAT working with a 2nd Kandak was a valued unit to his battalion. We were neither a drain on his resources nor a distraction from another part of his mission. In practice, we were a central part of his mission and vice versa."

The first operations near COP Muqor had pounded the Taliban's "B Team," so that by early summer, the Quetta Shura in Pakistan sent in A-Team commanders and fighters. Concurrently, our paratroopers were rapidly learning how to make the most of their superior weaponry, communications, and surveillance capabilities.

After hearing of the four paratroopers hit on the same patrol, I knew I had to get to Muqor. I travelled with Alpha Company's Captain Driskell, who had led the debacle of "Operation Goodyear." By mid-June, Driskell was a much different commander.

With the death of Corporal Burnside, Colonel Stock required every route-clearance patrol to be accompanied by an infantry maneuver element. For the Warrior-Muqor area, that mission fell to Driskell's Alpha Company.

Before deploying, Driskell's direct boss Salome had brought in a former commander of the 75th Ranger Regiment, and for seven days, ten hours a day, his company commanders and staff studied southern Ghazni in a "white room" with zero outside distractions. As a result, they arrived in Ghazni with a plan to take the focus off of Highway 1 by establishing several joint security stations like JSS Hasan on the periphery of the relatively secure corridor surrounding the highway. Pull the fight away from the highway, in other words.

Driskell interpreted Stock's order as a call to become a lethal maneuver force that didn't just attack the device but rather, defeated the network. "I came up with all these sexy concepts, like setting up mortar positions with LRAS (a high-tech surveillance system) overlooking sites, putting in sniper positions, doing baited ambushes, doing disruption operations, doing 'tornado operations' with other companies as I moved through their area of operations, and I was immediately shut down by my battalion," he said. "They said no, you are strictly a guard force."

In a chance meeting at the chow hall, Colonel Stock sat down to eat dinner with Driskell. The young captain decided to take a chance, and he said, "Sir, I've got to ask you something." He described his interpretation of the order and the types of offensive operations he had dreamt up to execute it.

"That's exactly what I want you to do," replied Stock.

From that point forward, there wasn't another IED strike on Highway 1 in Gilan or Muqor while 1-504 owned it. Driskell used his three native infantry platoons and Stock's handpicked PSD element to blaze across insurgent forces unaccustomed to being on the defense. Driskell's team continually analyzed and planned against emerging enemy patterns, trying to stay at least seven days ahead of them. They never did anything the same way more than twice because the enemy adapted quickly.

The area became more and more dangerous for insurgents, and they took much less care in planting IEDs. In fact, between Alpha Company and the RCP unit, sixty-five IEDs were identified and destroyed. "Operations were never the same, but they were always offensive," Driskell said.

They might maneuver to make it look like they were reacting to contact, but Driskell would have other elements prepared to assault, whether it was Apaches hidden over a ridgeline or heavy artillery set on the enemy's only avenue of retreat, or snipers sitting in *karez* holes as other paratroopers moved through the open as bait. The baiting worked. "Toward the end of the deployment, we were destroying the enemy left and right, and we were finding his IEDs like nothing," Driskell said.

That was about the time that I linked up with Driskell and the PSD for a ride to Muqor. He and his paratroopers just happened to be heading north to The Playground to pick a fight. The Playground was a loose collection of Taliban-friendly villages just northeast of Muqor right off Highway 1. It was so-named for a reliable insurgent presence, but also because the expansive empty ground separating the villages allowed for the effective use of snipers, artillery, and mortars, attack helicopters, and even Air Force bombers.

Being on patrol with Driskell's paratroopers was like sliding through a Rube Goldberg machine. The motion never stopped, and there always seemed to be a plan, albeit not an obvious one. Over here he deployed snipers with the long-barreled .50-caliber Barrett. Over there, he had a pair of 240 Bravos set in, overwatching not only a squad moving through a village to the front, but also the likely escape route when they flushed. Apaches were inbound. A UAV was overhead, feeding video of a dozen Taliban preparing an ambush from the roof of a mosque, and at Warrior, 155mm howitzers were locked on predetermined escape routes.

The PSD's platoon sergeant, Sergeant First Class Alan Sutton, was a formidable NCO on any battlefield. Sutton was platinum blonde and turned red in the sun. He was Ranger-tabbed as was Driskell, and he inspired his men not like a quarterback or coach, but like the big, burly linebacker whose mission is always to seek and destroy as part of a team that enjoys seeking and destroying, a well-organized roving hoard.

None of Driskell's paratroopers hesitated in combat. It helped that their commander planned missions such as: bait the Taliban in, then hit them with artillery from the right, machine guns from the left, and when they try to escape on motorcycles, call in the Apaches hovering behind the hill, out of sight and sound.

The day that I joined Driskell on The Playground, the Taliban fled from the roof of a mosque where they were lying in wait, and the Apaches weren't yet on station so there was no catching them as they fled on motorcycles. Perhaps the Taliban recognized Sutton's bushy blond eyebrows. I don't know. Before returing to Warrior, Driskell dropped me off in Muqor.

COP Muqor was as odd a base as I had ever visited. Its centerpiece, a 19th-century, three-story British mansion, was the tallest man-made habitation in southern Ghazni. Many of the Afghan troops of 2nd Kandak lived inside, and though stately from a distance, the interior was a hundred-year-old slum. An enemy mortar round once pierced the roof and passed through several stories to blow up the refrigerator on the first floor, surely as demoralizing a blow to troops as there ever was.

The mansion was set back from Highway 1 at the end of a long Hesco-walled corridor that separated two US compounds, Bravo Company's to the north and Charlie Company's to the south. The battalion TAC, company CPs, gym, chow hall, and shower tent were on the Bravo compound, while the motor pool, aid station, and HLZ were on Charlie's.

Sergeant First Class Zachary Moon of Corvallis, Oregon, helped me move gear into the "transient" tent that was divided by a haphazard plywood wall to give women on the other side privacy. Moon was a battalion "fires" NCO, meaning that he helped coordinate artillery support from Warrior and mortar fire on Muqor for wherever it was needed. At Muqor, that meant supporting infantry patrols and acting as a counter-battery against insurgent mortars targeting the COP. Muqor received substantial IDF (indirect fire, including mortars and rockets).

Like many steadfast senior NCOs, Moon seemed to be involved with every important battalion function, whether in garrison or downrange. As a smart guy caught up in the inanity of battalion operations, his only respite was a substantial talent for dry sarcasm, which he shared liberally due to his rank.

Moon pointed to a nearby bunker. "The Taliban's got this old relic mortarman who fought the Russians. He is shit hot," he said. "If we do take IDF while you're here, make sure you get in that bunker before the second round hits. It will already be full of local nationals who work here because they're the ones calling in fire, so there won't be any room for you. You're basically already screwed. Any questions?"

All the sleeping quarters were mid-sized canvas tents. The chow hall, laundry, and showers were tents. The company and battalion buildings were made of plywood. Anything that a mortar hit was going to be destroyed. In comparison, my berth at Warrior was like a bomb shelter.

I ran into a buddy of mine, Staff Sergeant Ron Hartford, whose infantry squad was quartered a few tents over on the opposite side of the concrete bunker. Hartford, 45, was an older soldier with a diverse life back in the States that included golf, riding Harleys, growing a sports memorabilia business, and enjoying his family. He had spent over sixteen years on active duty. Had he not smoked a Joe in a non-airborne or "leg" unit for badmouthing the 82nd in his early years, he would have been a platoon sergeant or first sergeant by now. His was a voice of maturity in a young man's world.

Hartford's squad had helped build Joint Security Station Nawah, a soil-berm and Hesco basket checkpoint on the main road leading east from Muqor toward the district of Nawah. For his infantrymen, life at Muqor involved rotations manning the gate and towers, pushing out for rotations at JSS Nawah, and patrols that lasted anywhere from a few hours to several days.

"Except for the IDF, it ain't bad here," Hartford said. For IDF in Ghazni, Muqor was second only to JSS Hasan. Between April and July, the COP was hit at least seventeen times, three of which were attacks of ten rounds or more. While about 90 percent of patrols outside of the city received some form of contact with the enemy, it was the defenselessness against IDF that made soldiers revile the place. Occasionally, the 120mm mortars at Muqor were able to lock onto the enemy mortar position and return fire, which in one incident accounted for the head of the mortarman getting blown into a nearby field.

My first patrol out of Muqor was not violent, but it was telling of the nature of the fight that our paratroopers were engaged in. With Bravo Company's First Platoon, I traveled to the village of Ati Kheyl not far from JSS Nawah to check out a possible meeting of local Taliban at the village mosque. Captain Brian James, the company commander, explained that on their first visit, his paratroopers found stocks of HME in the compound next to the mosque and IED packaging in the mosque's basement. Nearby, they also uncovered a PKM machine gun, ammunition, and tactical vests. During another operation, they found four hundred pounds of HME just two hundred meters from the mosque, behind a wall in a field where the camels are now. The last time one of his lieutenants shared tea and bread with the owner of the mosque, his paratroopers were hit with machine-gun fire as they exited the village.

The following day started off innocuous enough with a patrol through the bazaar and two of Muqor's suburbs, Juni Kheyl and Qaleh ye Godom. I walked with Hartford's squad in Third Platoon as they tried to stay alert and on task through the chaotic third-world shopping district with its open-air butcher shops, push-cart street vendors, racks of cheap shoes, bargain electronics, clay and ceramic-enameled cooking pots, and busy young boys everywhere, put to some task by a father or uncle. Wheeled traffic was constant—a family of five on a single motorcycle, the mother draped in a powder-blue burka; a three-wheeled pickup truck loaded with empty plastic jugs for sale; four goats prodded by a boy with a stick.

Mid-morning, there was distant gunfire to the north, but nothing in Muqor. The patrol moved slowly south for a ways along Highway 1, weaving through over-laden jingle trucks, crossing the road and past a large elementary school, looping around to the backside of the COP. While Hurley and his fire team searched a farmer and the hay cart attached to his tractor, other paratroopers and Afghan soldiers picked up a game of sandlot soccer with schoolboys. Mother never said don't run with machine guns, did she? The patrol was back inside the wire by noon.

At 2:45 p.m., the first mortar round slammed into the COP near the laundry tent as Staff Sergeant Rodenay Joseph, a Haitian friend of mine in the battalion legal section, was picking up his clothes. The 82mm high-explosive round impacted six feet away, knocking him out cold. I was in the transient tent, barefoot. Remembering Moon's admonition to beat feet to the shelter after the first round, I found a pair of flip-flops and dashed out of the tent.

I'll be damned. The narrow concrete IDF shelter was already packed with local nationals. I crouched near the entrance. Standing nonchalantly in the entryway next to me was Staff Sergeant Michael Benson, a squad leader with Second Platoon. Crouching behind me was Staff Sergeant Bounhieng Phongsay of Laos, Muqor's head cook. We were in the shelter less than two seconds when the second round struck the MP tent ten feet from Benson.

The blast ripped a gaping hole in the canvas, blew sandbags off the plywood roof over the bunker entrance, and sprayed hot, jagged shrapnel into the shelter. Benson was struck in the left shoulder, the right flank, and the chest—near the heart. He fell and began quaking violently, like a deer struck by a hunter's bullet. Behind me, Phongsay was hit in the leg. Someone else caught a piece of shrapnel in the chest. Master Sergeant Zachary Schuman, a National Guardsman who was on the FOB that day, saw Benson from a nearby bunker and rushed to pull him under cover, even as a third round exploded less than fifteen meters away, destroying several more tents. Specialist Christian Contreras applied a tourniquet to Benson's leg and began patching up the other wounds. Eventually—and I mean within those first sixty seconds—medics arrived to give aid.

It's easy to share the details of a mortar attack. It's almost impossible to describe the crushing feeling that incoming mortars have on one's sense of self, as in no more self. Imagine standing in a circle with twenty people. In the center is a blindfolded man armed with a shotgun who spins around, stops and shoots where he thinks you are. No one is allowed to move. He will spin and shoot until he runs out of ammunition. He may have two shells. He may have twenty.

If you know how mortars work, it's even worse. Mortarmen can "walk" rounds into a target just like artillerymen do, and once they are on target, the mortarmen keep feeding the tube. Wind, munition variance, and whatever unaccounted-for derivatives that might be referred to as chance, will cast serial mortars in a shot pattern similar to that of a rifle grouping. The problem is, after the first or second mortar, one never really knows if the mortarman is adjusting the tube or just feeding the beast. Are you safer staying put or moving? It's like dodging lighting aimed by a god. And you can't shoot back.

Base survival instincts take over. Inside the bunker, bodies crushed ever inward like stampeding cows away from the openings, whores to their own self-preservation. The partly barricaded entrance, just a narrow slit, seemed like a gaping hole. Young sergeants screamed at the fear-numbed mass of bodies that was pushing in on the wounded. I wished I had my camera.

In the distance, mortar and artillery shells sound with a *carrump*, like plywood falling on lumber, but close at hand, they explode with a crack, like a point-blank lightning strike. With each shattering impact, one imagined the worst: limbs hacked off or heads, bodies bleeding from Soviet steel turned hot and explosive by a smelly, uneducated goat farmer or sneaker-wearing Punjabi holy warrior.

The author John Cheever, who barely missed being part of an infantry company destroyed on the beaches of Normandy, writes that "fear tastes like a rusty knife," but that "courage tastes of blood." In the bomb shelter, there was no doubt what cowardice smelled like.

A round landed outside the perimeter in the bazaar, injuring several civilians including children. Rounds crashed among the armored MRAPs in the motor pool. More tents were destroyed. The MWR tent was hit, splattering half of the eight computer monitors with shrapnel.

After the first round impacted, Moon and the mortar team had the enemy mortar's position fixed and their tubes "laid on," but they could not acquire permission from division in Bagram to fire back. To stop the mortar attack, they had to get the okay from an officer who was sitting behind a computer screen several provinces away. But that computer screen had gone down, so there was no way of knowing whether the airspace was clear of traffic before counter-firing. Thus, our mortar team held their fire as a dozen more rounds rained down on the COP, unabated.

When the all-clear signal was given, Schuman and Contreras helped carry Benson and the other wounded soldiers to the HLZ for medevac. Hartford, Hurley, and the rest of the infantrymen of Bravo spread out on a plywood parapet along the perimeter wall, half-dressed in boots and shorts, armed to the teeth and prepared to meet any follow-on attack. A Red Crescent ambulance (the Islamic equivalent to Red Cross) rushed into the COP to pick up injured Afghan soldiers. Someone hollered to search the ambulance in case it was a car bomb.

Captain James told a lieutenant to shoot anyone on the roof who appeared to be recording the medevac birds coming in. The lieutenant rushed to the wall and yelled, "Anyone on the roof dies!" There was a pregnant pause of about two seconds.

In one of the towers, a squad-designated marksman fired the first shot at a man on a roof. The conflagration that followed included just about every caliber and weapons system smaller than .50 caliber. In seconds, a thousand rounds raced through the air at some poor soul who was unlucky enough to be on a rooftop with his cell phone held out to record a video—or to get better reception. There is a lot to be said for being at the wrong place at the wrong time. He must have been living right though, because he wasn't hit.

The MP's tent was a sinus-assaulting slew of bitter cordite, busted TVs, and computers, smoldering blankets and a ravaged watermelon. A three-foot hole gaped in the roof over one soldier's cot. On the next bunk, shrapnel had blown through a helmet left there. From the splintered doorway, one of the MPs surveying the mess said, "We got here fourteen days ago and were almost hit by a rocket within twenty minutes. We climbed right back into our trucks. Now this." He shook his head and added, "This is no place for watermelons."

There is an elastic nature to fear in combat, and mine had been drawn tight in the open-ended bunker waiting to get fragged by the next mortar round. The feeling would recede by evening, but then and there, if I'd had the chance to step into the magic transporter, I would have left Ghazni and Afghanistan and returned home. I had renewed appreciation for the kind of terrors that must have strip-mined the souls of 82nd soldiers in earlier wars during sustained artillery barrages—in the 1918 St-Mihiel offensive in France during which the division lost eight hundred men, in the Argonne Forest, and at Anzio and the Ardennes during World War II.

Charlie Company's First Platoon investigated the mortar site, a mosque a few kilometers to the south. There, in a grain bag, they found over a dozen cylindrical cardboard "tootsie rolls" that had recently contained 82mm mortars. The paratroopers detained the mullah, and though his fingers tested positive for explosive residue, he was released a few days later.

That night, the men won a consolation prize for the IDF attack. Lieutenant Colonel Mouton announced that US involvement in the 2nd Kandak was responsible for the arrest of ten corrupt officers, including Wazeel.

"You think today's IDF was bad? Wait until the Afghans realize Wazeel has been arrested," quipped Moon. "Then we're really gonna get hit. I can't wait."

CHAPTER 13:
ON KILLING

On June 30, I shot a man in the face. I know this because I could see in my ACOG sight what must have been the back of his head blowing out. I may have also killed a man next to him, but I'm not sure.

After the mortar attack, I hung around the base a few days on the doc's orders until a persistent headache cleared up. I was one of about twenty soldiers checked out for traumatic brain injury. Oddly, Joseph was not examined, even though he was coldcocked by the concussion. Over the next week, as he complained of nausea and a terrible migraine, his condition deteriorated until Command Sergeant Major Billy Chaney ordered him to report to the TBI recovery center at FOB Arian, where he recovered.

While at Muqor, I wanted to get out with Captain Ling's Charlie Company, one of the few infantry units that I'd not patrolled with, so I asked one of his platoon sergeants if I could tag along on the next patrol. Sergeant First Class Frank Downing, a self-assured, accomplished wrestler from upstate New York and four-deployment veteran working on his fifth, told me that his platoon's next mission would be a long, boring snoozer—route clearance on the Janube Road.

"You might want to wait for something better, but we have a seat for you if you want to come along," said the stocky but deep-voiced New Yorker. Downing had only been a platoon sergeant for a few weeks. The man he replaced, Staff Sgt. Jerry Sczymczyk, had his back broken in the blast that killed Private First Class Christian Sannicolas.

Downing was pulled up from Alpha Company where he'd been a squad leader. He had enjoyed managing two fire teams as a squad leader and being integrally involved in the fight. The verdict was still out on the job of platoon sergeant. "I enlisted in the army because my family is a military family. It's what we do," he said. Downing's father, brother, and cousins all served in the navy, but he couldn't see himself sequestered on a boat for months at a time. "I'd rather jump out of planes and shoot the bad guys."

At the time of our deployment, Frank Downing and wife Casey were married eleven years and had two sons and a daughter. They are the bedrock of our military, these families such as Downing's, who pass along military service from generation to generation as the family business. Nick Fredsti's family has served in every major war dating to the Civil War.

There was nothing else going on that day at Muqor, so I linked up with First Platoon and rode out of the gate late in the morning in the back of a MaxxPro MRAP with Sergeant Carl Sowdon and his crew. Sowdon was keen to go on patrols. Every day off the COP was a chance to kill the insurgents who mortared his platoon's tent two weeks earlier, he said.

The platoon was led by Downing and his PL, Second Lieutenant Nick Prieto of Rockingham, North Carolina. Prieto was a tall, dark-skinned, muscular fellow with a broad, short neck and a head like a helmet. He came to the platoon halfway through the deployment, but coming from a stint on battalion staff at Warrior, he was ecstatic to command his own platoon. A former sheriff's deputy, he was more wary than most of ulterior motives and criminal intent. He was modest, dependable, and loved being a leader of paratroopers.

Up to that point, the highlight of Prieto's deployment had been using a loudspeaker issued for psychological operations to blast Michael Jackson's *Thriller* in a remote Afghan village and watching the children dance. At Muqor, Prieto quickly proved his mettle as a combat leader. On June 16, he moved through heavy machine-gun fire to reach wounded paratroopers during the day's many gunfights and effectively maneuvered the platoon even when his squad leaders were taken out of the fight. For his actions, he was nominated by his platoon sergeant and company commander for the Army Commendation Medal with Valor.

Prieto's headquarters element included radioman Private First Class Blaze Glocar, somewhat of an introvert, and an equally extroverted forward observer, redhead Specialist Jonathan Myers. Wherever Prieto was, there was Glocar and Myers. Prieto's squad leaders included Staff Sergeants Phil Shore and Justin Himes, and Sergeant Michael Gamble. (Shore and Himes had been hit by bullets to the body armor the same day Hadley had been wounded while patrolling The Playground. Prieto had also been grazed, and another paratrooper, Batcher, was hit in the body armor. Battalion Intel suspected the gunner in some or all incidents to be a Turkish sniper, eventually identified by signal intelligence.) Gamble had taken Hadley's place.

Like the Nawah Road, the Janube Road left Highway 1 at a right angle, heading southeast toward the mountains of Paktika Province through a belt of Taliban-friendly villages that paralleled the highway. "The further out you go, the worse it gets, like *Apocalypse Now*," Downing told me. "You cross a magical line, and you'll get hit every time." I was already appreciating Downing for his matter-of-fact assessments.

The two neighboring villages that marked the day's turnaround point, Asghar Kheyl and Asghar Kheyl-Jonubi, lay within that apocalyptic belt, which seemed to pose the question of why Downing thought the mission might be boring. Turns out, he had been there before and had taken no contact.

It says a lot about how the army struggles to get the detail down to the lowest man that not until three years later have I learned the true intent of the mission. Captain Ling had planned it as a reconnaissance to the Jonubi School to see if the building could support a water silo. It was one of five fresh water silos that Ling had proposed with the district council to provide the local populace a way to store clean water to prevent the dysentery common among their children. The overarching intent was to build rapport with the villages nearest the Muqor market to push back the Taliban disruption zone. But for Joe, the mission was all about what *they* had to do, which was route clearance.

After leaving Highway 1, a dozen soldiers dismounted to sweep in front of the trucks for IEDs using collapsible green gadgets called "Gizmos" that resembled commercial metal detectors. At the front of the column were Sergeant Sowdon, Sergeant David Pickard, and Private First Class Eric Batcher, sweeping the hard-packed roadbed. Behind them was squad leader Shore who was coordinating additional riflemen, SAW gunners, and grenadiers. From Winder, Georgia, Shore was one of those American sons who enlisted shortly after the Twin Towers came down. He deployed with the 82nd during the early years of the War in Afghanistan, got out of the Army for a short spell, reenlisted, and finally found his way back to "The Eighty Deuce." Thirty-year-old Shore had been married a dozen years and had two daughters.

Specialist Shane Storey was on the left flank with a SAW, walking, stopping, and scanning. On the right was Private First Class Blake Hagert. Behind the front security element were more paratroopers and a handful of Afghan soldiers, followed by creeping gun trucks—American MRAPs and Afghan Humvees mounted with medium and heavy machine guns and an MK19 grenade launcher.

After a kilometer, the Janube Road left the last dwelling of Muqor and struck off across a broad corduroy of ripening wheat fields. Young boys passed by asking for candy and pens. The paratroopers searched every adult coming and going in light traffic of motorcycles and bicycles.

It was sunburn weather with windless, desiccating heat throbbing from ripening, waist-high grain, and in the midday sun, tracks of salt and dust soon lined the faces of the lead paratroopers around me as they squinted into the shimmering horizon. Ahead, where the rutted road crossed a creek, were two concrete bridges. Thin lines of trees bordered the only open water source for some distance. Beyond the second bridge was a sagging ruin to the right of the road, a snaking, shoulder-high mud wall to the left, and a hundred meters further, a single-story, U-shaped building that was a schoolhouse. Its gated courtyard faced the bridges.

I was dismounted just behind the lead element. As we neared the first bridge, Shore noticed that all motorcycle and foot traffic seemed to avoid the center and north side of the span. A man, with a short-cropped beard and typical white man-jammies and blue vest and riding a red, Chinese-built motorcycle, approached the pointmen. He stopped and was trying to explain something to them when Shore told his men, "Send him back to the terp." The Afghan motored on to the MRAPs, where the terp explained to Lieutenant Prieto that the man was a local who was trying to warn them that both bridges were mined with IEDs.

"You think he's bullshitting us?" Shore asked the LT over the radio.

Prieto, the former deputy, asked why the man was divulging the information.

"I am a good Muslim, sir, and I wanted to let you know there is danger ahead," he replied. Sometimes it seemed that villagers "warned" of IEDs just to slow soldiers down so that others could prepare an ambush, Shore explained. It was hard to call. Clearly the traffic pattern suggested the man was telling the truth.

We scanned the horizon. Here and there, farmers worked the fields as they did every day. Yet to the north and south, motorcycles and the occasional white minivan—the preferred assault vehicles of insurgents—raced east on roads that paralleled ours, as if the Taliban were rushing in fighters ahead of us. Fresh in the platoon's memory was Operation Pinball Wizard, when on the last night, several teams of black-clad insurgents surrounded their patrol base near the village of Khamat Kheyl. The Taliban knew the American paratroopers were bound by strict rules of engagement. As long as they kept weapons hidden, the Americans would not fire. Over a confiscated Taliban radio, the paratroopers heard a fighter at a mosque requesting permission to fire RPGs at them. Still the paratroopers could not fire.

Through my long telephoto lens, I glassed along the creek as it headed north from the bridges. Near a dogleg bend, a man appeared in a white man-dress and muted turban. He walked with the stilted stride of one who is accustomed to striking the forefoot first, common to those raised barefoot. He was tall and bony, and he appeared to be a farmer moving from a wheat field beyond the trees into the shade. He seemed to have an implement in his hand, perhaps a shovel, perhaps a rifle. I couldn't tell. I assumed he was a farmer.

With the ripening wheat and ribbon of trees, I hoped to frame an iconic photo of the farmer surveying his land and waited for him to pass into the right light. He was walking at a considered pace without a threatening posture. Once he reached the shade, he stopped near a tiny mud shelter, the kind built for shepherd boys to escape the elements. The shade killed my photo op.

I pointed him out to the soldier nearest me. He waved me off, "Yeah, got it." He and the others were more interested in the vehicle traffic streaming past our flanks in the distance. I felt like a POG for pointing out a single farmer when I had seen processions like the ones he was watching deliver Taliban fighters to Giro and Hasan. The white minivan is the Taliban's helicopter.

Prieto and Downing moved up to Shore's position to powwow. Downing told the others that only weeks earlier as part of Alpha Company, his squad had set up a traffic checkpoint near the bridges. Both bridges had been wired and mined with explosives, and EOD was called out. The man was probably telling the truth. "It jibes with what I've seen," said Downing.

Two young boys on a single bicycle pedaled across the bridges in our direction. They followed the same route as the man had. When questioned by the terp, their account was the same as that of the good Muslim. American soldiers wanted to trust Afghans, but in general, they did not. Whether villagers lied due to Taliban sympathies or threat of life made little difference for a single patrol on a single day.

Prieto signaled for the patrol to continue. "Just be careful," he said.

As we neared the first bridge and the line of trees, Shore called a SAW gunner forward. He ordered everyone except Storey and two of the minesweepers to get down in the prone and take up security while they pushed to the bridge. Downing, Prieto, his radioman Glocar, and Myers the forward observer moved up to the right side of the road and took a knee. Prieto was talking to Staff Sergeant Alan Hubbard back at Muqor, who was operating a Puma unmanned aerial vehicle flying above us.

The minesweepers were almost to the foot of the first bridge when Prieto hollered, "Hold up!" Hubbard had seen what appeared to be insurgents aiming a mortar tube at our position. Prieto conferred with Downing for a brief minute while the forward three stood exposed on the road. "Get them back in the vehicles," Prieto ordered. "I want everyone inside if mortars start coming in."

Downing and Shore called all elements back to the vehicles, which were fifty meters to our rear. As soon as the minesweepers reversed course, insurgents opened fire from both tree lines.

We all turned and ran for cover behind the gun trucks, but arriving at them, few mounted up. Instead, riflemen and SAW gunners crouched in hasty firing positions around the big armored rigs and oversized tires, even as enemy fire raked head-high along the steel flanks. The paratroopers immediately returned fire. "Where's it coming from?" everyone seemed to yell at once. In the absence of a known enemy, soldiers were laying down suppressive fire into both tree lines. Afghan soldiers rushed from the rear to get in the fight.

I was taking pictures almost immediately. I have photos of Sowdon, Downing, and Pickard in a dead sprint to the vehicles, of a paratrooper tripping and rolling as he cut across wheel ruts between the first and second trucks and fear on the faces of both Afghans and Americans that he had been shot (he was not). Storey was off to the left, tongue out, rocking the SAW. Several trucks back, an Afghan gunner in a Humvee was pounding the north tree line with a .50 caliber heavy machine gun. Sowdon was on the left shoulder in the prone, firing his carbine behind the slightest of berms. Next to him, an Afghan soldier stood with a PKM machine gun and fired it from the hip, his eyes squinted against the noise and hot flying brass. Enemy fire was snapping all around us and ricocheting off the bulletproof MRAPs.

Remembering the farmer, I looked through my camera to see if he was still there, but I forgot that I had switched to a wide-angle lens. To better see, I raised my M4 and braced against the side of the MRAP. It was a familiar movement to steady my sight picture—one that I had learned in the mountains of Montana chasing elk and deer but that was reinforced in the army.

There in my reticle was the "farmer" and a shorter, fatter man in black, firing at us from behind the little mud hut. Both were well within the 500-meter range of my M4. Again, my first impulse was out of context. I felt betrayed, as if the man had actually told me he was a farmer rather than me assuming it. The emotion caught me at the top of an inhale. At the bottom of the exhale, I squeezed off a round at the only part of his body that I could see, his *shemagh*-wrapped head. The man went down immediately, with the weapon still in his hands.

I have no recollection of seeing a weapon in the shorter man's hand, but I didn't hesitate in moving the little red crosshair onto him. Because of his height, he was standing more to the side of the pillar. I pumped the trigger twice. The man disappeared in a cartoon-like manner, not straight back, but pirouetting dramatically to one side and careening over backward. I believe that I hit him in the way that hunters do when they know they've made a good shot, but he could have been ducking awkwardly. This all happened in about five seconds.

I had never killed a man in combat before, not even close. War kills in random, capricious ways. This man died because he was seen by a photographer who thought he might make a good subject for a picture. After firing, I didn't stop or even pause what I was doing, but from the moment the second man disappeared, my recollection of what I did is sharp but disjointed until the I reached the inside of the MRAP, where Sergeant Sowdon and his crew were pumping MK19 rounds into the same tree line.

Fortunately, I have a visual, time-stamped record in my photos, even in the absence of an orderly cognitive one. I have photos of Storey in the prone, on a knee, and standing, firing his SAW with his tongue out. Sowdon is firing his M4, but 5.56mm cartridges jam in the ejection port. He does "SPORTS"—slaps the magazine, pulls the charging handle, observes the chamber for whatever is binding (several jammed cartridges), taps the forward assist, and squeezes the trigger.

Behind me, Sergeant Pickard is taking cover behind the front end of a massive MaxxPro. Enemy rounds kick up dirt in front of the tires. Pickard rises and squares off with his M4. His body language is complete aggression. He fires, brass flies. Fires, brass flies. Fires, brass flies. To the rear is a dark green Afghan Humvee with a tricolored green, red, and black flag rising from each fender. The gunner is pounding on the Ma Deuce (M2 .50-caliber heavy machine gun). Prieto is on the radio behind Pickard's feet, elbows in the dirt, trying to bring order to the fight. The terp, a terrified young Afghan from Kabul, is ducking in a roadside ditch. With each of Pickard's shots, swirling tongues of dust are sucked off a stretcher attached to the front bumper of the truck. It's a striking photo of a paratrooper in battle, though I only vaguely remember taking it.

Eventually I found my truck. The gunner was pumping 40mm grenades from his MK19 into the woodline, while Sowdon prepped the Carl Gustav recoilless rifle. I have photos of a steady stream of shot-glass-sized empties cascading from the gunner's turret. The grenade launcher jammed. "Are you fucking serious?" the gunner yelled.

From the rear, Captain Ling's truck appeared on our left flank and raked the woodline with machine-gun fire. A truck on our right was doing the same thing. The gunfight was over. Fifteen minutes later, the drone operator spotted insurgents fleeing nine hundred meters to the south.

So what of the good Muslim? He was long gone. His job had been to slow down the patrol as it entered the kill zone near the two lines of fire. Had it not been for the gun trucks, the insurgents might have pinned us down with little cover. Taliban commonly employed even children to spread disinformation to lure troops into IEDs and ambushes. During Prieto's first mission on June 15, Afghan kids warned them of IEDs planted in a field, tricking the platoon into sweeping it for nonexistent mines, only to be hit by withering machine gun and mortar fire. Whether the kids had been coerced or played along willingly was beside the point. The results were the same.

Yet our soldiers never gave up wanting to trust Afghans. The young Joes had little patience for what they saw as a simple black-and-white issue. Lie to us when we are here to help you? Well, fuck you. Yet the younger soldiers were also more ready to believe the initial deception. Older infantrymen like Downing understood in their bones that good and evil are woven into the human condition, and to win the counterinsurgency fight, a soldier must steadfastly raise the good and beat down the evil wherever he finds it. Winning the hearts and minds of the people is always a moral imperative.

Now mounted, our patrol moved to the creek and pushed south (to the right). We dismounted and searched for brass and other telltale signs of a firefight. Downing warned us to keep an eye out for unexploded MK19 rounds. He had seen a soldier get his leg blown off from stepping on one. Some found a few brass casings—some old, some new—but if insurgents had been firing there, they had retrieved most of their brass.

Prieto pushed his paratroopers across the creek on foot to the eroding ruins on the right of the road. Walking in each other's footsteps to avoid stepping on mines, we crossed the road and took cover along a low mud wall that roughly paralleled the wooded creek to the north of the bridges. Meanwhile, EOD had arrived and was poking around the concrete spans with a small tracked robot. A fire team moved into the trees to investigate where the insurgents had been firing from there, but they did not make it as far as the dogleg before turning around. (Even if they had, the forty-five minutes since the firefight was plenty of time to move bodies and brass.) The LT seemed to be in a hurry to make the schoolhouse.

We sprinted in small groups across a hundred meters of open ground to the U-shaped, single-story building. Inside the iron gate of the fenced courtyard, Prieto ordered his men to search every room. Pickard and some others climbed onto the roof to provide additional security. The school contained nothing at all—no desks, books, paper, or any trace that the building had ever been used as a place of learning, at least by our standards.

While Prieto's men continued to clear the building, I found the platoon's medic, Private First Class Adam Abraham, standing near the gate. Abraham was on his first deployment. I asked him what his most difficult medical situation had been so far. He considered the question for a minute, as if he were hesitating not about what to say but, rather, whether he should say it at all. He finally replied, "During a firefight at JSS Nawah, this one ANA was shot in the groin by another ANA high on drugs. When I cut off his pants, his testicles came rolling out into my hands." Joe jokes about getting his balls blown off all the time. In fact, in BAF we had been issued special underwear to protect our testicles from bomb blasts. They wouldn't stop a bullet.

Still in his MRAP on the Muqor side of the bridges, Captain Ling ordered Prieto to check out some unusual orange bundles in the road between the schoolhouse and the bridges. Ling wanted to make sure the bundles near the culverts weren't IEDs so he could maneuver the vehicles with heavy weapons forward to support the dismount movement.

Staff Sergeant Shore took Sowdon, Batcher, and Hagert with Gizmos to investigate. Downing stood watch at the open gate as his paratroopers crossed no-man's land.

Automatic weapons fire erupted from the south, this time, accurate fire bearing down on the four exposed men. They dropped the Gizmos and hit the prone. Two made it behind a pile of rubble and provided suppressive fire for the other two to fall back, one at a time. In one of my photos, an enemy round is kicking up dirt inches behind a running paratrooper's boot. Prieto sent more men up to the roof to provide support by fire for his pinned soldiers. With the extra firepower covering them, the four dashed back to the building.

On the roof, the security element was now taking fire from several directions, but mostly from the village of Ashgar Kheyl Janube, two hundred meters to the south. The lip of the roof was less than a foot high, meager cover for our riflemen, yet they continued to return fire. Hubbard reported to Ling that Prieto's platoon was being surrounded by a handful of fighters. He also said that insurgents had broken contact to the south near a mosque and appeared to be establishing a mortar tube. Those who were not on the roof moved into the building and braced for the crack of incoming, but nothing came. EOD had cleared the bridges—neither was mined. We had been duped. But why?

The gun trucks crossed the bridges and pulled up to the schoolhouse. With rounds still zinging in from multiple directions, we loaded up and pushed down a narrow lane into Ashgar Kheyl Janube. The firing almost immediately abated. Since IEDs were always a threat, a small team of dismounts kicked out and swept the road in front of the lead vehicle. Near a grove of trees fifty meters from the village, they investigated a disturbed spot in the road with the Gizmos. Nothing. Somebody swept away soil with a hand. Still nothing. Well, just don't step on it, somebody else said. They waived the mineroller through. The second truck crossed, and the third. In the fourth truck, Downing called an immediate halt. (I was in the fifth truck.) He saw an object burning in the road where the third truck had just passed. The platoon was effectively cut in half, but Downing decided to park and wait for EOD to investigate. It had to be some kind of IED, he thought, and with that, the earlier firefights suddenly made sense. Insurgents had sent the man and the boys down the road with false information about mined bridges so the patrol would slow down at the natural choke point between the two lines of trees. The small-arms fire from Ashgar Kheyle Janube was meant to lure the paratroopers into the kill zone of the IED, which it had. Fortunately, the explosives had been poorly sealed against the weather. Had the bomb gone off, at the very least, it would have caused a mobility kill to a truck, bottling the convoy in a natural swale just outside the village, where insurgents could have hit it with mortars, RPGs, and machine-gun fire while in good cover themselves.

Downing's immediate concern was to reunite the two halves of the platoon. He led a squad of dismounts on a bold sweep to the southwest through a wheat field along the village periphery and joined up with Prieto and the others inside the village. By then, it was nearing evening of what was becoming a long day.

Set on a slight rise that overlooked expansive golden wheat fields with ribbons of creek-fed woodlines, faint forms of neighboring villages, and lithic ramparts jutting from behind Muqor, the village of Ashgar Kheyl Janube was idyllic and pastoral. The people, not so much. According to overhead surveillance, a dozen or more villagers were gathering at a mosque just ahead, so Captain Ling ordered Prieto to get the ANA soldiers to search it. Our soldiers were finding it commonplace for insurgents to cache weapons in mosques. Just as the patrol moved forward, Myer, the forward observer yelled, "Stop!"

Hubbard had just warned him of a likely IED in the road a dozen meters ahead. The ANA were still walking forward.

Downing yelled at the terp to tell the ANA to halt, but the terp was frozen with fear and would not move. The platoon sergeant grabbed the young man by the shoulder and said, "Get the fuck up there before they get blown the fuck up!" Begrudgingly the terp moved forward, but only with Downing yanking him along. They stopped the Afghan soldiers in time.

Meanwhile, two EOD technicians had reached the burning spot in the road. They identified it as an anti-personnel mine placed upside down on a hundred pounds of HME. They said that the mine had "low-ordered," meaning that it had weathered to the point where it slowly burned up instead of detonating. They were going to blow the main charge in place.

Inside the village, our patrol moved into an alleyway around the corner and a hundred meters from where the first three gun trucks had stopped. A short, tottering Afghan man tried to scurry past the American troops while casting his eyes at his feet.

"Hey, tell the ANA to grab that guy," yelled Staff Sergeant Shore. "Where the fuck is he going so fast?" In ten minutes, Shore had collected a dozen military-aged males into our alley for questioning. Some were frightened, but others just squatted with caustic grins, knowing full well that soon they would be free to go, and free to shoot at us again.

Through the terp, Shore was questioning the first man. The Afghan's whole body was trembling, and his eyes were tunneling in on Shore's forehead. "Why are you shaking?" Shore asked him.

"What? I am not shaking," the man replied.

Sergeant Sowdon unpacked the HIIDES and asked the man to remove his turban for a photo. On the man's weathered face grew a thick black beard and bushy eyebrows, but his dome was bald and white—the Afghan farmer's tan. With his fingers, he held his right eye open as Sowdon scanned the iris. A taller man in white man-jammies and only scruff for a beard was smirking and talking to the others in spite of Shore's admonitions to stay quiet. (The five S's of detainee ops are search, segregate, silence, separate, and safeguard.)

A familiar pop sounded from the north. Instinctively, we all pressed against the earth as an RPG streaked into the village and exploded fifty meters away. A second RPG popped off. Again we flattened. It landed just short of the third gun truck without exploding.

In our alleyway, we couldn't tell where the rounds were coming from or even where they were impacting, but back at Muqor, the drone operator saw it all. Two men had walked into a compound a hundred meters from the vehicles. One shouldered an RPG, aimed, and fired. After the explosion, his companion took a turn. The gun trucks returned fire with machine guns and 40mm grenades.

The smugness of some of the detainees melted away as they realized that our safety was their safety. Despite repeated warnings by Shore, the taller man with the baby face continued to instigate talk. The HIIDE process was taking forever, and it was beginning to get dark. Worse yet, many of the riflemen who had initially accompanied us into the village had left with Captain Ling.

Prieto was talking on the radio. "Controlled det in sixty seconds," he warned. "Hey, tell the terp, what's his name? Tell him to tell the ANA we're blowing up an IED."

At that point, most of the ANA were ready to return to their base at Muqor. In the waning light, with more of "them" out there and fewer of us, their faces were drawn with worry.

The IED detonation wasn't a sharp crack like incoming mortar rounds, but it was still jarring. It blew a familiar two-toned plume of dirt and smoke high in the air. It's what victory must look like to insurgents.

"Captain Ling wants us to clear the mosque," Prieto relayed to his men. The mortar team that had been shelling COP Muqor had been recently using the Mosque to hide a mortar tube. In fact, Bravo Company had seen the mortar team fire a few rounds and move east towards the mosque a few days prior.

"I don't like this situation at all," Downing replied. "It's getting dark. They sure as hell don't want to be here," he said, nodding at the ANA.

"I know it," said the LT, "but he wants us to clear the mosque first."

The mosque was only a hundred meters away, but it was sequestered by kalats and vineyards on the front side and who-knew-what on the backside. We could see villagers gathered on the side facing us. "This is fucking nuts," Downing said. "Even if there was something in there before, there's not going to be anything now."

Not wanting to risk his men for a task more culturally suited to Afghans, Prieto and Downing asked the ANA if they would search the mosque on their own. The Afghan lieutenant shook his head and put his two index fingers side by side. No, only together.

Prieto wanted a show-of-force before sending his men in. There was a B1-B Lancer on station, Myers said. "Sar'nt Shore, get your squad ready," Prieto ordered. "When the bomber comes in for a low pass, escort the ANA over there and get back as quick as you can."

Every bit of ground so far had been contested. "I had no reason to think that the last hundred meters through the village would have been different, but that was what we had to do," Shore said later. "As far as what I thought was going to happen? I wasn't really sure. By then, we had been in so many firefights, most of it was muscle memory."

The bomber skimmed over, north to south, higher than we'd have liked, but still a threatening check for any jihad heroes. Shore's team shuffled quickly around a walled vineyard to the mosque, while the remainder of us watched the detainees. Glancing at the Afghan civilians, Prieto said, "They're staying with us until we get out of here."

I looked around, and with Shore's squad gone, noticed how few rifles were left among the many Afghans. My camera hung limp as I pulled security to the south, hoping the infantrymen would return quickly. It took almost fifteen minutes.

"Nothing," Shore said, clearly relieved for the safety of his men. The squad leader held his paratroopers to a high standard and was articulate in his dissection of fucked-up situations or people, but always professional. He was proud of how his men never failed to move *toward* the sound of gunfire and always leaned into the fight. They were warriors, and he loved them for that, but the mission seemed to be devolving into needless risk.

Prieto could not agree more and had the platoon and dozen detainees moving quickly, returning to the edge of the village where the IED had been destroyed. There, he had the detainees sit along a mud wall and out of harm's way while the two EOD soldiers walked forward with their robot and an "exploratory charge" of C4 to blow up the second IED. In the army, EOD is almost a rank. They can dress almost however they want, wear whatever kind of boots or shoes they want, roll up their sleeves, and even grow stubble so long as they show up to dismantle the bombs. They are gutsy Americans, often nerdy, saving other American soldiers from terrible deaths.

The ANA were happy again. Hot chow and beds were in the foreseeable future. Sundown was burnishing the day's last convective clouds above the hills. Thrushes and larks sang from the still woodlots. Dusk was a long affair in the Afghan summer, often a pleasant unwinding of the day as the sun blithely beat it for the far side of the planet, the side with featherbeds, green lawns, backyard grills, and fat robins.

In the fields, top-heavy MRAPs labored to turn around without foundering in the soft soil, ready to drop their ramps and take in soldiers for the short ride to base, where they will laugh and replay the day in the chow tent as if the tent were a magical umbrella, as if IDF didn't exist in the quickening of dusk into starlight.

Tomorrow we may find ourselves the quick or the dead, but tonight that's just a tale we tell to explain our days. Tonight we may even dream of home.

CHAPTER 14:
SCHOOLHOUSE
REPRISE

Two days after the Jonubi Road mission, Lieutenant Shane Joyce and the boys of Third Platoon returned to the schoolhouse before dawn, with several sniper rifles, sniper netting to make decoy positions, and two M240 Bravo machine guns. In Joyce's view, the abandoned schoolhouse was an ideal fortification for counter-mortar interdiction and surveillance operations in an insurgent stronghold. The empty building was built of thick concrete walls and roof, with a courtyard that opened westward toward the Jonubi Road, the only direction from which insurgents could not mount an attack. The roof was specious and flat, with a low palisade that formed a nearly ideal defense for the sharpshooters he emplaced there—Hatfield and Buhl armed with M14s. It also afforded Hubbard, the fire support NCO, an ideal vantage of the battlefield, and the schoolhouse's isolation from the villages of Asghar Kehyl Jonubi to the north, Barankhan Kheyl to the east, and Asghar Kehyl Shomali to the south, provided a buffer against collateral damage should Hubbard need to call in mortars, artillery, or air support.

Little concerned with the partnership aspect of his mission so late in the deployment, Joyce brought along three token ANA soldiers who quickly cost the mission its covertness. One of the soldiers wandered over to a well and was shot in the arm by an insurgent. The soldier's buddy returned fire with a machine gun in the general direction that the shot had come from.

The best-laid plans were still unraveling, however. After sunup, three hundred children showed up at the schoolhouse gate for classes. Joyce apologized profusely to the bewildered headmaster, explaining that they had been told the school was no longer in use. Well, it was, the headmaster said, with dramatic understatement. Joyce suggested he give students the day off. "Would that be okay?" The headmaster turned and spoke in Pashto to the colorful throng of children, who erupted with cheer. "At that point, I knew the mission was fucked," said Joyce.

It was going to be a long day, because he was determined only to exfil (leave) to Muqor in cover of darkness. "Yes, we were hopelessly compromised, and my plan to be covert was blown, but we were set up well in the best fighting position of the deployment." Joyce made the decision to hold what they had in hopes that the Taliban would be pulled into *his* engagement areas, rather than the norm of walking blindly into theirs.

By midafternoon, there was activity to the east in Barakhan Kheyl. People were seen scurrying in and out of the mosque. On the rooftop, Hatfield and Buhl had been baking in the July heat for hours. Inside the courtyard, Joyce climbed the ladder and crawled to Hatfield's position to give his squad leader a reprieve from the sun. The roof was ideal to view the activity at the mosque. Before climbing down, Hatfield warned him, "Be careful with my M14." Since procuring the souped-up EBR model of the venerated Vietnam-era sniper rifle from Staff Sergeant Percefull, Hatfield had yet to fire it in battle.

The lieutenant settled in, removing his helmet to better fit beneath the sniper position. With a piece of scrap metal balanced on his head, he propped up the camo netting just enough for his weapon and scope. Suddenly, PKM and AK fire erupted from a long, thin wood line 250 meters east of the schoolhouse toward Barakhan Kheyl, targeting the school's many windows. A Taliban sniper began hitting targets on the schoolhouse roof with his Dragunov, smacking the false sniper blinds one after the other.

For once, Joyce was not worried about the outcome of a battle. He started moving through his echelon of fires, beginning with the hand-held 60mm mortars. His mortarman, an "eleven bravo" infantryman named Specialist Mark Kluk, was the best in the company. Kluk plastered the tree line with both surface-detonating rounds and proximity fuses (airbursts), but the moondust, poplar trunks, and foliage afforded the Taliban fighters too much protection. Joyce had Hubbard call in 81mm and 120mm mortars from Muqor, even though they were in the gun target line, meaning that if a round were "short," it might hit them.

Hubbard and Moon, the dry-witted fire support NCO at Muqor, had predetermined likely targets in the event that Joyce's platoon would need steel from the sky, applying short-hand labels to the eight-digit target grids for more efficient communication. Thus, Hubbard told Moon to fire for effect on target "Trebeck." On the roof, Joyce's paratroopers heard each round streak in on its plenary arcs before the thunderous *kerrump* of impact. "That tree line was just getting fucked up," said Joyce. Yet, unbelievably, insurgents continued to rake the schoolhouse with fire even after three calls to fire for effect.

Through the scope of Hatfield's M14, the lieutenant noticed a man on a cell phone a thousand meters to the northeast near some trees, intently watching the battle. Battalion commander Rob Salome had recently adjusted the rules of engagement so that observers on cell phones or motorcycles during an engagement were legitimate targets.

No longer were the "unarmed" Taliban leaders afforded free command-and-control of their battlefields.

Joyce took a potshot at the man, and he briefly disappeared, only to pop up again two hundred meters closer, still "prairie dogging" on the cell phone. He ducked again and reemerged still closer. This time, Joyce estimated the man's distance at about 550 meters and took a carefully aimed shot at center mass. The 175-grain bullet raced across the half-klick in less than a second. The man suddenly sat down.

Buhl heard Joyce fire.

"Do you see that guy?" Joyce asked him, pointing to the northeast.

Buhl turned his weapon on the man, who was standing again and still on his cell phone. Buhl fired. The man spun around but came up again. Joyce and Buhl fired another round, and each time, the man came back up. From the north, they watched another man run to evacuate the stricken Taliban leader. Buhl zeroed in on the man, and with a single shot, dropped him.

About that time, the Dragunov sniper shot the scrap metal off Joyce's helmetless head. The same thing happened to Buhl. Both men were hit with bullet fragments. Enough, Joyce thought. Joyce asked the pilot of a roving B1-B Lancer to drop a five-hundred-pound GBU-38V1 bomb on the tree line. To minimize the risk to his own men, he requested a delayed detonation. The GPS-guided warhead would not explode until it was a foot in the ground to localize the shrapnel blast pattern.

"Put your fingers in your ears and open your mouths!" Hubbard yelled. He counted down. The horizon lifted into the sky, casting great sheets of black soil into the unaltered blue sky. The roof shook. Joyce looked up, but free soil was still precipitating from a boiling black fog.

Following the shockwave, the collective focus of the platoon was on the crater.

"I shit you not," said Joyce, "two guys ran out of that crater like cockroaches. I'm sure they were full of holes and mush on the inside, but

I was astonished that anything could have survived that blast." Following the bomb, two Apache gunships came on station. For the first time in the deployment, Joyce had all the firepower he could ever want.

He took Hatfield's squad to investigate the slash heap that was once a wood line. There was no sign of life or death, just a copse of trees distended and turned inside out with the earth from which it once grew. The crater was large enough to accommodate an eight-wheel HEMTT heavy wrecker.

From the eastern village, a man dressed in white manjams approached, covered in blood from head to toe. Joyce ordered him to approach. The man had shrapnel wounds across his entire body and two bullet holes in his back. He was walking as if nothing had happened. Clearly he was one of the fighters who had managed to escape before the bomb was dropped. Joyce had him walk back to the schoolhouse, where his men tended to his wounds.

After clearing the tree line, the squad turned north to find the wounded Taliban leader. A man stood up in the wheat waving a white shirt. He was shot through the thigh. At his feet lay the cell-phone guy, bloodied and in excruciating pain. He was a younger guy dressed in athletic pants and running shoes, with a neat, cropped beard, very out of the ordinary for locals. His face was cleaner and somehow harder. The man's left thigh was split from his knee to hip flexor. He was also shot in the buttocks and the shin, but his worst injury had come from Joyce's first shot, which impacted low due to the lieutenant's underestimate of the distance by at least a hundred meters. The bullet had passed through the man's penis and blown out his buttocks. He was lucky to be alive, considering that he'd been bleeding for thirty minutes.

Doc Wells went to work on the wounds, stabilizing both by the time Prieto's First Platoon arrived with gun trucks to take the detainees back to Muqor. Joyce found out later that the man with the perforated organ had just been married the day before. He died, but his would-be rescuer was seen by Joyce's paratroopers two weeks later in the Muqor bazaar a free man.

There was apparently another victim of Third Platoon's schoolhouse reprise, likely killed by the bomb. Two weeks later, a farmer who lived near the schoolhouse brought in the head of the Turkish sniper who had nicked Prieto and hit three of his paratroopers.

Two weeks after that, I was in America. There was no flag ever planted on a mountaintop, no conquered enemy or freed people, just me and my fellow soldiers plucked from the battlefield at a predetermined date and sent home.

AFTERWORD

The last major clearing operation of the war in Afghanistan was nearly over. The Devils in Baggy Pants killed and captured hundreds of Taliban fighters, upended their safe zones, and addled their command structure.

In early summer, a high-level Intel report came down from higher headquarters: "Quetta Shura in Pakistan has passed a directive to Ghazni-based TB to reduce or stop direct-fire attacks on the US paratroopers in Ghazni due to the aggressiveness of their efforts and losses being suffered by the TB fighters. The [Quetta Shura] directed them to use IEDs as main source of attacks until further notice."

The report was strikingly similar to the German officer's diary entry at Anzio sixty-eight years earlier: "American parachutists . . . devils in baggy pants . . . are less than a hundred meters from my outpost line. I can't sleep at night; they pop up from nowhere and we never know when or how they will strike next. Seems like the black-hearted devils are everywhere . . ."

In Ghazni, the fighting abated until the 82nd began to leave and our Kansas-based replacements from the 1st Infantry Division took over. In Nick Prieto's deployment journal, he writes, "We would leave COP

Moqur on the morning of Wednesday, 15 August 2012. One thing is for sure, I will certainly not miss this place . . . not even in the least bit."

As the 82nd Airborne Division pulled out of Ghazni, JSS Hasan was abandoned, but JSS Nawah was maintained. FOB Warrior was taken over by Italy-based paratroopers of the 173rd Airborne Brigade, and soldiers continued to operate out of Arian and Giro.

At Muqor in Charlie Company's former area of operation, Captain Adam Cowan led the soldiers of Company D, 2nd Battalion, 16th Infantry Regiment, until he was hit with a terrible wound to the leg by a sniper and evacuated to the States. His replacement, Captain James D. Nehl, thirty-seven, of Gardiner, Oregon, was shot in the head and killed north of Jonubi Road, November 9, 2012.

Nehl was the 106th soldier to die in Ghazni province, and the 1,723rd American service member to die in Afghanistan from hostile action since September 11, 2001.

That fall was the peak of my army experience, photographing flight after flight of returning paratroopers greeting loved ones at Pope Army Airfield. The homemade signs, the eager children, the welcome-home dresses, and parents crying because they didn't outlive their sons and daughters, their heroes.

All of life's poignancy was there in those fifteen minutes that paratroopers were allowed to share with their loved ones before being bused off to turn in weapons, get de-briefed, etc. There was joy, love, and romance, of course, but also redemption and reconciliation, regret and sorrow, feelings of fulfillment, and sometimes, faithlessness, abandonment, and betrayal. Families had survived another deployment intact, so there was thankfulness, rebirth, and celebration. For parents of returning soldiers, there was relief and perhaps realignment of priorities. Some soldiers stood alone because nobody at all was there for them. After *that*.

Most of all, there was recognition and thankfulness of the service and sacrifice born by the few for the many at the end of an Odyssean journey. A general was always there to shake the hand of every returning soldier. It was an abiding rectitude that today's military has rightly deemed important, and one that we as a free nation should never fail to observe. After the flights came the military balls, changes of command, changes of station, schools, reclasses, retirements, and discharges. Then came block leave, our brigade's official month of post-deployment time off. I went fishing in a hurricane.

My fishing buddy was "Wild Bill" Sciotti (pronounced "Scotty"), a Department of Defense photo editor who I began working with shortly after arriving at the 82nd. Bill's job was to find and publish the best, most current photos of military men and women to the DOD website. A civilian now, Sciotti did his twenty as a photographer, working mostly in Korea for the 8th Army. He was also an expert martial artist, joining Bruce Lee in *Enter the Game of Death*. Bill was Italian. (He and his brothers promised to "take care of" my daughter's boyfriend if the need arose.)

From Ramadi to Ghazni and beyond, Bill edited and published my photo essays of the Devils in Baggy Pants, making me one of the most published army photographers of the last decade. Even through a bout of kidney cancer, the old soldier kept getting my photos out. Even from a cruise ship while vacationing with his wife. Bill always had time to support soldiers.

We were both fly fishermen. When I returned to the States, we planned to meet on a river near his hometown of Hornell, New York, and that is exactly what we did. Because my leave dates were fixed, we were forced to fish while Hurricane Sandy ripped across New York State. We had the rivers to ourselves.

On the knee-deep Cohocton River in the late October woods, I unfurled my flyline for the first time since fishing in Montana a week before I enlisted in the army. It was my first real down time in over four years, the stream, my own Big Two-Hearted River.

Much had changed. I had joined the army in part to leverage my age and experience to "tell the soldier's story" in a way that the typical enlisted person of fewer years could not. Yet the army had changed me too, and for the better. I had joined to write about service, and in the process, learned to serve. I came to understand that, regardless of why men and women become soldiers, there is so much ass-pain and sacrifice involved in *being* a soldier, so much bureaucratic stupidity, so many "shit shows" and "goat ropes," and such grievous heartbreak when buddies die and mothers have their hearts ripped out that a soldier's initial reasons for serving are commonly replaced by more sustainable motives. Patriotism becomes brotherly love. College tuition becomes vocational skills. Adventure becomes mission. Vainglory becomes self-lessness. Service becomes a way of life.

The best soldiers were good soldiers not because they worked well in a bureaucracy, but rather, because they soldiered well in spite of bureaucracy. They soldiered on because they embraced the nature of military life, which is service.

When I first arrived at the 82nd, I was convinced that the army could save all the bonus money it was paying soldiers to reenlist if it just got rid of all the sergeants major (my first brigade sergeant major literally "showed me my place in the army" by actually putting me into the cargo hold of a mostly empty SUV). But I was wrong. I have served with command sergeant majors like Chuck Gregory of Tennessee, a seven-time deployer who would do anything for a dedicated soldier, and Kurt Reed, a sustainment soldier and a rock of enlisted muscle and for-titude who could chew ass like a bionic hemorrhoid but who never took a soldier's dignity. These men inspired soldiers because their business was serving soldiers and their families. They believed to their core in the nobility of service. Because these men exist, I believe nobility does too.

When I joined the Army, I had 102 contacts in my phone. Now I have 592. Welcome to the brotherhood. "You're going to miss it," Major Mike Labrecque said to me on a jump just before I left the Eighty-Deuce. Well, maybe some of it.

On the Cohocton River, I cast a dry fly above a logjam and watched it float back to me on a patient current. There were brown trout in the stream with backs the color of water rushing over pebbles. I could only see their shadows.

I cast again.

I had time.

On a steep ridge above the river, gale winds were stripping the year's last leaves from hardwoods that grew boldly along the edge of a cliff. On the river, Bill was around the bend, always there but like a good father, giving me my own water to work. Before I went to war, I would hear combat vets say not a day went by that they didn't remember their betters lost downrange. Not possible, I would say to myself. But you don't think of them. They come to you, on a breeze, in a theater, over lunch, on a trout stream. Many times a day. Every day. In these words.

For the families of fallen paratroopers, grief becomes a constant companion. Chase Marta's mother, Karen Stone, recalled bringing her son's ashes to Arlington. "You look at all of those headstones, and you say, my gosh, how did all of these people—the mothers and fathers, the sisters and brothers, aunts and uncles—live through this?" she asked herself then. "But you take strength from the fact that they did."

A quiet, compassionate young man with a Samaritan spirit, Chase had loved military history. In spite of Karen's best efforts, he got what he wanted: the army, airborne, and Afghanistan. She gets by knowing that her son did not live his life wanting to do something he didn't do.

When Charlie Company came home from Muqor, I met Christian Sannicolas' mom, Deanna Howard, who had flown in from Anaheim to welcome her son's platoon mates home. I hugged her, and she cried. Many people strive their entire lives for an accomplishment as meaningful as Christian's, I said. As a soldier, I did not feel sorry for him, only for the hole he left in the lives of Deanna's family and Christian's friends.

"I agree," Deanna replied, "but I also mourn the loss of his dreams."

His dreams. What does a paratrooper dream of? What were the dreams of Christian Sannicolas? Christian had told his mother that he was enlisting to belong to something greater than himself. "Mom, I could die walking across the street and have nothing to show for my life, contributing nothing back."

Deanna was a single parent, and Christian knew on his own that he needed male guidance to become the man he wanted to be. He believed the army could provide that. "He wasn't going to sit back and be a victim," Deanna said. "He sought out guidance."

Christian was her social butterfly and always made sure that his friends knew he cared about them. To his army friends, "Saint" was a guy who would literally give you the food off his plate or take your twenty-four-hour weekend guard duty at the last moment. Christian's immediate dreams included going to Ranger School, and later becoming a combat medic. "He knew he was going to have to take life," said Deanna. "As a medic, he would be able to give life back to be in balance." Christian was close friends with Blake Hagert, who survived the Janube Road firefights, getting shot in the body armor, and an IED strike that destroyed the vehicle he was riding in, but he never got over the loss of his pal.

War is full of ironical twists. After I enlisted, TC asked me why I hadn't joined Special Forces. I was smart enough, strong enough, and my age could have been waivered. "Jesus, Tom. I don't want to actually kill people," I had told him. So I became an army journalist and shot a man in the face. I never wanted to be an unlikely thread of chaos akin to mortar shrapnel. Who gets shot by a photographer? Sometimes it works out that way. I have never regretted killing the man or even felt bad about it. He was trying to shoot me and my fellow paratroopers. We were warriors, and like Hurndon says, that's what we do. Soldiers kill and sometimes die.

Yet, when I find myself in peaceful places such as the Cohocton, a clip begins to run in my head. A bullet comes in quickly. It hits my right cheek, and my head blows apart into many pieces. In spite of casting gray matter and the rather disastrous entropy that follows, it's not painful, frightening, or even disturbing. It is there, and then it's gone.

I know it's not real because I am about to use my multitool pliers to unhook another ruby-flecked, mustard-bellied trout, slimy and squirming in my fingers. The scene is there all the same, an apparition from some common sepulcher of soldier memories, brought to life only if the moral code is breeched. I am fortunate. The men, or man, that I killed were clearly enemy combatants trying to kill me and the young Americans around me. It could not have been less complicated. For many of my fellow soldiers, especially those who lost very close friends, or who fought in urban settings in Iraq, it is more complicated.

Civilians are sometimes killed and crippled in war, their homes destroyed and families ripped apart. Soldiers sometimes die by friendly fire. Some soldiers blame themselves for not doing enough in combat, or doing the wrong thing. When the moral code is perceived to be violated, a soldier becomes a perpetrator, at least to himself. That's when things get bad. The day he began the outprocessing paperwork to leave the army, Christian Sannicolas' friend Blake Hagert killed himself. "My sweet Blake was on an emotional roller coaster, and he carried the guilt of Saint's death to his grave," said Blake's wife, Chelsea.

(Two months after Sannicolas' passing, Hagert received a Traumatic Brain Injury when his truck was hit by IED near The Playground. Back at Bragg, he was reassigned to the Warrior Transition Unit and was being medicated to treat his TBI, PTSD, and a post-deployment sports injury.)

I was very fortunate. I had none of that to carry, only a shadow of myself doing a soldier's job and a photo that I took immediately afterward of Sergeant Pickard squared off against the enemy that would become the quintessential image of our deployment to Afghanistan. A giant print of it would hang in the halls of the US Army Infantry School at Fort Benning before the year's end. A T-shirt company would use it as the basis of a new design, engineers who build MaxxPros would hang the photo in their offices, officers and senior NCOs who I haven't heard from in years—or ever—would email me about the iconic image. Like millions of others in the army, one sergeant would see it online and then email me:

SGT,

What is wrong with this picture? As a senior NCO and as a Master Driver Instructor who has taught this vehicle for years, I am totally blown away by what I have seen here.

This vehicle is specifically designed to protect the Soldiers that ride in it and yet I see two of them outside of its hull and with a perfectly good Crow system on top.

I want to know who trained these individuals to step outside of their protection. Are they there just to get a CAB or Purple Heart? I sure hope not.

I know you are just a PAO person but this is total foolishness on the Commanding Officer's part to allow this to happen. No wonder people are getting hurt or killed.

One guy is even on the ground under a high centered vehicle. There is no protection there from a ricocheting bullet. These Soldiers should really be reprimanded and so should all of their chain of command.

Captain Ling and Lieutenant Prieto, consider yourselves reprimanded. Following my fishing trip, life back home "in garrison" was complex and, at times, it seemed overly complicated. Eat, sleep, and complete the mission became traffic, bills, juggling family and work, and the inevitable loss of "big boy rules" we had grown accustomed to downrange. In Afghanistan, we left the FOB armed like gladiators, Bad Muldoons all. Back at Bragg, we were just traffic. No weapons, no combat uniforms, no real responsibility, no mortal mission. Memories of combat walled off like insect galls, no longer worth the effort of remembering. And for civilians, even wives, there was just too much backstory and context required to explain what it was like, and then it still wouldn't come out right.

In July 2013, I finished my five year enlistment and returned home to Montana, stepping into a life nearly identical to the one I'd left, building houses and operating a photo studio. Instead of being middle schoolers, our children are in high school and college. I volunteer a good bit of time with Warriors and Quiet Waters, a Montana-grown nonprofit that uses fly fishing to help treat traumatically wounded warriors of the Iraq and Afghanistan conflicts. It's ironic, given my experience on the Cohocton. Being around the veterans—the young participants and the old volunteers—is good for me, for I'm learning that what veterans need more than anything is time with other veterans.

Joey Driskell returned from deployment to find himself a single parent of four. After 18 years of service, including sixty months deployed, he retired from the army and is applying for medical school. After another deployment to Afghanistan in 2014, Nick Prieto earned a master's degree in law enforcement and a year later, came off active duty to attend special agent training with the US Department of State Bureau of Diplomatic Security. Justin Boardman became a Special Forces operator, and Shane Joyce joined the 75th Ranger Regiment and returned to Afghanistan. Justin Lansford became engaged to a woman he met while rehabbing, and he is attending Catholic University. Pat Malone recenty returned to the 82nd Airborne Division Public Affairs Office, where he is serving as the top enlisted soldier there.

In a final twist—a didn't-see-that-coming moment—when Trey Gacke separated from the army in 2015, he was inspired by the book

Lonesome Dove to move to Montana for the slower pace of life, wildlife, and wide open spaces once found in his native Texas. While he and wife Marie hunted for jobs and housing, we were fortunate to have them stay at our house for several weeks. I am amazed at how many interests Trey and I share, and we have since become good friends.

My wife tells me that I dreamt a lot those first few weeks back from Afghanistan. One night I pulled her out of bed and told her to "stay the fuck down," we were being mortared. Several nights, I called up a medevac bird for Fredsti, complete with an eight-digit grid of the location. I began taking my showers in the dark, and three years later, I still prefer it.

But the dreams faded. Though I turn my head to the future, I cherish nothing so much as those years that I was allowed to serve alongside the paratroopers of the 82nd Airborne Division. Before deploying to Ghazni, I asked Lieutenant Colonel Salome, commander of 1-504, whether he believed that soldiers of the Greatest Generation were a breed apart from today's soldiers, the Xbox Generation. He turned the question around and asked me what I thought. I said I believed that American soldiers have always done what needed to be done. What continues to make soldiers the "nation's best" is not aptitude but attitude.

He agreed and added that, perhaps in some ways, they are even greater. "Their country does not perceive itself to be at risk, their peers are not rushing to defend against an ominous threat to the American way of life, and they are volunteers not swept up by a rising tide of patriotism but instead leaning into a tide of complacency," he said.

Anyone can be born beautiful, smart, well-heeled, or even lucky, but very few—less than 1 percent—will step out of the pursuit of the American Dream to defend the American Dream. They are the brave ones. They are my heroes.

I think Salome was right when he predicted that in twenty years we will look around and see hundreds of veterans serving in leadership positions across the nation who learned the true value of liberty, freedom, and representative government through the most difficult of tasks—explaining, and sometimes defending, those values to others who could not conceive of the free gift of freedom offered by a nation of volunteer soldiers.

It may be our flag, but it's their blood in the red threads, their fidelity in the field of blue. That's why they wear America on the right shoulder stars first, as it goes into battle. They carry it forward. Like the Willy's Jeep, the P-51 Mustang, and Ka-Bar knives, paratroopers are part of that iconic force that won a future for America back in the cataclysmic 1940s. Seventy years later, silver jump wings still represent arduous training, brash determination, and a promise of overwhelming violence of action on the battlefield.

"That's right," a sergeant friend blustered. "We kill hajji until there's no more hajjis to kill. And then we police up our brass." It's a paratrooper's dream and his requiem, for bravery on the battlefield doesn't come from brash words, but from brave hearts.

It's been said that "all battles are fought by scared men who'd rather be someplace else." Though my young brothers-in-arms may miss combat later, in the heat of battle, I know this to be mostly true. I think it also makes them brave. I, for one, am glad they are not someplace else.

GLOSSARY

A

Afghan National Army (ANA) – Divided into five combat corps. Together with the Afghan Air Force, it makes up the Afghan Armed Forces.

Anbar Awakening – September 2006 alliance and uprising of thirty Sunni tribes of the Anbar Province in Iraq against Al Qaeda.

Ask, Care, and Escort (ACE) – Suicide prevention effort by the US Army.

Assalamu alaykum – "Peace be upon you," an Arabic phrase commonly used by Muslims the world over as a greeting.

B

Blue Force Tracker (BFT) – A GPS satellite-based system that displays the positions of all US forces.

boot-up – To get ready for a physical challenge.

brown rounds – A hat worn by drill sergeants.

burka (or burqa) – The long, loose cloth worn as facial and body covering by Muslim women in public.

butter bar – A single gold bar insignia worn on the uniform to identify a second lieutenant.

C

c-wire – Short for concertina wire, which is like barbed wire.

Charlie Mike – A term used to mean "continue the mission."

chicken sandwich; or, gagging chicken – Those who have two combat patches from the Screaming Eagles, one on each shoulder.

Combat Infantry Badge – A badge received when an infantry soldier is shot at and returns fire.

combatives – Hand-to-hand combat exercises.

commissary (PX) – A store that sells food and supplies to the personnel on a military base.

cut slingload – To head for home.

D

danger close artillery fire – To be so close that one's own troops could be hit by shrapnel.

Dari – A variety of the Persian language spoken in Afghanistan.

Desert Shield – The US operational name for the buildup of US and other international armed forces and Saudi Arabia's defense from August 1990 to January 1991.

Desert Storm – The name used for the military operation of the US and other international armed forces in which Iraq was attacked in the Gulf War, starting on January 16, 1991, and lasting for one hundred days.

duty status, whereabouts unknown (DUSTWUN) – A term used to indicate the possibility of kidnapped soldiers.

E

Election Day – Reference to the March 2010 Afghan presidential election.

end of tour medals – Awards granted to soldiers for their service during a combat tour.

explosive ordinance disposal (EOD) – The bomb squad.

eye pro – Ballistic sunglasses, eyeshields, and goggles.

F

Fallschirmjäger – The German word for a paratrooper.

Family Readiness Group – A military-sponsored organization, usually at the company level, whose goal is to keep military families informed before, during, and after deployments.

Fertile Crescent – The crescent-shaped and relatively fertile region in the Middle East stretching from the Persian Gulf through modern-day southern Iraq, Syria, Lebanon, Jordan, Israel, and northern Egypt.

G

GIRoA (Government of the Islamic Republic of Afghanistan) – The official name of Afghanistan.

gizmos – Slang for a device that detects IEDs.

H

hajjis – (pl.) An honorific title given to Muslim who have successfully made the pilgrimage to Mecca, but used as slang by American and other occupying troops to denote any Iraqi.

Haqqani Network – A guerrilla insurgent group fighting against US-led NATO forces and Afghani troops.

hashish (hash) – An illegal extract from the cannabis plant containing psychoactive resins; a narcotic.

Hazaras – Afghan ethnicity descended from the Mongols.

heavy shoulder – Slang for the location of the "combat patch" on a soldier's uniform.

hescoes – (pl.) Protective barriers, like giant, upright sandbags.

Hextend – Resuscitative fluids used in medical situations in combat.

HIIDES – An identity verification device to scan the iris, fingerprints; used for facial recognition.

Homemade Explosives (HME) – Chemical based explosives; the Taliban would smuggle large quantities of the base chemicals to rural areas and mix them up on site. HME was the propellant of most roadside bombs and car bombs.

hook-pile tape – Velcro.

I

Imam – A Muslim religious leader.

J

Jaysh al-Mahdi, or JAM – Militants; foot soldiers of the radical Shia cleric Moqtada al Sadr.

jihadist – An armed Muslim fundamentalist.

jingle truck – Afghan trucks with chains hanging off the bumper.

Joint Prioritized Effects List – Taliban most-wanted list.

Joint Readiness Training Center (JRTC) – The training center at Fork Polk, Louisiana, where our troops war-game immediately before a deployment.

K

kalat – A mud-brick compound.

karezes – (pl.) Ancient, subterranean tunnels used for irrigation.

Karmageddon – Deserving shitstorm.

Hamid Karzai – The president of Afghanistan from 2004 to 2014.

Kuchi – Afghan ethnicity.

L

LRAS – A high-tech surveillance system.

lungee – A cloth worn as a turban.

M

Meal, Ready-to-Eat (MRE) – A food pack used by the US military.

mujahedeen – Islamic guerrilla fighters.

mullah – An educated Muslim trained in religious law or doctrine and usually holding an official post.

MultiCam uniforms – Uniforms employing camouflage designed to work well in Afghanistan, especially compared to the much-reviled grayish-green Universal Combat Pattern employed on the standard-issued Army Combat Uniform.

Muqtada al-Sadr's Mahdi militia – The name of a Taliban leader and his militia group.

O

on digits – Uploading a digital photo or other type of file, i.e., put it "on digits."

optempo – Operations tempo.

P

Pashto – An Indo-Iranian language spoken in Afghanistan, Pakistan, and Iran.

Pashtun – The Pashto-speaking people residing in the region from northeastern Afghanistan to the Indus River in northern Pakistan.

Pashtunwali – The code the Pashtun live by.

pogey bait – A slang term for candy or other sweets, often used to barter.

pop smoke – A military term meaning to head for home.

Persistent Threat Detection System – A surveillance blimp suspended by a cable over a base.

Prop Blast - A term that refers to the blast of air that a paratrooper feels when he jumps out of an airplane into the prop wash of an engine; it is also the name of a physically arduous, 24-hour rite of passage training exercise for officers new to the 82nd.

prop wash – The turbulent air behind a propeller.

pugil sticks – Padded poles for fighting.

Punjabi – Indo-Aryan people and language from the Punjab, northern India.

Q

Q-tip – A device that's used to hook howitzers to the belly of a helicopter for transport to another part of the battlefield.

Quetta Shura – A militant organization of the top leadership of the Taliban in Pakistan.

R

Ranger graves – Individual foxholes dug specifically for sleeping.

River City – The twenty-four-hour communications blackout following the death of soldier to prevent his or her family from learning about it accidentally via social media or the internet.

S

salwar kameez – A long tunic worn over a pair of baggy trousers, often worn by women in Pakistan.

Screaming Eagle(s) – A nickname for the members of the US Army 101st Airborne Division.

Seabees – Navy engineers who build bases and airstrips.

Security Force Assistance Teams (SFATs) – Military personnel who act as trainers and liaisons to the Afghan security forces with whom our infantry battalions are partnered.

shemagh – A traditional Afghan scarf; US soldiers wear them against the sun and sand.

shura – The Arabic word for "consultation."

silver jump wings – An award granted upon successful completion of the Basic Airborne Course.

snivel gear – US Army slang for warmer clothing for colder conditions.

SPORTS – An acronym representing the steps used to fix a jammed gun (slaps the magazine, pulls the charging handle, observes the chamber for whatever is binding [several jammed cartridges], taps the forward assist, and squeezes the trigger).

Spur Ride – A 24-hour rite of passage in a cavalry unit (much like a Prop Blast).

Stan Taliban – A nickname for Taliban operatives.

T

T10 Delta parachute – The standard-issue round parachute for US Army paratroopers since 2000, currently being replaced by the square T11.

TA50 – An individual soldier's basic issued equipment.

terps – Slang for interpreters.

Triangle of Death – An area south of Baghdad.

V

voluntold – Slang for being told to volunteer.

W

wadi – The bed of a stream that's usually dry.

wag bags – Portable latrine devices, of sorts: single-use, zip-closed toilet bags.

Warriors and Quiet Waters – A nonprofit group that uses fly fishing to treat traumatically wounded veterans.

wooby – A poncho liner.

Y

Young Turk – Slang for the new guy with all the bright ideas and energy.

BIBLIOGRAPHY

1. Baldor, Lolita C, "Military Recruitment Costs, Bonuses Up 25%," *CBS News/AP*, Oct. 2, 2008.

2. "Army Exceed Recruiting Goal for Fiscal Year 2008," United States Army, October 10, 2008, http://www.army.mil/article/13228/Army_Exceed_Recruiting_Goal_for_Fiscal_Year_2008/

3. Stevens, Terry, "The All-Volunteer Force," United States Army, November 7, 2008, http://www.military.com/opinion/0,15202,178777,00.html.

4. Michaels, Jim, "More Army Recruits Require 'Conduct' Waivers," *USA Today*, April 7, 2008, http://www.usatoday.com/news/military/2008-04-06-Waiver_N.htm.

5. Pawlik-Kienlen, Laurie, "The Benefits of Video Games," *Suite 101*, January 24, 2007, http://www.suite101.com/content/they-psychology-of-gaming-a12214.

6. "Those Who Exercise When Young Have Stronger Bones When They Grow Old," *ScienceDaily LLC*, July 15, 2010, http://www.sciencedaily.com/releases/2010/05/100503111744.htm.

7. Vargas, Jose Antonio, "Virtual Reality Prepares Soldiers for Real War," *The Washington Post*, February 14, 2006.

8. Grossman, David, *On Killing: The Psychological Cost of Learning to Kill in War and Society*, New York: Back Bay Books, 1995.

9. Tanielian T and Jaycox LH, eds., *Invisible Wounds of War: Psychological and Cognitive Injuries, Their Consequences, and Services to Assist Recovery*, Santa Monica: RAND Corporation, 2008.

10. Jenkins, Henry, "Reality Bytes: Eight Myths About Video Games Debunked," *PBS*, http://www.pbs.org/kcts/videogamerevolution/impact/myths.html.

11. Junger, Sebastian, *War*, New York: Twelve, 2010.

12. Couch, Dick, *The Sheriff of Ramadi: Navy SEALs and the Winning of al-Anbar*, Annapolis: Naval Institute Press, 2008.

13. Daly, Thomas, *Rage Company: A Marine's Baptism By Fire*, Hoboken: Wiley, 2010.

14. Yon, Michael, *Moment of Truth in Iraq*, Minneapolis: Richard Vigilante Books, Inc., 2010.

15. Frederick, Jim, *Black Hearts: One Platoon's Descent into Madness in Iraq's Triangle of Death*, New York: Broadway Books, 2011.

16. Giunta, Salvatore, and Joe Layden, *Living with Honor: a Memoir by Medal of Honor Recipient Salvatore A. Giunta*, New York: Threshold Editions, 2012.

17. Megellas, James, *All the way to Berlin: a Paratrooper at War in Europe*, New York: Presidio Press, 2003.

18. Ruggero, Ed, *The First Men In: US Paratroopers and the Fight to Save D-Day*, New York: William Morrow Paperbacks, 2007.

ACKNOWLEDGMENTS

For a work like this book, acknowledging everyone who helped shape it and contributed to it is an impossible task, so let me take it wave by wave. To my wife, Barbara, and children Mattie Marie, and Douglas. You risked everything, and you waited a long time. T.C., this book is almost entirely your fault. Wild Bill Sciotti, you compounded it. Andy Zack, contacting you was the best advice I've received in six years. Charlie and Mattie Warlick, this book simply wouldn't have happened without your support. To the families of Corporal Antonio Burnside, Private First Class Michael Metcalf, First Lieutenant Jonathan Walsh, Private First Class Christian Sannicolas, Sergeant Jacob Schwallie, Specialist Chase Marta, Private First Class Dustin Gross, and Staff Sergeant Nick Fredsti, may everyone know what great men you raised. A special thanks to Amy Hosford at Amazon Publishing for deftly guiding the publishing process, to Tom Wallace for your expert eye at spotting sloppy expression and gently telling me to stop already, and to Jennifer Blanksteen and Montreux Rotholtz for putting an Airborne spit-shine to everything. ATM, Pat, and Cookie, you were my first Army family. To Corey Deer, Nick Prieto, Shane Joyce, Ron Hartford, Caleb Ling, Brian Freeman, Elizabeth Trobaugh, Thinh Huynh, Sarah Fredsti, Deanna Howard,

Ceejay Metcalf, Scott Shepro, Jonathan Brooks, Bryan Butler, Chuck Gregory, and Dan Loeffler, your chat box was always open, helping me along. Steven Noonan, you are the standard. To the paratroopers with wounds from Ghazni Province, you carry the heavy ruck for the rest of us. To the Devils in Baggy Pants and our fellow All Americans, you were and continue to be my inspiration. Thanks to Ed Ruggero, who shared important details of the 505th's time in Normandy. To Command Sergeant Major LaMarquis Knowles. No lie, you were my least favorite paratrooper for a long time and that only changed because you left. However, I learned more from you than from any other what it means to be a paratrooper in the 82nd Airborne Division.

Task: to acknowledge every service member who has played a role in the development of this book. Conditions: one parachute landing fall, and RPG-addled brain. Standards: Achieve 90 percent accuracy, leave off ranks because they change all the time and I really don't care anymore. For the inspiration, corrections, camaraderie, and insight, I thank Victor Aguirre, Neil Alcaria, Miguel Alfaro, Jonay Alvira, Michael Ames, William Anger, Alain Ayan, Lee Bagan, Brian Baggett, Russell Bagley, Anthony Barbina, Adam Barlow, Sean Barrett, Rick Bavis, Bill Bellomy, Dan Benick, Steve Berlin, Kris Berube, Russell Blackwell, Justin Boardman, William Boddie, Robyn Boehringer, Steven Boer, Danny Boivin, Brad Boothby, Ralph Boyd, Steve Brabner, Josh Bracey, Jason Brashears, James Brawley, Trevor Bredenkamp, Katie Bridge, Scott Brinson, Jonathan Brooks, Jeff Brown, Kevin Brown, Kyle Brown, Scott Brzak, Jeffery Buhl, Calen Bullard, Eric Bullard, Bryan Butler, Nick Cage, Deny & Catilina Caballero, Max Caylor, Edward Cellitti, Billy Chaney, Roy Chapman, Greg Cheney, Reid Chitty, Phil Churchill, Tom Cieslak, Joe Coker, Jermell Coleman, Jason Condrey, Christian Contreras, Alex Corby, Trey Corrales, Jeff Cosola, Neal Cunningham, Nicholas Curry, David Danielson, Alan Davis, Andy Davis, Johnny Davis, Lee Davis, Juan Declet, Dana Dennis, Fede Despiau, Billy Dewberry, Felix Diaz, Shanne Dill, Derrick Dillon,

Harry Dixon, Mark Dotson, Frank Downing Jr., Joey Driskell, Jared Dudley, Chris Duprey, Towanga Dyson, Robb Eaton, Jeff Edgington, Walter Embich, Matt Feigenbaum, Carl Felton, Jenie Fisher, Brendan Fitzgerald, Martin & Maggie Fox, Travis Franklin, Gary Frey, Trey & Marie Gacke, Nalise Gaither, Orlando Garcia, Chris Gardea, David Gardner, Anthony Gilbert, Jose Gilbert, Josh & Shaleen Gillen, Joe & Yenny Giusto, Jason Glemser, Jason Gregory, Tom & Renee Groves, Shad Grunloh, Mark Gunn, Frank Hacker, Emile Hakime, Thomas Haskins Sr., Samir Hassan, Kristina Hayden, Douglas Hayes, Tim Heckerman, Sean Heidgerken, Gregg Heil, Chad Hendricks, Nathan Henry, Louis Herrera, Mark Heyliger, Richard Hill, Matt Hinds, Gary Hoffman, Richard "Jason" Holmes, Scott Hooper, Jim Horn, Steven Horsley, Allen House, Corey Howard, Bob Huckabee, Chad Hunt, Jacob Hurndon, William Hutchens, Arvi Insto, Shamsuddin Jabbar, Wenderson Jangada, Grace Jeanne-Pierre, Marc Jensen, William Johnson, Jeff Jones, Kenneth Jones, Ric Jones, Tim Jones, Mike Jordan, Robert Jordan, Jonathan Joseph, Rodenay Joseph, Darren Keblish, Ogbonna Kenyatta, Jason Ketchum, Steve Kim, Jeremy King, Russell Klika, Reed Knutson, Chris Kompier, Kyle Koncaba, Paul Krasulski, Cory Kroll, Clint Kupari, Mike LaBrecque, Steven Laire, Rick Lancaster, Justin Lansford, Jared Larpenteur, Michael Larsen, Jessica Larson, Paul Larson, Johnny Layba, Bob Leines, Bobby Lieske, Michael Lindsay, Reece Lodder, Dave Lowrey, Corey Luffler, Richard Ly, Matt MacClellan, Matt Madison, Vladimir Makarov, Michael Marlow, Carla Marrero, Terry Matz, Ginny McCabe, Terry McCray, Jeff McFarland, Sonny McGee, Lee McMooain, Abraham Medina, Pablo Michel, Chris Midberry, Ray Middleton, Danny Miller, Forsti Miller, Jason Miller, John Miller, Mick Miller, Richard Mills, Chris Mitchell, Jose Molina, Zachary Moon, Cedric Moore, Bryan Morgan, Linda Mosley, Chris Naglieri, Paul Narowski, Michael Natalino, Kathy Nguyen, Steven Noonan, Dare O'Ravitz, Michelle Orley-Elliott, Michael Ortiz, Raymond Ostil, Barrett Overton, James Ozsomer,

Nate Palisca, Gabriel Paniagua, Dale Papka, Abe Passetti, Maira Patino, Preston Patton, Patrick Percefull, Marshall Pesta, David Pickard, David Pierce, Will Pittman, Randy Randolph, Kurt Reed, Winston Rhym, Adam Rice, Chris Richelderfer, Daniel Ritchie, Tim Rodgers, Corey Rose, Hannah Rosenthal, Grant Rothberg, Zachary Rozar, Jose Salcedo, Joshua Salem, Marlen Salinas, James "Rob" Salome, Chris Saltsgaver, Carlo Sanchez, Perry Saunders, Jayson Sears, Jonathan Shaw, Kirk Shoemaker, Phillip Shore, Jody Shouse, Shawn Smith, Nurdin Sobari, Hugh Sollom, Phillip Sounia, Carl Sowdon, Mark Stammer, Jennifer Starnes, Rudy Stevens, Jeffrey Stitzel, Mark Stock, Marty Stufflebeam, James Sullivan, Alan Sutton, Marlena Syvertsen, Theron Tingstad, Daniel Torres Sr., Elizabeth Trobaugh, Jerry Tucker, Eric Valentine, Praxitelis "Nick" Vamvakias, David Ventura, Tiari Ventura, Tyler Vest, Juan Carlos Villarreal, Richard Walker, Michael Wallace, Roger Wang, Abby Ward, Jesse Ward, Josh Warrick, Matthew Watson, Joel Watts, Billy Wells, Cody Williams, Delarick & Jane Williams, Earnest Williams, Garrett Williams, Wavell Williams Jr., Gary Wilson, Crystal Wint, Jason Yanda, Troy Yard, Young Yi, Harley Young, Joshua Zaruba, and Brandon Zylstra.

Additional thanks to civilians Dawna Gepner, Robert Rivera, Reginald Rogers, Ahmad Al Samarraee, Lee Bagan, Mohamad F., Aqeel H., Sandy Harrison, James Robinson, Drew Brooks, David Wood, David Gilkey, Blaire Harms, David Gilkey, Tyler Merica, Faiz Dawood, Sandy Aubrey, Vincent Orrière, Terry Leist, Lee Rimkus, Matt & Becki Orrell, Greg Stewart, and Rocky Pearson.

ABOUT THE AUTHOR

Michael J. MacLeod is one of the most published military photographers of the last decade, a recipient of both a Bronze Star and a Meritorious Service Medal from the US Army, and an active supporter of war veterans' groups. His work has earned dozens of military journalism awards, including Military Journalist of the Year in 2012, and has been published online at Time.com, the *Huffington Post*, *Mother Jones*, Fox News, CNN, Corbis Images, *Army Times*, *Business Insider*, the *Atlantic*, and the *Long War Journal*. He holds a bachelor's degree in biology and a master's degree in wildlife biology. In addition to being a combat correspondent with the 82nd Airborne Division, he has worked as a photographer, magazine editor, carpenter, and college professor. MacLeod also spent three years living in a wilderness cabin in Montana studying elk, wolves, and mountain lions. Married for twenty-four years to his college sweetheart, he has two children and resides in a small town near Bozeman, Montana.